COLLECTIVE BARGAINING IN HIGHER EDUCATION

This is one of the first compilations on collective bargaining in higher education reflecting the work of scholars, practitioners, and employer and union advocates. It offers a practical and comprehensive resource to higher education leaders responsible for developing, managing, and maintaining collective bargaining relationships with academic personnel.

Offering views from an experienced and diverse group, this book explores how to manage relationships in collaborative, transparent, and equitable ways, best practices for meaningful outcome measures, and approaches for framing collective bargaining as a long-term process that benefits the institution. This volume provides an overview of the contemporary landscape, benchmark measures of success, and practical advice focusing on advancing collaborative, equitable, and sustainable labor relations approaches in higher education.

Designed for administrators, union leaders, elected officials, and policy makers at all stages of their careers as well as for faculty and students in graduate programs, this volume serves as an invaluable resource for those who endeavor to conceptualize, conduct, manage, and implement collective bargaining in more mutually effective and beneficial ways for all parties.

Daniel J. Julius is the former Provost and Senior Vice President, now Professor of Management at New Jersey City University, Adjunct Professor at University at Albany, SUNY, and affiliated as a Visiting Fellow at the School of Management at Yale University.

COLLECTIVE BARGAINING IN HIGHER EDUCATION

Best Practices for Promoting Collaboration, Equity, and Measurable Outcomes

Edited by Daniel J. Julius

Routledge
Taylor & Francis Group

NEW YORK AND LONDON

First published 2022
by Routledge
605 Third Avenue, New York, NY 10158

and by Routledge
2 Park Square, Milton Park, Abingdon, Oxon OX14 4RN

Routledge is an imprint of the Taylor & Francis Group, an informa business

© 2022 Taylor & Francis

Library of Congress Cataloging-in-Publication Data
Names: Julius, Daniel J., editor.
Title: Collective bargaining in higher education : best practices for promoting collaboration, equity, and measurable outcomes / edited by Daniel J. Julius.
Description: First Edition. | New York : Routledge, 2022. | Includes index.
Identifiers: LCCN 2021020429 (print) | LCCN 2021020430 (ebook) |
ISBN 9780367680527 (Hardback) | ISBN 9780367687748 (Paperback) |
ISBN 9781003138990 (eBook)
Subjects: LCSH: Collective bargaining--College employees--United States--
Case studies. | Universities and colleges--Employees--Labor unions--
Organizing--United States. | Universities and colleges--United States--
Administration--Case studies.
Classification: LCC LB2335.875.U6 C65 2022 (print) | LCC LB2335.875.
U6 (ebook) | DDC 331.89/041371100973--dc23
LC record available at https://lccn.loc.gov/2021020429
LC ebook record available at https://lccn.loc.gov/2021020430

ISBN: 978-0-367-68052-7 (hbk)
ISBN: 978-0-367-68774-8 (pbk)
ISBN: 978-1-003-13899-0 (ebk)

DOI: 10.4324/9781003138990

Typeset in Bembo
by Taylor & Francis Books

CONTENTS

ILLUSTRATIONS

Figures

Tables

CONTRIBUTORS

James N. Baron is the William S. Beinecke Professor of Management at Yale's School of Management and Professor of Sociology (by courtesy) at Yale University.

Ernst Benjamin previously served the national AAUP as General Secretary, Director of Research and chair of its Collective Bargaining Congress.

Tracy Bigney teaches Human Resource Management in the Maine Business School following a career in higher education labor relations, human resources, and governance.

Mathew Bodah is Vice Provost for Academic Personnel and Budget at the University of Rhode Island, where he earlier served as a professor of industrial relations.

Neil Bucklew, President Emeritus and Professor Emeritus, West Virginia University.

Timothy Reese Cain is an associate professor at the University of Georgia's Institute of Higher Education. He studies historic and modern issues involving students and faculty.

Shelly Chabon, Vice Provost Academic Personnel and Dean of Interdisciplinary General Education at Portland State University (PSU) represents PSU's administration with its academic unions.

William Connellan is assistant provost at University of Florida. Previously he was at Oakland University; and working in higher education for 51 years.

Jeffrey F. Cross is Associate Vice President for Academic Affairs and Associate Professor Emeritus at Eastern Illinois University and founding co-editor, Journal of Collective Bargaining in the Academy.

Joel Cutcher-Gershenfeld is Professor at the Heller School for Social Policy and Management at Brandeis University and Former Dean, School of Labor and Employment Relations, University of Illinois.

Nicholas DiGiovanni, Jr. is a partner in the Boston labor and employment law firm of Morgan Brown & Joy. He represents colleges and universities around the country.

Adrienne E. Eaton is Dean, School of Management and Labor Relations, and Distinguished Professor in Labor Studies and Employment Relations at Rutgers University.

Nadine Baron Fishel is chief negotiator for academic bargaining at the University of California, Office of the President and serving as the current President, Academy of Academic Personnel Administrators (AAPA).

Wassim Garzouzi (2006, LLL, 2008 LLB) is an Adjunct Professor at the University of Ottawa's Faculty of Law. He is a partner at a national union-side labour firm.

Janet Gillman is the State Conciliator at the Oregon Employment Relations Board serving as program administrator and chief mediator for the State Conciliation Service.

James M. Glaser is Dean of the School of Arts and Sciences and Professor of Political Science at Tufts University, and a scholar of electoral politics and political behavior.

Joseph Glover is Provost and Senior Vice President of Academic Affairs at the University of Florida since July 2008, and on the faculty since 1982.

Raymond L. Haines, Jr. is the former SUNY System Associate Vice Chancellor for Employee Relations, Emeritus. He worked for nine SUNY Chancellors over a 42-year career.

William A. Herbert is Executive Director of the National Center for the Study of Collective Bargaining in Higher Education and the Professions and a Distinguished Lecturer at Hunter College, City University of New York (CUNY). He is also a Faculty Associate at the Roosevelt House Public Policy Institute at Hunter College.

James R. Johnsen is Senior Fellow at the National Association of System Heads and former President of the University of Alaska.

Daniel J. Julius is former Provost/Senior Vice President at New Jersey City University, now Professor of Management, and a Visiting Fellow, School of Management at Yale University. He is a Past President of CUPA/HR and the Academy of Academic Personnel Administrators

Dale Kapla is the Associate Provost for Academic Affairs at Northern Michigan University, and the Dean of the College of Health Sciences and Professional Studies.

Adrianna Kezar, PhD, Wilbur Kieffer Endowed Professor and Dean's Professor of Leadership, USC, Director of the Pullias Center (pullias.usc.edu) and Director Delphi Project.

Matthew Kinservik is the Vice Provost for Faculty Affairs at the University of Delaware.

Michael W. Klein is a Richard P. Nathan Public Policy Fellow at SUNY's Rockefeller Institute of Government, and a part-time lecturer at Rutgers University.

Paula Knopf has arbitrated and mediated in the private and public sectors since 1980. She is also very involved in arbitrator training and education.

Thomas A. Kochan is a Professor at the MIT Sloan School of Management and Faculty member in the MIT Institute for Work and Employment Research.

Jason E. Lane serves as Dean of the College of Education, Health and Society and Professor of Educational Leadership at Miami University in Oxford, Ohio.

Barbara A. Lee is a Distinguished Professor of Human Resource Management and previously served as Senior Vice President for Academic Affairs at Rutgers University.

David Lewin is Neil H. Jacoby Professor Emeritus of Management, Human Resources and Organizational Behavior at the UCLA Anderson School of Management.

Risa L. Lieberwitz is Professor of Labor and Employment Law at Cornell University ILR School and General Counsel of the American Association of University Professors.

Ira B. Lobel spent over 30 years as a mediator with the Federal Mediation and Conciliation Service. For the last 20 years, he has been in private practice as an independent arbitrator, mediator and factfinder. Graduate of Cornell IL & R and Catholic University Law School.

Bill Lyne is Professor of English at Western Washington University and the President of the United Faculty of Washington State.

Terrence MacTaggart is former Chancellor of the University of Wisconsin-Superior, former Chancellor of the Minnesota State University System and on two occasions served as Chancellor of the University of Maine System.

Jude Paul Matias Dizon studies higher education at the University of Southern California. His research agenda explores carcerality in higher education.

Michael Mauer, Senior Labor Advisor, AAUP; visiting lecturer at Ton Duc Thang University in Ho Chi Minh City, Vietnam.

Derryn Moten is a Professor of History and chair of the Department of History and Political Science at Alabama State University, the Birthplace of the Civil Rights Movement.

Scott L. Pratt is Professor of Philosophy, Union Executive Vice President, and former Executive Vice Provost for Academic Affairs and Graduate Dean, University of Oregon.

Patricia A. Prelock is Provost and Senior Vice President, Professor of Communication Sciences and Disorders, and Professor of Paediatrics, at the University of Vermont.

Leanne Serbulo is a non-tenure track professor and union member. She's been a collective bargaining team member and leader for three rounds of negotiations.

Pamela S. Silverblatt is CUNY's Senior Vice Chancellor for Labor Relations; she negotiates the 20,000 faculty member contract and manages labor matters for 14 bargaining units.

Daphne Taras, Dean and Professor of Labour Relations, Ted Rogers School of Management, Ryerson University, Toronto, Canada.

Eve Weinbaum is President of the Massachusetts Society of Professors, the faculty and librarians' union at UMass Amherst, and on the faculty in Labor Studies.

Margaret E. Winters is former Provost and Professor Emerita (French and Linguistics) at Wayne State University.

FOREWORD

Adrienne E. Eaton

As an academic leader in a large university, I am keenly aware that I inhabit a world that is significantly different from most other sectors or organizations, one where authority in particular is typically widely dispersed: the use of the term "herding cats" to talk about managing faculty is commonplace for a reason. The widely discussed corporatization of the university is argued – by both critics and supporters – to push universities toward being more like other, typically profit-seeking organizations. Governing boards, often populated largely by representatives from those other worlds, no doubt see merit in that push. Faculty and students defend the unique character of shared governance and decision-making while staff often experience the organization as much like any other. Of course, the extent of faculty governance varies widely within the higher education world and faculty at community colleges or less well-resourced institutions may also experience very different working conditions and authority. As a faculty member and now a Dean, I tend to share the faculty view that faculty governance and freedoms are well worth defending. But despite my broader defense of that character, I also think that higher education has things to learn from the private sector. But as a Dean of a school focused on human resource management and labor relations (and other aspects of work), it appears to me that higher education tends to lag far behind best practice in the organization and management of work and that university leadership could benefit from better understanding things our fields have established through years of rigorous scholarship.

I believe that this volume's editor, Daniel Julius, whom I did not know before being invited to contribute to the book, asked me to write this foreword because of the unusual intersection of expertise and experience I hold. With a PhD in industrial relations from the university which helped found the field (Wisconsin) I have conducted research for over three decades, much of it focused on labor-management partnerships and worker and union involvement in managerial decision-making. I've also studied the impact of unionization on graduate student employees and have contributed letter briefs to the NLRB drawing on that research. I have been collecting data from graduate student employees at private universities for a yet unpublished study. After I achieved my full professorship at Rutgers, I became involved in the faculty union, serving on or co-leading multiple bargaining teams and eventually serving as union president. And since the summer of 2017 I have been the Dean of the Rutgers School of Management and Labor Relations, joining – as many friends have noted, including other academic leaders at Rutgers – the "dark side." (I note that a disproportionate number of members of my field have gone and continue to go into academic leadership, the most notable from the past being Clark Kerr, the well-known president of the University of California system and Derek Bok, president of Harvard) I offer the following observations drawing on all that experience and knowledge, observations that I think are consistent with the overall message of this volume.

There is ample research evidence that more constructive, problem-solving approaches to labor relations are associated with better organizational outcomes and outcomes for employees too. The most developed of these approaches, ones that involve extensive consultation and even decision-making roles for both the union institutionally and workers, are typically called "labor-management partnerships."[1] There are many parallels between hospital systems and universities, especially around the hierarchies and the high levels of education of many, though not all, occupational groups. From my intimate knowledge of several formal labor-management partnerships in health care, it is clear that consultation with unions and employees has moved the needle on important organizational outcomes like service quality, patient safety, immunization rates and many more.[2] Indeed, I would argue that labor-management partnership is a best practice across many different sectors. While many employers would prefer to avoid or escape unions, avoidance is typically not possible in the public sector and creates a whole other set of problems, and escape is typically not possible in the service sector. If collaborative approaches improve outcomes in manufacturing and service sector jobs where the workforce is relatively less educated, it is even more true when the workforce hold PhDs. Given those realities, it is far better to approach unions as potential partners in reaching organizational goals.

This less oppositional approach can and should be established even during union organizing campaigns. My own research, conducted in the private sector across many different unions, employers and industries, makes clear that union organizing campaigns that take place under agreements by the employer to remain neutral or use simpler, non-election methods of demonstrating majority support for the union lead to better outcomes once the union is established.[3] More broadly, unions do not necessarily produce negative outcomes and often produce positive ones. There is a decades-old research literature on this, much of which suggests those outcomes (ranging from productivity to patient deaths) are contingent on the nature and quality of the labor relationship. My research on graduate student employee unions in public sector universities, for instance, shows a positive relationship between the presence of a union and student perceptions of the support they received from faculty and, perhaps less surprising, pay fairness and adequacy (higher pay adequacy was associated with less outside work). There was neither a positive nor a negative relationship between unionization and perceptions of academic freedom.[4] There are various theories about why unions can have a positive outcome of some organizational outcomes. An important one is that unions force managers to be better at their jobs, something sorely needed in higher education in my observation. No wonder an employer representative I interviewed years ago for a research project described unionization as a "smoke monster", something that seems very scary to managers from a distance, but often isn't up close.

Another benefit for employers in taking a partnership approach, and one that underpins the opposition to partnership by some more militant or left-leaning union leaders or activists, is that bringing unions and employees into decision-making processes can soften up resistance to organizational change. I experienced this dynamic more than once as union president. One case involved changes in ethics requirements forced on my university by the state of New Jersey. In this case, bringing me and our union's executive director into the multi-stakeholder negotiations with the state made clear to me that the university had no real interest in adopting the state's new rules but that neither the university or the union were going to be able to resist these changes. The best thing we could do – jointly – was carve out exceptions for faculty. I would argue that this strategy led to far better outcomes for my members and for the university in reducing, though not eliminating, faculty resistance. There is a broader point here that unions can be powerful allies of the university in negotiating or working with state leaders (in the public sector) and even the federal government. (The national unions that represent the majority of faculty maintain active lobbying efforts and local union leaders often join in those efforts.) Academic unions and universities are often on the same side of public policy issues like immigration, research funding and possibly student debt; working together on those issues will not prevent either side from leveraging politicians and regulatory agencies when they are not on the same side.

Another area where I think academic unions can be an asset is social justice and faculty diversity. I would argue that while unions can be obstacles to gender and racial equity and raising the standards of non-tenure track and adjunct or part-time faculty, most often through support for seniority as a principle in a range of decisions, when they are serious about supporting equity, that is a good thing for higher education more broadly and our individual institutions. (Editor Daniel Julius discusses these complexities in useful detail in Chapter 8.) When I was active in the union at Rutgers, one of the union's two national affiliates, the American Federation of Teachers, issued three excellent guides for local union leaders around gender, racial and LGBTQ equity.[5] Academic unions have pushed to create career paths and provide better salaries and working conditions more successfully for full time non-tenure track faculty and less successfully for part-time faculty, both of which provide a significant quantity of instruction and research on our campuses. There is a literature in human resource management called "HR architecture." This literature suggests that occupational groups, which are as central to the organization's core mission as these non-tenure track faculty groups are, ought not be treated as casual labor if that organization is concerned about core outcomes.

Academic leaders are often unfamiliar with the potential benefits of constructive labor relations. In this regard, this book is sorely needed. Leaders often turn to attorneys, either internal or external to the university, to help develop and implement labor relations strategy. While there are labor lawyers who appreciate the relationship part of labor relations and who know something about the positive approaches discussed above and throughout this volume, many more do not. Further, few lawyers, even those employed by universities, thoroughly understand the work of faculty, how decision-making is structured in the academic enterprise, and how faculty are "managed." In other cases, academic leaders are distanced from the bargaining table when systems or clusters of public sector institutions bargain directly with state authorities who know even less about how these institutions function but are, at least, expert in labor relations. Faculty union leaders can perceive, rightly or wrongly that lawyers and labor relations staff have a thinly veiled hostility to the incredible freedom faculty tend to have in their work lives and the privilege of tenure, and lack appreciation for how hard most faculty work. Lawyers will also tend to argue against certain proposals on legal grounds. This is particularly detrimental if labor and management are trying to forge a labor-management partnership or simply engage the union in constructive discussion outside the formal bargaining process or where unions have successfully mobilized community groups to bargain for the "common good."[6] These strategies will involve the union in decisions traditionally viewed as outside the narrow scope of bargaining as defined by labor laws both public and private which can be a very good thing and yet something with which management side attorneys will be uncomfortable. Similarly, "bargaining" either in the traditional sense or a more collaborative sense does not have to be confined to the traditional multi-year cycle that ends with a new collective agreement; if some aspect of the contract or the relationship isn't working or management needs the union's help, management should not be shy about reaching out between agreements.

To conclude, academic leaders need to think "strategically" about labor relations and about their broader human resource management policies and practices too. This involves thinking more deeply about how unions and employees can contribute to the strategic goals of the institution while at the same time respecting the needs and goals of employees. As some of the contributors have noted, higher education is under enormous strain right now in the face of the COVID crisis and under longer term disruptive challenges. It is again interesting to note that health care organizations are facing their own short or medium term COVID along with longer term systemic challenges. There are excellent models in that sector for engaging with healthcare unions to better adjust to those challenges as well as negative models leading to several nurses strikes in recent weeks. This volume is an impressive effort toward shifting practice in higher education toward the positive end of the spectrum.

Notes

1 It should be noted that faculty, at least full time tenure track faculty, typically have many other forums for such participation including university Senates and the other practices of faculty governance at different levels of the institution. Chapter 3 in this volume discusses this issue in detail. I will note here that my own model for thinking about this as a union leader was based in my understanding of best practices for how German unions interact with mandated employee representation bodies in that country known as "works councils."
2 See for example, Adrienne E. Eaton, Rebecca Kolins Givan, and Peter Lazes, "Labor-Management Partnerships in Healthcare: Responding to the Evolving Landscape," in, *The Evolving Healthcare Landscape: How Employees, Organizations, and Institutions Adapt and Innovate*, A. Avgar and T. Vogus (eds.), Labor and Employment Relations Association/Cornell University Press, 2016.
3 Steven Abraham, Adrienne E. Eaton, and Paula B. Voos, "Card Check Recognition: Resulting Labor Relations and Investor Reaction," *Advances in Industrial and Labor Relations*, Vol. 17, 2010. This paper focuses on investor reactions to unionization looking at stock market prices, and on the impact of employer approaches to organizing on subsequent negotiations based on survey and interview data.
4 Sean E. Rogers, Adrienne E. Eaton and Paula P. Voos, "The Effects of Unionization on Graduate Student Employees: Faculty-Student Relations, Academic Freedom and Pay", *Industrial and Labor Relations Review*, April 2013, Vol. 66, No. 2, pp. 487–510.
5 As of November 2020, these guides (*Promoting Racial and Ethnic Diversity in the Faculty, Promoting Gender Diversity in the Faculty*, and *Creating a Positive Work Environment for LGBT Faculty*) could still be found here: https://www.aft.org/highered/resources.
6 For a good basic description and a discussion of some of the issues involved see *Public Law Journal*, Vol. 43, No., 4, Fall 2020/*California Labor and Employment Review*, Vol. 34, No. 6, November 2020, *Special Joint Issue*, pp. 6–8.

PREFACE

This volume offers views and ideas from an unusually experienced and diverse group of Americans and Canadians. It is one of the first compilations on collective bargaining in higher education reflecting the work of scholars, neutrals, employer and union advocates, newer voices, and those of individuals whose work spans a half century: a significant period of time during which unions representing faculty and graduate students have become fully integrated in many academic environments. During my career I have been privileged to work with a number of the individuals in this distinguished group of contributors and I thank all of them sincerely for their thoughtful responses and additions to the literature on unions in four-year post-secondary institutions.

The book is organized into three parts. Part I presents an overview of the contemporary landscape. The chapters in Part I feature history, shared governance, legal affairs, mediation, graduate student unionization (including the recent negotiations at Harvard), how to accommodate social justice in negotiations, and updates on contingent, part-time, and adjunct faculty organizing. Part II contains selections largely written by the chief employer negotiators and focuses on particular histories, organizational design, innovative practices, contract administration and negotiation dynamics in select institutions and systems. Part III is separated into three sections and provides shorter reflections from distinguished faculty/scholars, institutional leaders and employer representatives and union/employee advocate voices. Contributions in Part III also contain reflections from individuals who have been involved in collective bargaining in higher education from the 1960s, the era considered to be the time when unions entered academe in massive numbers.

Today, post-secondary education remains one of the most unionized sectors in Canada and the US. In the United States, very few industries are as organized for purposes of collective bargaining although the overwhelming majority of organized faculty and academically related personnel work in approximately 15 states, in large public institutions and systems. Newer unionization drives are occurring in the more elite private sector (where many non-faculty employees have been organized for many years, some dating back to the 1920s and 1930s) and involve adjuncts, term faculty, graduate students, and teaching assistants.

Contributors were asked to consider the following questions:

- How might the parties better promote collaboration, innovation, and equity in the conduct of labor-management relationships?
- How might the parties accommodate contemporary social justice issues in labor-management relationships and collective bargaining agreements?
- Can collective bargaining outcomes be evaluated and measured in meaningful ways?
- What were the seminal events and issues the parties confronted in select institutions or systems, and can recommendations be made concerning "best practices" to address these matters?
- What impact has the pandemic had on collective negotiations and labor-management relationships this past year and going forward?

The questions above are important and timely. Unfortunately, they have not been given the attention they deserve in much of the literature on collective bargaining in higher education, particularly in recent years. While I do not agree with a number of the views expressed by contributors, I felt it important for readers to have the opportunity to evaluate a myriad of opinions and ideas; each contribution stands on its own merits.

If there is anything we know about collective bargaining in higher education it is that outcomes are shaped by institutional and demographic variables (which constrain the individuals serving as spokespeople or those who manage these processes) associated with particular types of colleges, universities, or systems where employees are unionized or seek representation. Colleges and universities where academic employees are organized have many organizational features, governance, and administrative processes in common. In this realm, and where bargaining occurs, there are more similarities than differences in enabling state (or federal) labor legislation, the rules and procedures governing bargaining, dispute resolution processes, contract administration, and legal precedents (the latter not always confined to a particular jurisdiction). While it is true that labor-management relationships sometimes unfold differently at times in various institutional settings, influenced by particular leaders, the culture, or local political conditions, it is my experience, after nearly 50 years, that few, if any, of these relationships or situations are unique. This observation stands in contrast to what many continue to believe about "their" institution, union, leadership, history, or labor-management culture: that "what occurs here could not possibly be the same anywhere else." But more frequently than not, it is!

It is my expectation this volume will serve as an invaluable resource for students, faculty, administrators, and leaders from all perspectives, at (or away from) bargaining tables. The book is designed for those who endeavor to conceptualize, conduct, manage, and implement collective bargaining in more mutually effective and beneficial ways for all parties, and I hope, without rediscovering the wheel in doing so.

Daniel J. Julius
New Jersey City University
Yale University
University at Albany, SUNY

ACKNOWLEDGEMENTS

I wish to extend my gratitude to all contributors for their insight, time, and work. A special thank you is given to my Teaching Assistant, Jai Abrams from Woodstock Connecticut, who was instrumental in helping with the technical aspects involved in assembling this book. I also wish to express my appreciation to my colleague at the School of Management at Yale University, Jim Baron. This book is modeled on an earlier volume published by Routledge edited by Adrianna Kezar and Julie Posselt. Adrianna Kezar offered advice on the conceptualization of this book. Others were particularly helpful, Adrienne Eaton, Dean and Professor at the School of Management and Labor Relations at Rutgers University, David Lewin, Professor Emeritus at UCLA Anderson School, and William Herbert, Executive Director of the National Center for the Study of Collective Bargaining in Higher Education and the Professions, Hunter College, CUNY, for their suggestions and advice. The enthusiasm and support of Heather Jarrow from Routledge was invaluable. Both of my late parents were AFT members and faculty at the City University of New York. They instilled a sense of respect for all parties; their influence continues. Lastly to my family and grandchildren in particular, always supportive and enthusiastic, and who wait patiently for their obsessive-compulsive grandpa (Zaidy) to finish emails and edits before going out to play.

PART I

An Overview of the Contemporary Landscape

1

THE HISTORY AND STUDY OF FACULTY UNIONS AND COLLECTIVE BARGAINING IN THE UNITED STATES

Timothy Reese Cain

Academic unionism has a long history in the United States, and the study of it was once a flourishing subfield of research. Faculty unions grew from idiosyncratic and underappreciated associations to more powerful and influential legally recognized bargaining agents. As they did, they were met with optimism, confusion, and derision. They were also met with academic research aimed at understanding the reasons why faculty joined, what they gained through contracts, and how bargaining might affect campus relations. Unions were normalized on college campuses by the late 1970s, but their rapid growth slowed amid legal and legislative constraints. Research on them soon cratered. In the 21st century, academic unionism remains a significant feature of higher education with as much or more than a third of the faculty working under collectively bargained contracts. Moreover, while the unionization of instructional workers has remained contested in some circles, it is also an area of burgeoning excitement and innovation, including efforts to organize contingent faculty on city-wide bases. And, yet, it remains understudied and too often overlooked.

This chapter serves as background and context for the ensuing contributions focusing on collective bargaining in modern U.S. higher education. As such, it takes on two distinct but related tasks. The first is exploring and conveying the development of faculty unions over more than a century. In so doing, it addresses their deep history but emphasizes the rise and spread of bargaining in the second half of the 20th century. The second primary purpose is to consider how faculty unions have been studied.[1] Throughout, the main argument is that faculty unions were important but underappreciated before the rise of collective bargaining and have been that much more so in the more than half century since. As such, they deserve more scholarly attention than they currently receive.

DOI: 10.4324/9781003138990-2

"The Professor Becomes a Union Man"

The seeds of faculty unionization date to the turn of the 20th century when great institutional growth was joined by the centralization of power in the hands of domineering presidents and powerful boards of trustees. Faculty, who had come to see themselves as experts and professionals, sought standing and institutional voice commensurate with their contributions. They were dissatisfied enough with their working conditions that a "professors' literature of protest" emerged (Teichgraeber 2015). Although most viewed it as unbecoming of the professoriate, some advocated unionization as the faculty's best hope. When, in 1915, established faculty founded the American Association of University Professors (AAUP) to protect their interests, they did so on professional lines, explicitly rejecting unionism. Beginning with a small group of faculty at Howard University in late 1918, however, others pursued affiliation with organized labor. Within three years, faculty founded 20 American Federation of Teachers (AFT) locals on college campuses or on city-wide bases. Even though all but one soon closed, they hinted at a unionized future for the faculty (Cain 2010).

Amid the financial devastation and changed political climate of the 1930s, AFT faculty unionization returned in a more prominent form. More than 60 college locals attracted faculty for political, economic, and social justice reasons; a number were founded to signal support for organized labor more broadly. They existed at the full range of colleges, including elite private universities, midwestern land-grants, and small regional and liberal arts college (Cain 2012c). With the founding of the Cambridge University of University Teachers, the College Section of the New York Teachers Union (n.d.) declared "The Professor Becomes a Union Man" and proclaimed the local's importance in negating "the myth that college professors do not need trade unions; the myth that they will not join even if they need it; and above all, the myth that college professors will not affiliate with the organized labor movement" (3). While many college locals were small and largely symbolic, some had significant local effects. Among them was the successor to the original AFT campus local at Howard, which influenced the institution's crafting of new tenure and shared governance policies (Cain 2012b). The local at the University of Wisconsin was particularly effective, raising concerns about the most vulnerable of the instructional staff and working to ensure that they were not discarded to protect administrators' and senior faculty members' salaries. Its broader work to better societal conditions demonstrated elements of what might now be considered social movement unionism (Cain and Wilkinson 2019). The AFT's greatest national contribution to higher education in this period was becoming powerful enough to set the stage for the AAUP and Association of American Colleges to negotiate the "1940 Statement of Principles on Academic Freedom and Tenure." The 1940 Statement is a fundamentally important document whose writing and terms—including the creation of a seven-year tenure clock—were partially shaped by the AFT's activism (Metzger 1990; Cain 2012a).

Yet by the time the 1940 Statement was finalized, faculty unionism was in retreat. The perpetual challenges to organizing were evident in the Pittsburgh College Teachers Federation secretary's comment that "College teachers here, in or out of the union, are either pressed down under too heavy schedules, or inert from defeatism" (Wing 1940). Moreover, the combined effects of the AFT's split over communism and the loss in membership due to World War II led to the shuttering of many campus locals. As Lester (1968) noted, "the college locals had gone from a position of considerable influence and stature in the late 1930s to one of relative unimportance in the AFT" (141). Of those that persisted after the war, the Wisconsin local remained notable. It extended its influence in the late-1940s and 1950s by producing high quality institutional research that was relied on by both the faculty and the administration (Cain and Wilkinson 2019).

Even as AFT faculty unionism retreated, campus unions affiliated with the Congress of Industrial Organizations (CIO) grew, some as direct replacements for former AFT locals. A pair of CIO unions at Historically Black Colleges and Universities led the way to collective bargaining. In 1944, the same year that Howard University's AFT local closed, faculty in the institution's medical school formed a branch of the United Federal Workers of America (UFWA). By the following October, almost 75% of the institution's eligible staff were members, including over half of the faculty. In December, the non-teaching staff voted 203–0 to be represented by UFWA Local 10 for bargaining purposes; it signed its first contract in April 1946. Almost a year later—after the UFWA had merged with the State, County, and Municipal Workers of America to form the United Public Workers of America (UPWA)—the university's faculty likewise voted 130–1 for representation in an election overseen by the National Labor Relations Board (NLRB). It signed the first faculty contract of its type in the nation in May 1947 (Cain 2012b). By then, faculty and other workers at Hampton Institute were likewise negotiating their first contract with the UPWA as their representative ("Hampton Institute in negotiations" 1947; Herbert 2017). Union leadership claimed that not only did the contract improve compensation and working conditions for all employees, "through the influence of our local, turnover has been reduced, morale has been improved, and a greater spirit of democracy pervades our campus" ("UPW locals take the floor" 1949, 4).

These efforts took place amid broader attacks on communism that led to the UPWA's expulsion from the CIO in early 1950 and the end to these first bargained contracts. Still, the contracts were important, as were the short-lived salary scale negotiated by the AFT local at Tri-State College in late 1947 and the contracts negotiated by UPWA-affiliated faculty at the New School for Social Research's Dramatic Workshop beginning in 1948 (Lester 1968; Herbert

2017). They demonstrated the possibility and promise of collective bargaining for college faculty. At the same time, administrations entered into negotiations voluntarily, rendering them fragile and precarious.

"Era of Collective Bargaining"

This early bargaining occurred at the very beginnings of broader changes that would eventually, in the words of Wisconsin Federation of Teachers president William Herziger (1967), usher in education's "era of collective bargaining." Those shifts were uneven but included great growths in the numbers of colleges and universities, students, and staff members. In 1949–50, there were 1,851 degree-granting institutions in the U.S.; 20 years later there were more than 2,500. Over the same range of time enrollment rose from 2.45 million to over 8 million and the instructional staff increased from 190,353 to more than 550,000 (Snyder 1993). And while this growth in higher education signaled its centrality to U.S. society, it simultaneously caused conditions that would, by the 1960s, lead students to question why they were in higher education and what they were getting out of it. The bureaucracy that allowed large institutions to function also de-personalized college going and fostered student unrest at a number of universities (Thelin 2018). Noteworthy among this expansion was the spread of community colleges, where collective bargaining would make an early mark. In the 1960s, many were founded with ties to local school districts and lacked the traditions associated with shared governance and faculty rights. Of course, those traditions were not as prevalent across institutional types as recollections of a "golden age" of higher education might imply. Moreover, by the late 1960s, strains were showing that would only be exacerbated when the bullish faculty job market contracted.

The forces contributing to the rise of faculty bargaining extended beyond higher education, including the changing legal and legislative landscape. In 1958, Mayor Fiorello La Guardia issued an executive order allowing New York City's public employees to collective bargain and, the following year, Wisconsin became the first state to pass such enabling legislation (Murolo 2018). The initial Wisconsin law and successor legislation in 1962 were, in Joseph E. Slater's (2004) terms, "an opening salvo and a historic watershed in Wisconsin and the nation" (191). Other states followed, especially after President John F. Kennedy's Executive Order 10988 extended the right to federal workers in 1962. While these legislative and related efforts often had limitations—Kennedy's order, for example, did not permit bargaining on wages—they still launched new possibilities for faculty and other public sector employees.

The AFT commitment to pursuing bargaining in the 1950s provided a further impetus. Then, in the early 1960s, New York City's United Federation of Teachers (UFT; AFT Local 2) twice violated anti-strike legislation to first demand an election for a bargaining agent and then force a contract. The events were catalytic; UFT president Charles Cogen called the day of the second strike, "the most glorious day in the history of American education" (Buder 1962, 370). It helped galvanize teacher unionism across the country, including for college faculty who soon began pursuing their own bargaining rights with new fervor (Murphy 2000). The AFT reported a surge in college faculty membership in New York and chartered the United Federation of College Teachers (UFCT) in early 1963; it soon challenged the Legislative Conference (LC), the existing faculty body at the City University of New York (CUNY), for recognition as the bargaining agent for CUNY faculty. The two organizations battled until late 1968, when LC was elected as the agent for tenure-line faculty and UFCT was elected for non-tenure-line faculty. They each negotiated their first contracts in 1969 ("College teachers in city join union," 1963; Yellowitz 1987).

Carr and VanEyck (1973) argued that "faculty collective bargaining made its appearance at four-year college on a scattered, somewhat spotty basis" and argued that the "starting point might be marked as September 1969" (17) when the CUNY contracts took effect. The CUNY contracts were significant developments that portended the staying power of collective bargaining in higher education, though important steps had already taken place. In 1963, faculty at a two-year vocational school that would eventually become Milwaukee Area Technical College (MATC) voted to collectively bargain, facilitated by the school's operation under the authority of the local school district (Garbarino 1975; Hutcheson and Kidder 2011). Shortly after enabling legislation passed in Michigan in 1965, faculty at multiple community colleges in the state pursued and achieved representation. The following year, 140 faculty members at Henry Ford Community College participated the first faculty strike in U.S. higher education, and the AFT local bargained its first contract. Other faculty unions in the state soon agreed to contracts, as well, including some that also resorted to strikes (Kroeger 1967; Levine 1967). Following two short work stoppages, one in late 1966 and one in early 1967, the AFT local covering the City Colleges of Chicago agreed to a contract, launching the rise of multi-campus contracts (Cain 2017b). In all, faculty at 21 two-year institutions had bargained contracts by the end of 1969 and many more had achieved recognition as a bargaining agent (Hutcheson 2000).

The "scattered" efforts at four-year institutions in the 1960s included two faculty contracts before those at CUNY. Operating under the rights afforded by Kennedy's executive order, faculty at the United States Merchant Marine Academy began bargaining in 1966 and agreed to a contract in 1968. In 1967, faculty at Rhode Island's Bryant College used the threat of both a grade strike and an appeal to the college's accreditor to convince the institution to bargain on a voluntary basis (Carr and VanEyck 1973). Of course, not all of efforts unionization were successful—the AFT local that experienced success at Chicago's two-year institutions was unable to gain widespread faculty support for bargaining in its four-year institutions, for example (Cain 2017b). Still, even setbacks could prove important. Most notable was the UFCT's lengthy 1966–67 strike at St. John's University after the dismissal of 31 faculty members. St. John's faculty did not receive immediate redress, but the effort helped propel faculty action more broadly (Kugler 1997).

The AFT emphasized bargaining early but was soon joined by the National Education Association (NEA). In 1962, the historic association of administrators and teachers, first endorsed "professional negotiations" as an alternative to collective bargaining. Its approach evolved in ensuing years to the extent that its 1965 "Guidelines for Professional Negotiations" argued for exclusive representation rights, signaling a significant turn toward bargaining. And, in fact, many of these early community college bargaining units were affiliated with the NEA either through shared units with K–12 teachers or as stand-alone entities. In 1967, the National Faculty Association of Community and Junior Colleges (NFACJC) was established within the NEA and, in 1968, the organization committed to supporting collective bargaining in two- and four-year colleges. Yet, divisions lingered until the full embrace of collective bargaining with the 1972 constitutional convention (Con-Con) and then the formal adoption of a new constitution the following year. While much of the focus was on organizing K–12 classroom teachers, higher education work continued and, in 1974, NFACJC and National Society of Professors merged to form the NEA National Council for Higher Education (Keck 1992; Urban 2007; Urban 2013). Though it did not join the AFL-CIO, the NEA was operating as a union and, according to *Phi Delta Kappan* editor Stanley M. Elam (1981), its "emphasis on bargaining had become almost obsessive" (170).

The AAUP's entry was more halting, torn between its traditional role as a professional voice of the faculty and changing power relations in higher education. By the mid-1960s, it allowed that, under certain conditions, chapters might be granted the right to act as bargaining representatives. In 1967, faculty at Belleville Junior College selected the AAUP as its bargaining agent without previously consulting with the association. They made the choice in part to clearly identify as college faculty after having separated from the K–12 system and its AFT local. The association agreed to assist its "wayward chapter" but did not initially publicize its role (Davis 1967; Cain 2017b). As pressures mounted, the AAUP continued to reconsider its stance—in a 1966 statement, it had publicly rejected faculty strikes but in 1968 "dramatically reversed its position" and allowed that such actions might be warranted in extreme situations (Benjamin 2015, 42). Still, while some saw bargaining as a useful tool and one that would secure the AAUP's role in providing faculty voice, others saw it as potentially disastrous. A report by its Committee A on Academic Freedom and Tenure, for example, warned of the "manifest unwisdom" of entering bargaining, including that it could cause substantial change in the character of its membership, its identity, and its image, sharp impairment of its ability to carry out its historic role and an indeterminately severe curtailment of the effectiveness of the Association's staff and of Committee A.

(Kadish, Van Alstyne, and Webb 1972, 59)

Yet, in 1972, the association formally adopted bargaining as an important element of its work and the following year released its "Statement on Collective Bargaining." For the AAUP, embracing bargaining was both about maintaining the association's place as a key representative of the faculty amid changing conditions and seeking to ensure that bargaining conformed to professorial values (Hutcheson 2000).

Academic collective bargaining grew at a tremendous rate throughout much of the 1970s. With three main organizations competing to represent faculty, and additional units operating without a national affiliate, it was a significant enough trend that Ladd and Lipset began their 1973 report for the Carnegie Commission on Higher Education with the claim

if student activism and reactions to efforts to politicize academe explicitly proved to be the major development affecting American campuses in the latter half of the 1960s, faculty trade union organization and formal collective bargaining are likely to constitute the most important new intramural issues in the 1970s.

(1)

Indeed, Garbarino (1975) reported 47,300 faculty in 177 institutions in bargaining units in 1970; by 1974, the numbers had almost doubled to 92,300 faculty at 331 institutions. By the end of 1978, there were 382 agents at more than 600 campuses, with more than 300 signed contracts ("Faculty Unionization in 1978—A Review," 1979). Garbarino and Lawler (1979) estimated that roughly 25% to 30% of all faculty were covered by contracts. The majority of these contracts were at public institutions, but some were at private colleges, enabled by the NLRB's 1970 decision to oversee faculty bargaining in the sector. They were also far more likely to be at two-year institutions than at four-year institutions and, as would be expected, clustered in states with enabling legislation.

"A New Industry—Academic Studies of Academic Unionism"

The 1960s saw consternation over the rise of faculty bargaining and handwringing over what it would engender; by the end of the decade, large-scale research on the issue had started to emerge. Then, it exploded in the 1970s. Major foundations and educational associations sponsored studies of the topic and long-term research trajectories developed. These were joined by numerous smaller and more localized projects. The amount of work was such that Morand and McPherson (1980) announced the existence of "a new industry—academic studies of academic unionism" (34).

With outcomes difficult to study, much of the early work examined faculty attitudes toward bargaining or tried to assess the reasons behind its spread. A 1969 survey under the auspices of the American Council on Education and the Carnegie Commission, for example, found that only 40% of faculty agreed that faculty bargaining "has no place" in higher education. A follow up study two years later found that the number had dropped to 34% (Bayer 1970; 1973). Ladd and Lipset (1973) used this data and additional research to determine that younger and more liberal faculty were more likely to support collective bargaining. Ladd and Lipset also pointed to the stratification of higher education that afforded faculty in different sectors both different rewards and different access to governance roles. More broadly, Ladd and Lipset relied on the "rapidly burgeoning group of experts on faculty bargaining" (4) to locate the rise of faculty collective bargaining in four trends: economic and marketplace shifts that negatively affected job opportunities and working conditions; structural changes that saw the centralization of power in large institutions and multi-campus systems; legal advancements that protected public sector bargaining; and the broader activism of the 1960s (including as a counterbalance to the rise of student power).

Numerous other studies also considered attitudes and trends, including Kemerer and Baldridge's extended work as part of the Stanford Project on Academic Governance. In *Unions on Campus*, they pointed to the complexities of union support: "It is possible to believe in unions but refuse to join one. Alternatively, one can have a lukewarm attitude toward collective bargaining in general but be very involved in the union movement because of environmental and institutional conditions" (1975, 62–63). Indeed, they noted environmental (e.g., pay differentials, centralized control, challenges to tenure, active work by unions), institutional (e.g., sector, prestige, public control, insufficient faculty roles in governance), and individual (e.g., age, rank, trust in institutional administrations) factors encouraging collective bargaining. Although not all authors agreed on the specific details, by the end of the 1970s, patterns in findings were evident. Younger faculty and those without tenure were generally more supportive of bargaining, though institutional and state contexts mattered. Faculty in the humanities, social sciences, vocational fields, and education were more likely to support unionization than those in other fields. And, while salary considerations were significant, so too were concerns over the consolidation of power in administrative hands and expanding systems (Cain 2017a).

Amid inconsistent labor board rulings, substantial—though often descriptive or legal—work considered the pressing issue of unit determination (i.e., whether tenure-line and non-tenure-line faculty share a community of interest or whether faculty and non-faculty employees should be in the same unit). Often these raised questions of whether joint units would serve all parties or be dominated by one group to the detriment of others (e.g., Shannon 1973; Moore 1975). As bargaining spread, scholars began analyzing the resulting contracts. Garcia (1975), for example, considered 64 contracts and related documents from community colleges, cataloguing what and who they covered. The vast majority covered not just faculty but librarians, counselors, or other workers; department chairs were largely excluded. A wide range of governance, education policy, working condition, and economic issues were present in the contracts; many included statements of administrator rights and allusions to collegiality. Other work looked more deeply at the content of contracts, especially around issues of personnel policies and formalized grievance procedures. Mortimer (1974), for example, found that the vast majority of contracts included explicit mentions of tenure, and those that did not often alluded to it. Chandler and Julius (1979) used both contracts and select interviews to understand faculty and administrator rights. They found that consistent with craft unionism, unions had focused on traditional faculty roles and rights. They were "only modest inroads into decisions in the administrative and personnel areas. By and large faculties were incorporating existing governance mechanisms into the contract" (79). The bulk of the studies that included contract analyses in the 1970s suggested that bargaining was associated with better job security and greater procedural protections for faculty, including increased (though not definitive) roles in retrenchment processes (Lee 1978; Cain 2017a). Kemerer and Baldridge (1975; 1975–1976) argued that the inclusion of these personnel policies was among the most positive outcomes of bargaining. At the same time, they hedged on whether grievance procedures might be the best fit for academe, cautioned that benefits were not equally spread, and warned that part-time faculty could be disadvantaged in contracts bargained by largely full-time units.

Many early studies of bargaining's effects on compensation relied on attempts to match institutions with bargained contracts and those without; they often found at least the suggestion of a union wage premium. These studies, though, can be critiqued due to the quality of the data, the methods of analysis, and the difficulty in assessing salary differentials in light of spill-over effects. Particularly important are concerns over cost-of-living differentials in the comparisons, the effects of short-term economic changes, and the distortions caused by faculty contracts linking wages to K–12 salaries (Cain 2017a).

Worries that faculty bargaining would undercut campus collegiality or interfere with shared governance were prevalent in the debates over faculty unions and caused some to oppose bargaining. The early evidence regarding climate and collegiality was conflicted. Some studies showed that bargaining caused or exaggerated tensions; others found little evidence that such was the case. Numerous studies found that relationships were more formalized through the bargaining process, though authors differed on whether this was a positive or negative development (Cain 2017a). The research on governance demonstrated that early fears were largely misguided. For example, Begin (1974) found that "there is no evidence to support a conclusion that collective bargaining has led to significant dismantling of the traditional institution-wide or system-wide governance procedures" (584). By the end of the decade, multiple studies indicated what Kemerer and Baldridge captured in the subtitle of their 1981 article: there was an "unexpected peaceful coexistence" between senates and unions. Where governance was already strong, unions stayed out of it; where it was weak, collective bargaining offered benefits to the faculty.

Kemerer and Baldridge's work on these issues culminated in a monograph that synthesized the existing research literature and offered findings from an extension of their earlier work. In addition to the "peaceful coexistence," their main findings were: faculty bargaining had not produced revolutionary change; some union local leaders were disappointed with its outcomes; personnel policies had been standardized; and there was the possibility that hostility could ensue amid significant financial and personnel cuts (Baldridge, Kemerer, and Associates 1981). Though published in 1981, the work largely was based on research undertaken in the 1970s and helped cap a decade of enthusiasm about unionization, hopes and fears about potential outcomes, and research into its causes and outcomes. More research on faculty unions was undertaken and published than in any decade before or since, and more attention was paid to the causes and outcomes of faculty collective bargaining. Yet many questions remained unanswered. While it was clear that bargaining was neither the panacea that some had hoped, nor the catastrophe that others had feared, the full scope of what it meant was still unknown. As Ponak and Thompson (1979) wrote, "A decade after the advent of unionism in North America, its impact on university life is still unclear" (97). As the causes and effects of complex social phenomena are difficult to ascertain, such a conclusion should not be unexpected. It is, though, concerning that such a conclusion was reached as the sustained and widespread research on faculty bargaining was nearing an end.

"The Going Gets Tougher"

With the rapid expansion in the number of public institutions having ended and a lack of new enabling legislation, the great surge in collective bargaining in higher education began to fade in the late 1970s (Garbarino and Lawler 1979). In "Unions in Higher Education: The Going Gets Tougher," Kemerer and Baldridge (1980) suggested that the inability to prevent retrenchment was partly to blame for disillusionment with unionization. Before that piece appeared in print, another development that would fundamentally reshape faculty unionization occurred. The U.S. Supreme Court's February ruling in *NLRB v. Yeshiva University* (1980) upheld an appeals court ruling that declared tenure-line faculty at Yeshiva University were not just professionals but were "managerial employees," and therefore not eligible for the protections of the National Labor Relations Act (NLRA) and ensuing legislation. Organizing new locals for bargaining purposes became excruciatingly difficult and a number of private institutions refused to bargain when existing contracts expired; some moved quickly for decertification. By the end of the decade, roughly 40% of private college bargaining units had been decertified (Thomas and McGehee 1994). Still, while organizing new tenure-line units at private colleges was fundamentally impeded and unit decertifications took place, bargaining did continue at some private institutions. Julius (2012) argued that this was because "unionized institutions can be easier to manage that non-organized schools" (3).

While new bargaining for tenure-line faculty at private colleges was hamstrung, it continued in public colleges and universities, despite initial fears that *Yeshiva* might affect practices across higher education (Franke 1984). The rate of growth, though, was slow. In 1984, the National Center for the Study of Collective Bargaining in Higher Education and the Professions termed faculty organizing "virtually non-existent," in part due to unions' new emphasis on lobbying and legislative activity in light of *Yeshiva*. In the previous year, there had been one new bargaining agent elected and 11 new contracts ("Unionization among college faculty–1983" 1984). At the end of the decade, the National Center conveyed somewhat similar findings in a more positive light:

> Faculty unionization continued to increase in 1989 marking the sixth consecutive year in which such growth was recorded. Although the increases were minimal, they should be contrasted with an environment which continues to show decreases in the overall unionized sector. The percentage of unionization in the American work force is estimated at 17 percent, while organized faculty constitute approximately 30 percent of the professoriate.
>
> *("Unionization among college faculty–1990" 1990, 1)*

Maintenance and servicing remained a more prominent foci than organizing new faculty units, as did the organizing of non-faculty employees in higher education. All told, the number of bargaining agents increased from 427 to 460 from 1980 to 1990; the number of contracts increased from 359 to 440. In the middle of the next decade, Hurd and Foerster noted the "continued slow but steady increase" of faculty unionization. There were 504 agents and 481 total contracts, most of which were at public community colleges. Yet because units at two-year colleges are frequently small, more than half of the 246,206 unionized faculty were at four-year institutions (Hurd and Foerster with Johnson 1996, V).

One key area of union growth was among non-tenure-line faculty. Prior to 1980, almost all part-time and non-tenure-line faculty who worked under bargained contracts did so as part of larger units including tenure-line faculty. By the middle of the 1990s, however, there were almost 18,000 members of 35 units of non-tenure-line faculty at more than 90 institutions. Many more remained in mixed units. At the very end of the decade, with the founding of the Coalition of Contingent and Academic Labor (COCAL) and its work with multiple groups on organizing non-tenure-line faculty across Boston, a new direction in organizing was initiated (Zabel 2000).

A second growth area by the 1990s was in graduate student unionization. Graduate student unions date to the mid-1960s, when students at the Universities of California–Berkeley and Wisconsin–Madison organized; the former folded in the early 1970s but the latter operated under a series of contracts until 1980. There were some successes at large public institutions in the 1970s (e.g., Rutgers University and the Universities of Michigan and Oregon), though NLRB rulings denied students at private institutions protections for bargaining. At the very end of the 20th century, graduate student unionization was a vital but contentious issue. The number of graduate students in unions more than tripled in the 1990s, including through the addition of new units at both the State University of New York and the University of California (Berry and Savarese 2012). Yet despite the successes, opponents argued—and still argue—that graduate students were not primarily employees and that bargaining would upend student/faculty relations. They also criticized graduate students' frequent election of the International Union, United Automobile, Aerospace and Agricultural Implement Workers of America—commonly known as the United Auto Workers (UAW)—as a bargaining agent. The attempts to organize at private universities were most contested as the protracted efforts of Yale University's Graduate Employees and Students Organization demonstrated. The years-long fight for recognition, a 1995 grade strike, and allegations that the administration undertook unfair labor practices attracted considerable attention. Only in 2000, in a case involving graduate students at New York University (NYU), did the NLRB rule that students were, in fact, employees and deserving of protections. As the two decades since have shown, however, the situation was far from settled (DeCew 2003).

Taken together, at the end of the 20th century, the unionization of faculty and other instructional workers was well established. It may have "taken higher education by surprise" (Carr and VanEyck 1973, 1) when it first arrived, but it had stabilized and continued to slowly grow in public higher education. By the 1990s, heightened activity by educators without tenure or the ability to earn it pointed to a key direction of unionization in the new century.

An Emerging "Lacuna"

In 1994, Maitland and Hendrickson (1994) noted a "lacuna" in attention to faculty unions:

Bargaining on campus at first was the subject of considerable scrutiny and speculation. Would unions change decision-making patterns on campus, or affect collegiality? But the post-*Yeshiva* scholarly and polemical commentary on bargaining conditions and agreements diminished considerably.

(61)

Their point is an important one that helps capture the state of the field both to that time and since. Still, for a short period, significant work continued. Some was specifically about *Yeshiva* as numerous authors sought to understand the ruling and what it would mean for faculty, higher education, and professional workers more broadly. As Deitsch and Dilts (1983) contended, the treatments "for the most part, either focused upon the normative issues of whether the Court erred in its reasoning and why, or upon the closely related proper tack the NLRB should have taken" (34). Such emphasis on *Yeshiva* continued for several years.

Some of the early 1980s work was based on longstanding research projects and interests. As mentioned, Baldridge, Kemerer, and Associates (1981) monograph was built on research undertaken in the 1970s, but it did consider the challenges posed by *Yeshiva* and foretold a slowing of the expansion of faculty bargaining. Researchers focused some attention on faculty attitudes toward and reasons for unionizing, with studies pointing to both economic and non-economic correlates with views and behaviors. Hammer and Berman (1981), for example, found that satisfaction with economic issues correlated with voting behaviors but that faculty voice in governance, tenure protections, and grievance procedures were more important to those who voted to unionize. Dayal (1984; 1989) found that attaining academic freedom was the most important individual bargaining goal for faculty but that, overall, economic goals were more important than non-economic goals. Williams and Zirkel (1989) considered 75 studies undertaken over almost two decades, finding that initial unionization efforts might have been driven by economic factors but as apparent economic returns diminished, non-economic goals grew in importance. In the ensuing decade, small-scale studies on the issue continued, most often involving faculty at a single institution. As a whole, this work pointed to the importance of satisfaction with compensation and governance, beliefs in individual and union efficacy, and political liberalism as related to faculty members' propensity to support collective bargaining (Cain 2017a).

New techniques and the availability of large datasets pushed the work on compensation forward; many of the new studies found small union wage premiums at two-year colleges and smaller ones at four-year institutions. Across studies, a common theme was that faculty at research and doctoral universities were least likely to achieve a wage premium. Concerns still remained about potential spill-over effects, appropriate comparisons, and whether results were confounded by institutional conditions that might have been tied to the very decision to unionize. Some researchers examined differential wage effects, most often finding that bargaining benefitted those who were already relatively advantaged and only rarely finding a levelling or equity effect. A smaller body of work on satisfaction with salaries produced mixed results, though leaned toward unionized faculty being more satisfied (Cain 2017a). Important among these was Lillydahl and Singell's (1993) study using data from the National Survey of Postsecondary Faculty, which found that at four-year institutions associate and full professors saw the greatest wage premiums and that unionized faculty were more satisfied with compensation than non-unionized.

Limited evidence showed that there might be small gains for women in terms of both salary and tenuring rates, though, as Sosin, Rives, and West (1998) concluded, "Unions matter, but not to an extent that is likely to be considered satisfactory by the unions or by women" (40). The studies that examined tenure more broadly found weak evidence of increased satisfaction with processes. Some of the most significant work at the end of the century examined contract language related to faculty reductions. Together, the studies showed an increase in policies regarding retrenchment that provided faculty with more protections than would otherwise have existed. At the same time, the protections were limited, benefitted more senior faculty, and were more likely to establish policy than provide faculty a role in enacting it (e.g., Rhoades 1993; Williams and Zirkel 1988).

Contract analyses provided further findings beyond retrenchment policies, including that the scope of the issues covered in bargaining was increasing over time (e.g., Andes 1982; Julius and Chandler 1989). The most comprehensive of these studies was Rhoades's (1998) *Managed Professionals* based on 212 faculty contracts that were part of the NEA's Higher Education Contract Analysis System (HECAS). In an important book for the study of faculty unions and higher education more broadly, Rhoades examined the restructuring of higher education, including issues involving the shift to part-time labor, intellectual property concerns, control of faculty time, compensation and merit, and the impacts of technological change. His findings, informed by literature in the sociology of the professions and the field of higher education, pointed to increased managerial discretion and the negotiated restructuring of higher education. In short: "Unionized faculty are managed, stratified professionals. The contractual terms of faculty employment are such that managers have considerable flexibility to restructure academic labor" (257). Unions had achieved some gains for faculty in important areas yet had not been able to prevent the larger reorganization of higher education that was—and is—threatening the faculty writ large.

Of course, as in previous decades, scholars looked at additional issues. With strikes being among the most visible union actions (though not the most typical), they garnered attention, especially as related to determinants of and attitudes toward strikes. Studies found multiple factors related to militancy, including belief in strike efficacy, union commitment, and views of colleagues (e.g., Douglas 1988; McClendon and Klass 1993). Meador and Walters (1994) argued that faculty at unionized institutions produce less scholarship than those at non-unionized institutions; while they only considered Ph.D. granting public institutions, the findings did not account for the institutional differences within that broader group. Cameron (1982; 1985) examined organizational effectiveness more broadly, finding that unionized institutions appeared less effective, though he could not determine whether ineffectiveness was a cause of unionizing or a result. He also found that bargaining could decrease collegiality. More often, studies found that differences in collegiality or satisfaction with campus relations either between unionized and non-unionized faculty or before and after bargaining were weak or insignificant (e.g., Ormsby and Ormsby 1988). Considerations of non-tenure-line faculty were largely confined to those based on contract analyses, such as Rhoades's work and Maitland's (1987) analysis of two-year contracts in California.

Taken together, the research on unions and bargaining in higher education in the last two decades of the 20th century was idiosyncratic. Increasingly advanced methods and better data allowed for more complicated analyses, for example, and individual pieces and authors offered significant insight. But despite some important works, overall attention to these issues diminished in the 1980s and then did so even further in the 1990s.

"More Energy Among Faculty for Organizing"

The 21st century has seen continued gains in bargaining and increased efforts by non-tenure-line and graduate student workers. As Rhoades and Torres-Olave (2015) wrote,

> U.S. higher education was on the cusp and indeed in the midst of experiencing more energy among faculty for organizing local bargaining units than at any time in over 30 years. Not since the inception of collective bargaining for academic employees in the late 1960s and 1970s, had there been such interest and success in faculty organizing and voting for union representation.
>
> *(412)*

Indeed, more than 100,000 faculty were newly covered by collectively bargained contracts in the first decade of the new century. The best evidence indicates that 368,473 faculty were represented by 639 bargaining units on 1,174 campuses of 519 institutions or systems by 2010. Most were in public four-year colleges, but many were in public two-year colleges or other institution types. They remained localized in a small number of states with enabling legislation; California and New York combined for 58% of the organized (Berry and Savarese 2012). Over the next decade, the unionization of faculty continued to grow; in 2020, the National Center reported 411,921 faculty covered by bargained contracts (Herbert, Apkarian, and van der Naald 2020).

Much of the early 21st century growth was among non-tenure-line faculty, including many in the private sector. Herbert (2016) termed it "a major new shift in higher education" (1). This growth in non-tenure-line unionization implicated the larger move to a predominantly contingent faculty, as well as increased organizational efforts by both the traditional higher education bargaining agents and other unions. In the 2010s, the Service Employees International Union (SEIU), particularly, was active in organizing non-tenure-line faculty both at individual campuses and on city-wide bases. Of the 65 new units at private institutions that were recognized or certified between 2013 and 2019, 56 were affiliated with SEIU; 90% of the newly covered faculty at private institutions were in SEIU units (Herbert, Apkarian, and van der Naald 2020). These efforts were aided by increased activism among non-tenure-line faculty and their advocates, including unions and organizations such as COCAL and the New Faculty Majority, the latter of which was founded in 2009.

Other tenuously employed academic laborers also turned to bargaining, often with the UAW, SEIU, or other non-education-specific labor unions. Workers at the University of California (UC) formed the first unit of postdoctoral workers in 2005 and were soon joined by postdocs at the University of Massachusetts and Rutgers University. The National Center's most recent data indicates more than 14,000 postdocs and academic researchers in bargaining units, most of whom are at UC (Herbert, Apkarian, and van der Naald 2020). Graduate student unions likewise grew, with nine new units at public universities in the first few years of the new millennium, including one at the California State University system composed of more than 6,000 students (Berry and Savarese 2012). At private institutions, unionization was buffeted by competing NLRB rulings. The aforementioned 2000 ruling affording students at NYU bargaining protections both led to a contract at NYU and increased graduate student organizing more broadly. A 2004 reversal in a case involving Brown University, though, eliminated such protections. A 2016 decision involving Columbia University returned bargaining rights to student unions at private institutions, leading to a new surge in organizing. Eleven new units including almost 15,000 members were recognized in the next two years. The most recent numbers indicate more than 83,000 members of recognized graduate student unions, some of whom are actually undergraduates (Herbert, Apkarian, and van der Naald 2020).

Even with this growth, larger environmental and legal conditions worked against faculty and organizing. Beginning with Wisconsin in 2011, multiple states passed legislation that undercut public sector union rights. With exclusions for firefighters and many law enforcement workers, Wisconsin's Act 10 limited public sector contracts to one year and restricted negotiations to wages. It further required unions to recertify every year and explicitly eliminated faculty collective bargaining in the University of Wisconsin system. Indiana,

Michigan, and Wisconsin then passed so-called "right-to-work" legislation, barring requirements that non-union members pay fees to unions for their representation. In 2017, Iowa legislation most closely followed Act 10, limiting bargaining to salary for those unions whose membership did not include at least 30% public safety employees (Deviantz 2015; Taylor 2015; Flaherty 2017). These increasing attacks on and restrictions of public sector unions were joined by the Supreme Court's 2018 ruling in *Janus v American Federal, State, County, and Municipal Employees, Council 31*. By a 5–4 margin, the court ruled that required agency fees were unconstitutional, thereby depriving unions of resources while maintaining their responsibility to serve workers who refused to pay. While the initial effect on membership has not been as severe as many predicted, the ruling still poses significant challenges ("Unions fend off membership exodus in 2 years since Janus ruling" 2020). Moreover, excitement that the NLRB might relax rules on bargaining for faculty at private colleges proved unwarranted (Jashik 2015; Flaherty 2016).

In 2018, President Donald Trump appointed two new members of the NLRB, shifting the board in a conservative direction with implications for workers' rights writ large and in higher education. In 2014, the NLRB had ruled that non-tenure-line faculty at Pacific Lutheran University were covered by the NLRA but in a 2020 ruling, the reconstituted NLRB found that non-tenure-line employees at religious colleges were not entitled protections for bargaining. Anticipating that the new NLRB would reverse the 2016 ruling providing graduate unions protections, other organizing locals soon withdrew their petitions for recognition. In response, the NLRB took the unusual (and lengthy) step of proposing its own rules to strip graduate students of their rights. While these efforts were abandoned in early 2021, they highlighted the precarity that graduate workers face. Advocates of graduate workers' rights are hopeful that President Joseph Biden's appointments to the NLRB will further secure them (Marotti 2018; Myerson 2020).

"Paucity of Contemporary Scholarship"

The growth and continued importance of bargaining in the 21st century has opened up multiple avenues for research, but most have not been thoroughly explored. As William A. Herbert (2013), Director of the National Center, wrote, "The relative paucity of contemporary scholarship examining collective bargaining and labor representation issues is not due to a shortage of engaging and important topics" (3). Engagement with those topics has remained sporadic and has frequently not penetrated the scholarly field of higher education. Over the past decade, for example, less than 1% of the research papers at the Association for the Study of Higher Education's annual meetings have focused on unions or collective bargaining—most often there was one paper per year at the leading scholarly conference on higher education.

To be clear, it is not that scholarly writing on academic unions has not been produced in the 21st century, just that not enough has been done. The

National Center's *Journal of Collective Bargaining in the Academy*, conferences, and directories are intentionally intended to encourage and share such research. Moreover, books and other scholarly considerations do exist. DeCew (2003), for example, usefully conveyed the history, landscape, and contested issues surrounding faculty and graduate student unionization. Benjamin and Mauer's (2006) edited volume likewise provided context for unionization in higher education but more clearly focused on the practices of, approaches to, and experiences of organizing and bargaining. Wickens's (2008) review of the literature captured the state of research on faculty unions in the U.S. and Canada. Rhoades and Torres-Olave's (2015) "Academic Capitalism and (Secondary) Academic Labor Markets" was about more than unionization but included significant insight into the context and patterns of organizing. Like Wickens, Herbert, and others, they argued that there is a great deal more to know.

Some of the studies that were undertaken explored salaries. Findings include that wage premiums are smaller than previously thought at two-year colleges, and not statistically significant at four-year institutions (Henson et al. 2012; Hedrick et al. 2011). Katsinas, Ogun, and Bray (2016), though, cautioned that comparison groups matter and found evidence that among regional comprehensive public colleges, premiums do exist. Krieg et al. (2013) found that unionized faculty were more satisfied with their wages, even if the wages were not necessarily higher. Findings on gender-related wage gaps were mixed but more promising for gender equity was May, Moorhouse, and Bossard's (2010) finding that women were better represented across ranks at unionized public research universities.

Twenty-first century studies of satisfaction and unionization continued to show complicated relationships. While some found unionized faculty to be more likely to report dissatisfaction, others did not (Cain 2017a). Studies of faculty roles in governance—or at least perceptions of them—showed either no difference between unionized and non-unionized environments or increased faculty influence in the former. Kater and Levin's (2004) analysis of two-year college contracts, for example, showed the establishment of faculty governance roles, though mostly consulting rather than decision-making roles. Porter, though, found significant evidence of a "strong, positive difference" in faculty influence at unionized institutions.

As indicated by Rhoades and Torres-Olave's (2015) chapter, the larger shift to a contingent faculty generated attention in academic and related writing, some of which included significant consideration of unionization. Berry's (2005) *Reclaiming the Ivory Tower*, for example, was an important early book on organizing adjunct faculty. Much more recently, Tolley's (2018) edited *Professors in the Gig Economy* built on both research and experience to offer contextual and practical treatments of adjunct organizing and bargaining. Kezar, DePaola, and Scott's (2019) *The Gig Academy* was broader in scope but included treatment of unionization and calls for more collective and social justice-oriented action. These and other works have been joined by studies of specific events, issues, and outcomes involving non-tenure-line faculty organizing and bargaining, though not nearly enough considering its scope and importance.

Contract analyses constitute a key part of the recent research, much of it showing improved provisions for non-tenure-line faculty over contracts from earlier periods but still with limitations (e.g., Maitland and Rhoades, 2005). Rhoades (2013) found enough evidence of contractual language regarding "just-in-time higher" and "just-at-will nonrenewal," to "suggest that collective bargaining can provide a path" (11) to redefining hiring and continuation policies and practices. In a study of both HECAS and SEIU contracts, Rhoades (2017) found "there have been some significant gains in the contracts in due-process rights for adjunct faculty, but much managerial discretion remains" (664). Moreover, there were differences in contractual protections by sector, type of unit, and union. A cautionary piece by Klein (2010) argued that institutions had tightened control on intellectual property but Julius and DiGiovanni (2019) viewed contract outcomes more positively, arguing that unions' craft-like approach protected tenure and academic judgment.

Case studies offered further understandings of the processes of organizing and bargaining; many acknowledged the challenges but argued that the outcomes were positive for non-tenure-line faculty and postdocs (e.g., Camacho and Rhoads 2015; Stubaus 2015). Some found conflict between unionized non-tenure-track and tenure-track faculty (e.g., Ruiz 2007). Surveys by both the Coalition on the Academic Workforce (2012) and Gehrke and Kezar (2015) found perceived compensation and working condition benefits for unionized non-tenure-line faculty. Elsewhere, in a study of how non-tenure-line faculty construct support, Kezar (2013) found both the belief that the union was beneficial and some distrust. Life conditions and organizational features were key.

Graduate student unions likewise received useful but limited attention in the first two decades of this century. Firsthand accounts such as Krause et al.'s (2008) edited volume on organizing and striking at NYU offered insight into politics, ideology, and actions of unionizing graduate students, as well as the industry and administration that opposed them. Research studies often focused on reasons for graduate student unionization and members' ideological perspectives. Several found that compensation and working conditions were the primary drivers of graduate student organizing and primary points of negotiation (e.g., Rhoades and Rhoads 2003). Julius and Gumport (2003) argued "though the words 'dignity and respect' fly off the pages of much of the campaign literature of graduate student organizers, our data show that the unionization of these individuals is driven fundamentally by economic realities" (195). Still, as Rhoads and Rhoades (2005) argued, "bread-and-butter" issues might be the most important drivers of graduate student unionization but they are joined by a larger critique of the corporate practices of higher education.

Studies of graduate unions effects were rare but often focused on compensation and/or faculty-student relations. While firsthand accounts often conveyed success in economic outcomes, the small body of existing research is less clear. Ehrenberg et al. (2004) found that the "the impact of graduate assistant unions on economic outcomes does not appear to be very large" (230) and Schenk (2010) found a wage premium but not an overall compensation premium. Rogers, Eaton, and Voos (2013) though, found "some support for the notion that unionization improves the economic terms of graduate student employment" (507). The work on faculty–student relations is more decisive. Multiple studies found little or no evidence that unionization significantly impairs them; Rogers, Eaton, and Voos are among those who argued that it might actually improve them.

Like that in the last years of the 20th century, the 21st century literature is sparse but includes useful works that add to our understandings of unionization and faculty and graduate students more broadly. The best of them were theoretical rich and methodologically advanced, including deep qualitative analyses. Their findings sometimes conflicted, but they often showed some benefits from bargaining. Throughout, these pieces shared the common understanding that there is much more work left to do.

Conclusion

Academic unions are important. From the activist beginnings of non-bargaining campus locals a century ago to the activist efforts of graduate students, adjuncts, and others today, they have provided mechanisms for educational workers to assert their voices and affect the conditions of their work. In some cases, they have pushed further in pursuit of broader social justice. They were contested at the outset and in some corners remain so, but they are an established facet of U.S. higher education. Currently, there are a half a million workers covered by contracts bargained by faculty, postdoctoral researcher, and graduate student unions. As the discussion above indicates, there is evidence that academic unions have provided benefits for their members and have not caused the problems some feared, yet the research is mixed and much of it is dated. It is a great detriment to the scholarly field of higher education that the modern research on the topic is not more robust. It is even more problematic for the practice of higher education.

Note

1 For a more comprehensive discussion, see Cain (2017a), on which this chapter draws.

Bibliography

Andes, J. 1982. A decade of development in higher education collective bargaining: Changes in contract content. *Journal of Collective Negotiations in the Public Sector 11*, no. 1: 285–295.

Angulo, Z. 2020. The NLRB and graduate-worker employee status: Past, present, and future. *Berkeley Journal of Employment and Labor Law 41*, no. 1: 187–217.

Baldridge, J. V., Kemerer, F. R. and Associates.1981. *Assessing the impact of faculty collective bargaining.* AAHE-ERIC/Higher Education Research Report 8. Washington, DC: American Association of Higher Education.

Bayer, A. E. 1970. *College and university faculty: A statistical description.* ACE Research Reports 5, no. 5. Washington, DC: American Council on Education.

Bayer, A. E. 1973. *Teaching faculty in academe: 1972–1973.* ACE Research Reports 8, no. 2. Washington, DC: American Council on Education.

Begin, J. P. 1974. Faculty governance and collective bargaining: An early appraisal. *Journal of Higher Education* 45, no. 8: 582–593.

Benjamin, E. 2015. How did we get here? The AAUP's evolving emphasis on collective bargaining. *Academe* 101, no. 1: 38–45.

Benjamin, E., and M. Mauer, eds. 2006. *Academic collective bargaining.* Washington, DC: Modern Language Association and the American Association of University Professors.

Berry, J. 2005. *Reclaiming the ivory tower: Organizing adjunct to change higher education.* New York: Monthly Review Press.

Berry, J., and M. Savarese. 2012. *Directory of U.S. faculty contracts and bargaining agents in institutions of higher education.* New York: National Center for the Study of Collective Bargaining in Higher Education and the Professions.

Buder, L. 1962. Report from New York City: The teachers revolt. *Phi Delta Kappan* 43, no. 9: 370–376.

Cain, T. R. 2010. The first attempts to unionize the faculty. *Teachers College Record* 12, no. 3: 875–913.

Cain, T. R. 2012a. *Establishing academic freedom: Politics, principles, and the development of core values.* New York: Palgrave Macmillan.

Cain, T. R. 2012b. "Only organized effort will find the way out!": Faculty unionization at Howard University, 1918–1950. *Perspectives on the History of Higher Education* 29: 113–150.

Cain, T. R. 2012c. Unionised faculty and the political left: Communism and the American Federation of Teachers on the eve of the second world war. *History of Education* 41, no. 4: 515–535.

Cain, T. R. 2017a. Campus unions: Organized faculty and graduate students in U.S. higher education. *ASHE Higher Education Report Series* 43, no. 3. San Francisco: Jossey-Bass.

Cain, T. R. 2017b. Collective bargaining and college faculty: Illinois in the 1960s. *Perspectives on the History of Higher Education* 32: 116–145.

Cain, T. R, and P. J. Wilkinson. 2019. Influence without bargaining: Unionization at the University of Wisconsin, 1930–1957. *Labor: Studies in Working-Class History* 16, no. 2: 99–122.

Camacho, S, and R. A. Rhoads. 2015. Breaking the silence: The unionization of post-doctoral workers at the University of California. *Journal of Higher Education* 86, no. 2: 295–335.

Cameron, K. 1982. The relationship between faculty unionism and organizational effectiveness. *Academy of Management Journal* 25, no. 1: 6–24.

Cameron, K. 1985. Investigating the causal association between unionism and organizational effectiveness. *Research in Higher Education* 23, no. 4: 387–411.

Carr, R. K., and D. K. VanEyck. 1973. *Collective bargaining comes to the campus.* Washington, DC: American Council on Education.

Chandler, M. K. and D. J. Julius. 1979. *Faculty vs. administration: Rights issues in academic collective bargaining.* New York: National Center for the Study of Collective Bargaining in Higher Education and the Professions.

Coalition on the Academic Workforce. 2012. A portrait of part-time faculty members: A summary of findings on art-time faculty respondents to the Coalition on the Academic Workforce survey of contingent faculty members and instructors. Retrieved from http://www.academicworkforce.org/CAW_portrait_2012.pdf.

College Section of the New York Teachers Union. n.d. [1936]. *The college teacher and the trade union.* New York: The College Section of the Teachers Union.

"College teachers in city join union." 1963, April 27. *New York Times*, 23.

Davis, B. H. 1967, September 12. Memo to File. Box 3, Folder REI Specific Insts. Belleville Junior College (Illinois), Committee N Papers. Committee N Papers, American Association of University Professors Archives, Gelman Library, George Washington University.

Dayal, S. 1984. Unionized professions and bargaining priorities: An exploratory study of unionized professions. *Journal of Collective Negotiations* 13, no. 1: 55–65.

Dayal, S. 1989. Collective bargaining among academic professionals: An analysis of issues and outcomes. *Journal of Collective Negotiations* 18, no. 3: 207–216.

DeCew, J. W. 2003. *Unionization in the academy: Visions and realities.* Lanham, MD: Rowman & Littlefield Publishers.

Deitsch, C. R., and D. A. Dilts. 1983. NLRB v. Yeshiva University: A positive approach. *Monthly Labor Review* (July): 34–37.

Deviantz, V. G. 2015. Right-to-work laws, the southernization of U.S. labor relations and the U.S. trade union movement. *Labor Studies Journal* 40, no. 1: 297–318.

Douglas, J. M. 1988. Professors on strike: And analysis of two decades of faculty work stoppages—1966–1985. *Labor Lawyer* 4, no. 1: 87–101.

Ehrenberg, R. D., D. B. Klaff, A. T. Kezsbom, and M. P. Nagowski. 2004. Collective bargaining in American higher education. In *Governing academia: Who is in charge of the modern university?*, ed. R. G. Ehrenberg, 209–295. Ithaca, NY: Cornell University Press.

Elam, S. M. 1981. The National Education Association: Political powerhouse or paper tiger? *Phi Delta Kappan* 63, no. 3: 169–174.

"Faculty Unionization in 1978—A Review." 1979. *National Center for the Study of Collective Bargaining in Higher Education Newsletter* 7, no. 1: 4–5.

Flaherty, C. 2016, January 21. Failing the test for faculty unions, *Inside Higher Ed.* https://www.insidehighered.com/news/2016/01/21/proposed-faculty-union-carroll-college-first-be-rejected-under-new-guidelines.

Flaherty, C. 2017, February 10. Collective bargaining in the crosshairs. *Inside Higher Ed.* https://www.insidehighered.com/news/2017/02/10/iowa-lawmakers-push-bill-severely-restrict-collective-bargaining-public-campus.

Flaherty, C. 2020, June 11. No NLRB jurisdiction at religious colleges. *Inside Higher Ed.* https://www.insidehighered.com/news/2020/06/11/no-nlrb-jurisdiction-religious-colleges.

Franke, A. H. 1984. Two trends in academic collective bargaining: A faculty representative's perspective. *Journal of Law and Education* 13, no. 4: 651–668.

Garbarino, J. W., with B. Aussieker. 1975. *Faculty bargaining: Change and conflict.* New York: McGraw Hill Book Company.

Garbarino, J. W., and Lawler, J. 1979. Faculty union activity in higher education. *Industrial Relations* 18, no. 2: 244–246.

Garcia, E. H. 1975. Community college labor contracts and the issues: An analysis of 64 agreements. *Journal of Collective Negotiations* 4, no. 1: 83–100.

Gehrke, S. J., and A. Kezar. 2015. Supporting non-tenure-track at 4-year colleges and universities: A national study of deans' values and decisions. *Educational Policy* 29, no. 6: 926–960.

Hammer, T. H., and M. Berman. 1981. The role of noneconomic factors in faculty union voting. *Journal of Applied Psychology* 66, no. 4: 415–421.

"Hampton Institute in negotiations." 1947. *The Public Record* 2, no. 1: 11.

Hedrick, S. E., D. W. Henson, J. M. Kreig, and C. S. Wassell Jr. 2011. Is there really a faculty union salary premium? *Industrial and Labor Relations Review* 63, no. 3: 558–575.

Henson, S. E., J. M. Kreig, C. S. Wassell Jr., and D. W. Hedrick. 2012. Collective bargaining and community college faculty: What is the wage impact? *Journal of Labor Research* 33, no. 1: 104–117.

Herbert, W. A. 2013. Shelter from the storm: Rekindling research on collective bargaining and representation issues. *Journal of Collective Bargaining in the Academy* 5, article 2. http://thekeep.eiu.edu/jcba/vol5/iss1/2.

Herbert, W. A. 2016. The winds of changes shift: An analysis of recent growth in bargaining units and representation efforts in higher education. *Journal of Collective Bargaining in the Academy* 8, article 1. https://thekeep.eiu.edu/jcba/vol8/iss1/1/.

Herbert, W. A. 2017. The history books tell it? Collective bargaining in higher education in the 1940s. *Journal of Collective Bargaining in the Academy* 9, article 3. https://thekeep.eiu.edu/jcba/vol9/iss1/3.

Herbert, W. A., J. Apkarian, and J. van der Naald, 2020. *2020 supplementary directory of new bargaining agents and contracts in institutions of higher education, 2013–2019.* New York: National Center for the Study of Collective Bargaining in Higher Education and the Professions.

Herziger, W. A. 1967, June 29. Letter to H. A. Juris, Folder 4, Box 2, U.S. Mss. 77a, Wisconsin Historical Society.

Hurd, R., and A. Foerster with B. H. Johnson. 1996. *Directory of faculty contracts and bargaining agents in institutions of higher education,* Vol. 22. New York: National Center for the Study of Collective Bargaining in Higher Education and the Professions.

Hutcheson, P. A. 2000. *A professional professoriate: Unionization, bureaucratization, and the AAUP.* Nashville: Vanderbilt University Press.

Hutcheson, P. A., and R. D. Kidder. 2011. In the national interest: The college and university in the United States in the post-World War II era. In *Higher Education: Handbook of theory and research,* Vol. 26, ed. J. C. Smart and M. B. Paulsen, 221–264. Springer.

Janus v American Federal, State, County, and Municipal Employees, Council 31, 585 US ___.

Jashik, S. 2015, January 2. Big union win. *Inside Higher Ed.* https://www.insidehighered.com/news/2015/01/02/nlrb-ruling-shifts-legal-ground-faculty-unions-private-colleges;

Julius, D. J. 2012. Universities should continue to bargain. *Journal of Collective Bargaining in the Academy* 3, article 1. https://thekeep.eiu.edu/jcba/vol3/iss1/1/.

Julius, D. J., and M. K. Chandler. 1989. Academic bargaining agents in higher education: Do their achievements matter? *Journal of Collective Negotiations in the Public Sector* 18, no. 1: 9–58.

Julius, D. J., and N.DiGiovanni, Jr. 2019. Academic collective bargaining: Status, process, and prospect. *Academic Labor: Research and Artistry* 3, article 11. https://digitalcommons.humboldt.edu/alra/vol3/iss1/11.

Julius, D. J., and P. J. Gumport. 2003. Graduate student unionization: Catalysts and consequences. *Review of Higher Education* 26, no. 2: 187–216.

Kadish, S. H., W. W. Van Alstyne, and R. K. Webb. 1972. The manifest unwisdom of the AAUP as a collective bargaining agency: A dissenting view. In B. H. Davis, Council position on collective bargaining, 57–61. *AAUP Bulletin* 58, no. 1: 46–61.

Kater, S., and J. S. Levin. 2004. Shared governance in community colleges. *Community College Journal of Research and Practice* 29, no. 1: 1–23.

Katsinas, S. G., J. A. Ogun, and N. J. Bray. 2016. Monetary compensation of full-time faculty in American public regional universities: The impact of geography and the existence of collective bargaining. *Journal of Collective Bargaining in the Academy* 8, no. 3: https://thekeep.eiu.edu/jcba/vol8/iss1/3.

Keck, D. J. 1992. The higher education roots of the NEA, 1957–1991. In *The NEA 1992 almanac of higher education*, 118–126. Washington, DC: NEA.

Kemerer, F. R., and J. V. Baldridge. 1975. *Unions on campus: A national study of the consequences of faculty bargaining.* San Francisco: Jossey-Bass, Inc.

Kemerer, F. R., and J. V. Baldridge. 1975–1976. The impact of faculty unions on governance. *Change* 7, no. 10: 50–51, 62.

Kemerer, F. R., and J. V. Baldridge. 1980. Unions in higher education: The going gets tougher. *Phi Delta Kappan* 61, no. 10: 714–715.

Kemerer, F. R., and J. V. Baldridge. 1981. Senates and unions: An unexpected peaceful coexistence. *Journal of Higher Education* 52, no. 3: 256–264.

Kezar, A. 2013. Non-tenure-track faculty's social construction of a supportive work environment. *Teachers College Record* 115, no. 12: 1–47.

Kezar, A., T. DePaola, and D. T. Scott. 2019. *The gig academy: Mapping labor in the neoliberal university.* Baltimore: Johns Hopkins University Press.

Klein, M. W. 2010. Ten years after *Managed Professionals*: Who owns intellectual property now? *Journal of Collective Bargaining in the Academy* 2, article 2. http://thekeep.eiu.edu/jcba/vol2/iss1/2.

Krause, M., M. Nolan, M. Palm, and A. Ross, eds. 2008. *The university against itself: The NYU strike and the future of the academic workplace.* Philadelphia: Temple University Press.

Krieg, J. M., C. S. Wassell, Jr., D. W. Hedrick, and S. E. Henson. 2013. Collective bargaining and faculty job satisfaction. *Industrial Relations: A Journal of Economy and Society* 52, no. 3: 619–644.

Kroeger, F. 1967. The effect of a negotiated contract on the relations of the faculty to the administrator. *College Composition and Communication* 18, no. 2: 85–87.

Kugler, I. 1997. The 1966 strike at St. John's University, a memoir. *Labor's Heritage* 9, no. 2: 4–19.

Ladd, Jr., E. C., and S. M. Lipset. 1973. *Professors, unions, and American higher education.* Washington, DC: American Enterprise Institute for Public Policy Research.

Lee, B. A. 1978. *Collective bargaining in four-year colleges: Impact on institutional practice.* AAHE-ERIC/Higher Education Research Report 5. Washington, DC: American Association of Higher Education.

Lester, J. A. 1968. "The American Federation of Teachers in higher education: A history of union organization of faculty members in colleges and universities" (EdD diss.). University of Toledo.

Levine, M. J. 1967. Higher education and collective action: Will professors unionize? *Journal of Higher Education* 38, no. 5: 263–268.

Lillydahl, J. H., and L. D. Singell. 1993. Job satisfaction, salaries, and unions: The determination of university faculty compensation. *Economics of Education Review* 12, no. 3: 233–243.

Maitland, C. 1987. Temporary faculty and collective bargaining in higher education in California. *Journal of Collective Negotiations in the Public Sector* 16, no. 3: 233–257.

Maitland, C., and R. Hendrickson. 1994. Trends in bargaining. In *The NEA 1994 almanac of higher education*, 59–78. Washington, DC: NEA.

Maitland, C. and G. Rhoades. 2005. Bargaining for contingent faculty. In *The NEA 2005 almanac of higher education*, 75–83. Washington, DC: NEA.

Marotti, A. 2018, February 14. "University of Chicago graduate students want to bypas sGOP-controlled labor board in contract talks." *Chicago Tribune.* https://www.chicagotri bune.com/business/ct-biz-university-of-chicago-graduate-student-union-20180214-story. html.

May, A. M., E. A. Moorhouse, and J. A. Bossard. 2010. Representation of women faculty at public research universities: Do unions matter? *ILR Review* 63, no. 4: 699–718.

McClendon, J. A., and B. Klass. 1993. Determinants of strike-related militancy: An analysis of a university faculty strike. *Industrial and Labor Relations Review* 46, no. 3: 560–573.

Meador, M., and S. J. K. Walters. 1994. Unions and productivity: Evidence from academe. *Journal of Labor Research* 15, no. 4: 373–386.

Metzger, W. P. 1990. The 1940 Statement of Principles on Academic Freedom and Tenure. *Law and Contemporary Problems* 53, no. 3: 3–77.

Moore, E. 1975. The determination of bargaining units for college faculties. *University of Pittsburgh Law Review* 37, no. 1: 43–62.

Morand, M. J., and D. S. McPherson. 1980. Unionism's effects on faculty pay: Handicapping the data. *Monthly Labor Review* 103 (June): 34–36.

Mortimer, K. P. 1974. *Research data on tenure and governance under collective bargaining.* Speech delivered at the Annual Meeting of the American Federation of Teachers (1974). Retrieved from ERIC database. (ED100200).

Murolo, P. 2018, June 11. Five lessons from the history of public sector unions. *Labor Notes.* https://www.labornotes.org/2018/06/five-lessons-history-public-sector-unions.

Murphy, M. 2000. *Blackboard unions: The AFT & the NEA, 1900–1980.* Ithaca: Cornell University Press.

Myerson, H. 2020, November 19. What a Biden labor board could do. *The American Prospect.* https://prospect.org/day-one-agenda/what-a-biden-labor-board-could-do/.

National Labor Relations Board *v.* Yeshiva University, 444 U.S. 672 (1980).

Ormsby, J. G., and S. Y. Ormsby, 1998. The effect of unionization on faculty job satisfaction: A longitudinal study. *Journal of Collective Negotiations in the Public Sector* 17, no. 2: 153–160.

Ponak, A. M., and M. Thompson. 1979. Faculty attitudes and the scope of bargaining. *Industrial Relations* 18, no. 1: 97–102.

Porter, S. R. 2013. The causal effects of unions on institutional decision-making. *Industrial & Labor Relations Review* 66, no. 5: 1192–1211.

Rhoades, G. 1993. Retrenchment clauses in faculty union contracts: Faculty rights and administrative discretion. *Journal of Higher Education* 64, no. 3: 312–347.

Rhoades, G. 1998. *Managed professionals: Unionized faculty and restructuring academic labor.* Albany: State University of New York Press.

Rhoades, G. 2013. Bargaining quality in part-time faculty working conditions: Beyond just-in-time employment and just-at-will non-renewal. *Journal of Collective Bargaining in the Academy* 4, article 4. https://thekeep.eiu.edu/jcba/vol4/iss1/4/.

Rhoades, G. 2017. Bread and roses, and quality too? A new faculty majority negotiating the new academy. *Journal of Higher Education* 88, no 5: 645–671.

Rhoades, G., and R. A. Rhoades. 2003. The public discourse of U.S. graduate student employee unions: Social movement identities, ideologies, and strategies. *Review of Higher Education* 26, no. 2: 163–286.

Rhoades, G., and B. M. Torres-Olave. 2015. Academic capitalism and (secondary) labor markets: Negotiation a new academy and research agenda. In *Higher education: Handbook of theory and research*, Vol. 30, ed. M. Paulsen, 383–430. Springer.

Rhoads, R., and G. Rhoades. 2005. Graduate employee unionization as symbol of and challenge to the corporatization of U.S. research universities. *Journal of Higher Education* 76, no. 3: 243–275.

Rogers, S. E., A. E. Eaton, and P. B. Voos. 2013. Effects of unionization on graduate student employees: Relations, academic freedom, and pay. *ILR Review* 22, no. 2: 487–510.

Ruiz, E. A. 2007. *The stone that struck goliath: The Part-time Faculty Association*, Washington State Community and Technical Colleges, and class-action lawsuits. In *The current landscape and changing perspectives of part-time faculty. New Directions for Community Colleges, no. 140,* ed. R. L. Wagoner, 49–54. San Francisco: Jossey-Bass.

Schenk, T. L. Jr. 2010. The effects of graduate-student unionization on stipends. http://dx.doi.org/10.2139/ssrn.1831975.

Shannon, K. E. 1973. Labor law—Determination of the appropriate faculty bargaining unit in a private university—New York University. *Boston College Law Review* 15, no. 2: 423–442.

Slater, J. E. 2004. *Public workers: Government employee unions, the law and the state, 1900–1962.* Ithaca: Cornell University Press.

Snyder, T. D., ed. 1993. *120 years of American education: A statistical portrait.* Washington, DC: U.S. Department of Education, Office of Educational Research and Improvement, National Center for Education Statistics.

Sosin, J. R., J. Rives, and J. West. 1998. Unions and gender pay equity in academe: A study of U.S. institutions. *Feminist Economics* 4, no. 2: 25–45.

Stubaus, K. R. 2015. The professionalization of non-tenure-track faculty in the United States: Three case studies from public research institutions: Rutgers, The State University of New Jersey, University of Illinois at Urbana-Champaign, and University of Oregon. *Journal of Collective Bargaining in the Academy* 0, article 14. http://thekeep.eiu.edu/jcba/vol0/iss10/34.

Taylor, D. 2015. Can renewal emerge from destructions? Crisis and opportunity in Wisconsin. *Labor Studies Journal* 40, no. 1: 396–418.

Teichgraeber, III, R. F. 2015. Introduction. In Thorstein Veblen, *The Higher Learning in America: A Memorandum on the Conduct of Universities by Business Men*, 1–32. Baltimore: Johns Hopkins University Press.

Thelin, J. R. 2018. *Going to college in the sixties.* Baltimore: Johns Hopkins University Press.

Thomas, S. L., and V. McGehee. 1994. Faculty bargaining in private colleges and universities: Beyond Yeshiva. *Employee Responsibilities and Rights Journal* 7, no. 4: 297–315.

Tolley, K. ed. 2018. *Professors in the gig economy: Unionizing adjunct faculty in America.*Baltimore: Johns Hopkins University Press.

Unionization among college faculty–1983. 1984. *National Center for the Study of Collective Bargaining in Higher Education and the Professions Newsletter* 12, no. 1: 1–3.

Unionization among college faculty–1990. 1990. *National Center for the Study of Collective Bargaining in Higher Education and the Professions Newsletter* 18, no. 1: 1–7.

"Unions fend off membership exodus in 2 years since Janus ruling." 2020, June 26. *Bloomberg Law*. https://news.bloomberglaw.com/daily-labor-report/unions-fend-off-membership-exodus-in-2-years-since-janus-ruling.

"UPW locals take the floor." 1949. *The Public Record* 4, no. 2: 4.

Urban, W. J. 2007. Higher education and the National Education Association: A sesquicentennial review. In *The NEA 2007 almanac of higher education*, 27–40. Washington, DC: NEA.

Urban, W. J. 2013. *Gender, race, and the National Education Association: Professionalism and its limitations.* New York: Routledge.

Wickens, C. M. 2008. The organizational impact of university labor unions. *Higher Education* 56, no. 5: 545–564.

Williams, G. B., and P. A. Zirkel. 1988. Academic penetration in faculty collective bargaining contracts in higher education. *Research in Higher Education* 28, no. 1: 76–92.

Williams, G. B., and P. A. Zirkel. 1989. Shift in collective bargaining issues in higher education: A review of the literature. *Journal of Collective Negotiations in the Public Sector* 18, no. 1: 73–88.

Wing, H. A. 1940, January. Monthly report. Box 23, Folder Pittsburgh College Teachers Federation, Pittsburgh and Allegheny County, PA, #646, AFT Defunct Locals, Archive of Labor and Union Affairs, Wayne State University.

Yellowitz, I. 1987. Academic governance and collective bargaining in the City University of New York. *Academe* 73, no. 6: 8–11.

Zabel, G. 2000. A new campus rebellion: Organizing Boston's contingent faculty. *New Labor Forum* 6 (Spring–Summer): 90–98.

2

SYMBIOSIS AND TENSIONS

Shared Governance and Unions

Adrianna Kezar and Jude Paul Matias Dizon

Shared governance (which is an administration/faculty partnership that pro-motes collaboration, shared decision-making, and accountability in the opera-tions of a campus) and unionization have long been considered incompatible and seen as emerging from very different views of the role of faculty within their institutions and the ways they accomplish influence and help to define professional working conditions (Burgan, 2006). There is over 50 years of lit-erature describing the relationship between these two entities and generally taking two very different positions – that they are incompatible or compatible. While the thesis of incompatibility drove the narrative and views in early years from the 1970s through 1990s, in the last 20 years there has been a shift to considering the compatibility of these two processes. During that time period, higher education underwent a transformation, particularly, the rise of academic capitalism which has re-shaped the labor relations on campuses. It is perhaps not a coincidence, that in the same time period that the compatibility thesis became popular that academic capitalism was reshaping campuses so that the faculty influence was in decline through shared governance and their working condi-tions being dramatically undercut, becoming contingent, deprofessionalized, and unbundled.

In this chapter, we reflect back on this 50-year discussion about the rela-tionship between shared governance and faculty unions, exploring the empirical literature on the topic, which is scant. Most of the scholarship in this area has been arguments for a particular perspective. In examining the empirical research, the notion that these processes are wholly incompatible or completely compatible are brought into question. Instead, studies that examine the process

DOI: 10.4324/9781003138990-3

in detail identify ways that they are both complementary and supportive of each other but can at times be at odds with each other. The devil is in the details as they say. Therefore, it is important that campus leaders in shared governance and unions carefully orchestrate the relationship between the two so they can maximize the ways they can complement each other and avoid or best navigate the tensions. This chapter also demonstrates the historical and context-related impact on these processes. And we conclude that few universal recommendations can be made, situations change based on context and time period.

In the Beginning: Hesitation and Cautious Optimism – Late 1960–late 1970s

As noted in the introduction, placing this discussion in historical context helps to appreciate how and why the relationship between these two processes has changed over time. Almost all discussions of the relationship between shared governance and unions starts by noting that shared governance predates unionization by decades going back to the 1920s as well as noting that in 1965 there were virtually no unionized campuses. Shared governance is typically defined as the extent to which faculty participate in decision-making processes involving academic policies, programs, and other key issues at higher education institutions (Schwartz 1980). Shared governance is based on notions of collegiality, where faculty work with administrators to make decisions often through a faculty senate, as well as norms of professionalism, where faculty should have input on their work environment as they know best how to structure their work (Burgan, 2006).

The most widely cited definition and standard practices of shared governance were established in the mid-1960s by the American Association of University Professors (AAUP) in the Statement on Government in College and Universities. This document outlines the faculty's role in governance in detail, noting that the faculty should have the primary oversight regarding areas such as curriculum, subject matter and instructional methods, research activities, and faculty status.

Unionization often emerged on campuses where faculty were not experiencing shared governance and their voice was diminished by autocratic presidents and central administrations (Cohen & Brawer, 2003; Kater & Levin, 2004). They emerged within community college settings that were expanding as a sector throughout the 1960s and early 1970s. As unionization emerged, it was assumed it would clash with traditional definitions of collegiality where faculty and administrators work together on policy; especially at more elite institutions and universities where faculty often had the most power. Throughout the 1970s and 1980s, unionization was viewed as potentially destructive to the long-time tradition of shared governance. Thus, a gulf emerged between two-year institutions that became unionized and four-year institutions and universities where shared governance was still the prevalent model.

Some of the early literature on unions suggested they were undercutting the power of senates on campuses (Kemerer & Baldridge, 1975). Some feared collective bargaining would enable unions to take over or replace faculty senates (Kemerer & Baldridge, 1975). There was even some speculation about the end of faculty governance (Kemerer & Baldridge, 1975). Although the notion of a complete demise of faculty senates was not widely held, it was clear that unions did have the power to curtail faculty senate influence over economic issues and that unions had the potential to share jurisdiction with senates in a number of key areas such as personnel decision-making (Kemerer & Baldridge, 1975). The early narrative was characterized as one of unions violating principles of collegiality that were part of shared governance and leading to the decline of shared governance and administrative and faculty relationships.

The Stanford Project on Academic Governance (1975) provided some of the first large-scale empirical data and identified that unions tended to exist on campuses where there was weak or virtually no shared governance contradicting the idea it was usurping collegiality. Unionization was occurring because of the lack of shared governance not that it was replacing it. Community colleges that emerged out of K-12 governance systems often lacked a history with shared governance and were among the first to unionize. The study also identified that the campuses where unions and shared governance existed tended to take on different issues – dual tracks. In the "dual track" unions focused on economics and working conditions, while senates focused more on academic matters. Areas of joint responsibility or "concurrent jurisdiction"included various aspects of personnel issues and decision-making. And research revealed an "unexpected peaceful coexistence" (Kemerer & Baldridge, 1981), faculty were committed to shared governance and a division of decision-making emerged between senates and unions, with senates having responsibility for a range of academic, curricular, and educational matters, and unions having responsibility for wages, working conditions, and a range of other non-academic matters

Over Time: Incompatibility, 1980s–1990s

Over time, research studies identified that unions tended to expand into areas where shared governance was prominent creating overlap and tensions (Keller, 1983). So the original proposition of dual tracks became challenged in the 1980s. Evidence of union expansion into the faculty senate's purview is found early on. For example, a 1979 survey showed that over half the presidents and faculty union chairpersons polled agreed with the statement, "Our union is gradually moving into educational issues, trying to influence curriculum and program decisions" (Kemerer & Baldridge, 1981). They note that faculty unions may pursue issues that are historically in the purview of the faculty senates when they are hard-pressed to deliver on matters typically within the traditional scope of bargaining, in an effort to secure some deliverables for union members, it can often mean securing contract provisions that can over-step what was previously the domain of the campus senate. Studies throughout the 1980s and 1990s saw the encroachment of unions increasingly into deci-sions that have been part of shared governance related to curriculum, educa-tional matters, and policy.

Several studies throughout the 1990s found evidence of the ways unions were reshaping shared governance away from collegial discussions and delib-eration and becoming more legalistic and bound by collective-bargaining tra-ditions. Research identified that unions produced an overemphasis on rules and regulations, decline in debate and a perceived decrease in collegiality (Ponak, Thompson, & Zerbe, 1992). Drummond and Reitsch (1995) found that col-lective bargaining redefined the governance process so that rules reigned and collegiality was sometimes discouraged. Studies seem to also identify that col-lective bargaining and unionization were changing the culture of campuses, particularly building antagonistic relationships between faculty and adminis-trators. For example, Signorelli (1997) conducted a case study of Union County College exploring its unionization process. The campus unionized as a result of no longer having adequate involvement in shared governance. In the 1980s, faculty went on strike over the administration's decision to increase class sizes. The researcher documents how the collective-bargaining process seems to have intensified the division between faculty and administration, and negatively affected the climate of shared governance. The researcher concludes that col-lective bargaining by its very nature and its roots in the industrial world creates antagonism and results in overly prescriptive roles for faculty and limitations for both parties. Many proponents of shared governance found evidence that col-lective bargaining was reshaping the process in ways they felt was problematic. Yet union supporters looked at the same case study and saw that it was insti-tuted because shared governance was being violated and faculty had no voice in decision-making so that pursuing unionization was not really threatening to collegiality and professionalism (Castro, 2012). So the same evidence was often interpreted differently.

Additionally, White (1998), using a case study methodology, compared the experiences of two community colleges in California in which the unions pre-vented a strong faculty senate from developing, and even as the senate devel-oped the union had strong hold over and influence over shared governance. Castro's (2012) study suggest that academic senates' power of influence is often diminished by unions. Some senators reported that when senates are viewed by the campus administration, the Chancellor's office, and the Board of Trustees, as aligned with the union, their influence is diminished. Many participants reported occasions when the senate faced competition with, or a challenge of, their authority by the union, and of them, most shared a view that the union was seeking to assert influence in more and more areas that were traditionally considered to be the purview of the senate. The incompatibility argument was often based on single case studies of institutions where conflicts emerge between the two processes. The degree to which incompatibility is widespread or deeply problematic is not empirically known.

Others have pointed to legislation that prevent shared governance from supporting unionization. At private institutions, faculty members, being seen as managerial employees, prevented the unionization of these campuses. The Supreme Court ruled that Yeshiva University faculty were not covered by the National Labor Relations Act (NLRA) because they were "managerial" employees. In its almost evenly split decision, the court determined that the university administration had no statutory obligation to bargain with the union because it found that faculty at Yeshiva possessed a degree of management authority appropriate to exclude them from protection under the NLRA. The court's decision stemmed from what it considered evidence of Yeshiva faculty's managerial functions and authority through the role faculty play in the university governance process which put the shared governance and collective-bargaining process at odds. And there were others (Devinatz, 2001) who argued that shared governance and professionalism can prevent faculty from unionizing and has done so historically. So shared governance is incompatible with unions as it is not supportive of this approach. Case studies demonstrate how this logic can be utilized by administrations to undermine unionization efforts. Faculty affiliation with professionalism makes them antagonistic to being seen as laborers, want to align with being seen as managers, and do not see the need to organize as employees on the job. A case study of Illinois State University also illustrates that faculty committed to shared governance opposed bargaining, arguing it would destroy the relationship between faculty and the campus administration. Failed union drives became evidence the two groups could not exist in support of each other.

When collective bargaining was gaining ground in higher education, shared governance was at its peak in terms of influence at many institutions. The 1960s–1980s were considered the golden age of shared governance but this eroded with the growth of academic capitalism on college campuses in the late 1980s into the 1990s.

Times Change: Academic Capitalism and Shared Governance/Unions

A major force in the changing relationship between shared governance and unionization is academic capitalism. The shift has happened because shared governance has declined under the academic capitalist regime. Slaughter and Rhoades (2004) document how neoliberal logic, which privileges a corporate orientation to university operations, took hold in the 1990s. Academic capitalism brought many systemic changes to universities from a market orientation that sees students as customers trying to maximize revenues to a centralization of decision-making power among a few senior administrators to changes in academic workers with faculty becoming increasingly contingent, part-time, and deprofessionalized. The corporate model of governance in higher education has made faculty "managed professionals" who have much less input into working conditions and a professional autonomy to do their work (Rhoades, 1998). Therefore, the management style is one that does not embrace shared governance and is working actively against it. Furthermore, the corporate model rejects the need for and benefit of the deliberation, reflection, and compromise of shared governance processes.

This amplification of the capitalist orientation to higher education management has fundamentally altered the way faculty think about their work is and the importance of shared governance. As academic capitalism is translated into people's consciousness, it drives faculty to see themselves as small business that must generate their own revenues through grants, and sees contributions to the overall organization through service as unimportant (Rhoades, 1998). For example, surveys and interviews of faculty in recent years have revealed that faculty are spending very limited time on meaningful and influential service activities within the college or university (Finkelstein, Conley, & Schuster, 2016). Finkelstein, Conley, and Schuster (2016) document how faculty are spending much less time in overall institutional governance and decision-making and are bogged down in local departmental administrative work, like course scheduling and managing adjuncts. In short, participation in shared governance takes time and under academic capitalism time spent on shared governance is seen as unproductive. Part of the cultural impact of academic capitalism is to focus more of the time and energies of professionals in the academy on economic production, and less on community service and involvement in democratic decision-making processes. As Rhoades (2003, pg. 30) notes,

> part of the aim of sharing authority between professionals and managers is to serve the public good, and to ensure that decisions are driven by careful consideration of the public good. However, as both parties increasingly pursue academic capitalism, as they focus on and search for flexibility to capitalize on economic opportunities for revenue generation, that ideal is undermined.

Another challenge to shared governance is the increased use of part-time and contingent faculty, who are largely excluded from governance and as a disproportionate burden of governance activity falls to fewer full-time faculty who are increasingly focused on other revenue producing activities (research, teaching).

Extending Slaughter and Rhoads thesis, Nelson (2008) argues that shared governance has been whittled away so thoroughly that it is not viable to support faculty interests anymore and collective bargaining must increasingly take its place or be in support of shared governance. Administrators have developed shadow task forces and groups to conduct most work on campuses outside of shared governance, administrators develop relationships with third-party groups to get around the need to work with faculty on curriculum. All of the various workarounds suggest that bargaining is a better place for asserting faculty rights then shared governance in its deteriorated state. Nelson (2008) argues that young faculty do not realize that faculty once had more power and are too busy worried about staying in a secure tenure-track job or are off the tenure track so vulnerable and distraught that they have no ability to contribute.

And various studies identified that collective-bargaining emerged to help support weakened shared governance. Wickens (2008, pg. 547) found that

> many of the reasons cited for collective bargaining in the academic environment involve the improvement of working conditions including faculty power and university governance, workload and support services, job security, equity issues, due process and grievance issues, promotion procedures, and academic freedom.

Similarly, Castro (2012) found, "faculty dissatisfaction with job security, compensation, and governance issues provided the historical impetus for collective bargaining in higher education" (pg. 47). So collective bargaining is a natural outgrowth of declining shared governance and faculty power and a recognition they are workers like everyone else and vulnerable to management and corporate power. Rhoades (1998) documents how this consciousness of being "managed professionals" has taken several decades to take hold in higher education and has shaped the relationships between shared governance and unionization.

Collective Bargaining Supporting Shared Governance: Complementary – 2000–2020

With the decline of shared governance, the relationship between collective bargaining and shared governance was re-examined. In the late 1990s, the AAUP advocates and presents data that the two can exist (Ramo, 1998) which is detailed in their Redbook (updated in 2015), which provides guidance for campuses to reconcile conflicts that have been identified over time between the two groups. The inclusion of a section in the handbook about the relationship between shared governance on unionized campuses marked a turn in the relationship between the two. This argument was labeled by (Douglass, 1995) as "Symbiosis" in which the relationship between faculty unions and faculty senates has the potential to be mutually beneficial. The challenge for the union is to develop a legislative system that encourages faculty involvement and protects faculty representation rights (Douglass, 1995). Faculty unions generally strive to work in cooperation with traditional faculty governance systems. Those who take a symbiosis approach try to challenge the false dichotomy that unions weaken the role of faculty in governance (or that shared governance prevents unionization); or that the governance is antagonistic to unions (Aronowitz, 2006; Balkun, 2011; Lyne, 2011).

Taking this lead, others have tried to provide empirical evidence in support of these arguments of complementarity. Porter and Stephens (2010) found that unionization greatly increases faculty influence over decision-making in areas such as setting faculty salary scales, individual faculty salaries, appointing department chairs, and appointments to institution-wide committees. Maitland and Rhoades (2001; Maitland, Rhoades, & Smith, 2009) attempted to challenge the argument that unions and senates are antithetical, and suggest that bargaining unit members and teams often negotiate for expanded professional involvement in campus decision-making. In fact, they document the ways that collective-bargaining agreements can and do designate specific supports for shared governance in terms of outlining governance bodies, protections for senates being disbanded, describe voting rights, ensure compensation for involvement and shared governance, and outline specific areas that faculty have authority in so that they have influence over decisions. And they document that institutions with collective bargaining faculty were more involved in governance, not less so.

Maitland and Rhoades and Maitland, Rhoades, and Smith's studies review hundreds of collective-bargaining agreements and lended arguments in favor of the ways that collective bargaining can support shared governance, especially as administrators were moving to centralize power and take away decision-making from faculty. They highlight how the faculty role in decision-making is almost always an issue in collective-bargaining elections. They also illustrate how faculty members support bargaining when they perceive erosion of their governance role. Contrary to common fears, unions do not preclude or supersede collegial patterns of decision-making. Maitland and Rhoades (2001) conclude that collective-bargaining agreements have accorded faculty at a wider range of institutions more decision-making responsibility collectively in key financial and planning realms; and extended shared governance rather than compromised it. In colleges and universities with a history of limited faculty involvement in governance, contract provisions often work to strengthen – not just maintain – faculty participation in organizational policy and decision-making. The encroachment that was documented by researchers on shared governance by unions was intentional to make up for declines in shared governance on campuses. As faculty were losing power in shared governance over certain decisions, the unions were asserting themselves and trying to gain back influence in those areas. The loss of the dual tracks was a result of the breakdown of shared governance, not that the systems were incompatible or inherently in competition.

Increasingly the overlap between the two processes was not seen as incompatible, but a way that the two approaches can support each other (Douglass, 1995; Ramo, 1998).

Another argument that emerged is that it is hard to completely separate issues into dual tracks. Academic issues, from teaching methods to curriculum, also have an economic component and therefore are a potential subject of negotiation (Ramo, 1998). Job security and tenure, promotion procedures, and due process are issues that reside in the overlapping territory of governance and unions. For example, academic freedom is central to both governance and unions. Over time the ability to keep issues on separate tracks became harder and harder to establish and maintain. And the narrative shifts to how to reconcile the many gray areas that are emerging between the two processes. As a result of the abundance of "gray areas", policy documents increasingly emerge such as AAUP's Redbook policies, that designate the extent to which the contract supplements institutional policies found elsewhere through shared governance. And community college governance structures, which harbored vestiges of secondary education's authoritative decision-making processes, continue to give way to more participatory processes over time (Cohen & Brawer, 2003). At many community colleges the collective-bargaining process has allowed for the development of shared or participatory decision-making (Levin, 2000).

Maitland and Rhoades (2001, pg. 31) conclude

> that faculty members must combine involvement in institutional governance with the power of collective bargaining. These mechanisms can work effectively to support each other. But without the force of the contract, the advisory role of faculty in "shared governance" has limited efficacy in an era of reorganization and restructuring. The real threat to faculty's role in collegial decision-making lies in management, not in unions.

Much of the complementary argument, similar to the incompatibility argument, is rhetorical and there are limited empirical studies in support of this premise beyond the work of Maitland and Rhoades (2001), Maitland, Rhoades, and Smith (2009) and Porter and Stephens (2010).

Complementarity and Tensions

One might read the earlier empirical studies about compatibility and incompatibility as both being true and both empirical insights worth considering. Some studies and scholarship lead credence to this reading of the literature (Castro, 2012; Hartley, 2010). One of the few empirical studies that identifies this trend is by Castro (2012) who shows that the two are complementary but also exist in tension with shared governance sometimes being minimized. The study explored the Cal State system and the role that the union played in shared governance. The study documents how the union impacts who gets elected to the senate, shapes informal senate committee proceedings, impacts the policy discourse and policy development, curtailed senate discussion on issues where there was overlap with the bargaining agreement, and resulted in the senate not being seen as an independent body by some faculty and administrators. Many people interviewed talked about the challenge of union representatives that are on senate bodies being unable to separate their role in the union and independently address issues in their senate role. Most people interviewed believe that the two existed in support of each other and had collegial intentions but that in certain circumstances, tensions did arise where there was lack of clarity around who had responsibility. And in other instances, if contingent faculty members were not included in shared governance then the unions tended to have a larger voice, diminishing shared governance. And on some campuses where shared governance was weakened by administrative leaders, the unions ended up having more power in decision-making. The study points to the need to identify and work through areas of tension so that the two processes can best work together.

Study participants noted that it is not uncommon to have contractual provisions in many of the same areas already covered by senate policy and vice versa. In these situations, some provisions reflect a mere duplication while others build upon the other. A consequence of this is that the senate and the union alike are often unclear about which party possesses the primary, if not exclusive, purview on a matter. Campus culture and context shapes if tensions emerge or not. When collegial relationships exist between the parties, the process works and boundaries are seemingly irrelevant. The result under these circumstances is a set of senate policies that mesh with the collective-bargaining agreement. At the same time, when adversarial relationships exist, the purview of one party is regularly challenged by the other and competition ensues in an arena in which boundaries are ambiguous, if not deliberately obscured. Therefore, making universal statements about the compatibility of the two is challenged by evidence that they work compatibly if there are good working relationships between the two entities. Few studies have explored the relationship between unions and shared governance at this level of depth to understand how they can both complement each other yet also end up with challenges that can compromise each other. We highlight the study as it indicates the type of research needed to help bridge these two processes going forward. The study focuses mostly on how unions can compromise shared governance and not the other direction, which likely also needs exploration. More research about the interactions of these two groups is needed to identify the types of tensions that need to be worked through so they can be maximally coordinated.

Various studies have identified how there are dwindling numbers of tenure-track faculty on campus and many campuses have excluded non-tenure-track faculty, meaning their voice can only be represented through unions (Kezar & Maxey, 2013; Rhoades, 1998). And on campuses that include non-tenure-track faculty, often their number is extremely limited and only includes full-time not part-time faculty. These exclusionary behaviors of shared governance processes have created tension between unions and shared governance that needs to be resolved for the two to work together. The AAUP Redbook has also addressed the need for inclusion of non-tenure-track faculty members. This is an issue that continues to need to be resolved so that the two processes can work well together.

Another tension is that newer non-academic unions (UnitedAuto Workers, SEIU- Steelworkers) from industrial backgrounds often do not know about the tradition of shared governance (Kezar, DePaola, & Scott, 2019). These non-academic unions are expanding and their knowledge and interest in shared governance is not always as strong as the traditional academic unions such as AAUP, National Education Association (NEA) or American Federation of Teachers (AFT). So the history, background, and traditions of the unions impacts their openness and understanding of shared governance and whether they will work in complementary ways or not.

And there are often issues where faculty unions have different interests or stances from faculty governance processes(Drummond & Reitsch, 1995; Ponak, Thompson, & Zerbe, 1992). Take the case of faculty evaluation or professional development. Unions have often been resistant to putting in place evaluation systems that they think might shape pay or promotions, whereas faculty under shared governance see an evaluation system as important to being a professional and obtaining feedback on performance. Similarly, professional development is a key component of a professional that helps a faculty member keep current on his or her discipline and scholarly activities, but collective bargaining is less likely to focus on professional development.

Reconciling Tensions: Working Together

In order to support the idea of symbiosis, various scholars provide arguments and approaches for the two processes to be engaged simultaneously often acknowledging the complexity of the interaction of these processes due to local contexts, legal issues, social changes, and evolving views of both processes. Many of these more recent proposals are grounded in the research that sees these two processes as having the potential for symbiosis but needing to work through tensions that remain, and some tensions might be inherent unless shared governance and/or collective bargaining are modified.

Rethinking Union Approaches and Relationships to Shared Governance

Mutual gains bargaining is advocated as more aligned with shared governance. Many of the early arguments against collective bargaining is that it came out of an industrial and antagonistic model of working relationships (Ponak, Thompson, &

Zerbe, 1992). Thus, different approaches to bargaining are recommended as a way to reconcile shared governance and collective bargaining (Wagner & Borgstrom, 2012). Common ground can include student success, institutional effectiveness, academic quality, financial viability, and the like. These areas of common ground support and understanding of the ways that the processes can be symbiotic can be built upon for further action in the future.

Another approach is social justice unionism as a way to get more support for unions that have sometimes been considered self-serving (Kezar, DePaola, & Scott, 2019). Social justice organizing focuses on public or broader interests (e.g. student learning, changing demographics, diversity/equity, social and community development, democratic and civic engagement) to support collective-bargaining efforts. Rhoades (2003) argues for union's role in supporting public purposes such as research, community development, and civic engagement and connecting to communities, government, business and students' interest as a way to align unionization with a broader set of interests to gain greater support – and this support can be both external but also internal among faculty participating in shared governance. The connection of work issues and social justice issues also provides a point of connection for shared governance efforts that are increasingly taking up issues of racial justice, community engagement and other broader social issues. But as noted above, non-academic unions are often unfamiliar with shared governance so bridging work still needs to be done to ensure that the two work well together even as new approaches to collective bargaining are engaged.

A More Dynamic View of Dual Tracks

Others have suggested reworking the dual tracks argument to acknowledge the complexity of the policymaking process and inherent overlaps that have developed over time. Mauer (2016) provides guidance for sorting through the tensions in the interactions of the two groups. The fundamental starting point is determining the division of responsibility between the senate and the union:

> But the typical arrangement would have the darker area of overlap be the largest, with each faculty body having some responsibility. So, for example, the faculty functioning through their governance mechanisms might determine standards for promotion and tenure, while the faculty in their union capacity might establish the procedural aspects of the process, including applicable time frames and the functioning of appeal mechanisms.
>
> *(Mauer, 2016, pg. 3)*

Additionally, Messier (2017) also challenges the perceived conflict between collective bargaining and faculty governance, noting the clear dual tracks path is overly simple. The dual tracks approach weakens both endeavors by driving a wedge within the faculty. Collective bargaining is an asset, a tool that can help strengthen and support shared governance. He takes up a set of different issues and argues how both shared governance and collective bargaining are needed to adequately address the issue. But he does not ignore conflicts between the two either and suggests ways that leaders within both groups can work together to support each other. And he brings up the challenges of the rise of contingent faculty that need to be included in governance, which is often why faculty who have no decision-making influence rely on unions, because so many faculty are no longer represented in shared governance when it's exclusive to tenure-track faculty. Another related approach cedes authority over academic matters generally to the existing governance structure, but establishes contractual oversight or protection of these processes in some manner (Ramo, 1998). So, for example, a collective-bargaining agreement may specify that governance changes may not be made without the approval of the union.

Messier and Mauer also point to ways to bridge the two processes. Collective-bargaining agreements can include language that recognizes faculty governance and supports its existence. This gives legal standing to practices so that administrators cannot overstep or ignore the process. Faculty leaders can strengthen the culture of shared governance by including materials on the topic in new faculty orientations and holding training sessions. Faculty are often unaware of their rights and responsibilities under shared governance. Faculty leaders can explore the common areas of governance and collective bargaining by documenting all the contract language that memorializes shared governance. Faculty need to understand the extent of the current overlap between these areas and how they support each other to support faculty rights. And faculty should be oriented and trained about their shared governance and collective-bargaining rights at annual events and through professional development for faculty about their roles in these two processes at their responsibilities in helping them work together.

A Typology That Recognizes Multiple Relationships

Bucklew, Houghton, and Ellison (2012) help move beyond the typical polarized argument between the two processes being complementary or incompatible to create a typology that provides varying ways the two processes can come together that are responsive to institutional context, different histories, and the culture of campuses. The models provide a framework for understanding the co-existence of faculty unions and shared governance and defines boundaries in collective-bargaining agreements. The typology includes four models that are detailed in the Appendix, including the comprehensive model, the co-determination model, the permissive model and the restricted or limited model (Bucklew, Ellison, & Houghton, 2013).

In the comprehensive model, both traditional labor-management contract issues and shared governance issues are addressed in the contract. They note:

"the union fulfills the primary faculty representation role in place of traditional faculty governance, such as the faculty senate…matters that were traditionally decided by the faculty senate are now explicitly spelled out in the collective-bargaining agreement" (2013, pg. 8). This would include: wages, promotion and tenure, teaching load, academic rank (job classification), peer evaluation committees and processes, academic governance advisory process, retirement policies, pension programs, health insurance, life and disability, insurances, sick leave, vacation and holidays, and academic freedom rights and responsibilities (Bucklew, Ellison, & Houghton, 2013).

In the co-determination model "parties negotiate over traditional collective-bargaining topics, but also create enabling language in the contract concerning the continuation of shared governance activities. Here, language exists in the contract that authorizes faculty senates to continue to oversee traditional governance items, such as promotion and tenure processes, teaching load, and curriculum committee structures" (Bucklew, Ellison, & Houghton, 2013, pg. 8). A benefit to this model is that it not only allows traditional faculty senates to exist but also clarifies the responsibility between the two entities.

The permissive model tries to establish the relationship between collective bargaining and shared governance but in a less explicit way – allowing more room for issues to be worked out overtime and be more dynamic (Bucklew, Ellison, & Houghton, 2013, pg. 9). The collective-bargaining agreement references the faculty governance issues and is supportive of the entity, mentioning its traditional role as a governing body. However, the explicit parameters and boundaries of traditional faculty governance are not established.

The fourth is the restricted or limited model (Bucklew, Ellison, & Houghton, 2013). The collective-bargaining agreement

> is silent on matters that are traditionally handled by the faculty senate. There is no language in the contract to address how these issues will be decided; instead, the contract only addresses traditional labor topics, such as wages, benefits, etc. This model may be adopted voluntarily, or, in some cases, it may be mandated by law.
>
> *(Bucklew, Ellison, & Houghton, 2013, pg. 9)*

What is helpful about this typology is that it allows varying types of relationships between shared governance and collective bargaining based on contextual issues, legal statutes, institutional histories, and the like. This type of typology is helpful for understanding existing relationships but falls short of offering an aspiration for the relationship between these two entities which is offered above under the new approaches to collective bargaining, rethinking of dual tracks, and greater inclusion of non-tenure-track faculty in governance. An important area for future thinking and research would be ways that the existing typology might be tweaked to create greater synergy for campuses over time. It might appear that the co-determination model provides the most ability to reconcile tensions, for example, and research about how campuses might move over time from the limited model, for example, to a model that might ensure greater symbiosis would be helpful.

These three areas provide a path for campuses to consider moving forward. But Castro (2012) suggests there are more nuances in the details of shared governance and collective bargaining working together that also need further research. And of course, as times have changed the dynamics around these processes also have been altered. The global pandemic and ensuing recession create a very difficult environment for working relationships between administration and faculty. The political environment in the last four years has not been supportive of unions and we have yet to determine what the political environment will be like over the next decade in terms of workers and unions. Much is in flux and the possibilities for symbiosis may become much clearer over the next year or so. But there is certainly emerging evidence for campuses that the two processes have potential for synergy when harnessed under the right conditions.

References

American Association of University Professors (AAUP). (2015). *Policy documents and reports*. The John Hopkins University Press.

Aronowitz, S. (2006). Should academic unions get involved in governance? *Liberal Education*, 92(4), 22–27.

Baldridge, J. V., & Kemerer, F. R. (1976). Academic senates and faculty collective bargaining. *The Journal of Higher Education*, 47(4), 391–411.

Balkun, M.M. (2011). Making shared governance work: Strategies and challenges. *Pedagogy* 11(3), 562–569. https://www.muse.jhu.edu/article/450854.

Blake-Hudson, C. (2007). *Unions and faculty senates: A cross-case analysis of governance within private universities*. https://core.ac.uk/download/pdf/154486987.pdf.

Bucklew, N., Ellison, C. N., & Houghton, J. D. (2013). Shared governance and academic collective bargaining in American higher education: A potential model for US participation in the global experience of works councils and codetermination. *Journal of Collective Bargaining in the Academy*, 4(1), 3.

Bucklew, N., Houghton, J. D., & Ellison, C. N. (2012). Faculty union and faculty senate co-existence: A review of the impact of academic collective bargaining on traditional academic governance. *Labor Studies Journal*, 37(4), 373–390.

Burgan, M. (2006). *What Ever Happened to the Faculty? Drift and Decision in Higher Education*. Baltimore, MD, The John Hopkins University Press.

Castro, R. (2012). *Faculty unions and their effects on university shared governance*. Long Beach, California, California State University.

Cohen, A. M., & Brawer, F. B. (2003). *The American Community College*. John Wiley & Sons.

Devinatz, V. G. (2001). Unions, faculty, and the culture of competition. *Thought and Action*, 17, 87–98.

Douglass, J. A. (1995). Shared governance: Shaped by conflict and by agreement. *Notice*, 20, 4–5.

Drummond, M. E., & Reitsch, A. (1995). The relationship between shared governance models and faculty and administrator attitudes. *Journal for Higher Education Management*, 11(1), 49–58.

Finkelstein, M. J., Conley, V. M., & Schuster, J. H. (2016). *The faculty Factor: Reassessing the American Academy in a Turbulent Era*. The John Hopkins University Press.

Hartley, M. (2010). Reconcilable differences: Conflict and collegiality in a unionized community college environment. *Community College Journal of Research and Practice*, 34 (4), 318–336. https://www.tandfonline.com/doi/full/10.1080/10668920701382427? scroll=top&needAccess=true.

Kater, S., & Levin, J. S. (2004). Shared governance in the community college. *Community College Journal of Research and Practice*, 29(1), 1–23.

Keller, G. (1983). *Academic Strategy: The Management Revolution in American Higher Education*. The John Hopkins University Press.

Kemerer, F. R., & Baldridge, J. V. (1975). The impact of faculty unions on governance. *Change: The Magazine of Higher Learning*, 7(10), 50–62.

Kemerer, F. R., & Baldridge, J. V. (1981). Senates and unions: Unexpected peaceful coexistence. *The Journal of Higher Education*, 52(3), 256–264. https://www.jstor.org/stable/pdf/1981034.pdf.

Kezar, A., DePaola, T., & Scott, D. T. (2019). *The Gig Academy: Mapping Labor in the Neoliberal University*. The Johns Hopkins University Press.

Kezar, A., & Maxey, D. (2013). The changing academic workforce. *Trusteeship*, 21(3), 15–21.

Levin, J. S. (2000). What's the impediment? Structural and legal constraints to shared governance in the community college. *Canadian Journal of Higher Education*, 30(2), 87–122.

Lyne, B. (2011). Campus clout, statewide strength: Improving shared governance through unionization. *Pedagogy*, 11(3), 558–562.

Maitland, C., & Rhoades, G. (2001). Unions and faculty governance. *The NEA 2001 Almanac of Higher Education*, 27–33.

Maitland, C., Rhoades, G., & Smith, M. F. (2009). Unions and senates: Governance and distance education. *NEA Almanac of Higher Education*, 75–84.

Mauer, M. (2016). Protecting shared governance through collective bargaining: Models used by AAUP chapters. *Journal of Collective Bargaining in the Academy*, 8(1), 7.

Messier, J. (2017). Shared governance and academic freedom: Yes, this is union work. *Thought & Action*, 33(2), 63–76.

Nelson, C. (2008). The future of faculty unionization. *Journal of Collective Bargaining in the Academy*, (3), 10.

Polishook, I. H. (1982). Unions and governance the CUNY experience. *Academe*, 68(1), 15–17. https://www.jstor.org/stable/pdf/40248897.pdf.

Ponak, A., Thompson, M., & Zerbe, W. (1992). Collective bargaining goals of university faculty. *Research in Higher Education*, 33(4), 415–431.

Porter, S. R. (2013). The causal effect of faculty unions on institutional decision-making. *ILR Review*, 66(5), 1192–1211.

Porter, S. R. & Stephens, C. M. (November 8, 2010). *The Causal Effect of Faculty Unions on Institutional Decision-Making*. Available at SSRN: https://ssrn.com/abstract=1705713 or http://dx.doi.org/10.2139/ssrn.1705713.

Ramo. J. (1998). *Assessing the Faculty's Role in Shared Governance: Implications of AAUP Standards*. Washington, DC, American Association of University Professors.

Rhoades, G. (1998). *Managed Professionals: Unionized Faculty and Restructuring Academic Labor*. SUNY press.

Rhoades, G. (2003). *Democracy and Capitalism*, Academic Style: Governance in Contemporary Higher Education. Prepared by the Center for Higher Education Policy Analysis (Los Angeles, CA). Paper presented to the Governance Roundtable (Santa Fe, NM).

Schuster, J. H. (1989). *Governing Tomorrow's Campus. Perspectives and Agendas*. New York, NY, Macmillan Publishing Company.

Schuster, J. H., & M. J. Finkelstein (2008). *The American Faculty: The Restructuring of Academic Work and Careers*. Baltimore, MD, Johns Hopkins University.

Schwartz, S. J. (1980). Governance: Another view. *Labor Law Journal*, 31(10), 645.

Signorelli, A. (1997). *Has Collective Bargaining Damaged Shared Governance?* Issues of Education at Community Colleges: Essays by Fellows in the Mid-Career Fellowship Program at Princeton University.

Slaughter, S., & Rhoades, G. (2004). *Academic capitalism and the new economy: Markets, state, and higher education*. The Johns Hopkins University Press.

The Stanford Project on Academic Governance (1975). https://eric.ed.gov/?id= ED098876.

Wagner, S. C., & Borgstrom, C. H. (2012). Negotiating within a shared governance format. *Journal of Collective Bargaining in the Academy*, 3(1), 6.

White, K. B. (1998). Shared governance in California. *New directions for community colleges*, 102, 19–29.

Wickens, C. (2008). The organizational impact of university labor unions. *Higher Education*, 56(5). Yildirim, A.K.

Appendix

Comprehensive Model

This model is characterized by a situation in which the parties enter into collective bargaining as the process for determining the full range of policies and formal practices between the faculty and the university (as their employer). The topics covered by the bargaining parties in this model include traditional labor-management contract issues and substantive coverage of shared governance issues. In this model the exclusive bargaining agent, the union, implements a non-symbiotic relationship with the faculty senate if such a structure was already in place. The matters covered include, but are not limited to: wages, promotion and tenure, teaching load, academic rank (job classification), peer evaluation committees and processes, academic governance advisory process, retirement policies, pension programs, health insurance, life and disability, insurances, sick leave, vacation and holidays, and academic freedom rights and responsibilities. The parties recognize that their relationship represents an "exclusive agent" arrangement and that the university may not enter into formal or binding arrangements with other groups or organizations representing faculty. In essence, the union fulfills the broad faculty representation role in lieu of other faculty organizations such as the faculty senate. This model is often found in colleges and universities with limited traditions of structured faculty involvement in academic governance. Community colleges are most likely to adopt this model.

Co-Determination Model

In this model, the faculty union bargains with the university, while serving as official and legal co-determiners regarding shared governance on the campus. The parties negotiate over traditional collective bargaining topics but also create enabling language in the contract regarding the continuation of shared governance activities. The collective bargaining agreement contains provisions for traditional labor-management topics such as wages, benefits, pensions, and grievances, while also including "authorizing or enabling" language regarding shared governance topics. These shared governance clauses include, but are not limited to: promotion and tenure processes, faculty senate structure, and curriculum committee structures. The contract language is normally general in nature and often takes already established policies and practices and incorporates them by reference. The union reserves the right to negotiate over these topics as needed and takes the position that the employer cannot modify them unilaterally. Within this model, the relationship between the faculty union and faculty senate is generally symbiotic in general but can easily shift to a non-symbiotic nature. The fact remains that the arrangements for shared governance are a matter of contract negotiations between the faculty union and the university.

An example of this model is the contract at Evergreen State College. In this agreement the parties designate that the union will be responsible for "wages, hours, and working conditions." It also acknowledges that the College has a "history of shared governance" and specifies that the Faculty Agenda Committee (their version of the faculty senate) will continue to participate in behalf of the faculty on curriculum matters; admissions, retention, and graduation of students; honorary degrees and student awards; and priorities for faculty hiring and search policies. Other institutions that follow this model include Central Michigan University and the University of Montana.

Permissive Model

The parties negotiate over traditional collective bargaining topics, but any topic relating to shared governance is treated as a non-required or permissive topic. If the shared governance topics are included it is normally by reference only. The university reserves the right to modify these policies outside the collective bargaining process according to traditional provisions and practices that ensure faculty involvement. If the shared governance topics are in the contract, those provisions are often excluded from the contract grievance and/or arbitration clauses. Under this model the faculty union and faculty senate co-exist in a symbiotic state. There remains an opportunity for a non-symbiotic nature to develop because the faculty union often seeks the inclusion of contract language regarding shared governance issues. The contractual impact is limited, however, because the topics are permissive, and even if they are included those clauses are not open to grievances and arbitration processes.

This model is implemented in a number of public university contracts in Florida. The approach uses a preamble clause in which both parties acknowledge the existence of a shared governance tradition and system on the campus but set this joint affirmation aside from the formal (and grievable) collective-bargaining agreement itself. The Florida Gulf Coast University agreement is a good example of this approach. In the Preamble the parties recognize "the desirability of a collegial system." They specifically identify the Faculty Senate and its role in curriculum, degree requirements, admission of students, grading policy, and academic program approval. The final paragraph of the Preamble states, "This preamble is a statement of intent and policy and is, therefore, not subject to the Grievance procedure." The permissive model is also used at other institutions including the University of Alaska, Wright State University, Kent. State University, Florida Atlantic University, and Oakland University.

Restrictive or Limited Model

Within this model, the parties limit the subjects of bargaining and the content of the collective bargaining agreement to traditional labor-management topics. Faculty governance subjects are reserved for their faculty organizations (faculty senate, faculty assembly, etc.). This restricted or limited approach can be voluntary by the parties, or it may be mandated by law. Under this model the faculty union and faculty senate co-exist in a permanent state of symbiosis.

An area of academic staffing where you might predict a restrictive model would be adjuncts, lecturers, and teaching assistants. There are several such contracts where that is the case. The agreement between the University of Michigan and the University of Michigan Lecturers (AFT) contains no language on shared governance issues and is limited to salaries, benefits, and basic conditions of employment. That is also true of the New York University contract with the New York University Adjuncts (UAW). However, this model is not restricted to adjunct or lecturer bargaining units. The regular faculty contract between the University of Florida and the University Faculty of Florida adopts this model. The contract provisions are limited to traditional union issues, and the contract does not incorporate academic governance issues.

3

GRADUATE STUDENT UNIONIZATION

Nicholas DiGiovanni Jr.

Introduction

We begin with a recognition that graduate student assistant collective bargaining is simply like no other type of union negotiations in academia. It stands alone as presenting the most complex and confounding challenges to administrations, largely due to the very nature of the bargaining unit members. In all other types of campus negotiations, be it with full- or part-time faculty or other academic staff, the essential nature of the members of those units is that of an employee, pure and unalloyed. Differences exist, of course, between the employees in such bargaining units. But in all cases, those unit members have no other relationship to the employer but that of an employee – one who works under the direction of the employer and receives compensation for their efforts.

Not so with graduate student assistants. They are not simply employees; they are also students. Indeed, it is their *student nature* that is primary and essential and without which nothing else follows. Unlike other employees, they come to the employer, not through a competitive hiring process that sifts out applicants based on resumes, references and personal interviews, but instead through their admission to the institution as students seeking an advanced degree. They are selected through an examination of their academic capabilities, measured by past performance and test scores. They are not recruited as employees; no one cares about their work skills or work history. Any "work" responsibilities that may come later in their student career are always secondary to their academic progress towards a graduate degree.

DOI: 10.4324/9781003138990-4

In short, without first becoming a student, they simply cannot be an employee, and once they cease being a student, they can no longer be a bargaining unit employee. It is because of this reality that labor boards, especially the National Labor Relations Board (NLRB), have struggled mightily for years with the very idea that, despite their paramount student status, they might still be able to bargain collectively for better working conditions during those times when they do perform work functions.

Thus, when a university first faces negotiations with a graduate student employee union, it is immediately confronted with a conundrum. How can academic administrators bargain a contract that addresses "wages, hours and other terms and conditions of employment" – the essential topics of labor negotiations – when the people they see across the table are students and have always been treated as such? To now meet the legal duty to bargain in good faith, an administration will have to try to approach student employee collective bargaining with a suspension of disbelief, namely, that the *employee component* of their nature can be isolated and that the basic provisions of a labor contract can be negotiated in the same manner as with any other employee group without regard to their synchronous status as a student.

Of course, it just isn't that easy. To put it succinctly, it is like trying to separate a person from their shadow.

History

Collective bargaining for graduate students made its first appearance in public sector universities over 50 years ago at the City University of New York (CUNY) system when the New York Public Employment Relations Board certified a union to represent a bargaining unit of teaching assistants, research assistants and research associates.[1] Many more such units followed closely behind.[2] Today, some 35 bargaining units of graduate assistants have been established at public sector universities in 14 states throughout the country.[3]

In the private sector, however, the path to graduate student unionization has been wildly erratic, with shifting decision-making over many years by the NLRB as to whether or not such individuals were even employees covered by the National Labor Relations Act (NLRA).

The NLRB took jurisdiction over private colleges and universities for the first time in 1970.[4] In the aftermath of that decision, the Board began to tackle a variety of bargaining unit issues unique to higher education, such as the supervisory status of department chairs, or whether adjunct faculty belonged in the same bargaining unit as full-time tenure-track faculty, to name two.[5]

In 1972, the Board was confronted for the first time with the question of whether graduate student assistants were entitled to collective bargaining rights. In *Adelphi University*,[6] the Board held that graduate student assistants were primarily students and should be excluded from a unit of regular faculty. The

Board noted that the graduate students were all working towards their advanced academic degrees and that "their employment depends entirely on their status as such."[7]

In *Leland Stanford*[8] decided two years later, the Board went further. It held that graduate student assistants "are not employees within the meaning of Section 2(3) of the Act" because, like the graduate students in *Adelphi*, they were "primarily students."

For over 25 years, the Board adhered to the *Leland Stanford* principle.

But in 2000, the Board dramatically switched gears, and in *New York University*[9] held for the first time that graduate student assistants were indeed employees within the meaning of the Act and entitled to collective bargaining. The Board applied the common law definition of master–servant in interpreting Section 2(3) of the Act and concluded that in such a relationship "a servant performs services for another, under the other's control or right to control, and in return for payment."[10] Using this baseline definition, the Board found that graduate assistants performed services for and under the direction of the university and received compensation for such services, and therefore clearly fell within the definition of Section 2(3).

However, just four years later, in *Brown University*,[11] the Board, now with a majority of Republican appointees, reversed its *New York University* decision and held that graduate students working as teaching or research assistants were *not* employees. The Board held that such individuals "have a predominantly academic rather than economic relationship with their school."[12]

Fast forward 14 years later, and the Obama Board in the *Columbia University* decision overturned *Brown University* and determined that both graduate and undergraduate students who perform services at a university in connection with their studies are employees and have the right to unionize. The *Columbia* decision not only overturned *Brown* but also overturned the *Leland Stanford* decision that had found externally funded research assistants were not employees under the Act. Reiterating the earlier *NYU* decision, the Board said that the key inquiry is whether the employer has control over the employee's work that is performed in exchange for compensation, *regardless* of whether or not a student–educator relationship also concurrently exists.

In applying this standard, the Board found that Columbia oversees and directs student assistants' teaching activities and that they receive compensation for their duties (through a stipend) with receipt of their stipend dependent upon their teaching.

Contrary to the *Brown* decision, the Board ruled that *a graduate student can simultaneously be both a student and an employee, and a university can be both the student's educator and employer*, noting also that collective bargaining by graduate student employees is "increasingly a fact of American university life" in the public sector.[13]

The Board decision unleashed a flurry of union activity. In the wake of *Columbia*, petitions for representation were filed at multiple private universities, including Harvard, Yale, Tufts, Brandeis, Duke, Boston College and the University of Chicago. NLRB elections were held at these institutions and various unions won certification rights. Some of these institutions went on to negotiate initial contracts with their graduate assistant unions. However, others, such as the University of Chicago and Boston College, refused to bargain with their newly certified units and contested the graduate student assistants' employee status, hoping to bring their cases ultimately to a newly constituted, management-friendly NLRB appointed in the wake of President Trump's election.

Then, in a significant coordinated move to blunt those appeals, all of the involved labor unions, including the United Auto Workers and the American Federation of Teachers, fearing a reversal of *Columbia* at the Board level, withdrew their petitions from the NLRB in February 2018, even in cases where they had already won elections and been certified. Their orchestrated withdrawals removed any possibility of a case reaching the full Board and providing an opportunity for a reversal of *Columbia*.

However, in one final twist, the NLRB, utilizing its rule-making authority, announced a proposed rule on September 23, 2019 that would essentially strip away NLRA rights from students. The proposed rule states:

> ...students who perform any services for compensation, including, but not limited to, teaching or research, at a private college or university in connection with their studies are not "employees" within the meaning of Section 2(3) of the Act.

The Board set a public comment period before issuance of any final rule, which expired in early March 2020. No action was taken on the proposed rule throughout 2020 and into the new year, but on March 12, 2021, the NLRB announced that they were withdrawing their rule making procedure in this case. Thus, as things currently stand, the right of student workers to unionize remains intact in the private sector.[14]

Negotiations: The Initial Challenges

The case history of the issue of the graduate student assistant's employee status over the past 50 years is not just important as a picture of how we got to the present state of affairs in the private sector, but also because within those decisions, one can see the struggle that various Board members had with the very notion of student negotiations. And while these points were raised by NLRB members regarding *private* sector graduate student assistants, most apply to public sector graduate student bargaining as well.

The concerns of various Board members have proven accurate to those who are on the ground trying to negotiate such agreements. Most importantly, the primary problem that permeates the entire bargaining process is the reality that they are fundamentally students first and employees second. This makes it difficult to separate employee issues from student issues, often complicated by graduate student unions bringing issues to the table that are clearly student matters, not employment matters. These include issues such as housing, financial aid and residential life. In addition, social justice issues that reflect the latest societal discussions are often found at graduate student bargaining tables as well.

Thus, when the Harvard Graduate Student Union–United Auto Workers (HGSU-UAW) first began negotiations with the university in 2018, they entered bargaining with no less than 80 well-publicized goals, many of them well beyond the scope of obligatory bargaining, including issues dealing housing issues, immigration policy concerns, the desire for inclusion of "vulnerable populations" on campus and certain areas of shared governance.[15] At Columbia, the UAW local proposed making that university a "sanctuary university" for immigration purposes,[16] with the student union leadership explaining:

> We believe in the power of strike action to further struggles for real solutions to the climate crisis, immigrant rights and dignity, free on-demand abortion, Medicare for All, civil rights for all people, no matter race, religion, gender, sexuality, national origin, physical ability, immigration status.[17]

Such agendas that reach beyond typical bargaining topics are not unusual with student worker negotiations.

In addition to the effort to expand bargaining topics, a further complication is that the nature of the bargaining unit is by definition unstable. Graduate students are not regular employees; they are a transitory population.[18] These are not career positions; no one aspires to be a graduate teaching assistant as a career goal. Their work life is fleeting, existing for no more than the time it takes for them to get their advanced degree. Further, even within these limited time frames, they may be moving in and out of the bargaining unit depending on whether they are working or not. This fluidity and turnover of the unit will present problems that simply are not present in most bargaining settings.

Graduate students are also in a younger demographic group overall compared to other workers. While people of all ages pursue graduate degrees, the typical graduate student is in their twenties or early thirties. As noted above, they thus bring with them all of the issues of their generation, especially social justice issues such as affordable housing, childcare, diversity concerns, racial justice, protections from harassment and retaliation, and immigration protections.

Finally, given who they are, their idealism and heightened expectations going into negotiations will often make it difficult for them to compromise. This becomes a particularly acute problem in those situations where the bargaining agent yields the actual negotiations to the students themselves rather than have their business agents control discussions at the table, as the UAW has done in some cases.

Negotiations: Organizational Issues

When student workers unionize, the administration will face a variety of immediate issues in terms of how to prepare. The first challenge is organizational.

For administrations approaching negotiations with a new graduate student employee union, they are understandably not prepared as to how to deal with such a unit. To add to the complications, such a round of negotiations may also be the very first time that the university has had to deal with academic collective bargaining *in any form.*[19]

Logistical and organizational issues deserve special attention in the beginning of the process, and they include the following items for consideration:

1. **The need to develop clarity as to the lines of authority.** As in all bargaining, there must be clarity at the outset as to which part of the institution is in charge of the process. In university-wide units, this likely falls upon the provost's office or sometimes the president, but the degree to which the deans of the various schools must be involved in terms of decision-making will vary from university to university.

2. **Interaction between human resources and/or labor relations; involvement of the student side of the institution.** In many cases, the human resources department (and, in some universities, the labor relations department) may exercise considerable authority in *non-academic* employee and labor relations, but what their role should be when it comes to academic units will need clarity.

3. **Selection of a bargaining team.** University bargaining teams for graduate student worker negotiations should include individuals who have the time to devote to the process; bring knowledge, information and creativity to the issues that will dominate the discussions; demonstrate a willingness to engage in table discussions and not merely sit in the background; and have the needed patience to withstand the challenges – and the tedium – of negotiations. Since these are academic negotiations, the team should include academic administrators as well as human resources/labor relations representatives. Others may become part of a backup working group to lend their expertise. Finally, the institution should consider whether to engage the assistance of outside labor counsel to lead or assist the negotiations.

4. **Create a working group that will meet between bargaining sessions to develop proposals and counter proposals and brainstorm solutions to table issues.** A working group will be invaluable in terms of keeping the institution focused on the process; what needs to be done and by when; and to coordinate needed information with other parts of the institution. Members of such a group should involve all of the bargaining team members plus other administrators and support staff.

5. **Coordination with the schools and colleges of the universities in terms of review of proposals.** Each school within the university should have a contact person to coordinate with the bargaining team and working group. These individuals can be activated to provide answers to particular questions that may come up at the table; to collect information that may be needed from a school or department; and to test the feasibility of possible proposals on either side.

6. **Be clear about how data will be generated, be it for the administration or in response to union requests for information and data.** Data drives all negotiations and no less so for graduate student negotiations. Since institutions are not accustomed to thinking of their students as employees, sources of information relevant for bargaining may be scattered in various places. Coordination as to how relevant data can be accessed will be important.

7. **Coordination with the press and related public relations.** Experience shows the graduate student unions are particularly focused on public relations and will spread their positions through campus newspapers and the wider press; through social media; through advertising and other methods. Thus, involving the public relations department in the bargaining process will be essential during a round of bargaining.

8. **Ground rules.** Preparation for negotiations should also consider whether or not the administration will propose specific ground rules for bargaining with the union. Such ground rules can cover topics such as where and how frequently the parties will be meet; whether observers will be allowed at negotiations sessions; whether the press can be in attendance; whether there will be any restrictions on public comments about the progress of negotiations; whether there should be release time from duties for the student workers to attend bargaining; and many more.

Negotiations: Administration Goals

What goals should animate the administration's bargaining platform in approaching these types of negotiations? Every institution should decide such matters before entering into any round of negotiations and each will be based on its own culture. In my view, however, best practices in this regard can be condensed into a handful of basic principles and guidelines.

First and foremost, the administration team should enter into negotiations with a respect for the process, a recognition of the appropriate role of the union and an understanding of some of the intangible factors in negotiations.[20]

Second, as with any collective bargaining situation, the university should preserve management rights to the extent possible, especially in negotiating the initial contract.

Third, the institution should limit the contract to mandatory subjects of bargaining. This includes but is not limited to the avoidance of contract provisions that involve faculty assessments of students as students; issues that are purely student matters (such as admissions, retention, housing and financial aid); and social justice issues not anchored in the employment relationship.

Fourth, as a guiding principle, the university should preserve all matters of academic judgment to the institution. The contract should not limit the faculty's primary authority to control the educational process; to make judgments on student performance; and to decide what is necessary in lab and classroom settings.

Fifth, with regard to "workload," the contract should be as clear as possible about the separation of "employment work" from "academic" work recognizing that it may be difficult to do so in all cases.

Sixth, the compensation articles should be carefully negotiated. Ideally, the contract should separate true compensation – payment for work performed – from student financial aid.

Seventh, the Family Education Rights and Privacy Act (FERPA) cannot be ignored. Care should be taken not to violate student privacy rights by agreeing to provide information to the union that is protected by the Act.

Within the context of negotiating an "employee/employer" contract, institutions should remember that union bargaining team members are still students, and the institution should remain motivated to create a welcoming educational environment and do what is best for them as students. The intensity of their academic work, the uncertainty about their future job market, the economic challenges that many of them face, especially those who are starting families during this period, and many other factors can contribute to heightened anxiety and cases of depression for this group.[21] Listening with an empathetic ear to all of their concerns is important and can lead to a less contentious round of bargaining.

All of this means that many of the issues that the students will raise at the table – even if they involve subjects over which the institution should not bargain – might nevertheless be addressed through different means. In this manner, the process of bargaining can be collaborative *even as the boundaries of what the union contract contains can be limited.*

Management Rights

General Importance in Contract Negotiations

Despite the particular complexities and nuances of graduate student negotiations, there are some elements of this type of bargaining that are no different from any other type. A collective bargaining agreement, from a management perspective, should have "good bones," and nowhere is this more important than in the negotiations of the management rights article.

The management rights article is the fountainhead for all administrative action under the agreement and serves as the cornerstone of the contract for the administration. It sets forth the basic rights of management in terms of directing and assigning work, making appointments, disciplining employees, issuing rules and regulations, etc. This article serves as a counterweight to all of the other contract provisions that are negotiated that define employee or union rights.

The best of management rights articles provides an illustrative list of rights that management has retained in the contract but not to the exclusion of others. The management rights article can serve as a default provision if there is some doubt about the existence or extent of a certain management function. Beyond serving as a means of providing clarity to an arbitrator in a given grievance case, a strong management rights article can also serve as evidence that a certain change in the status quo or a newly issued work policy does not require mid-term bargaining.[22]

Usually, the union's counterpoint to strong management rights articles is a proposed past practices clause under which a union will seek to preserve whatever it failed to specifically reference in contract language. Such clauses should be avoided. Such clauses serve as a kind of safety net for unions and, if they end up in the contract, they will be cited whenever management tries to alter a policy or practice in a way that impacts employees.

Importance in Graduate Student Negotiations

In graduate student negotiations, the management rights article is especially important because, among its other benefits, it can also be a likely landing spot for the administration to highlight that matters of academic judgment and student issues are entirely retained by management. A good example of a very strong management rights clause can be found in Harvard contract with the UAW.[23] The Management Rights article in the Tufts University graduate student worker contract with the SEIU has an equally strong provision, highlighting the retention of the institution's rights over academic and student matters and providing examples.[24] See also the Brown University contract with its AFT graduate student local.[25] Strong management rights clauses that retain administrative control over academic and student issues can be found as well in many public sector graduate student contracts.[26]

Mandatory Subjects

With any of its campus unions, an administration may be confronted by union demands to negotiate over items that are not mandatory subjects of negotiation under state or federal law. But graduate students are more likely to bring non-mandatory subjects to the table than any other labor organization. Consequently, depending on the union's agenda, an administrative bargaining team may spend time at the table listening to demands relating to student housing, financial aid and even consequential social justice issues like immigration policies.

An employer is required under the NLRA and most public sector statutes to negotiate over compensation, hours and other terms and conditions of employment. It is not required to negotiate over other subjects, and at the table, the administration should be careful not to introduce into their contracts areas that are permissive subjects at best. There are multiple reasons for this approach.

First, collective bargaining takes long enough fighting over topics that must be bargained under law. To add new topics that do not have to be bargained can lead to extensive delays in the process and a further opportunity for the parties to reach impasse.

Second, while technically an employer who agrees to language on permissive subjects in the contract is free to not do so in the next agreement, it is difficult, on a practical level, in future rounds to reject talking about a topic that the parties agreed to discuss once before.

Third, adding extra layers of protections on non-bargainable topics can and will lead to grievances and arbitrations over such matters when there is a claimed violation.

Fourth, it's a slippery slope. Being willing to talk about one or more permissive subjects, such as housing, can invariably lead to discussions of others that affect students in their "non-labor" status. It may be hard to draw a consistent line as to what the administration will discuss and what it will not in terms of permissive subjects.

On the other hand, if an administration wants to address a non-mandatory subject either due to union pressure or because it feels it is the right setting to do so, one method would be to address the issue via side letters that are not permanent parts of the agreement. For example, agreeing not to change financial aid policies during the life of the agreement or waiving certain student fees as part of obtaining a deal can be placed in side letters that essentially self-destruct with the expiration of the contract.

Matters of Academic Judgment

The overlap of academic and employment status of graduate students creates ample opportunity for confronting the question of whether a union proposal could lead to an arbitrator sorting out matters of faculty academic judgment. For example, a union proposal to allow a student worker to decide what type of software they should be provided to accomplish an assignment could lead to grievances over the principal investigator's refusal to agree and why that particular software was not necessary for the academic project involved.

As another example, a claim of "academic retaliation" by a student worker, e.g. claiming that the faculty member issued a negative academic assessment to a student because they filed a grievance against the faculty member, will inevitably involve the arbitrator in academic matters.

In the end, it is perhaps impossible to exclude every potential situation where the academic judgment of a faculty member could be litigated. But a thoughtful administrative bargaining team should consider every union proposal in that light and decide whether it could lead to litigating underlying academic decisions.

Workload

Perhaps nowhere is the tension more visible between the graduate assistant as "student" as opposed to "student worker" than in the workload article of the contract. The teaching assistant who conducts a section of a class as part of their work is providing a service to the institution and teaching students in every sense of the word. But they are also doing so as part of a post-graduate learning experience in pursuit of the Ph. D. Is such work academic in nature or is it employment work?

At least with a teaching assistant, the hours in which they are "working" are somewhat visible in terms of meeting a class or holding office hours. But what about a research assistant who works all day every day in a lab performing services under the direction of a principal investigator (PI) working on a grant? Are they pursuing knowledge in pursuit of their degree? Or are they assisting the PI in conducting experiments as a worker bee in the lab? Or both simultaneously?

Most student employee contracts make reference to limits on how many hours a student employee must work, such as "student workers shall not work more than 20 hours a week." But how can an institution neatly sever the total effort of the student into academic bucket and employment work bucket? How can it assure that a student in a biochemistry lab is only "working" 20 hours in a week while at the same time not putting any limits on the amount of time the student should spent on their academic work?

Some contracts try to thread this needle. The University of Washington contract, for example, starts with very detailed restrictions on the number of required hours "per quarter." But later such restrictive language is softened:

> Workload assigned to an ASE under this article is separate from the academic expectations associated with thesis and dissertation research that is expected pursuant to 600-, 700-, and 800-level course work. This Agreement should not in any way be construed as imposing a limit on the amount of academic work necessary for a student to make satisfactory academic progress toward their degree.[27]

The University of Rhode Island contract with the AAUP states:

> The average weekly workload for all full-time Graduate Assistants shall be twenty (20) hours. It is understood that Graduate Assistants are engaged in

professional activities of such a nature that the output produced, or the results accomplished, cannot be precisely standardized or measured in relation to a given period of time and that the time necessary to accomplish an assignment may vary.[28]

See also the Tufts contract with the SEIU[29] and the University of Illinois contract with the AFT.[30]

Harvard's contract with the UAW provides:

> Salaried/stipended appointments. For all such appointments, the University will not require more than an average of twenty (20) hours per week of effort for students in their roles as student workers over the course of their employment appointment period where the appointment period is a traditional semester, academic year or calendar year.[31]
>
> The time spend by a student worker on their academic efforts associated with degree requirements and academic expectations are not part of this collective bargaining agreement.

While it is difficult to avoid some mention of hours, some flexible language, like the examples above, should be desired. Further, administrations should avoid a strict "number of hours per week" limitation and seek more generalized "average number of hours over the appointment period" to allow for the ebb and flow of work, especially in lab settings.

In addition to the delicacy of negotiating time limits in these agreements, administrations may want to seek other provisions in the workload article, such as discretionary control of assignments.

For teaching assignments, any limits on hours worked should ideally not include prep time for class but only the hours associated in the class or section meeting. Harvard's contract with the UAW illustrates this point.[32] The parties were also clear that the compensation paid for teaching a section "includes, in addition to class time, preparation, grading, meeting with and advising students on course work and all other matters attendant to teaching the course."

Compensation

When the NLRB and other labor boards decided that graduate student assistants are employees, one linchpin of such rulings was that students received compensation for work performed. But what is that compensation? In *Columbia*, the Board found the annual stipend to be the compensation needed to create an employee–employer relationship, since "receipt of a full financial award is conditioned upon their performance of teaching duties."

But there is an uncomfortable feel to this logic. In other workplace settings, compensation is measured by *the value of the work that the employee performs*, molded and shaped by such other factors as market comparability, individual experience, and merit. But by simply referring to the stipend as the "compensation," the Board was stating that the financial aid that the student *already receives* will now be re-labeled as "compensation" since the student has to work in order to receive the financial aid. The Board's designation of the stipend as compensation, then, is simply used as a working convenience to circumvent the fact that stipends are not designed to measure the intrinsic value of work but rather serve as financial support to a graduate student in order to help them live while completing their degrees.

Nonetheless, at many bargaining tables, the negotiations over compensation articles often devolve into what the stipend should be. Thus, contracts at Florida State, University of Connecticut and the University of Iowa, among many others, work off the stipend approach when it comes to the compensation articles of the contract.

But it is also perfectly reasonable to limit contract "compensation" to some reasonable measure of what to pay someone for the worked performed. For example, how much is teaching a section of a course worth? Some contracts, such as the NYU/UAW agreement, consider such teaching compensation as comparable to pay per course for adjuncts.[33] The contracts at Harvard and Brandeis similarly provide for a per course or per credit rate of pay for teaching assistants.[34]

With research assistants, it is more difficult to segregate the stipend from the compensation due to the complete overlap of academics and employment. Thus, while Harvard separated out the teaching fellows for a per course compensation, the contract uses the stipend rate as the compensation rate for research assistants.

For those bargaining units that include hourly workers, the best practice may be to bargain over minimum hourly rates rather than fixed rates. This is recommended because hourly workers may have widely variable hourly rates, often dependent on how much funding their mentor may have available for them to do spot research assignments.

FERPA

The Statutory Conflict

Under the Family Education Rights and Privacy Act (FERPA), colleges and universities are precluded from disclosing certain personal student information. There are severe penalties that can be imposed on schools for violating FERPA, including the loss of federal funding.

FERPA protects the privacy of student "education records." An education record is defined as "those records, files, documents, and other materials which (i) contain information directly related to a student; and (ii) are maintained by an educational agency or institution or by a person acting for such agency or institution."[35] The records of graduate students – even if they are also employees – are education records as defined under FERPA.[36]

Except for certain directory information, FERPA only allows such education records to be disclosed to third parties under certain conditions: (1) where the student has provided written consent or (2) pursuant to a lawfully issued subpoena.[37]

The problem that arises with unionized graduate students is that an exclusive bargaining representative is entitled by law to information that the university maintains that is necessary and relevant for the union to carry out its representational functions.[38] Thus, when a union asks for information from a university that includes the "educational records" of the students they represent, an immediate conflict with FERPA arises. Normal union requests for pay rates and disciplinary records of the people they represent become suddenly complicated when disclosure of such information could violate FERPA.[39]

Interpretations of FERPA by the Department of Education do not provide any special exemption for when a union asks for such information. Disclosure of educational records to a union without a student waiver or a subpoena will still be considered a FERPA violation.[40]

Dealing with the Issue at the Table

In negotiations, unions will invariably propose specific contract language that the university will provide them with information on a regular basis about the student workers they represent, clauses that often appear in union contracts. Because of the potential for a FERPA violation, an administration must be extremely careful not to agree in the collective bargaining agreement to these standard provisions without also delineating FERPA limitations. While it is permissible to include directory information to the union (assuming the student has not otherwise blocked such disclosure) on a regular basis, any other information should only be provided with a student waiver, and the contract should have provisions for how that will be done.

Sexual Harassment and Discrimination

Sexual harassment of graduate students by faculty is a particularly acute problem, and the litany of well-publicized cases of faculty members sexually harassing students is quite long. In many cases, the reality of such harassment becomes a motivating factor for student protests and labor organizing. To compound the problem, graduate students especially are often hesitant to report cases to Title IX coordinators and administrative officials in light of the enormous power that their faculty hold over them.[41]

In negotiations, it is not uncommon for a graduate student union to seek ways of strengthening their protections from gender discrimination and harassment over and above a simple non-discrimination clause in the contract. Graduate student unions may seek the inclusion of other provisions, such as a demand for training of faculty and employees; interim relief measures when reporting cases of harassment; protection from being pressured by administrators to drop their cases or settle for a modest accommodation; and direct student involvement in setting university policies and procedures over such matters. Often such provisions are already contained in university policies, but more often than not, unions will seek enhanced protections. Whether the university chooses to agree to such contract provisions or to amend its policies to address such demands is an individual choice for each administration.

Another related issue that universities will face is whether to allow such claims of discrimination and harassment to be grieved and arbitrated. Most contracts allow for such claims to move forward as grievances; some, on the other hand, keep resolution of such matters internal and prohibit such claims from being pursued to arbitration.[42] This is an issue that arises not only in graduate student contracts but others as well. For those administrations that argue against grievability, a common rationale for doing so is that the agencies provide ample protection for such claims and the institution will not want to be faced with duplicative proceedings on defending against such claims. An additional reason is the avoidance of separate processes for students with harassment complaints, with the student worker potentially having access to outside arbitration while other students have no such avenue. Title IX policies and procedures are not drafted with such a dichotomy in mind and agreeing to different procedures can create administrative and legal problems.

Finally, paying attention to Department of Education regulations is also important on this topic. Title IX has become a statute heavily regulated by the federal government. It is a worthwhile caveat that administrations should seek to avoid specific language in the contract that may be at odds with university policies that may have to be modified from time to time to deal with changing agency regulations.

Short Takes: Other Special Areas of Concern

Discipline and Discharge

While this chapter will not cover every type of article that might appear in a collective bargaining agreement, there are a few contract areas that do warrant mention as especially troublesome articles to negotiate with graduate students. For example, while provisions on discipline and discharge are classic bargaining issues with all unions, the graduate student world requires careful distinctions in the contract language. Central to negotiating these articles is the guideline that academic discipline and poor academic performance must be separated from employment discipline. Article 16 of the Tufts University contract with the

SEIU emphasizes that conduct that can be viewed as both employment and academic in nature will be handled by two different procedures.

> 16.1 Discipline related to employment shall not include consequences to a Graduate Assistant's student status; any incidents that could affect both student status and employment must be handled separately. The Union acknowledges it has no right to interfere with or grieve decisions regarding student status, including such decisions that may impact a student's employment, unless the decision is prompted by employment activities.[43]

Clauses such as these effectively separate out student discipline from worker discipline, at least on paper, and underline the reality that a student worker engaging in misconduct may very well face two dual disciplinary actions.

Union Security

Union security provisions are especially important for labor organizations, with union shop articles that require membership in the union as a condition of employment serving as the gold standard. In the private sector, negotiations of such provisions are still allowed under the NLRA, except for right to work states.[44] In the public sector, such provisions are now illegal in light of the Supreme Court's 2018 *Janus* decision.[45]

The question for an administration in confronting such proposals where they are allowed is whether it wishes to agree to requiring its graduate student workers to be forced to pay dues and fees to the union as a condition of employment. And, if the answer is yes, it will be necessary to carve out language that makes it clear that failure to pay the dues does *not* mean that the graduate student is expelled from the program, but only that they cannot work.

In addition to outright opposition to such clauses, some administrations have agreed to them but with limited penalties short of discharge. The Tufts contract, for example, provides a penalty of a two-week suspension each year when classes are not in session for those graduate student workers who refuse to join the union.[46]

Given the importance of such an issue for the union, if an administration decides to agree to such a provision, it is well-advised to do so by packaging such a concession with a meaningful trade for some other management-desired provision.

No Strike Clauses

While labor strikes in support of bargaining positions during contract negotiations are not uncommon, including strikes by graduate student workers,[47] once a contract is signed, administrations will want to rest assured that such work stoppages will not occur during the life of the agreement. Thus, a strong no strike article is indispensable for management in every contract. Even in the public sector where strikes are illegal in most states, a no strike clause serves as a deterrent to illegal action and can spell out the particular consequences of violating the article. In any graduate student contract, the no strike clause should ideally prohibit withholding of grades – a typical pressure tactic by graduate students – as well as other withholding of services.

The no strike article should also specifically embrace and prohibit "sympathy strikes" to make it crystal clear that *all* work stoppages are prohibited, not just those related to contract issues. This latter sympathy strike prohibition is especially important in graduate student contracts, not only to protect the institution against strikes undertaken in support of other unions, but also for strikes undertaken to achieve social justice issues over which graduate students wish to rally. Indeed, the likelihood of graduate student strikes, even those in contravention of no strike clauses, is higher than with other workers, as has been demonstrated in numerous cases.[48]

The delicacy of handling student strikes can test both the resolve and the creativity of an administration. For example, in some cases, it may not be clear that the student workers are truly on strike. In other cases where it appears that they are withholding services by not conducting a class, for example, they may be doing so with the acquiescence of their faculty advisors, particularly where the strike may be over social justice issues that the faculty member also supports.

But at the very least, strong no strike clauses should be negotiated into such contracts to allow the administration the legal authority and full range of any necessary action to put an end to such activity when such strikes occur.

Benefits

The question with regard to bargaining benefits in graduate student contracts is that since their benefits are usually limited in nature and usually given to them as part of the same student health benefit plans that might be offered to thousands of other non-working students on campus, an administration facing demands for improved health insurance will be concerned that any change for the graduate students might lead to changes in the entire student health plan for thousands more – at a prohibitive cost. This will cause many administrations to steer clear of changing benefits at the bargaining table unless they are comfortable extending the changes to all other non-working students.

For those institutions who do not want to touch their overall student health insurance plans or other student benefits in negotiating with the graduate students, some have simply referenced their standard student health plans as a benefit but have then created pools of money to be designated just for unit members to assist them on expenses such as dependent premium contributions; co-pays and deductibles; and dental costs. In this manner, the administration can negotiate over and provide an enhanced benefit but without reconfiguring the entire student health plan. The amount of money set aside in such pools can be negotiated by the parties along with the criteria for application. Such pools can also be set up for other benefits, such as a pool to assistant student workers in childcare.[49]

Social Justice and Equity Issues – Ripe for Collaboration

As mentioned earlier in this chapter, graduate students will often come to the bargaining table with a roster of issues that expand well beyond the standard wages, hours and conditions of employment. Many of their issues also embrace "social justice" issues,[50] and these present special challenges.

The term "social justice" itself is capable of variable definitions. While at one time social justice issues included traditional bargaining topics such as a fair wage for all workers, the reality of today's social justice issues is that they usually extend well beyond the four corners of the particular working environment of the employee and into a much broader societal realm. They can arrive at the table under different banners, such as racial justice, immigration reform, the #MeToo movement, inclusiveness of minority groups into society, income disparity and wealth inequality, divestiture, to name a few. Sometimes they are tangentially connected to a more typical bargaining demand (e.g. greater benefits for socioeconomically disadvantaged student workers) but they can also be demands for university statements of support of a political agenda (e.g. a declaration that the institution is a sanctuary campus or condemnation of the actions or statements of a political leader). At bottom, this attempt at merging traditional bargaining issues with social movements is often a unique issue when dealing with graduate student unions.

Why is this? We previously noted the obvious demographic point that graduate students tend to be a younger population than most other employee groups on campus. With collective bargaining, they may for the very first time have a platform to not only express their views but to wield actual power in an effort to attain social justice goals. In addition, those students who unionize sometimes see their own institution as an emblem of society as a whole, a corporate capitalist entity that may be contributing to society's ills or, at best, one that shamefully remains silent in the face of injustice. The bargaining table provides a forum for pushing such universities to act to improve society.

Particular societal movements loom large in this regard. For example, the #MeToo movement and the need to address the injustices of sexual harassment was a driving force in the Harvard graduate student unionization movement and subsequent negotiations. The Black Lives Matter movement and its agenda for racial justice is another societal movement that will likely resonate in bargaining table discussions.

A member of the Harvard UAW team, reflecting back on the first round of negotiations with the university, wrote about their union movement, fueled by the cases of sexual harassment and the #MeToo movement but also calling for a continuation of seeking non-traditional goals at the bargaining table for the future. She gave voice to the hope for a long-range union movement that might transform the university itself.

> A private university with a fully unionized academic worker class can not only improve working conditions, but help determine the agenda of the university.... We must conceive of our organizing as class struggle—as a fight not only to win harassment protections, but also to reclaim the university and preserve the integrity of our work.[51]

But collective bargaining has limits. The labor statutes that authorize the very legal existence of collective bargaining establish those limits by defining mandatory topics of negotiations. If one party insists on negotiating over issues that transcend such mandatory subjects, they can be a violation of the statutory duty to bargain in good faith. The bargaining relationship is primarily established for the *worker as worker*, not the worker as a member of society. An institution is fully within its rights to refuse to engage in such political and social justice demands and calls for "equity" unless such demands are linked to the standards confines of collective bargaining or are in concert with the institution's own mission. With this perspective, the university can claim no greater authority – or duty – to improve society than any other business, and it should not be placed in a position of having to act otherwise.

To the extent a graduate student union seeks broad political stances from a university in the context of bargaining a contract, such efforts should be resisted as simply inappropriate no matter how expansive one's view of bargaining may be. But to the extent a graduate student union is seeking social justice *within the bargaining unit itself*, such objectives may be achieved – if desired by both parties – without compromising the integrity of traditional collective bargaining. For example, it may be possible for the university to find a way of continuing such discussions outside the four corners of the agreement on such topics as racial justice on campus and gender harassment. While limiting bargaining topics, an administration can nonetheless address these broader student issues through side letters on non-bargainable topics; through verbal understandings at the table; and through the utilization of labor management committees that might allow for broader agendas that address student concerns generally. Placement of graduate student workers on university-wide committees dealing with an array of issues can be done as well, particularly since many of the issues are *student* issues writ large and not just *student worker* issues.[52] With a good faith willingness on both sides to find other forums and approaches for addressing these issues, institutions and unions can collaborate on such issues for betterment of all.

Concluding Thoughts

Anyone who has experienced graduate student unionization understands the challenges laid out in this chapter. The running theme of separating out student issues from employment issues will present the biggest hurtle of all but it will be well worth the effort not to over expand the union contract to cover pure student issues and other non-mandatory subjects.

Nevertheless, as noted, there are still many avenues for addressing the concerns raised by student workers that exceed mandatory topics of bargaining. In the end administrators should not be at war with unionized graduate students and, with their best interests at heart, will find ways to make the relationship work.

Finally, the principles of good labor relations apply to the graduate student union context with no less force than in other negotiations. In addition to respect for the union's role and adherence to contract provisions, perhaps the foundation that supports all else is frequent communications between labor and management. The union does not have to become a partner with the administration. But if they understand in advance the issues that an administration may be facing or the rationale for certain planned actions, they can better deal with their own members and in many cases work out problems with administrators before they become major obstacles and sources of litigation.

Such good practices may not always lead down the road to harmony. But they can certainly remove some of the roadblocks along the way.

Notes

1 *Board of Higher Education of the City of New York*, 2 PERB Para. 3000, 1969 WL 1894424 (NY PERB, 1969)
2 See Public Comments by the National Center for the Study of Collective Bargaining in Higher Education and the Professions on the NLRB proposed rule on the Nonemployee status of University and College Students Working in Connection with their Studies (November 20, 2019). The Comments provide an exhaustive review of public sector graduate student unionization. http://www.hunter.cuny.edu/ncscbhep/assets/files/2019_Comments%20by%20the%20National%20Center%20for%20the%20Study%20of%20Collective%20Bargaining%20in%20Higher%20Education%20and%20the%20Professions-%20NPRM%20FR%202019-20510.pdf
3 See Public Comments, *supra*, pp. 12–14
4 *Cornell University*, 183 NLRB 329 (1970)
5 The most consequential issue of all, of course, was the question of the managerial status of full-time faculty, culminating in the Supreme Court's decision in *NLRB v. Yeshiva University*, 444 U.S. 672 (1980)
6 195 NLRB 639 (1972)
7 195 NLRB at 640
8 214 NLRB 621 (1974)
9 332 NLRB 1205 (2000)
10 332 NLRB at 1206
11 342 NLRB 483 (2004)

12 See 342 NLRB at 489, citing *St. Claire's Hospital*, 229 NLRB, 1000,1002 (1977) (emphasis added)

13 *Columbia, supra*, at p. 9

14 Even if the rule is finally issued and survived any legal challenge, it is likely that an NLRB with Biden appointees will have eventually reversed the rule at some point. Perhaps not until the Act itself is clarified one way or the other as to the employee status of student workers will the ping pong game on this issue finally end.

15 https://www.thecrimson.com/article/2018/9/26/grad-union-list-of-goals/

16 https://columbiagradunion.org/wp-content/uploads/InitialBargainingGoals_full.pdf

17 *Columbia Spectator,* Feb 18, 2019

18 Arguments to exclude them as temporary employees failed in the *Columbia* case.

19 Some private sector institutions, like Tufts, Georgetown and American University, have had adjunct or contingent faculty units for some time. But most other private universities have no academic unions. Thus, Harvard, Columbia and Brown, to name a few, encountered academic collective bargaining for the first time when their graduate students organized.

20 DiGiovanni, "This Much I Know I Know is True: The Five Intangible Influences on Collective Bargaining," *Journal of Collective Bargaining in the Academy*, Vol. 3, Issue 1 (2012) Available at: http://thekeep.eiu.edu/jcba/vol3/iss1/5/

21 Not surprisingly, then, in many settings, a graduate student union will focus on mental health issues at the bargaining table as one of their primary concerns.

22 The decision by the NLRB in *MV Transportation, Inc.*, 368 NLRB No. 66 (2019) adopts this general approach in assessing the duty to bargain during the life of an agreement.

23 http://harvardgradunion.org/our-contract/article-17-management-rights/

24 https://as.tufts.edu/union-resources-gsas-doctoral-students

25 https://brownsugs1.files.wordpress.com/2020/06/brown-sugse-final-agreement_061520.pdf

26 For example, see the agreement between *University of Connecticut and UConn GEU-UAW* contract at http://uconngradunion.org/geu-uaw-collective-bargaining-agreement/article-3-university-prerogatives-and-academic-rights/; see also *Wayne State University and Graduate Employees Organizing Committee (AFT)*, https://www.geocwsu.com/resources. This contract, along with those at University of Illinois and Michigan State, were cited by the NLRB in the *Columbia* decision as agreements in which administrations retained control in their management rights articles over academic and student matters.

27 https://hr.uw.edu/labor/academic-and-student-unions/uaw-ase/ase-contract

28 https://www.urigau.org/read-me/#article-6

29 https://access.tufts.edu/sites/default/files/documents/hr/2018-2023-GSAS-CBA-Signed.pdf

30 https://humanresources.illinois.edu/assets/docs/GEO-2017-22-Contract.pdf

31 http://harvardgradunion.org/our-contract/article-16-workload/

32 http://harvardgradunion.org/our-contract/article-16-workload/

33 http://www.2110uaw.org/cbas/NYU_CBA_2015-2020_Searchable.pdf

34 Referred to as "teaching fellows" at Harvard

35 20 U.S.C. § 1232g(a)(4)(A)

36 *See* 34 C.F.R. § 99.3(b)(3)(ii); accord LeRoy S. Rooker, *Letter to University of Massachusetts Relating to Teaching Assistants* (Feb. 25, 2002); LeRoy S. Rooker, *Letter of Technical Assistance to the Regents of the University of California re: Disclosures to Employment Relations Board* (Sept. 17, 1999) Found at https://studentprivacy.ed.gov/sites/default/files/resource_document/file/oaklandca.pdf

37 *See* 20 U.S.C. § 1232g(b)(1) & (b)(2)(A)

38 *NLRB v. Truitt Manufacturing Co.*, 351 U.S. 149 (1956); *NLRB v. Jacobs Mfg. Co.*, 196 F. 2d 680 (2nd Cir., 1952). Public sector labor boards have held to the same

position. See, for example, *Board of Higher Education and Massachusetts Community College Council, MTA/NEA,* 26 MLC 91 (2000); *State of Vermont v. VSEA,* 15 VLRB 13, 22 (1991)

39   This conflict was anticipated in the dissenting opinion of Member Miscimarra in the Columbia case. See *Columbia,* p. 27, footnote 29

40   See *University of Massachusetts opinion letter,* footnote 28 *infra*

41   https://www.huffpost.com/entry/grad-students-sexual-harassment_n_ 57714bc6e4b0dbb1bbbb37c7

42   The handful of graduate student contracts that prohibit such claims from being pursued as a grievance under the contract include Harvard, Georgetown, American, and Florida State, among others.

43   https://access.tufts.edu/sites/default/files/documents/hr/2018-2023-GSAS-CBA-Signed.pdf.
      See also NYU's contract. http://www.2110uaw.org/cbas/NYU_CBA_2015-2020_ Searchable.pdf

44   There are 27 right to work states currently.

45   *Janus v. AFSCME,* 585 U.S. ___, 138 S. Ct. 2448; 201 L. Ed. 2d 924 (2018)

46   https://access.tufts.edu/sites/default/files/documents/hr/2018-2023-GSAS-CBA-Signed.pdf

47   During the negotiations of the first contract at Harvard, the HGSU-UAW went out on strike for a month before returning to the table and engaging in mediation that ultimately led to settlement. At New York University, the UAW went out on strike for six months to protest the institution's refusal to voluntarily bargain following the NLRB's *Brown University* decision. An illegal strike by graduate teaching assistants at the University of Michigan in September 2020 ended only after court action. https:// www.detroitnews.com/story/news/local/michigan/2020/09/17/university-michigan-graduate-students-return-teaching-end-strike/3476868001/

48   Graduate students at the University of California Santa Clara walked out in the middle of their contract in violation of the no strike clause and state law. https://en. wikipedia.org/wiki/2020_Santa_Cruz_graduate_students%27_strike. In early September 2020 both professors and students on many campuses engaged in a two-day strike to promote racial justice. https://www.newsbreak.com/news/2057037638927/schola rs-on-strike

49   Such pools appear in the University of Washington, University of Connecticut, Harvard and NYU contracts with their graduate student workers.

50   See D. Julius, Chapter 8, "Untangling the Issues; Social Justice and Collective Bargaining in Higher Education," in (A. Kezar and J. Posselt, eds., 2019) *Higher Education Administration for Social Justice and Equity: Critical Perspectives for Leadership,* (New York, NY: Routledge)

51   Ege Yumusak, *#MeToo's Strike Test, The Harvard Graduate Student Union and the Limits of "Time's Up" Organizing,* https://www.thedriftmag.com/article_author/ ege-yumusak/ (June 24, 2020)

52   The Harvard contract, for example, provides for unit member participation on several university-wide committees dealing with sexual harassment and the creation of procedures to deal with other forms of discrimination.

4

LEGAL DEVELOPMENTS IN HIGHER EDUCATION COLLECTIVE BARGAINING

Michael W. Klein

The Relationship Between Federal and State Labor Laws

The National Labor Relations Act of 1935 (NLRA) governs collective bargaining between private employers and employees, leaving state governments to decide whether to allow public employees to unionize.[1] Generally, in states that allow public collective bargaining, public employees have the right to organize and select a representative to negotiate on their behalf with their employer over terms and conditions of employment (explained in more detail below). Once a majority of employees in a specific bargaining unit elect a representative, the employer must bargain with the representative, and individual employees may not negotiate with the employer over issues that are mandatory subjects of collective bargaining.[2] The NLRA requires employers and employee representatives to bargain in good faith regarding "wages, hours, and other terms and conditions of employment."[3]

In states that allow public employees to unionize and conduct collective bargaining, the laws generally mirror the NLRA's provision regarding the subjects that collective bargaining must cover. In these states, parties must negotiate over "mandatory" subjects of bargaining, which in most states include wages, hours, and terms and conditions of employment.[4]

Because the statutes themselves fail to define "terms and conditions of employment," it has been left to the courts and public-employment labor boards to decide the issues that are covered under this phrase. These issues often include tenure, faculty assignments, and strikes. This state-by-state approach makes it important for college administrators to consult with university counsel

DOI: 10.4324/9781003138990-5

to know the specific items that are subject to bargaining as expressed in statutes and decided by courts in their state.

"Right to Work" and the Retraction of Union Rights, 2010–2012

"Right to Work" States

In the private sector, the National Labor Relations Act of 1935 allows union security agreements, which are collective bargaining agreements between employers and labor organizations that require workers covered by the agreement to join the negotiating labor organization.[5] The U.S. Supreme Court has ruled that under these agreements, an employee cannot be required to join a union but must pay some portion of membership dues,[6] which have been narrowed to cover union activities that are germane to collective bargaining, contract administration, and grievance adjustment.[7] In the public sector, the U.S. Supreme Court has ruled that unions cannot require employees to pay such agency fees.[8]

Amendments to the NLRA by the Taft-Hartley Act of 1947 allow individual states to enact laws prohibiting union security agreements.[9] These state statutes are called "right to work" laws. In right-to-work states, workers covered by a collective bargaining agreement may choose not to join the bargaining unit.[10] As of 2017, 27 states – five between 2012 and 2017 – adopted right-to-work laws.[11] Of these, six states, through statute or court decision, made collective bargaining by public-sector employees illegal: Georgia, North Carolina, South Carolina, Tennessee, Texas, and Virginia.[12]

The growth in right-to-work states followed the reverberations of the Great Recession of 2008, which by 2010 was still causing significant unemployment, under-employment, and wage stagnation that in turn decreased tax revenues for many state governments.[13] Republicans – many affiliated with the Tea Party – won elections across the country in 2010 and, once in office, blamed public employees' salaries and benefits – often achieved through collective bargaining – as the source of their respective state's budget problems.[14] Targeting collective bargaining, Republican leaders in about 12 states, including Wisconsin, Indiana, and Ohio, aimed to reduce the political and bargaining influence of public-sector unions.[15] Common elements among their legislative reforms included repealing public-sector collective bargaining rights; restricting the scope of bargaining over an array of subjects, most prominently health care; and changing impasse procedures by expanding employers' ability to impose final terms of employment.[16]

Wisconsin's Act 10

The 2011 Budget Repair Act in Wisconsin increased public-employee contributions toward their pensions and healthcare, and removed collective bargaining rights from faculty and academic staff of the University of Wisconsin System, among other public employees.[17] Act 10 prohibits bargaining over subjects other than "base wages."[18] Act 10 also requires annual recertification elections for incumbent bargaining representatives, who must receive votes from at least 51 percent of the employees in the bargaining unit – rather than a majority of votes cast, the standard for elections conducted by the National Labor Relations Board – to maintain their status.[19] This provision aimed to weaken the unions themselves. In addition, the law prohibits payroll deductions for dues,[20] and fair-share fees for bargaining-unit employees who do not join the union.[21]

Unions representing teachers and public employees challenged the constitutionality of Act 10, claiming that the restrictions on collective bargaining, the prohibition on payroll deductions of union dues, the prohibition on fair-share agreements, and the annual recertification requirements violated the right of free association under the U.S. and Wisconsin constitutions and the equal protection rights of represented employees.[22] In 2014, the Wisconsin Supreme Court upheld the law, stating: "If a general employee participates in collective bargaining under Act 10's statutory framework, that general employee has not relinquished a constitutional right. They have only acquired a benefit to which they were never constitutionally entitled."[23]

Ohio

In Ohio, the legislature narrowly passed a bill in 2011 that authorized public employers to choose, rather than be required, to bargain with public-employee unions, and it prohibited public employees from striking. The bill allowed bargaining over wages, but not health care or pensions. The legislation defined faculty at state institutions of higher education as "management level employees" if they participated "in the governance of the institution" and were "involved in personnel decisions, selection or review of administrators, planning and use of physical resources, budget preparation, and determination of educational policies related to admissions, curriculum, subject matter, and methods of instruction and research," thereby exempting them from union representation and preventing them from participating in collective bargaining.[24] In a fierce public backlash, opponents collected over 5.6 times more signatures than they needed to place a referendum on the November 2011 ballot to repeal the law, and voters rejected the enactment 62 percent to 38 percent.[25]

Michigan's "Freedom to Work" Law[26]

As in Ohio the year before, Michigan significantly reformed its Public Employment Relations Act during a lame-duck legislative session in December 2012.[27] The amendments permitted public employees to engage in, or refrain from, collective bargaining, and prohibited individuals from being required to engage in or refrain from certain activities – like joining a labor organization or paying dues – as a condition of public employment (there are exceptions for police and fire department employees and State Police troopers and sergeants). The amendments also deleted a requirement for public employees in a bargaining unit to pay a service fee equivalent to union dues.

Religious Institutions

In 2020, the National Labor Relations Board (NLRB) ruled that it would not assert jurisdiction over religious institutions of higher education, overturning its six-year-old precedent. In the 2020 case, faculty members at Bethany College in Kansas alleged that the college's tenure process, its confidentiality agreement that prevented faculty from discussing the tenure process, and the termination of a faculty member for violating the confidentiality agreement were unfair labor practices.[28] The NLRB did not rule on the substance of these allegations but instead declined to assert jurisdiction because Bethany College – a ministry of the Evangelical Lutheran Church in America (ELCA) that is owned and operated by the Central States Synod and the Arkansas/Oklahoma Synod of the ELCA – is "a self-identified religious institution of higher education."[29] The NLRB reasoned that exercising its jurisdiction "over religious schools in matters involving faculty members will inevitably involve inquiry into the religious tenets of these institutions," thereby risking an infringement of "the protections set forth in the Religion Clauses of the First Amendment."[30]

In declining jurisdiction, the NLRB adopted the three-pronged test first used by the U.S. Court of Appeals for the District of Columbia Circuit in a 2002 case involving a petition by the Montana Federation of Teachers, AFT, AFL–CIO to be recognized as the collective bargaining agent for the faculty of the University of Great Falls, a private Roman Catholic university in Montana.[31] The DC Circuit Court held that the NLRB "must decline to exercise jurisdiction"[32] over an institution that (a) "'holds itself out to students, faculty, and community' as providing a religious educational environment";[33] (b) is "organized as a 'nonprofit'";[34] and (c) "is affiliated with, or owned, operated, or controlled, directly or indirectly, by a recognized religious organization, or with an entity, membership of which is determined, at least in part, with reference to religion."[35] The DC Circuit used this standard again in 2020 when it ruled that the NLRB did not have jurisdiction over Duquesne University, a Catholic university where adjunct faculty tried to unionize.[36]

By adopting the *Great Falls* test, the NLRB overturned its previous, more union-friendly jurisdictional standard for religious institutions established in 2014.[37] In *Pacific Lutheran University*,[38] the NLRB – in finding that Pacific Lutheran's faculty could unionize – used a two-part test to determine jurisdiction: (1) the institution "holds itself out as providing a religious educational environment," and (2) the institution "must then show that it holds out the petitioned-for faculty members as performing a religious function," which "requires a showing by the college or university that it holds out those faculty as performing a specific role in creating or maintaining the university's religious educational environment."[39] The first part of the test was based on a U.S. Supreme Court case.[40] Focusing on the second part of the test, the NLRB in *Bethany College* said it was "fatally flawed" because requiring the NLRB to analyze "whether faculty members at religiously affiliated institutions of higher learning are held out as performing a specific religious function entails an impermissible inquiry into what does and what does not constitute a *religious function*" [emphasis in original].[41]

The *Bethany College* decision makes it quite doubtful that the NLRB will take up cases from self-identified religious educational institutions. These include religious colleges and universities as well as parochial and other sectarian elementary and secondary schools. As a result, their faculty will find it difficult to unionize.[42]

Graduate Students

While the unionization of graduate students at private institutions has attracted recent attention, as detailed in Chapter 9, graduate students at public colleges and universities have been able to form unions for over 50 years. In addition to negotiating wages, graduate student unions have tried to expand the scope their negotiations to include several other issues. These include fair hourly work expectations; maternity/paternity leave and pay, along with childcare assistance; and equal access for undocumented graduate students.[43]

Transparency in negotiations helps to maintain an even-keeled relationship between a university and its graduate students. At the University of Washington, for example, notes from each bargaining session and meeting documents are published on the Union for Academic Student Employees (UAW 4121) webpage on the university's website. These practices "demystify the bargaining process" and ensure there is "a constant record of various positions presented in a nonhyperbolic way," according to the assistant dean for personnel at the University of Washington's College of Arts and Sciences.[44]

Following the ebbing of collective bargaining rights for public employees, as detailed above, graduate students at some public colleges and universities lost their statutory status to bargain collectively in some states. For example, in Michigan,

- For example, in Michigan, a law enacted in 2012 excluded graduate research assistants at public institutions from being considered "a public employee entitled to representation or collective bargaining rights."[45]

Against this tide, graduate assistants in Illinois gained collective bargaining rights under legislation passed in 2019. The antecedent law specifically excluded students from the definition of "educational employee," and an Illinois appellate court applied a "significant connection test" to determine whether graduate research assistants and graduate teaching assistants remained excluded for bargaining. If a graduate student's assistantship "is significantly connected to his or her status as a student, then he or she is a 'student'" within the meaning of Educational Labor Relations Act and "precluded from organizing."[46] The court concluded, "Proper application of the test will exclude from organizing those graduate students whose work is so related to their academic roles that collective bargaining would be detrimental to the educational process."[47]

Under the 2019 legislation, Illinois allowed certain categories of students to be considered an "educational employee." Under the new law, these categories included

> graduate students who are research assistants primarily performing duties that involve research, graduate assistants primarily performing duties that are pre-professional, graduate students who are teaching assistants primarily performing duties that involve the delivery and support of instruction, or any other graduate assistants.[48]

As employees, these students may unionize.

College Football

Given the value of the scholarships they receive, the amount of revenue they generate, and the level of control their coaches exert over them, student athletes – led by football players –are exploring their rights to unionize. For example, football players at Northwestern University won an initial victory at the regional level before the full National Labor Relations Board blocked their case. University administrators should understand the arguments behind the case because the labor rights of student athletes remain a hot-button issue.

In 2014, Northwestern's scholarship football players petitioned the NLRB for the right to be represented for collective bargaining. A regional director found Northwestern's football players who receive scholarships to be employees under the NLRA, based on the services they performed for the benefit of the university in exchange for compensation, and the control the university had over their performance, including practices, meetings, and games.[49]

In 2015, the five-member NLRB unanimously chose not to assert its jurisdiction in the case because doing so "would not serve to promote stability in labor relations."[50] The NLRB noted that the National Collegiate Athletic Association (NCAA) and leagues like the Big Ten, to which Northwestern belongs, exercise considerable control over individual teams and establish rules over eligibility, practice, and competitions.[51] Moreover, the NLRB does not have jurisdiction over public institutions of higher education, which are "Northwestern's primary competitors" within the Big Ten.[52] By declining to assert jurisdiction, the NLRB did not decide the essential issue: whether the players are employees.

University trustees and presidents largely oppose student-athlete unionization. In a brief submitted to the NLRB in the Northwestern case, several institutional advocacy organizations argued that giving student athletes the rights of employees would "undermine the relationship between students and their coaches and teachers. And it would entangle the board and courts in matters traditionally left to educators and would trench on academic freedom and disserve students."[53]

Some state government also oppose collective bargaining by student athletes. In response to the regional decision in the *Northwestern* case, Ohio and Michigan enacted legislation prohibiting college athletes from unionizing.

A state-by-state approach to collective bargaining rights for student athletes is unlikely to sustain itself. One of the leading experts on higher education law, Michael A. Olivas, said,

> I think it's going to come by Congress looking at this and legislating, because they're the only ones that can really consider this in the context of antitrust law, employment law, labor law, the variety of very specific subfields that are implicated.[54]

Some influential leaders in college sports see the need for radical reforms to the anachronistic notion of the amateur – unpaid – student athlete. John Thompson, Jr., the former basketball coach at Georgetown University, wrote in a posthumously published essay, "The amateurism of big-time college sports is antiquated and needs to be redefined." He suggested that "it's time for the N. C.A.A. to stop pretending that education is its top priority and pay college athletes" by sharing revenue with players.[55]

Best Practices for Negotiating and Administering Contracts, and Achieving Greater Social Justice Through Collective Bargaining in Higher Education

Overarching the labor considerations in this chapter is the need for labor and management to communicate effectively and build partnerships. Whether they are located in a pro-labor or pro-management state, university administrators should be mindful that achieving successful labor-management partnerships is ultimately a "risk-taking" exercise on both sides of the negotiating table.[56] Some recommendations to navigate these risks successfully are provided below.

Establish Trust

Developing and maintaining trust between management and labor has been called "attitudinal structuring," a vital subprocess of collective bargaining.[57] Enhanced trust facilitates communication between both sides and can ultimately help the parties put concessions on the table and reach consensus.

University administrators and union leaders can establish trust by meeting regularly away from the bargaining table and having an honest exchange of views and concerns. By working together "on an ongoing basis to share information, create employee participation processes, and consult on important issues," university managers and union leaders can develop trust that carries over to negotiations themselves.[58]

If a university is not required by law to enter comprehensive collective bargaining, administrators and union leaders can still negotiate memoranda of understanding. While such agreements are not legally enforceable, "they are usually complied with out of mutual respect and cooperation."[59]

Meet-and-Confer Sessions

Short of entering formal memoranda of understanding, management can use the structure of meet-and-confer sessions with employee unions "to ensure positive employee input in workplace decision-making."[60] For such sessions to be meaningful, they should include:

- notice to the employees' representative, and an opportunity to be involved, before the administration makes a decision;
- disclosure of pertinent information regarding the issues to be discussed; and
- good-faith consideration of the union's responses and, if they are rejected, an explanation for the reasons why.[61]

Making meet-and-confer sessions a regular routine can build trust and communication. Minnesota, for example, requires public employers to meet and confer with representatives of professional employees at least once every four months to discuss matters related to public services that are not mandatory subjects of collective bargaining.[62]

Lessons from the 2020 Coronavirus Pandemic

The COVID-19 pandemic in 2020 activated and strengthened union activity at colleges and universities across the U.S., even in right-to-work states that do not allow collective bargaining by public employees. Examples from Arizona, North Carolina, New York, and Michigan provide good examples of these dynamics, and how university administrators should respond.

Local 7065, the United Campus Workers (UCW) of Arizona

In April 2020, the president of the University of Arizona, facing a total budget shortfall exceeding $250 million from the pandemic crisis, announced plans for furloughs or salary cuts based on employees' salaries.[63] In response, a group of faculty, staff, and students formed the Coalition for Academic Justice.[64] Although the parameters and implementation dates for the furlough and salary-cut plan were eventually revised, the Coalition for Academic Justice spearheaded an election in September 2020 to form Local 7065, the United Campus Workers (UCW) of Arizona.[65]

Administrators should find ways to open channels of communication with brand-new unions. Even without a legal requirement to collectively bargain, institutions that establish mutual relationships with unions can resolve and even prevent contentious issues and set a campus-wide tone of cooperation. For example, at Arizona, the new union said that because of the harm suffered by employees from furloughs, pay cuts, and layoffs, "trust has been broken."[66] Sharing information on emergency measures, like retrenchment because of financial crises, and establishing routine, regular meetings with union leaders can go a long way to building and maintaining trust.

College leaders also need to anticipate that new unions will reach out to governing boards and elected officials, requiring reenergized communications of their own. In Arizona, Local 7065 – while acknowledging that state law and Arizona Board of Regents policy prohibit collective bargaining – intended to retain attorneys and lobbyists to engage with lawmakers and the Board of Regents.[67] Campus leaders of public institutions need to ensure their messaging regarding institutional finances and major personnel actions are clearly and regularly communicated with trustees, legislators, and governors, otherwise they will be reacting to the statements the unions put forward.

Lawsuits to Protect Vulnerable Employees

Research indicated that the COVID-19 pandemic and the resulting economic and health consequences disproportionately impacted Black Americans.[68] Black Americans experienced the highest overall actual COVID-19 mortality rates (80.4 per 100,000), more than twice the rate of white Americans and Asian Americans, who had the lowest COVID-19 mortality rates. Black Americans were at higher risk of exposure to the coronavirus because of the higher likelihood of performing "frontline, essential work during the pandemic."[69] For example, Black Americans are more than twice as likely as the average worker to work in the healthcare support service industry, most vulnerably in assisted-living facilities and nursing homes.[70]

Colleges campuses have their own frontline workers. Janitors, housekeeping staff, and security officers are integral to the operation of a campus, particularly keeping it clean and safe during the pandemic.[71] College leaders must be aware of the vulnerability of their frontline staff, whether they are unionized or not. Maintaining their economic security, despite the financial challenges that institutions faced during the pandemic from enrollment declines and state-budget cuts,[72] should be a priority. Otherwise, institutions could face lawsuits, like the two described below.

Class-Action Suit Against North Carolina System

In August 2020, as the University of North Carolina planned to reopen for the fall semester and prepared for tens of thousands of students to return, employees in the University of North Carolina (UNC) System filed a class-action lawsuit over unsafe working conditions, citing the rise in COVID-19 cases across the state.[73] As workers began testing positive for COVID-19, the UE150, NC Public Service Workers Union said the effects of the reopening plans "inevitably fall hardest on Black and Brown workers' shoulders, putting them at risk during a pandemic that disproportionately impacts their health."[74] The perceived lack of communication with campus constituencies about UNC's reopening plans, and the inability of workers to participate in those plans, preceded the lawsuit.[75]

City University of New York

Layoffs, often of adjunct faculty and part-time workers, spurred other lawsuits during the pandemic. The faculty and staff union at the City University of New York, the Professional Staff Congress/CUNY, sued the university for laying off about 2,800 adjunct faculty, lab technicians, and other professional and non-teaching staff.[76]

Nationally, one report indicated at least 224 institutions imposed layoffs or furloughs, or did not renew contracts because of the coronavirus pandemic, affecting at least 51,793 employees.[77] U.S. Department of Labor data indicated that between February and October 2020, public colleges and universities experienced a 13.7 percent downturn in employment.[78] As the pandemic persisted, labor relations in higher education continued to fray.

Strike Votes

To protest the University of Michigan's reopening plans during the coronavirus pandemic – as well as issues related to campus policing – the Graduate Employees' Organization went on strike from September 8 to September 18, 2020.[79] During the strike, members of the union refused to teach classes, did not hold discussion sections, and stopped doing some research. The union's demands to return to work included more rigorous testing for COVID-19, childcare subsidies, a right for instructors to work remotely, rent freezes, and diverting funds from the campus's Division of Public Safety and Security.[80]

The University of Michigan's response to the strike is instructive for ending such work stoppages, but it also shows the need to nurture relationships with unions. First, the university submitted a proposal to the union to address its demands, but after the union rejected it, the university invoked the state law prohibiting strikes by public employees,[81] and the "no interference" provision in the collective bargaining agreement between the union and the university.[82] On the day the strike began, the university filed an unfair labor practice charge against the union with the Michigan Employment Relations Commission. Six days later, the university filed a motion in state court for a temporary restraining order and a preliminary injunction to end the strike. Graduate students who continued striking could have been held in contempt of court, and the union could have been liable for civil damages.

The strike was formally settled, but more work still needed to be done to fix the relationship between the administration and the university's graduate students. Under a strike resolution agreement, the university promised, among other provisions, an extra $500,000 for childcare; more data regarding its surveillance testing for the coronavirus; guidelines for extensions of stipends, tuition, and benefits for doctoral students whose degree progress was disrupted by the COVID-19 pandemic; and the formation of a Task Force on Policing at the university.[83] Despite the agreement, hard feelings throughout the campus community resulting from the strike persisted. In a campus-wide email during the strike, President Mark S. Schlissel and Provost Susan M. Collins recognized the university "feels fractured," and on September 16, the faculty came close to voting no-confidence in Schlissel over his handling of the university's reopening, a central issue of the graduate students' strike.[84]

Conclusion

Over the first two decades of the 21st century, decisions by the National Labor Relations Board and legislative changes under Republican legislatures shaped the labor rights of faculty, staff, graduate students, and student athletes at colleges and universities in the public, private, and sectarian sectors. Given the distinctive characteristics and politics of each state, collective bargaining rights at public institutions in particular have been described as "a crazy-quilt patchwork of state and local laws, regulations, executive orders, court decisions, and attorney general opinions."[85] Facing these idiosyncrasies, college administrators need to be securely grounded in the details of collective bargaining in their state. Putting in the hard work to build mutual, trusting relationships with faculty, staff, graduate students, and student athletes will ultimately drive institutional success, with the rules of collective bargaining underpinning those relationships. In the words of a veteran personnel manager: "[P]artnership is the high wire and collective bargaining is the safety net."[86]

Notes

1 National Labor Relations Act of 1935, 29 U.S.C. §§ 151–69 (2020).
2 Kaplin, W. A., Lee, B. A., Hutchens, N. H., and Rooksby, J. H. 2019. *The law of higher education*. San Francisco: Jossey Bass, p. 342.
3 29 U.S.C. § 158(d) (2020).
4 Kaplin, W. A., Lee, B. A., Hutchens, N. H., and Rooksby, J. H. 2019. *The law of higher education*. San Francisco: Jossey Bass, p. 363.
5 29 U.S.C. 158(a)(3) (2020). See also Collins, B. (2014). *Right to work laws: Legislative background and empirical research*. Washington, DC: Congressional Research Service. https://crsreports.congress.gov/product/pdf/R/R42575
6 *NLRB v. General Motors Corp.*, 373 U.S. 734 (1963).
7 *Commc'ns Workers of Am. v. Beck*, 487 U.S. 735, 745 (1988).
8 *Janus v. American Federation of State, County, & Municipal Employees, Council 31*, 138 S. Ct. 2448, 2459–2460 (2018).
9 29 U.S.C. 164(b) (2020).
10 Quach, M. "The Janus Decision and the Future of Private-Sector Unionism." 16 *Hastings Bus. L.J.* 119 (2020).
11 National Conference of State Legislatures. 2020. Right-To-Work Resources. https://www.ncsl.org/research/labor-and-employment/right-to-work-laws-and-bills.aspx#legis
12 Kaplin, W. A., Lee, B. A., Hutchens, N. H., and Rooksby, J. H. 2019. *The law of higher education*. San Francisco: Jossey Bass.
13 Nack, D., Childers, M., Kulwiec, A., and Ibarra, A.. "The Recent Evolution of Wisconsin Public Worker Unionism since Act 10." *Labor Studies Journal* 45, no. 2 (2020): 147–165.
14 After the 2010 elections, Republicans held 53 percent of the total state legislative seats in the U.S., the most the party had held since 1928, and controlled at least 54 of the 99 state legislative chambers, the party's highest number since 1952. Dorsch, M. 2010, November 3. Republicans Exceed Expectations in 2010 State Legislative Elections. National Conference of State Legislatures. https://www.ncsl.org/press-room/republicans-exceed-expectations-in-2010.aspx
15 Greenhouse, S. 2011, March 30. Ohio Lawmakers Pass Anti-Union Bill. *The New York Times*. https://www.nytimes.com/2011/03/31/us/31ohio.html
16 Malin, M. H. "The legislative upheaval in public-sector labor law: A search for common elements." *ABA Journal of Labor and Employment Law* (2012): 149–164.
17 2011 Wis. Act 10 §§ 265, 279–280. Employees at the Wisconsin's flagship university, the University of Wisconsin-Madison, have historically been excluded from collective bargaining. University of Wisconsin System. 2018. UW System Administrative Policy 1262: Labor Relations and Collective Bargaining Procedures.
    Labor Relations and Collective Bargaining Procedures. https://www.wisconsin.edu/uw-policies/uw-system-administrative-policies/labor-relations-and-collective-bargaining-procedures/
18 2011 Wis. Act 10 § 314.
19 2011 Wis. Act 10 § 289.
20 2011 Wis. Act 10 §§ 227, 298.
21 2011 Wis. Act 10 §§ 219, 276. The U.S. Supreme Court, in *Janus v. American Federation of State, County, & Municipal Employees, Council 31*, 138 S. Ct. 2448, 2459–2460 (2018), subsequently found agency fees in the public sector to be unconstitutional because they infringed free-speech rights under the First Amendment.
22 *Madison Teachers, Inc. v. Walker*, 851 N.W.2d 337, 346 (Wisc. 2014).
23 *Id.* at 363.
24 S.B. 5, 29th Gen. Assemb. (Ohio 2011), amending Ohio Rev. Code Ann. §§4117.01(K), https://legiscan.com/OH/text/SB5/2011

25 Malin, M. H. "The legislative upheaval in public-sector labor law: A search for common elements." *ABA Journal of Labor and Employment Law* (2012): 149–164.

26 Michigan Department of Licensing and Regulatory Affairs. 2020. Freedom to Work. https://www.michigan.gov/lara/0,4601,7-154–292490–,00.html#

27 Michigan P. L. 2012, no. 349. http://www.legislature.mi.gov/documents/2011-2012/publicact/pdf/2012-PA-0349.pdf; Kaminski, M. "How Michigan became a right to work State: The role of money and politics." *Labor Studies Journal* 40, no. 4 (2015): 362–378.

28 *Bethany College*, 369 N.L.R.B. no. 98 (June 10, 2020), pp. 14–16.

29 *Id.* at p. 1.

30 *Bethany College*, 369 N.L.R.B. at 1.

31 *University of Great Falls v. NLRB*, 278 F.3d 1335 (D.C. Cir. 2002). The university changed its name to the University of Providence in July 2017. University of Providence. 2020. n.d. About: History. https://www.uprovidence.edu/about/history/

32 *University of Great Falls*, 278 F.3d 1347.

33 Id. at 1343, citing *Universidad Central de Bayamon v. NLRB*, 793 F.2d 383, 400 (1st Cir.1985).

34 *University of Great Falls*, 278 F.3d at 1343.

35 Id.

36 *Duquesne University v. National Labor Relations Board*, 947 F.3d 824 (D.C. Cir. 2020).

37 *Pacific Lutheran University*, 361 N.L.R.B. 1404 (2014).

38 361 N.L.R.B. 1404 (2014).

39 Id. at 1404.

40 *NLRB v. Catholic Bishop of Chicago*, 440 U.S. 490 (1979).

41 Bethany College, 369 N.L.R.B. at 5.

42 Nisenson, A. 2020. "Annual Legal Update." *47th Annual National Conference, National Center for the Study of Collective Bargaining in Higher Education and the Professions.* Hunter College, the City University of New York.

43 Botelho, S. 2016, October. Students or employees? Unionizing assistants. University Business. https://universitybusiness.com/students-or-employees-unionizing-assistants/

44 Id.

45 Michigan P. L. 2012 no. 45, § 1(e) (iii) http://www.legislature.mi.gov/documents/2011-2012/billconcurred/House/pdf/2011-HCB-4246.pdf

46 *Graduate Employees Organization v. Illinois Educational Labor Relations Board*, 733 N.E.2d 759, 762–763 (Ill. App. Ct., 1st Dist. 2000), appeal denied, 738 N.E.2d 925 (Ill. 2000).

47 Graduate Employees Organization, 733 N.E.2d at 765.

48 Public Act 101–0380 § 2(b), https://www.ilga.gov/legislation/publicacts/101/PDF/101-0380.pdf

49 *Northwestern Univ.*, 362 N.L.R.B. 1350, 1360, 1363 (2015).

50 362 N.L.R.B. at 1350.

51 362 N.L.R.B. at 1353.

52 362 N.L.R.B. at 1354.

53 Brief for American Council on Education and Other Higher Education Associations as Amici Curiae Supporting Employer, Northwestern Univ., 362 N.L.R.B. 1350 (2015), at 2, https://apps.nlrb.gov/link/document.aspx/09031d45817cc3d0

54 Grasgreen, A., and Lederman D. 2014, March 26. Football players win union, for now. *Inside Higher Ed.* https://www.insidehighered.com/news/2014/03/27/nlrb-office-backs-union-northwestern-football-players

55 Thompson, J. 2020, November 12. Drop the charade: Pay college athletes. *The New York Times*, p. SR7.

56 Malin, M. H. Life After Act 10? Is there a future for collective representation of Wisconsin Public employees?, 96 *Marq. L. Rev.* 623, 638–639 (2012). Available at: http://scholarship.law.marquette.edu/mulr/vol96/iss2/7

57 Katz, H. C., Kochan, T. A., and Colvin, A. J. S. 2015. "The negotiations process and structures." In *Labor Relations in a Globalizing World* (pp. 79–101), p. 131. ILR Press, an imprint of Cornell University Press. http://digitalcommons.ilr.cornell.edu/articles/1040

58 Id. at 132.

59 Id. at 641.

60 Id. at 654.

61 Id. at 654–655.

62 MINN. STAT. ANN § 179A.08(2) (2020). Public employers in Minnesota must "meet and negotiate" with representatives of public employees regarding terms and conditions of employment. MINN. STAT. ANN § 179A.07(2) (2020).

63 Leingang, R. (2020, April 17). University of Arizona plans furloughs, pay cuts for most employees due to expected shortfall. *Arizona Republic.* azcentral.com/story/news/local/arizona-education/2020/04/17/university-arizona-furlough-cut-pay-employees-due-shortfall/5154742002/

64 Burdette, S. 2020, June 12. Coalition raises concerns with UA furloughs and layoffs. *Daily Wildcat.* https://www.wildcat.arizona.edu/article/2020/06/n-coalition-for-academic-justice

65 Smith, C. 2020, September 7. UArizona faculty, staff officially launch labor union. *KGUN 9 On Your Side.* https://www.kgun9.com/news/local-news/uarizona-coalition-officially-launches-union

66 González de Bustamante, C. 2020, September 17. University-wide coalition responds to UA President's Announcement to Shorten the Timeframe of the Furlough Pay Cut Plan. Coalition for Academic Justice at the University of Arizona. https://static1.squarespace.com/static/5f1a1aa2a261bd312904a87b/t/5f685a77ae8624210b543c16/1600674423736/9.17.20.ResponsetoRobbinsAnnouncement.pdf

67 Smith, C. 2020, September 7. UArizona faculty, staff officially launch labor union. *KGUN 9 On Your Side.* https://www.kgun9.com/news/local-news/uarizona-coalition-officially-launches-union

68 Hardy, B. L., & Logan, T. D. 2020, August. Racial Economic Inequality Amid the COVID-19 Crisis. Hamilton Project, Brookings Institution. p. 2. https://www.hamiltonproject.org/assets/files/EA_HardyLogan_LO_8.12.pdf

69 Id. at pp. 3–4.

70 Id. at p. 4.

71 Ramirez, A., and Miller, K. 2020, August 27. The Future of the Academic Workforce: Putting the Community Back in Community College. *Chronicle of Higher Education.* https://www.chronicle.com/article/the-future-of-the-academic-work-force

72 National Center for Higher Education Management Systems. 2020, June. *Modeling the Impacts of COVID-19 on Public Institutions.* https://sheeo.org/wp-content/uploads/2020/07/COVID-19-Impact-Paper-200701.pdf

73 *Alston v. University of North Carolina System*, 20 CvS https://s3.amazonaws.com/snwceomedia/dth/ab34736f-aac7-4120-84ea-46a7b72bb3c1.original.pdf

74 Murphy, K. 2020, August 10. Campus workers sue UNC System, claiming unsafe working conditions during pandemic. *Raleigh News & Observer.* https://www.newsobserver.com/article244858712.html

75 Johnson, E., and Patel, V. 2020, August 19. How Covid-19 United the Higher-Ed Work Force. *Chronicle of Higher Education.* https://www-chronicle-com.proxy.libraries.rutgers.edu/article/how-covid-19-united-the-higher-ed-work-force

76 Pettit, E. 2020, August 26. Will Covid-19 Revive Faculty Power? *Chronicle of Higher Education.* https://www.chronicle.com/article/will-covid-19-revive-faculty-power

77 Chronicle Staff. 2020, July 2. As Covid-19 Pummels Budgets, Colleges Are Resorting to Layoffs and Furloughs. Here's the Latest. *Chronicle of Higher Education.* https://www.chronicle.com/article/were-tracking-employees-laid-off-or-furloughed-by-colleges/

78 Rosewicz, B., and Maciag, M. 2020, November 10. Nearly All States Suffer Declines in Education Jobs. Pew Charitable Trusts. https://www.pewtrusts.org/en/research-and-analysis/articles/2020/11/10/nearly-all-states-suffer-declines-in-education-jobs

79 Ross. M. 2020, September 7. University of Michigan's graduate student union to strike against in-person classes. *MLive*. https://www.mlive.com/news/ann-arbor/2020/09/university-of-michigans-graduate-student-union-to-strike-against-in-person-classes.html

80 Burke, L. 2020, September 15. U of Michigan Seeks Court Order to End Strike. *Inside Higher Ed*. https://www.insidehighered.com/quicktakes/2020/09/15/u-michigan-seeks-court-order-end-strike

81 MICH. COMP. LAWS § 423.202 (2020)

82 Graduate Employees' Union-University of Michigan Contract 2020–2023, Art. III. https://www.geo3550.org/rights-benefits/our-contract/

83 UM | GEO Strike Resolution Agreement, 2020, September 16. https://www.geo3550.org/wp-content/uploads/2020/10/UM_GEO_StrikeOfferFinalLanguage.pdf

84 Patel, V. 2020, September 16. A Grad Strike, a Court Fight, a No-Confidence Vote: U. of Michigan Struggles Over Its Campus Reopening. *Chronicle of Higher Education*. https://www.chronicle.com/article/a-grad-strike-a-court-fight-a-no-confidence-vote-u-of-michigan-struggles-over-its-campus-reopening

85 Lund, J., and Maranto, C. 1996, "Public Sector Labor Law: An Update," in D. Belman, M. Gunderson and D. Hyatt (eds.), *Public Sector Employment in a Time of Transition*, Industrial Relations Research Association, p. 21.

86 OPM Director Lachance Addresses Future of Federal Workforce, 36 GOV'T EMP. REL. REP. 418, 422 (1998) (quoting American Federation of Government Employees President John Sturdivant).

5

MEDIATION IN THE RESOLUTION OF COLLECTIVE BARGAINING DISPUTES

Ira B. Lobel

This chapter will examine how mediators help the parties resolve outstanding issues and bring about a settlement. Mediation is an extension of the collective bargaining process. Collective bargaining is a process in which management and unions negotiate over wages, hours, and working conditions. The very nature of the process creates conflict. For example, employees, speaking through their union representatives, may want more money than the employer wishes to give. The employer, speaking through its representatives, has a different view on what constitutes a fair and just wage. Employees normally want unlimited time off; the employer normally wants to restrict released time and maintain productive work time. Nevertheless, in the majority of cases, management and the union settle a contract amicably, with little fuss or fanfare.

In some instances, however, the parties have difficulty reaching a settlement. It may be that one party does not understand or agree with the other's dilemma or position. It may be that while both parties understand the problem, they have a serious disagreement on how best to resolve an outstanding issue or issues. This often happens on the issues of wages and/or health insurance.

Failure to reach agreement during negotiations can create antagonism and animosity in the work environment. In the private sector, failure to agree may result ultimately in an employee job action or a strike. Failure to agree can also result in an employer locking out employees as an economic lever to force a union to agree to management's position. In the public sector, a breakdown of negotiations often leads to fact finding or arbitration, where a settlement is imposed on both parties.

Although the failure to agree may not lead to a strike, lockout, or arbitration, an unsettled labor dispute may have a detrimental impact on the work environment.

DOI: 10.4324/9781003138990-6

While parties to collective bargaining agree that conflict is endemic to the process, both will similarly agree that ultimately, everyone must get along. In higher education, whether private or public, resolution of disputes is necessary to help maintain the *esprit de corps* that many believe is essential for a well running institution.

In striving to reach a settlement, the parties will often seek assistance. One means of assistance is a mediator, a neutral third party brought into negotiations. The mediator's responsibility is simply to help the parties reach an agreement. A mediator accomplishes this by serving as a go-between, timing a proposal, developing a suggestion, coming up with an innovative idea, or assisting a chief spokesperson with his/her bargaining committee. A mediator will do whatever is necessary within the law to help the parties reach a settlement. Mediators lack authority to tell the parties what to do; his/her power is merely that of persuasion. By making sensible comments and suggestions at the appropriate time, the mediator can help bring closure to negotiations.

The mediator does not make a judgment on what constitutes a reasonable settlement or what is the best practice. Based on his/her knowledge and experience, he/she may point out common practices, what other similar institutions do in similar situations, or even what may be acceptable to the other side. However, he/she has no authority to make a decision; such a decision remains with the parties. As such, the mediator does not care whether the settlement is appropriate or not. The mediator's principle concern is focused on what is acceptable to both sides so that the parties can reach an agreement. A determination of regarding the various provisions in the settlement rests with the parties.

There is nothing magical about the mediation process. We see it in various forms daily. A marriage counselor is often a mediator between husband and wife. Mediation has been used often in international relations. More and more, it has become useful in business transactions.

Labor mediation has been prominent in the United States since the U.S. Conciliation Service was formed in 1918. In 1947, the agency was re-organized to become the Federal Mediation and Conciliation Service, an independent agency of the Federal government still active today. This means mediators have been used in settling collective bargaining disputes for over 100 years. The mediation process involves shuttling back and forth between labor and management, seeking clarifications and compromises, asking questions, and making suggestions until a settlement can be reached.

Unlike mediators in the international arena, labor mediators do not have economic or political sanctions to use as a tool to encourage labor and management to reach settlement; the mediator has limited hardware to get the parties to agree, except the power of persuasion and timing. The mediator must rely on the parties' desire to reach an agreement or the fear of disagreement (and its consequences) as the principal lever to encourage and cajole the parties into taking positions that will ultimately lead to a settlement.

The inexperienced labor relations practitioner may envision mediation as a highly structured or clearly defined process. In reality, mediation is a fluid, seat-of-the-pants type process. Mediators can accomplish their goals simply by showing up and allowing the parties to claim that a mediator was present. Settlement is sometimes achieved by talking to one side privately for a lengthy period of time. It may be achieved by setting artificial deadlines for the collective bargaining process. In other cases, the mediator may make substantive suggestions.

The mediator's approach depends on the situation, the parties, the issues, the place, the timing and most of all, personalities. For example, a mediator may use a different approach with a group of steelworkers than with university professors. The mediator may be more concerned about the expiration date for employees in a paper mill, where no contract may mean no-work, than in the newspaper industry, where the parties traditionally negotiate well past the contract expiration date. Timing may become more of a factor in a seasonal business, such as a resort hotel, than in a year-round business, such as a coal mine. In higher education, timing usually is not a major factor; however, in some locations, the beginning or end of a semester may put some pressure on both sides to settle a dispute.

Once involved in collective bargaining, the mediator typically does not care what the industry or setting is. The differences in the collective bargaining process are more subtle than substantive. In a 24-hour-a-day, three shift operation, a mediator may be confronted with unresolved issues regarding scheduling and weekend work. A mediator is more apt to discuss issues of health and safety in an asbestos mine than in a high-tech manufacturing plant. A mediator is more apt to hear about questions of academic freedom in a university than in an automobile plant.

These differences are minor compared to the similarities in the mediation process, such as resolving disputes over wages, hours, insurance, and other economic issues. The dynamics of collective bargaining may depend more on the personalities of the people involved than on the industry or issue. For the mediator, many of the underlying dynamics of bargaining situations are similar.

People involved in higher education will often try to look at a measurable outcome, best practices, or equity. The union or management representatives may look at these values when deciding its position on various issues. The mediator is primarily looking at one thing: whether a settlement can be reached. His/her techniques for obtaining this objective will vary, depending on the industry, the timing, and the personalities of the people from both parties, including those who are at the table and those who influence and/or direct the people at the table. All of these must be considered from both the parties' and mediator's perspective. The mediator may point out, based on settlements have been in a certain industry, but it is not his/her job to push for a certain settlement. His/her job is simply to obtain a settlement.

During this COVID pandemic, another issue must be raised. How is the process performed? Many mediators will not conduct in-person mediation sessions. While most mediators would prefer an in-person session, many believe a virtual meeting is far preferable to a mediation session with social distancing and masks. Two examples can be used to help reach this conclusion: if one cracks a bad joke, it can be usually determined if it is not well received on Zoom; there is little chance to make such determination if the person is wearing a mask. The same thing is true if someone does not understand a question or a point being made. One has a chance of seeing if the person does not understand the question. There is significantly less chance if a facemask is being worn. After these concerns are raised, most parties agree to a virtual hearing.

A virtual hearing does lack the immediacy of an in-person event. In an in-person hearing, one can "feel" the dynamics of disagreement or the need to have an agreement. A virtual hearing lacks the ability to obtain these "feelings" that come about in a normal, in-person hearing. Unfortunately, at least for the foreseeable future, mediators and advocates may have to consider which is the lesser of two choices: virtual hearings or in-person hearings with social distancing and masks.

Who Are Mediators and How Do They Get Involved?

Most mediators are labor relations professionals who have a vast amount of experience, either as a neutral or a former representative of either management or labor. The availability of mediators and mediation services will vary depending on whether the employer is in the private or public sector and, if public, the legislation of the state involved.

In the private sector, mediators from the Federal Mediation and Conciliation Services (FMCS) are used for most mediation activity. Under the law under which it was established (the 1947 Taft Hartley Act), FMCS receives a notice 30 days prior to the expiration of any collective bargaining agreement. Upon receipt of this notice, an assigned mediator contacts the parties and discusses the progress of negotiations. During these conversations, either party may request the involvement of a mediator. In addition, either party may call the mediator and request assistance.

In the public sector, the availability of mediation varies. In some states, mediators are appointed, on request, by various state administrative agencies. Such is the case with the New York State Public Employment Relations Board, the Wisconsin Employment Relations Commission, and the Michigan Employment Relations Commission, and many other similarly titled state agencies. In other states, such as Vermont, Ohio, or Illinois, where a state administrative agency does not exist, mediators, if needed, are selected on an ad hoc basis by the parties.[1] Some of these states often use mediators from FMCS. In some situations, mediators practicing in the private sector are hired on an ad hoc basis.

As noted, the parties are always free to use a mutually selected mediator who may be more acceptable than mediators from the public agencies. Such a mediator may be more acceptable for reasons such as his/her reputation or previous experience with the parties. The cost of hiring a mediator from the private sector is usually shared by the parties, in contrast to a mediator from a public agency who is usually provided at no cost to the parties. Additionally, the parties know who the mediator will be; the public sector agencies often appoint the mediator randomly. There are advantages and disadvantages to both systems.

It is important to emphasize that mediation is a voluntary process. Both parties must agree on the intervention of a mediator, when the mediator should come in, and the method for the selection of the mediator. When one side has made a formal request for assistance, a mediator will typically call the other side and ascertain whether mediation will be acceptable. If it is acceptable, the mediator will schedule a meeting. If it is not, the mediator will try to determine why not and will discuss the issue with either party. To be effective, the mediator must have the cooperation and acceptance of both sides.

When a Mediator Gets Involved

In many industries, the mediator becomes involved close to the expiration date of the collective bargaining agreement but there are no firmly established rules. In some industries, including higher education, the expiration date of the collective bargaining agreement rarely has significant value. The parties invite the mediator to enter negotiations when they find that direct talks are no longer productive.

Nothing is more frustrating for a mediator than to be asked to enter negotiations when there are 150 issues left on the table and both sides are posturing for position. Mediators follow various strategies when confronted with the dilemma of too many outstanding issues. In some instances, the mediator may wade through all topics and lump various categories together in an effort to group issues and compromises from each side. Although this process can be slow and tedious, it is sometimes necessary when one or both sides are new to collective bargaining and literally must be taught how to negotiate. In other situations, a mediator may follow a more unusual tact.

In one case, where I knew both sides quite well and there was no threat of any work stoppage (the dispute involved a public sector college system negotiating in April for the following September), I informed both sides in joint session that I would not mediate a settlement with 85 issues on the table. In this instance, there were obviously a large number of "throwaway" items on the table. Each party was posturing. Unless either party got rid of the "garbage", I threatened to pick up and leave until both parties got serious. I then requested a proposal from each party reflecting the "serious issues." I then stated if I believed both parties were realistic, I would exchange the proposals. If not, I would recess until August. Here, each party caucused for several hours and handed over their serious issues. Unfortunately, one party kept proposing several items that obviously were throwaways. The meeting was recessed and the parties were admonished not to call the mediator until ready to negotiate seriously. Several days later, the parties followed the mediator's suggestion. Eighty-five issues were narrowed down to eight within several hours of negotiations. With eight items left, both parties were willing to concentrate their efforts on resolving these remaining issues.

While it is sometimes difficult to deal with an extraordinarily large number of issues, it can be equally frustrating dealing with only one issue, particularly where both sides are locked into a firm position. This is true when an issue is something one party must "win" and the other must "lose", such as a union shop or binding arbitration. It is important to understand that collective bargaining works best when both parties feel they have won or lost equally. When it is perceived that one party won and the other lost, the tendency in future years is for the loser to get even.

The mediator's function may be to tell one side or the other the facts of life. For example, several years ago, I was involved in negotiations where the union represented 80 members in a unit of 350 employees. (Employees had a choice whether or not to join the union.) In addition to the small percentage of members, these individuals lacked special skills or other power that could afford them additional clout. With this limited support and power, the union was not in a strong bargaining position. My job as a mediator was to convince the union that, in this case, the best course of action may be to take whatever the employer offered. A strike in this situation would not have been successful. While the union did not appreciate being reminded of its limited power, these comments brought about a settlement.

In another case, the union represented two different units at the same facility. One unit, comprising about 250 craftsmen, settled a collective bargaining agreement calling for a 7% wage increase. (This example occurred in the late 1970s; at that time, a 7% wage increase was routine.) The settlement of the other unit, consisting of 25 professional radiological technicians, had not yet settled when I became involved. While the union obviously wanted to obtain as much as possible for the radiological technicians, who held jobs that would normally pay higher than the craftsman, the union was confronted with a difficult political situation: if the 25 technicians received a higher wage increase than 250 craftsmen, the craftsmen would be upset; if the technicians got less than the craftsmen, they would be upset. The only solution for both sides was to provide the technicians with the same increase as the craftsmen. My role as a mediator was to articulate this dilemma in a tactful way to both sides. The union was unable to offer this proposal formally across the table (because of possible unfair labor practice implications). The mediator convinced the company to offer the same wage increase to both units and, simultaneously, to factor in different elements such as hazardous duty pay. This addition to the package offered professional employees more money, but not so blatantly as to create a political dilemma for the union. In this fashion, both parties were satisfied with the final settlement.

In another situation, the role of the mediator is to convince one party of the other's resolve on a particular issue. Recently, I was engaged in a university where the employer sought to increase the deductible for health insurance. The union intimated they would accept the concept only if a pool was established from the premium savings created from the increase in the deductible. Ostensibly, this pool would have made the employees whole for any increase in their liability. Once I was able to convince the employer of the union's resolve on this issue, settlement quickly followed.

Depending on the situation, it may be appropriate for the mediator to help create a crisis or deadline, or avert one by getting the parties to agree on an extension of the collective bargaining agreement. It may be appropriate for the mediator to initiate acceptability for a joint study committee, or force the parties to tackle the problems head on. It may be appropriate for the mediator to sit with the parties in joint session and keep tempers below the boiling point, or it may be appropriate to allow tempers to flair and meet the parties separately in order to assist in resolving settlement. A mediator's approach will vary, depending on the situation.[2]

In summary, the best settlement is one in which the parties can agree without the intervention of a third party. If it becomes obvious to one party that settlement is not possible without third party intervention, it is important to request the presence of a mediator after the throwaway issues are resolved and before the parties are so entrenched that further compromise becomes impossible.

Preparation for Mediation

Once the parties agree that the time is ripe for a mediator's involvement, how do the parties prepare for mediation. From a mediator's perspective, the answer is easy: exactly the same way you would prepare for negotiations. Before any negotiations begin, it is important for each party to draw up a list of demands. This may include language additions, deletions, or modifications. When I first started in this business, it would have been unusual for an employer to offer initial demands at the bargaining table. Today, this is no longer true. Such demands may include wage improvements, scheduling changes that will improve productivity, additions to health benefits, and the like.[3] If the prioritizing and costing of demands is done properly, the preparation for both collective bargaining and, if necessary, mediation should not be overly burdensome.

The process of re-evaluating positions and priorities should continue, possibly at a more concentrated level, due to the presence of the mediator. The mediator will attempt to force the parties to look closely at the implications of various proposals, as well as to examine new approaches and compromises.

Need for Coordination in Negotiations

The entry of a mediator into a dispute and the preparation for mediation has been briefly discussed. It is now important to identify exactly what happens once a mediator becomes actively involved. The mediator's style and approach will vary widely, depending on the personality of the mediator, the situation and the parties. No two mediators will do exactly the same thing at the same time. Even the same mediator will use different techniques and approaches in the same situation.

During any set of negotiations, there may be several other sub-negotiations taking place within the various labor and management teams and their constituencies. Resolution of these sub-negotiations may be essential to the ultimate goal of obtaining collective bargaining agreement. For example, the union's chief negotiator may bargain with both the union team and the membership to encourage settlement on a smaller amount than initially proposed (or even initially deemed the minimum acceptable for settlement). The employer's chief negotiator will constantly consult or "bargain" with the Board, President, Vice Chancellor, etc., to encourage a more realistic offer that the union will accept. Part of a mediator's job is to help both chief negotiators in their role with their teams at the table and their constituents not at the table. This may be accomplished by asking probing questions about educational policies, making comments about labor relations trends, or taking other actions that will encourage both parties to re-evaluate their positions. Sub-negotiations will begin at an early stage in bargaining and will continue until agreement is reached. Negotiating teams, especially the union, must constantly discuss various bargaining issues with their constituents. It is essential to have make sure that any settlement reached will be accepted by those people who have a vote in the ratification process. This is particularly true in a university where a Board of Trustees, a union, and sometimes the legislature, all have a legal right to reject an agreement that has been worked out by the negotiation teams.[4]

A mediator will help both sides with coordination by identifying, discussing, and probing questions, problems, and issues with both parties. A mediator will often use the approach of asking questions to identify both the problem and the source of such problems. With this method, a mediator can sometimes lead the parties to understand the other's perspective and ultimately to find areas of compromise. At times, the mediator may press to bring external decision-makers to the bargaining table so that people involved in the table dialogue better understand the source and seriousness of a particular issue.

Confidentiality

It is important to note that a mediator's private conversations are confidential, only to be revealed if the party with whom the conversation was held wants the matter revealed. A mediator will carefully guard the specifics of these conversations. He or she will attempt to point either party in a specific direction, however, as a result of these conversations. For example, if a particular issue is union security and the management team has emphasized its belief that no current employees should be forced to join a union, the mediator may encourage the union to seek other approaches to union security that may be acceptable to the employer. In this manner, the mediator may be able to protect the confidence of the employer, while at the same time, obtaining support for a proposal that will be acceptable to both parties.

Timing During Mediation

The parties can engage in collective bargaining over a period of several weeks or months before a settlement is reached. Factors that can affect the time needed for negotiations are the number of outstanding issues, the complexity and seriousness of the issues, the contract expiration date, a deadline date that may be affected by business conditions (such as the start of school in a university), prior bargaining history, whether the contract is a renewal or an initial agreement, the sophistication of the parties, and the ability and desire of the parties to make the difficult decisions that lead to settlement. All of these factors will affect the right time for settlement.[5]

During any session, a mediator must be careful to time suggestions properly. Often, the mediator will first discuss the problems and issues involved, without seeking a specific proposal, until either party is in position to consider them positively. For example, several years ago, I was assigned to mediate in a state college system. For several sessions, little if anything was accomplished. It was my perception that the negotiator for the employer had to discuss a number of pivotal issues with the Chancellor before progress could be made. Similarly, the union preferred to wait and see what management would offer a union in comparable system. It was apparent that both parties desired the presence of a mediator to permit each to tread water and delay the process. During this interim, the mediator was successful in setting the stage for agreement by identifying possible alternatives and approaches.

Conclusion

This chapter has discussed the role and technique used by mediators in the settlement of labor disputes. One of the fascinating aspects of the collective bargaining process is that the disputes are between people and groups of people.

Because of the various ways that people approach problems, problem-solving mediators will use different approaches and techniques. They will offer proposals or make suggestions based on their experience in dealing with people at various industries or other organizations. Some of the approaches and techniques discussed in the chapter are common; however, there is no certainty to a process that involves the attempt to convince individuals to modify positions.

Notes

1   There are several important differences in the nature of dispute settlement mechanisms between the public and private sectors. In the private sector, the strike always looms as a possibility if the negotiations breakdown. In the public sector, where the strike is often illegal, failure to agree may push the dispute beyond mediation to fact finding, or in some jurisdictions, to arbitration. Fact finders make written, non-binding recommendations that will hopefully form the basis for settlement of the dispute. If the parties fail to agree, there may be further bargaining, or a legislative hearing, or the employer may have the right to impose a settlement, or, in some jurisdictions, there may be a right to strike. With arbitration, a neutral third party is called in to make a written decision that will become binding on all parties. A decision may also be based on a compromise of the last positions of either party, or may be the final offer of either the employer or the union, with no right of the arbitrator to compromise either position. In any event, the actual form of the fact finding or arbitration procedure will depend on the enabling legislation in that state. Due to the strike possibility or impossibility, or the availability of fact finding or arbitrations, the strategies and techniques used by both the mediator and the parties may differ. An employer or union may decide to make their best positions known before the strike. In a fact finding or arbitration situation, the parties may tend to hold a proposal back so that they can give something up during fact finding or arbitration.

2   One of the major functions that a mediator will perform is to get both sides to question the risks of going out on strike and/or the risks of going to the next step in the impasse procedure process – the impact of a fact finding report or the dangers and risk involved in an imposed arbitration award. The answer to this risk/reward question may be more difficult in the public sector and/or a higher education setting because the risks are not as clear. But regardless of the sector, the mediator will attempt to raise questions about the cost of agreement versus the cost of disagreement. This will be done by relating his or her own experiences and by raising questions about the particular negotiation with which he/she is involved to induce the parties to question their own positions to modify their demands or proposals.

3   After demands are formulated, their impact and cost should be analyzed. They should be categorized into three kinds: an absolute yes, an absolute no, and a maybe. After demands are exchanged at the bargaining table, each party should evaluate the others' proposals in the same way. The "maybes" should be prioritized according to what is the most important or the least harmful to give. The initial priorities should set the stage for negotiations and should be constantly re-evaluated and modified. The process also depends on the exchanges that take place at the bargaining table and the apparent position and priorities of each party. For example, not too many years ago, employers would seek to have employees share the cost of health insurance. For some unions, this demand would elicit an absolute no, with both sides understanding that a strike would occur if the shared cost was part of the final package. For others, the sharing of health insurance would be a maybe, depending on the mix of the entire package. The priority of this item may change throughout negotiations, depending

on the ability of either party to force its will on the other. With regard to health insurance, the real position of either party may not emerge until the parties are close to a settlement. Once prioritization is accomplished, the parties should have a good idea of the economic and non-economic impact of all proposals. In a manufacturing plant, employees will often calculate to the hundredths of a cent the per-hour cost of each percent wage increase and each fringe benefit increase. No logical employer will offer a wage increase without knowing the cost of that increase. The same is true of health insurance, pension, and other economic improvements. In the non-economic areas, employer and union alike should evaluate the implications and impact of all new language to ensure that the final agreement is cogent and well-conceived. Mistakes at the bargaining table can be extremely costly.

4   For example, in a university, law and medical professors may have different working conditions than other members of the faculty. Negotiators from both sides must work to accommodate specialized interests. Both parties often engage in a practice of counting votes that will ensure ratification of a contract. For example, if the law and medical professors comprise a large percentage of the bargaining unit, their special needs may have to be dealt with to obtain a contract that will be ratified. If, on the other hand, they represent a comparatively small portion of the unit, both sides may choose to neglect their special interests, unless they have a relatively large amount of power that is not related to numbers of employees in the unit (such as members of leadership or fund raising capabilities). Particularly in public sector disputes or in industries that have public boards (such as universities or hospitals), it is crucial that the management negotiating team be aware of the goals of other groups within the university, the municipality. For example, in a public university, the legislature will most likely have the final say on the economic increase. The management negotiating team, before offering a package to the union, must have a good idea of what the legislature will ultimately agree to. If they agree on a package that the legislature does not pass, they will not only have a serious problem with the legislature, but also with the union, which will accuse the management of backing away from a tentative agreement.

5   There are numerous union and management representatives who attempt to settle contracts several weeks before the contract expires, only to have the settlement rejected by the union membership. This may be due to the perception that if the parties spend another week negotiating, there will be more money available. If this mind set is a realistic possibility, it may be a mistake to settle early.

6

A TALE OF TWO UNIVERSITIES, COMPLEX IN DIFFERENT WAYS

Margaret E. Winters

1 Introduction

It is safe to state that events in the United States during the last few months have elevated the perception of matters pertaining to diversity and social justice to a higher level than, perhaps, ever before. Underlying the public demonstrations have been increasingly urgent conversations about the need for examination (and self-examination) of American society and its views of race. And, without belaboring points being made virtually daily, public policy is changing as well, with new required training programs and legislation intended to modify police behaviors as a crucial example, along with workshops to increase other kinds of awareness. Industries small and large are publicizing their adherence to the goals of diversity, equity, and inclusion, some with related changes in anti-harassment and hiring policies.

Higher education is not immune to this newly heightened awareness, nor to the desire to act. Student groups are petitioning for specialized support systems, a request which is being met on various campuses, as well as for more faculty of color, often more difficult a demand to fulfill quickly. At universities and colleges with unionized faculty and staff, discussions are reaching as far as the negotiation table where labor contracts are crafted, increasingly, with statements in support for social justice and, perhaps more rarely, clauses reflecting concrete steps for increasing diversity and inclusion through collective bargaining.

DOI: 10.4324/9781003138990-7

1.1 Higher Education and Social Justice

There are various reasons why institutions of higher education may be slower to act despite good intentions. The present paper includes cases study of how decision-making occurs at two unionized universities, Southern Illinois University Carbondale and Wayne State University in Detroit (SIUC and WSU, respectively). There are two reasons why I have chosen these two institutions, of which the first is personal; I worked at both of them. The second is that these institutions are both complex entities including multiple units (schools, colleges, and divisions) but, in some ways, however, displaying quite different interactions between the university administration and the academic unions.

1.2 Background Information

As was stated above, my own professional experiences took place at both these universities. My traditional faculty life was largely spent at Southern Illinois University where, after gaining tenure and, eventually, promotion to Professor, I became an associate provost for academic personnel. The faculty unionized while I was in that position, with the result that I was tapped to lead the negotiations for the administration side. After the two years spent arriving at a first contract, I served as the university-side contract administrator and, subsequently, interim provost. With my move to Wayne State University, I served first as associate provost for academic personnel and, again, was named provost.

1.3 Plan for this Essay

The remainder of this essay will proceed as follows: following this introduction, the second part will look at the universities, first as to their shared characteristics as complex entities and then, individually, as to how they differ. While they have a very similar missions, since both are large public universities, and similar configurations of academic units, they differ crucially in the negotiated description of the bargaining unit. The third part will continue this case study, with an emphasis on how they have managed the complexities set out in the second part. Of particular note is the role of other kinds of shared governance and how these structures have evolved as partners and/or competitors in the collective bargaining setting. Finally, the fourth part will consist of a series of recommendations (perhaps better titled "lessons learned") for the leadership of similar institutions. Here we will discuss both issues specific to represented faculty members and also those which touch on unionization in general. Important to any consideration of unions in academia is their effectiveness, how they enhance the university or college and how we might (or find we cannot) measure these results.

The increases in union activity, particularly in community colleges and private colleges and universities, make these comments timely and, one hopes, useful. Woven into all of the description and discussion will be ways in which collective bargaining has or hasn't taken social justice (a short phrase encompassing diversity, equity, and inclusion) into account and what more it might be doing for the collectivity of a faculty and also the individuals who make up the union.

2 The Universities

2.1 Commonalities

Both universities are public, supported by state dollars. Wayne State currently has approximately 27,000 students, while Southern Illinois University has about 14,000. SIUC's enrollment has shrunk considerably in the last decade. At the time the faculty unionized in 1996, it had approximately 24,000 students, much closer to the WSU number; this is the period which will be discussed in detail. Each university grants bachelors, masters, and doctoral degrees, the doctorate in sufficient numbers to be classified by the Carnegie Foundation as "very high research doctoral" universities. Although the exact range of academic units is not the same, both have approximately 65 departments organized in schools and colleges, as well as research centers and institutes. In particular, in addition to liberal arts, sciences, performing arts, business, engineering, and education, both universities have schools of Law and Medicine.

Although SIUC is rural and WSU urban, they have very similar missions, both educating underserved populations at the undergraduate level while maintaining their prestigious research classification through their doctoral programs and research funding. The result of this dichotomy is that both universities have large numbers of support staff members (advisors, student success specialists, etc.) for their undergraduates and opportunities for their graduate students to gain teaching experience with students at all levels of preparation.

As was said above, the faculty at SIUC unionized in 1996. WSU, on the other hand, was one of the first universities to have an academic union; the election took place in 1972. In both cases the then-new union did not replace the structures already in place to support faculty involvement in the governance of their university. Both universities have senates, founded before unionization took place (SIUC in 1973, based on a Faculty Council founded in 1935, and WSU in 1966). Their stated missions of representing the faculty of the university are quite similar, although their membership and some of their functions differ.

2.2 Differences

Southern Illinois University Carbondale is part of the Southern Illinois University system with another campus in Edwardsville. While the School of Medicine is part of the Carbondale campus, students take only their first-year courses there and then move to the state capital, Springfield, to the teaching hospital where they complete the work for their degrees. It should be noted that, although the Edwardsville faculty are now unionized, the election occurred in 2016 and constitutes a separate local.

Not all faculty are represented by the union, an affiliate of the Illinois Education Association and the National Education Association. Membership includes all tenured and tenure-track faculty at appointments of 50% or greater, including librarians, who at SIUC hold tenure-track/tenured faculty rank. However, in addition to all other employees and administrators, including chairs, faculty in the Law School and the School of Medicine are explicitly excluded. The result is a mixed faculty governance system where the Faculty Senate plays a somewhat wider role than at institutions where all faculty are represented.

Wayne State University is, on the other hand, a single-campus university. All tenure-track and tenured faculty with appointments at or above 50% are represented by the union, affiliated both with the American Association of University Professors and the American Federation of Teachers (AAUP-AFT), including faculty in the Law School and the School of Medicine. Somewhat unusually for a research university, the unit also includes academic staff, that is, among them librarians (who do not hold faculty positions), admissions and financial aid officers, and advisors. Both the faculty and academic staff constitute the Academic Senate, officially with separate functions from the union, although the range of eligible members is the same in both organizations. It is also the case that the union president serves ex officio not only on the Senate, but also on the Senate Policy Committee, the executive group which meets weekly with the provost, sets the Senate agenda, and is generally considered to constitute the leadership group for faculty and academic staff.

A particular factor of collective bargaining at WSU is that the faculty in the School of Medicine are represented; this is, nationwide, a relatively rare circumstance. Wayne State does not, however, own a hospital, but provides clinical training through complex contracts with those in other hands in the Detroit region, both public and privately owned. Many of the WSU faculty, for example, have their own practice at the Detroit Medical Center and, as a result, belong to the University Physicians Group (UPG), their professional organization as practicing clinicians. In their role as clinicians, they are not represented by any union, although, for many of them, their teaching assignment for WSU is clinical supervision. Until recently, as well, their paychecks from the university and the practice plan were commingled, coming from Wayne State. While the status of these clinical faculty seems like an issue specifically to be resolved in the School of Medicine, claims from the union as to their right to represent the members of the UPG tend to come up more generally in negotiations, grievances, and less formal discussions.

2.3 Social Justice and Anti-Discrimination

Both the SIU and WSU contracts have anti-discrimination clauses which start off similarly, stating that the university and the union agree that there should be no discrimination on the grounds of race, gender/sexuality, age, religion, and other well-established classes. SIU, in addition, mentions explicitly the principles of equal employment opportunity, affirmative action, and freedom from sexual harassment, while WSU refers to sexual harassment and discrimination against members for exercising their rights under the contract. Further, SIU allows for grievances under this clause, but only to the level of the system president; there will be no arbitration in matters of discrimination; WSU's contract is mute on this point, with the result that alleged infractions can be grieved up to arbitration.

The most recent iteration of each contract at the time of writing of this essay predates renewed societal interest in social justice, that is, diversity, equity, and inclusion. As a result, other than listing race among other classes which may not be discriminated against, neither contract contains language about equity and inclusion, although in the last months the leadership of both universities has issued strongly worded statements as to the institution's stance. One can predict that language will be brought to the table in the next reopening of the contracts by the respective unions, although it is hard to forecast what form the language will take, particularly as to actions to be asked for from the administration in the form, perhaps, of new units or new protections.

3.0 Managing Complexity

The above section is meant to underline the complexity of various institutions of higher education and the fact that complexity, by its very nature, can take more than one form. The contradictory situations of, at SIUC, a School of Medicine (like the Law School) which is non-represented and, at WSU, a School of Medicine which is, both give rise to different complex problems. Spoiler alert: some of the issues do not have tidy answers and contribute to the on-going complications in the relationship between university administrations and unions.

3.1 WSU

3.1.1 Academic Staff

Wayne State's AAUP-AFT union consists not only of all full-time faculty (50% appointment and higher), but also of various classes of employees called "academic staff". As might be expected where all tenure-track faculty are in the unit, not only is the fact of tenure memorialized in the contract, but so is the process for earning it, set out in great detail. What is perhaps less ordinary is the parallel process for academic staff. Called Employment Security Status (ESS), it differs from tenure in several ways. First, it is held university-wide instead of in the department where the faculty member is employed. Since at least some of the academic staff functions are somewhat flexible in being widely applicable across units, that means that they may be transferred without losing ESS; a department considering a transfer of a faculty member with tenure (a rarer event) is required to hold a vote on tenure within this new department. Secondly, the level of job security is lower for academic staff, even with ESS. This status promises, essentially, that dismissal must be for just cause.

Otherwise, the assignments and duties of academic staff differ from those of faculty. This gives rise to different questions of compliance and different rationales for grievances, still within the confines of one contract. For many years, academic staff were unhappy, particularly, that their queries and complaints were handled by faculty member officers of the union who might or might not understand their assignments and hence the basis for their complaints. Approximately 20 years ago, this dilemma was recognized in the contract. Among union officers since the 2002 contract are both a faculty and an academic staff compliance officer and a faculty and an academic staff grievance officer, with each office held by a member of that represented subgroup. It has eased tensions within the union, particularly among academic staff who felt under-represented. The administration as well has found this division of responsibilities within the union beneficial in that non-compliance and grievances are often easier to understand and respond to.

3.1.2 School of Medicine

A more intractable situation is the status of members of the University Physicians Group and other practice plans which include faculty in the School of Medicine. In their role as faculty members, they are represented by the AAUP-AFT, but, at the same time, are not represented as members of the practice plans. In most cases these dual roles are clearly delineated between teaching/research, on the one hand, and medical practice, on the other. The conflict of interest arises most often in the area of clinical supervision of students and residents. The supervisor is, in these cases, both a faculty member working with students and a practitioner tending to patients in a clinical setting.

The union has long maintained that, since the same people simultaneously hold positions both as instructors and clinicians, the practice plan side should also fall under the definition of union membership. The university has resisted this idea for decades. One step toward a reconciliation of these views is that specifically the University Physicians Group of the Detroit Medical Center, whose members include WSU clinical faculty, now has a policy to address complaints arising from the teaching and clinical supervision duties of members vis-à-vis Wayne State medical students. The policy is separate from the grievance article in the union contract and was negotiated through an Unfair Labor Practice (ULP) case filed with the Michigan Employment Relations Council by the union against the practice plan. The university, although not directly involved, signed the settlement as a peripheral party to the ULP. Interestingly, in exchange for the development of the policy, the AAUP-AFT agreed not to make demands to the university for UPG members to be represented by them for a period of five years. As a solution to complexity, this new way of looking at grievances may not be ideal since it adds a new policy and set of procedures, but it has helped to resolve arguments as to jurisdiction and accountability.

3.2 SIUC

The issues at Southern Illinois University Carbondale are somewhat different. As was said above, only tenured and tenure-track faculty are represented, so the complexities stemming from having non-tenure-track faculty and academic staff under the same collective bargaining agreement do not arise. Other matters, however, have had to be resolved, again because of the make-up of the unit. At the time of the negotiation of the first contract, there was more or less tacit agreement that the policies and procedures in the Faculty Handbook had to be maintained since neither Law nor Medicine faculty fell under the membership definition.

The most crucial issue is the process for tenure and promotion. At SIUC the process is memorialized, as it had been for many years before the faculty elected a union, in Board of Trustees policies and in the "Employees' Handbook", both of which are incorporated by reference in the contract. Some relevant matters, however, were negotiated at the table and are explicitly part of the CBA; among those are how and when a tenure-track probationary period might be extended and the role of a chair in cases when s/he has not attained the rank which is applied for by a member of the department.

A second challenge arising from the faculty split between membership and non-representation is the way in which grievances are reviewed and adjudicated. Prior to the establishment of the union, an entity called the Judicial Review Board heard complaints, most usually between a faculty member and an administrator (chair, dean, etc.) and often pertaining to tenure and promotion decisions. The members of the Board were—and continue to be—selected through a process governed by the Operating Paper of the Faculty Senate. Each panel consists of one faculty member named by the complainant, one by the administrator in question, and one from a pool established by the Senate. The hearing is a formal one and both sides are allowed to bring legal counsel. The outcome is a ruling to uphold or deny the complaint, accompanied by a series of (non-binding) recommendations, forwarded to the campus Chancellor.

There are differences between the contract grievance procedure and the work of the Judicial Review Board. Grievances under the contract result in binding directives, not just as to the appropriateness of the complaint but also as to remedies. The decision may be appealed to arbitration. On the other hand, the Judicial Review Board hearing is a review by a panel of peers without administrative participation, although the outcomes are recommendations and not binding; the Chancellor may, however, take these recommendations, but if s/he does not, there is no appeal to outside arbitration. Most notably, the contract states that tenure may not be awarded through the grievance process; the complaints are limited to claims of procedural flaws; the Review Board, on the other hand, may recommend the awarding of tenure, although that recommendation is rarely if ever accepted by the administration. Law and Medicine faculty have the single path of the faculty panel for complaints. The represented faculty, however, choose between union or senate procedures, with the explicit directive in the contract that they may not use both routes for resolution of a complaint.

3.3 Other Complexities

In addition to the cases described in the preceding paragraphs, there are other ways in which complexity might be introduced into labor relations. These are not necessarily confined to large universities, but tend to be of greater import when more people, represented or not, are involved in finding resolutions and especially where there exist multiple academic unions.

3.3.1 Unit Definition

A variable across contracts is the inclusion or non-inclusion of academic chairs/ department heads. Neither of the units discussed above included chairs, but they are represented, for example, in the Professional Staff Congress contract with all branches of the City University of New York system. Universities have traditionally argued, on the one hand, that chairs serve primarily in administrative functions, in particular the supervision of other faculty, hiring, making recommendations on tenure and promotion, and, perhaps crucially, assigning work and evaluating that work. On the other hand, unions have argued that the chair is primus inter pares, first among peers, and is fundamentally a member of the faculty, destined eventually to return to that status. Whatever their situation, represented or not, chairs are called upon to represent the upper administration to the faculty and the faculty to the administration.

The title of Director is used very widely (and sometimes carelessly) to designate a fairly wide range including department-internal assignments (Undergraduate Director) and heads of sub-units (Director, Master of Public Policy in a Political Science department). These are usually considered faculty service and are held by represented faculty. There are, however, directors who head centers, institutes, even schools (a School of Music for example) who have much more extensive supervisory responsibilities. They are more likely to be non-represented. The multiple references of this title make descriptions of the bargaining unit more difficult to agree on and, occasionally, lead to confusion as faculty members move into and out of these assignments. In some cases, the individual in question may simply negotiate whether to stay represented or not; this may lead to a change in representation with a change in leadership for a given unit.

Finally, unit definitions may combine groups of employees who do not necessarily always have the same interests. The case of faculty and academic staff at WSU has already been discussed in some detail. Another example, perhaps more common, involves unions which represent all non-tenure-track faculty, both full- and part-time. This is the case at the University of Michigan, while at WSU full-time Lecturers are represented in the AAUP-AFT union, with tenure-track faculty and academic staff, and part-time faculty have their independent union. Since full-time faculty are salaried and part-timers often paid by the course, such basic bargaining matters as wages can become quite complex in these cases, as can assignments, course cancellation policies, and other matters. It is frequently the case as well that full-time faculty receive benefits and part-time faculty do not; this too has to be clearly sorted out in what might be called a mixed contract.

3.3.2 Relationships Among Unions

If a bargaining unit is not the only academic union, complexities may arise in finding the most precise definition, with the goal of ensuring that faculty and other academic staff belong to one and only one; this is much preferred for the administration of contracts both by the administration and the unions in question. The solution is often found in percentages; at Wayne State, for example, the unit definition, which has not changed since the unit was established, has been that it represents faculty and academic staff holding at minimum a 50% assignment. When the part-time faculty union came into being some 30 years later, the definition had to make it clear that members (only faculty in this case) were assigned to the new union if employed at up to but not including 50%. Such determinations may be established with the help of a state labor relations board (in the case of public universities), or in negotiation with the administration. Because the question involves other unions, the administration role is often that of go-between, helping to resolve what is in reality a matter of the co-existence of bargaining units.

3.3.3 Outside Forces

Thus far we have been considering the relationship between the university administration and academic unions. Added layers of complexity come from elsewhere as well. While most union activity, including the negotiation of contracts, tends to remain within the scope of university administration, faculty contracts may attract wider attention. One obvious locus of such attention is the governing board of the university. Whether appointed or elected, some members may have strongly held pro- or anti-union points of view, often coming from their interaction with trade unions in their own professional life. At the least, this may lead, first, to a greater level of attention, with requests for reports, particularly when new or even renewal contracts are being negotiated. In some cases, with more conservative members, this may result in directives to the administrative-side negotiation team to achieve a rather rigid, pro-administration contract, which may not take the university tradition of shared governance into account. In other cases, some more progressive board members may make themselves available to union members and argue, within the board, for the union side of negotiations.

In other states and at other times, the state legislature and even the governor have been a complicating factor in labor relations. Most often this takes the form of urging settlement and even offering to provide mediation or arbitration; this kind of intrusion (if that term is apt) is more likely to occur with larger universities in a state system, although the so-called "flag-ship" institution is often the one where the tenured and tenure-track faculty are not unionized.

Finally, complications may arise as a result of current events, where the union, more often than the administration, may want to incorporate matters into the contract which may not directly impact faculty members' economic or non-economic professional situation. As was said in the introduction to this essay, at this moment there is very much enhanced national awareness of issues of social justice, seen through close scrutiny of matters having to do with diversity, equity, and inclusion. As was also mentioned, most contracts have a non-discrimination article, pertaining narrowly to actions in retaliation for union activity and, more widely, to discrimination against protected classes. Some may, instead, incorporate a university statute or other statement addressing the topic.

Unions, by their very nature, seek to ensure equal treatment for all their members and may, at times, claim racial and/or gender discrimination as the cause for salary differential or even termination. Given the complexity of academic institutions, these claims are sometimes upheld in grievance or arbitration hearings and sometimes denied. It might be argued that diversity, equity, and inclusion are therefore already incorporated into collective bargaining agreements. On the other hand, other than the non-discrimination clause, it has been rare for there to be direct language in the contract supporting these values. It will be interesting to see, in the next rounds of bargaining at many universities, if diversity, equity, and inclusion are addressed more specifically.

3.4 A Few Closing Words

To summarize, this section considered in some detail collective bargaining at two large, public universities with Research 1 classification, where each has a range of disciplinary units including both Law and Medicine. They are similar in multiple ways, as are other unionized campuses of about the same size, but have developed some marked differences stemming to some extent from the original unit definition as approved in each case by the state labor relations board. Other differences arise from the nature of the universities and, in addition, as to when these faculty unions were elected.

While the next section will speak in generalities about academic unions in complex organizations, a couple of points can be made to conclude this section. First, there is a perception on both campuses that the roles of the academic/ faculty senate and the union are distinct and should remain so. In the case of SIUC, for example, since neither Law nor Medicine faculty are represented, many key points reside in the purview of the senate, while elsewhere, including WSU, such matters are addressed for all faculty (and others) in the contract. At WSU, as at many institutions, curriculum is in the hands of the senate, as are policies which affect not just those represented, but also a wider constituency (hiring, travel regulations, and so on). The need exists, therefore, to keep policy and contract agreements working together both to avoid direct contradictions and to make sure all members of the university community are adequately served in their professional roles.

The second general message, which will be expanded in the fourth section of the chapter, is that unions and their activity do not live in a vacuum. There is a need for a good level of awareness of and appropriate involvement with the world outside the scope of the contract, defined broadly to mean the rest of the campus, its governing board, other members of a system, if such exists, and even state governance. This is not to encourage administrators to go quietly (furtively, perhaps, is a better word) to state-wide or national union leaders or for union leaders to cultivate board members, but rather to suggest that, with greater awareness, both signatories of the contract can better anticipate what the other side might bring to the table, either at the time of negotiations or as newly extended interpretations of existing language. In this time of pandemic, as this essay is being written, various campuses have coped with changes to different delivery of courses, with unions representing their membership both as wanting to be protected from the disease and, at the same time, to be trained and equipped for remote teaching. In most cases the need has come up too quickly for full table negotiations, but both unions and administrations have had to accommodate new and sometimes conflicting needs (desire not to be exposed to illness and desire not to have to adapt quickly to remote instruction). Other examples of the need for wider awareness may come from legislative interest (perhaps excesses of interest) in what has traditionally been university business (at one point Ohio considered legislating teaching load) or the need to balance the outcomes of faculty negotiations with the outcome of issues brought to the table by graduate student organizations or even the more traditional trade unions on campus.

4.0 Lessons Learned

This final section will take the form of a series of suggestions of ways, not to negotiate a contract, but to think about the relationship between the administration and faculty unions. While some of the comments will be specifically about associations of tenured and tenure-track faculty, others will be more widely applicable, at least to other academic unions. And some, finally, are based in formulas for basic human interactions; what occurs in labor relations is, after all, a specific kind of human interaction, perhaps more rule-driven than many others.

4.1 Faculty: Senates and the Board

One of the crucial differences between faculty contracts (whether or not they also include other employees) and other collective bargaining relationships involving academic entities is that the faculty are also frequently represented (in the common language sense of the term) by a senate, that is, some elected or selected groups meant to be a means for providing the faculty point of view to the administration and, often, for the involvement of faculty in the development of academic policy. The relationship of the senate and union is a faculty (as opposed to administrative) matter. In some cases, the two entities, union and senate, may keep themselves completely separate as to mission or may overlap only to a small extent. In other cases, the two are very much intertwined, with, for example the union president as an ex officio member of the senate and even its leadership council.

The academic senate at WSU is of the latter sort, with official status for the union through the recognition of the union president both on the senate and as a non-voting member of the leadership group. The senate at Southern Illinois Carbondale has no such formal provisions and tends to alternate annually between a represented, often union-activist president and one who is non-represented and interested in matters which are orthogonal to collective bargaining. This alternation is neither a matter of official policy nor a product of negotiations, but has been a regular outcome of elections for the senate leadership.

It is important for administration members to be aware of these dynamics, especially those who interact directly with the senate. While the stated mission of this organization may indeed be markedly different from that of the union, issues that come up at the senate may, even so, overlap with contractual matters. If the mistake is made by an administrator, s/he is often called to task for not understanding boundaries. In other instances, it is often the administrator who points out the error, not to scold, but with the intention of steering the issue to the right path for resolution. In short, the balance of traditional shared governance and collective bargaining can be a delicate one, further complicated when senate leadership tends to swing, from year to year, from those involved with the union to those who are unrepresented and hence less invested.

The degree of interest from university governing boards, and even state legislatures, is higher when there are issues concerning faculty unions than with any other academic unions or others affiliated with colleges or universities. The share of faculty salaries is usually one of the highest in an institution's budget and faculty are perceived, rightly I would add, as the most important driving force of the university, hence this heightened interest. The more the administration—and the union—can articulate the role of the faculty (not always understood even by members of governing boards, let alone legislatures) and the reasons they may take one or another stance in bargaining, the more support the process will receive from these parties. While the progress of negotiations is often reported by the university CEO to the board, it is also the case that union leadership may also communicate directly—or attempt to—with board members, usually to apply pressure on the administration. When that is the case, the highest members of the administration may succeed in persuading board members that the issues must be settled at the table or, at least, through discussion between administration and union. There are instances, however, when the union will prevail through invoking this kind of pressure; the CEO and his immediate colleagues will have to decide when to accede and when to make further attempts to disengage the board or its members.

4.2 Unions in General

When we move from faculty unions as exceptional to union campus activity in general, there are several points to consider. First, a reality check: as with many other aspects of academic life, collective bargaining is a complex matter and has to be understood as having multiple facets. What seems like a simple question about interpretation of the contract, raised informally or through the grievance process, may lead to complicated explanations and solutions. The contract administrator is often the person who can better perceive this complexity through more experience with a wider number of aspects of the institution and may well be the one to bring this complexity in a response to what the union believes is a simple matter of compliance. These calls for what the union believes would be more perfect implementation while the contract is in place should not be taken as threats to be feared, but as items in need of resolution.

On the other hand, the administrator may often fall short in understanding collective bargaining and how it works. For example, s/he should know how lines of communication between the union and the administration function; it is tempting, as a chair or dean, to deal directly with complaints, and this approach may, after consultation, even turn out to be the best way to approach some issues. But it is extremely important as well for the administration-side contract administrator to be informed, preferably before any response is provided to the union. Further, within the guidelines of the contract, a chair or dean may meet with a represented member for some disciplinary reason. The faculty member may well want the support of a union representative. What is often not understood is that being accompanied to a disciplinary meeting is a right. The administrator in question should also have support, normally a fellow administrator who will serve as an auxiliary note-taker and, yes, a witness to the meeting.

Finally, particularly new administrators (and union leaders for that matter) need to have patience as processes take place; there are often many steps, particularly in union challenges of administrative action. Even when all deadlines are observed (not always the case), quite a number of days and even weeks may elapse before a resolution is reached. Where a matter is not guided by explicit contractual processes and deadlines, even more time may go by. Another desirable virtue is a spirit of compromise; all sides must understand that not everything will go their way. In an ideal world, the aim of collective bargaining, like shared governance, is arriving at a middle ground. This is often a remarkably hard lesson to learn, especially for those who are used to being independent actors who see themselves as issuing directives (chairs to some extent and deans all the more so) or as being independent of any hierarchy (many faculty members by the nature of their professional lives).

4.3 Measuring Effectiveness

Lack of total satisfaction on either side of the table is, in some ways, a measure of the effectiveness of the bargaining process. But can effectiveness be measured in other ways? A few possible criteria come to mind. First, we might consider the time it takes to complete the negotiations, on the assumption that a short period of bargaining indicates a small number of issues to be resolved, first, and, second, that those issues are quite straight-forward and thus agreement is easily reached. A second criterion might be the number of grievances which arise during the life of the contract: few grievances indicate, it could be reasoned, that problems have been solved and the tools necessary to carry out policies and personnel management are now clearly in place. A third measure of effectiveness might be how successfully the contract led to policy changes, expansions, revisions, and completely new directions. A related measure might be a consideration of what policies were dropped as a result of negotiations.

These potential criteria, however, need to be used with care, straight-forward as they may seem. The time to the completion of a negotiation may point to a lack of issues or to exceptionally straight-forward solutions, but it may also point to a decision not to address multiple matters at a given time, especially if other factors (usually financial) were occupying the campus at the time of bargaining. The conclusion across the table is that some matters are actually too complex to resolve may result in the formation of committees to move matters forward independent of bargaining. There have even been cases where the entire process was by-passed by agreement between the administration (not necessarily including those charged with labor relations) and the union leadership simply to extend the contract without any negotiation at all.

The number of grievances is also, in some ways, fraught as a measure, since other considerations may keep the number low, like real or imagined fear of retribution, which will have members complain to the union but refuse to take the further step of grieving formally. As for the development of or deletion of policies arising from contractual agreements, there is often a flurry of activity just after the completion of a negotiation with university policies added or deleted for compliance with the newly agreed-upon requirements. A clear-cut case in point would be the development of criteria and processes to implement new or modified articles addressing the evaluation of tenure-track faculty or post-tenure performance. It may well be the case, however, that such policies were already at least partially in place, again making it difficult to measure the direct effectiveness the bargaining process.

4.4 Human Interactions

It is far too easy when involved in collective bargaining to lose sight of a couple of essential points; they might well be described as fundamental or even philosophical. The first, often stated glibly to open negotiations but true nonetheless, is that both administration and unions do want the best for their university or college. Faculty members who become administrators do not actually go to the dark side and those who become union leaders do not automatically become the enemy! But, even with that in mind, it is an easy mental trap to view administration/union disagreements as a kind of game, clever competitions which one must win at all costs. Too often, human beings, and especially those who are not directly implicated—like students—get lost in the contest. This is not to say that shedding the game view of collective bargaining is easy or, even, always desirable. A positive outcome to an arbitration is to be celebrated: the team has played well and has won! And some victories really are victories for one side or the other, especially when someone's livelihood or even the support or closure of an academic unit may be at stake.

A second point, however, follows from the first. Winning the "game" is not the only goal, although that is easily forgotten at the negotiations table or when arguing before an arbitrator. There are times when justice and "victory" at the table are not the same thing, so that sometimes it is the right thing to cede. This point of view is easily seen in individual cases; an administrator may on occasion misapply a contract clause (pertaining to benefits, for example, or layoffs decided without taking contractual agreements into account) and the right reaction is to fix it. Most contract administrators have had the experience of calling a chair or someone in a support office to explain what the error is in order to remedy it without even invoking the formal mechanisms of grievance hearings.

More complicated are wider issues including, increasingly, issues of social justice. The administration at some university or college asks (as hypothetical examples) for a clause to be added to the article on hiring to have a person of color on all search committees or in the article on department committees for a student to be on all admissions committees. The union at another one might, arguably, make the same request. In a relationship which sees negotiations (at the table or in grievance or compliance discussions) as a game where one has to win, the response might well be a rapid "no", motivated by the desire to protect the status quo. It takes the ability to see beyond the (often unfortunate) competition aspect of collective bargaining to reach a truly shared vision of what is right for the institution and the people who work and study there.

5.0 Conclusions

5.1 Summary

This essay addresses academic collective bargaining in large, complex universities. Two such institutions were used as a basis for the first part of the discussion: Southern Illinois University Carbondale and Wayne State University (located in Detroit). Contributing to the complexity of labor relations in both institutions are the ways in which the bargaining units were defined when the unions were formed. The decisions made then have had repercussions in contract language, the configuration of union leadership, and the relationships between the union and other governance entities, internal and external to the academic side of the university. The essay also addresses lessons which might be learned from the nature of all these relationships, with some emphasis on the necessity to remember, on both sides, that decisions made at the negotiations table and elsewhere have immediate effects on individuals.

5.2 Orientation and Training

What follows, therefore, is that administrators and union officers new to their positions must be given orientation, even training, in the nature of collective bargaining. The goal is informational, first, but also meant to bring nuance to an often-held expectation that the other side is wrong and must be defeated at all costs. In addition to basic understandings of how unions and administration function both internally and in relationship to each other, two further notions need to be emphasized. The first is that collective bargaining does not live in a vacuum, but belongs to wider and more complex systems which should be understood if it is to be successful. And secondly, this union/administration relationship writ large is not warfare or simply an intriguing game; it calls for compromise, sometimes collaboration, and continued mindfulness as to why, as a relationship, it must succeed for the individual and for the entire institution.

7

A NEW MORNING IN HIGHER EDUCATION COLLECTIVE BARGAINING, 2013–2019

William A. Herbert[1]

Introduction

This chapter analyzes and contextualizes data concerning the growth in collective bargaining in higher education from 2013 to 2019, the interregnum between the economic fallout from the Great Recession and the health and economic consequences from the COVID-19 pandemic.

The chapter begins with a discussion of the democratic procedures established by collective bargaining laws for determining union representation, and the genuine choices higher education leaders have in responding to unionization efforts. It describes how institutional decisions over the decades to increasingly rely on contingent faculty, postdoctoral scholars, and graduate assistants to teach and research helped to create a ripe environment for the growth of union representation during the period under study.

The chapter demonstrates that between 2013 and 2019, represented faculty grew by 10%, with contingent faculty constituting over three-quarters of that growth. During the same period, the number of represented graduate assistants increased by over 30%, and there was an even larger percentage increase among postdoctoral scholars.

Historically, unionization growth and collective bargaining were centered at public colleges and universities, with bargaining units more prevalent at community colleges and representation provided by bargaining agents affiliated with three traditional academic unions: American Federation of Teachers (AFT), National Education Association (NEA), and American Association of University Professors (AAUP).[2]

DOI: 10.4324/9781003138990-8

This chapter reveals three important new trends: a groundswell of new collective bargaining relationships at private institutions; the rate of bargaining unit growth at four-year public institutions outpacing community colleges; and non-traditional academic unions, Service Employees International Union (SEIU) and the United Auto Workers (UAW), expanding their representational roles on campus.[3] The chapter also examines the frequency of work stoppages in higher education over the seven-year period. It also presents four illustrative negotiated agreements reached during the COVID-19 pandemic, demonstrating the role that collective bargaining can play even during an emergency. It ends with some final thoughts about the impact of the pandemic on collective bargaining in higher education.

These developments in collective bargaining come at a time when higher education faces multiple crises requiring informed and principled campus leadership dedicated to collaborative labor relations. Some crises have been long in the making: cutbacks in public funding, job and economic insecurities, racial, ethnic and gender inequalities, and student debt. These challenges have been exacerbated by the pandemic and require the recalibration of priorities by government policymakers, institutions, and unions.

A related crisis, the growing partisan-divide over higher education, is a new variant of American anti-intellectualism,[4] with growing skepticism about the role of higher education.[5] A 2019 Pew study found that close to 60% of Republicans and independents who lean Republican believe that higher education has a negative impact on our country.[6] The survey reflects Michael Sandel's observations about the deep corrosive divisions and prejudices over possessing a college degree,[7] which Arlie Russell Hochschild summarized as "[f] or the first time in recent history, the less education you have, the more you lean right and distrust higher education itself."[8] This ominous upsurge in anti-intellectualism requires collaborative advocacy in support of higher education's mission and the tenets of academic freedom and freedom of speech on campus.

Data Collection and Methodology

The chapter draws primarily from three datasets gathered by the National Center for the Study of Collective Bargaining in Higher Education and the Professions at Hunter College (National Center). One includes all new collective bargaining relationships created during the period 2013–2019 involving faculty, graduate assistants, and postdoctoral scholars.[9] The data was gathered from primary sources during the processing of representation cases at the National Labor Relations Board (NLRB) and at public sector labor relations agencies. The chapter contextualizes this data with findings from earlier National Center studies dating back to 1976.[10]

The second dataset is of work stoppage activity in higher education during the same seven-year period, gathered by the National Center from government information, news services, and other sources.[11] The third dataset is a collection higher education collective negotiated agreements related to the COVID-19 pandemic. The data was collected by National Center through submissions made in response to a solicitation sent to administrators and faculty representatives between May and November 2020 and supplemented by agreements downloaded from university and union websites.

Back to the Future: Collective Bargaining in Historical and Legal Context

The prominent role that collective bargaining laws play in the growth and shape of unionization on campus has long been recognized.[12] What is often forgotten by scholars and practitioners is that the system of unionization and collective bargaining established by those laws was intentionally modeled after our political system.[13]

A 1915 report from the United States Commission on Industrial Relations may have been the first to expressly draw the analogy between political democracy and workplace democracy: "Political freedom can exist only where there is industrial freedom; political democracy only where there is industrial democracy."[14]

Two decades later, representative workplace democracy was codified in the National Labor Relations Act (NLRA) in 1935, which states in part that it is "the policy of the United States…[to encourage] the practice and procedure of collective bargaining and by protecting the exercise by workers of full freedom of association, self-organization, and designation of representatives of their own choosing, for the purpose of negotiating the terms and conditions of their employment or other mutual aid or protection."[15] In the legislation, Congress concluded that collective bargaining rights were necessary because the lack of employee representation and bargaining power results in depressed wages, strikes, and other workplace disruptions.[16]

During the congressional debate over the bill, Senator Robert F. Wagner paraphrased former NLRB Chairman Lloyd K. Garrison, when he declared that

> democracy in industry must be based upon the same principles as democracy in government. Majority rule, with all its imperfections, is the best protection of workers' rights, just as it is the surest guaranty of political liberty that mankind has yet discovered.[17]

It took another three decades before the NLRA was applied to private nonprofit higher education industry, and states enacted state collective bargaining laws applicable to public institutions.[18] Although the NLRA applies to virtually all private higher education institutions, collective representation as a right exists only at public institutions in states with their own collective bargaining laws or regulations.

While clear differences exist between the NLRA and state laws, as well as between state laws, there are also fundamental similarities. Each law permits a republican form of exclusive representation in the workplace and defines the rights and obligations of labor and management. Representation is determined by the outcome of a democratic process that includes petitions, voting units, campaigning, secret ballots, and elections overseen by government officials.[19]

If a bargaining agent is selected by the employees, it has a legal duty to fairly represent the entire unit, despite conflicts and tensions that can exist between groups of represented employees.[20] The internal affairs of unions with private sector bargaining units are regulated under federal law, which mandates financial disclosures and grants a bill of rights for union members.[21]

An institution has several available options in responding to a representation effort by faculty and other employees.[22] University leaders can permit faculty or others to select a representative without litigation and by taking steps to avoid fears of reprisals such as limiting the school's actions and communicative footprints on the question of representation.[23] For example, this lesser approach was adopted by Cornell University two decades ago by avoiding electioneering when its graduate assistants attempted to unionize.[24] Another alternative is for an institution to remain completely neutral on the question of representation and allow the at-issue employees to make their own choice without input from their employer. This perspective was adopted as a policy by the University of Michigan Board of Trustees in 2020 and has been stipulated to by other institutions.[25]

An institution can also chose to voluntarily recognize a union representative, a procedure that predates the application of collective bargaining laws to colleges and universities. For example, in 1945 the University of Illinois Board of Trustees adopted a formal collective bargaining program for its non-academic employees.[26] Similarly, certain private institutions in the late 1940s recognized unions and negotiated contracts for their faculty and other employees.[27] The practice of voluntary recognition continues today under Nevada's rules and regulations[28] and agreements reached with Georgetown University, Brown University, New York University (NYU), and other institutions after 2012.[29]

Lastly, university leaders who view union representation on campus as antithetical to the mission of higher education can retain firms that specialize in union avoidance tactics to aggressively circumvent organizing efforts.[30] Many of those tactics are commonly employed by private companies. The tactics were developed by business professors and presented at university-hosted seminars in the late 1970s.[31]

Following recognition of a union, the parties must engage in good faith negotiations that includes an exchange of proposals and information over their terms and conditions of employment and other related decisions.[32] Collective bargaining is a more uniform process of decision-making than shared governance, with labor and management treated as legal equals for purposes of negotiations and arbitration. It is a bilateral system of checks and balances that necessitates compromises by both sides to reach an agreement, but there is no legal requirement that an agreement be reached. The subjects of negotiations can address campus workplace issues as well as broader issues impacting the common good.[33] Negotiations provide administrators with an opportunity to make proposals and exchange information to address managerial concerns.[34] Most subjects concerning terms and conditions of employment are mandatorily negotiable, while others are permissive or prohibited. When a final agreement is reached, the terms are codified into an enforceable written agreement for a finite period. The failure to reach an agreement can result in mediation, and in some circumstances, a work stoppage.

The trend in higher education unionization growth described in this chapter differs significantly from the steady overall national decline in union density since 1983.[35] In many ways, the recent unionization growth on campuses is a consequence of the "revolutionary" restructuring and redesign of academic appointments over the decades,[36] with the massive increase in contingent faculty appointments. While there are many external and internal factors that have influenced institutional decision-making, the result has been the creation of pool of insecure, low wage, and marginalized academics at private and public institutions who view unionization and collective bargaining as the means of enfranchisement "to gain influence over governance patterns and secure greater economic and professional benefits."[37]

Trends in Representation Growth by Institutional Type and Sectors Prior to 2013

Faculty

Before analyzing the data since 2012, it is important to place it in the context of historic trends in higher education unionization.

Since the 1960s, disparities have existed in the relative size and growth of unionized academic labor by institutional type and between public and private institutions. In the public sector, faculty representation steadily increased as the right to unionize expanded across the country, with the largest concentration and growth at the community college level.[38] Until the past decade, representation growth at private institutions was slow and uneven with periods of slight increases and decreases.

Data from earlier National Center studies based on survey results illustrate the differences in faculty representation between institutional-types and sectors over four decades. In 1976, there were 179 faculty bargaining units at community colleges, 56 at four-year public colleges and universities, and 66 at private institutions.[39] Data from a study ten years later showed a 62% (111) increase in bargaining units at community colleges, a 41% (23) growth at four-year public colleges, and a 16.6% (11) increase at private institutions from 1976.[40] By 1996, faculty bargaining units had grown again at public institutions but declined in the private sector: a 18.6% (54) increase at community colleges, a 13.9% (11) increase at four-year public institutions, and a −9% (−7) decrease at private colleges and universities.[41]

The 2006 National Center study found there were 300,644 represented faculty at public colleges and universities. The number of bargaining units increased from 1996 by 11.6% (40) to 384 at community colleges and 31.1% (28) to 90 at four-year public institutions with an additional nine units identified as 2/4 public institutions.[42] At private institutions, the number of bargaining units declined again by −7.1% (−6) with 17,860 represented faculty.[43]

By 2012, two new important trends emerged. For the first time, the number of represented faculty and bargaining units at private institutions substantially increased. There were 26,241 faculty in 83 units, constituting a 46.9% (8,381) increase in represented private sector faculty over 2006 and a 29.6% (19) increase in bargaining units.[44] Second, the percentage of relative growth at community colleges and four-year public institutions slowed. In 2012, there were 348,250 represented public sector faculty in 568 bargaining units, constituting a 15.8% (47,606) increase over 2006. The number of new community college bargaining units increased by only 8.3% (32) to 416 and there was a 20.3% (24) increase to 142 at four-year institutions, and one additional unit at a 2/4-institution.[45]

Graduate Assistants and Postdoctoral Scholars

Prior to 2013, graduate assistant and postdoctoral scholar representation was almost exclusively at public universities and affiliated research foundations.[46] The one exception was at NYU. Graduate assistants there were represented in collective bargaining for five-year period ending in 2005.[47]

By 2012, there were 62,656 graduate assistants represented in 30 bargaining at public institutions and four research foundations affiliated with public institutions.[48] There were no represented graduate assistants at private universities, and representation of postdoctoral scholars was limited to approximately 6,700 in bargaining units at three public universities.[49] Consistent with the trend identified by Julius and Gumport,[50] well over 50% of the graduate assistants and postdoctoral scholars were represented by non-traditional academic unions in 2012.[51]

Factors Shaping These Trends

There are three major factors that help explain these trends prior to 2013. Historically, support for unionization has differed based on status and rank, salary and benefits, autonomy, job security, and participation in institutional decision-making.[52] Therefore, it is unsurprising that unionization is greater at community colleges and among graduate assistants than among faculty at research universities and private elite institutions.

Second, differences in institutional responses by sector to representation efforts have played a role. Aggressive union avoidance strategies are more common in NLRB elections.[53] Leaders at public colleges and universities are less likely to employ the same aggressive tactics.

A related factor is the legal doctrines and precedent that developed under the NLRA as the result of successful litigation pursued by private institutions in opposition to union representation and collective bargaining.

The first doctrine was annunciated in the 1980 United States Supreme Court decision in *National Labor Relations Board v. Yeshiva University*.[54] In that ruling, the Supreme Court determined that tenured and tenure track faculty involved in shared governance are managerial and exempt from NLRA rights and protections. *Yeshiva* and its progeny led to a decline in faculty representation at private institutions,[55] as the data prior to 2006 reveals.

The successful use of the *Yeshiva* doctrine by private institutions resulted in traditional academic unions and full-time faculty becoming apprehensive about pursuing new organizing because of the costs and complexities of litigating managerial status,[56] and fear of retaliation without legal recourse if faculty are deemed unprotected by the NLRA. This explains, in part, why there were only 21 faculty representation petitions filed with the NLRB during the period 2006–2012.[57] One labor observer has described the situation under *Yeshiva* as "a legal quagmire" for faculty and unions "from which little good obtains."[58]

Another perennial legal issue affecting private sector representation is whether the NLRB can assert jurisdiction over religiously affiliated institutions without infringing on religious liberties protected under the First Amendment. This issue has been litigated for decades before the NLRB and the courts.[59] Some, but not all, religiously affiliated institutions have cited this precedent as a tool to block representation of faculty and graduate assistants on their campuses.[60] For example, Manhattan College has used litigation for a decade to thwart contingent faculty unionization, while LeMoyne College made a different decision and chose not to object to contingent faculty unionization on the grounds of a religious exemption.[61]

A third legal issue impacting union density in the private sector is whether graduate assistants are employees covered under the NLRA. As a federal appellate court noted, the NLRB "has been consistently inconsistently" over the decades on this legal issue.[62]

Beginning in 1972, NLRB precedent treated graduate assistants as primarily students. In 2000, the NLRB ruled for the first time that graduate assistants had the right to representation. This ruling led directly to the first private sector collective bargaining relationship at NYU. Four years later, the NLRB reversed itself finding that graduate assistants did not have a right to organize or engage in collective bargaining under the NLRA.[63] This remained the state of law prior to 2013, which is an important reason for the lack of represented graduate assistants at private universities prior to the period under study.

Growth and Trends in Higher Education Representation, 2013–2019

The seven-year period between 2013 and 2019 saw a continuation of the growth in representation of faculty, graduate assistants, and postdoctoral with some new and continuing trends.

Faculty Representation Growth

Overall, the number of newly organized faculty at the end of 2019 was 411,921, a 10% (37,468) increase over the number represented in 2012.[64] Figure 7.1 sets forth the annual and total rate of unionization growth since 2012.

The most significant growth in unionized faculty took place at private institutions. During the seven-year period, represented faculty in the private sector grew by 16,104, which is a 61.3% increase over 2012. The number of faculty bargaining units on private sector campuses expanded by 80.9% (68). Viewed in another way, the growth in represented faculty on private sector campuses between 2013 and 2019 is equivalent to 90.1% of the total number found in the 2006.

The private sector growth was primarily among part-time and full-time contingent faculty (see Figure 7.2). Over 95% of the new bargaining units were

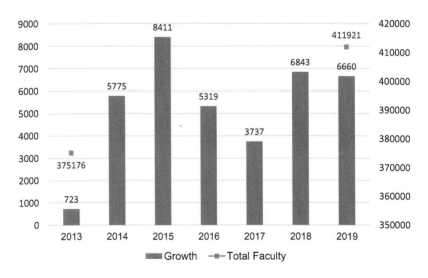

FIGURE 7.1

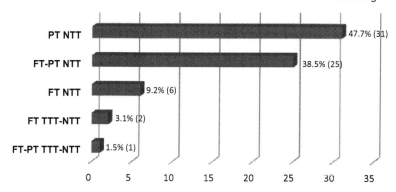

FIGURE 7.2

exclusively contingent faculty, with close to a half (47.7%) limited to those holding part-time appointments. The second largest group of new units included both part-time and full-time contingent faculty. Combined units with contingent and tenured and tenure track faculty were only 4.6% of the new bargaining units (see Figure 7.2). By the end of 2019, there were also three new bargaining units at for-profit institutions with a total of 206 represented faculty.[65]

In the public sector, there were 50 new faculty bargaining units formed after 2012 but only a 5.8% (20,160) increase in the overall number of newly represented faculty. Consistent with the trend first seen in 2006, faculty unionization growth at four-year institutions outpaced increases at community colleges. Over 70.3% (14,175) of the newly represented public sector faculty work at four-year colleges and universities, while less than 29.7% (5,985) are employed by community colleges.

As in the private sector, new successful contingent faculty unionization played a key role in the overall growth, representing over 65% of the public sector increase.[66] A majority (26) of new units were composed only of contingent faculty, with 42% (21) limited to those with part-time appointments. Another 34% (17) were units of tenured and tenure track faculty, with another 14% (7) combined units of contingent and tenured and tenure track faculty (see Figure 7.3). The inapplicability of the *Yeshiva* doctrine to the public sector enabled tenured and tenure track faculty to continue to unionize.

Factors Shaping New Faculty Representation

The recent growth in faculty unionization is the consequence of various factors, some old and some new.

The first factor is the restructuring of academic positions. In 1970, the vast majority of faculty were full-time tenured or tenure eligible.[67] By 2011, over

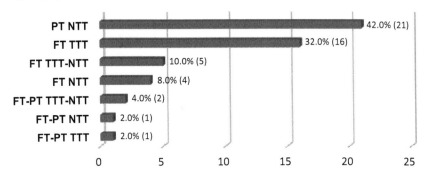

FIGURE 7.3

70% of faculty held contingent appointments with most working in part-time positions,[68] a group long known to be the most supportive of unionization. A related factor was the shift in national union priorities to aggressively support the growing demands by contingent faculty for representation.[69]

Another important factor is that the *Yeshiva* doctrine is largely irrelevant to contingent faculty representation because they are generally excluded from shared governance. Although the doctrine was invoked by some schools after 2012 to block representation efforts by tenured and tenure track faculty, and even some contingent faculty based on their role in shared governance, it was relatively infrequent.[70] The *Yeshiva* doctrine might become more pertinent to contingent faculty if AAUP's recommendations for contingent faculty to participate in shared governance are adopted on private campuses.[71]

In addition, the issue of NLRB jurisdiction over religiously affiliated institutions, was avoided when schools including Georgetown University,[72] Notre Dame de Namur University,[73] and Fordham University decided not to claim a religious exemption on First Amendment grounds.[74] Those choices are consistent with the view of scholars who believe that it is hypocritical for Catholic-affiliated institutions to challenge unionization efforts in light of the Church's social teachings.[75]

Other institutions have chosen the path of legal resistance including Duquesne University,[76] and Manhattan College, which have pursued litigation challenging the NLRB's assertion of jurisdiction over contingent faculty representation efforts. While a system of voluntary recognition is a legitimate compromise that would allow unionization without federal regulation, it has not been adopted at institutions seeking a religious exemption from the NLRA.[77]

Another key factor in the growth of faculty representation since 2012 is the new dominant role played by the SEIU, particularly at private sector non-profit institutions. Labor scholars have long recognized that union for its innovative and proactive strategies that identify "key sectors, industries, occupations, and local labor markets, and complementing this strategic planning process with extensive background research on the selected organizing targets."[78]

In 2006, SEIU represented no private sector faculty,[79] and by 2012 it represented only two units with a total of 2,573 contingent faculty.[80] By the end of 2019, however, SEIU represented over 86% (56) of the new private non-profit units (see Figure 7.4) and 90.3% (14,359) of the newly represented faculty.[81] It now represents faculty at private institutions in the District of Columbia and 11 states: California, Connecticut, Illinois, Massachusetts, Maryland, Minnesota, Missouri, New York, North Carolina, Vermont, and Washington.[82]

SEIU overwhelmingly eclipsed AAUP, AFT, and NEA in representing newly organized contingent faculty on those campuses although historically the traditional academic unions were the predominate national affiliates of bargaining agents representing all unionized faculty[83] (see Figure 7.4). SEIU's new role in contingent faculty unionization was not limited to the private sector. Over the seven-year period, it also organized 26% (13) of the new public sector units with 46.3% (9,347) of the newly represented faculty at public institutions.[84] It is fascinating, and perhaps telling, that contingent faculty chose to align with the same union active in organizing low wage workers in other industries and that has led the nationwide campaign to raise the minimum wage to $15.[85]

However, AAUP, AFT, and NEA remained dominate as the national affiliates for unions representing public sector faculty units (see Figure 7.5). Separately and jointly, the three traditional academic unions were the national affiliates of 72% (36) of the new public sector units with 52.7% (10,632) of the newly represented faculty.

Growth in Representation of Graduate Assistants and Postdoctoral Scholars

Since 2012, the number of graduate assistant bargaining units grew by 53.3% (16), representing a combined growth of 32.3% (19,627) in newly represented

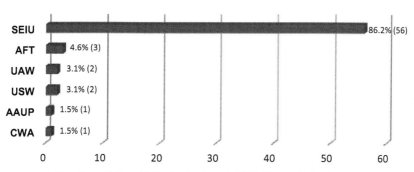

Number of New Units by National Affiliation at Private Non-Profit Institutions

FIGURE 7.4

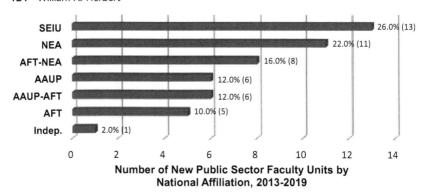

FIGURE 7.5

graduate and undergraduate employees.[86] Most (12) of the new bargaining units were limited to graduate assistants and one-third (4) also included under-graduate assistants.[87]

During the same period, postdoctoral scholar units doubled (3) with a 47% (3,181) increase in represented employees. Additional postdoctoral scholars were represented in new faculty bargaining units and there was a new recognized public sector unit of 4,110 academic researchers.[88] In the public sector alone, there was a 16.6% (5) increase in new graduate assistant bargaining units and a 66.6% (2) increase in postdoctoral scholar units.[89]

Factors Shaping New Representation of Graduate Assistants and Postdoctoral Scholars

This growth in representation is reflective of higher education's increased reliance on graduate assistants and postdoctoral scholars to teach and research.[90] A 2018 study by the Economic Policy Institute found that in the ten years ending in 2015, there was a 16.7% increase in the number of graduate assistants employed.[91] Other studies reveal an even greater growth in postdoctoral scholar employment over the past two decades.[92]

A significant new trend in the period ending in 2019 was the rise in graduate assistant and postdoctoral scholar collective bargaining at private colleges and universities. In 2012, there were no graduate assistant or postdoctoral bargaining units at private universities. By 2020, there were 11 certified or recognized private sector graduate assistant bargaining units and eight negotiated contracts at institutions including Harvard University, NYU, Georgetown University, and Brown University.[93] In addition, the first private sector postdoctoral unit was certified at Columbia University along with three new private faculty units with postdoctoral scholars.[94]

The new trend in private sector representation was primarily due to the change in NLRB precedent, which lifted the existing legal barrier to graduate and undergraduate assistant unionization. In 2016, the NLRB ruled in *Columbia University*,[95] a case brought by the UAW, that student employees had representation rights under the NLRA. The decision precipitated a massive number of new representation petition filings. Overall, the greatest level of growth (72.6%) in graduate assistant representation took place in the two years following the *Columbia University* decision.

Another notable trend in 2013–2019 was the expanded role of non-traditional academic unions in representing student employees and postdoctoral scholars.

In 2012, the UAW represented 43% of the organized graduate assistants and three units of postdoctoral scholars.[96] Seven years later, the UAW represented 70.2% (13,780) of newly organized student employees in 31.3% (5) of the new units. It also represented three new postdoctoral units and one academic researcher unit.[97] Although SEIU represented no graduate assistants in 2012, it now represents 37.5% (6) of the new graduate assistant units and 11.7% (2,287) of the newly represented student employees. SEIU also represents two of the four new faculty units with postdoctoral scholars.[98]

The AFT and AAUP, separately and jointly, were the national affiliates of three new graduate assistant bargaining units at Georgetown University, Brown University, and Portland State University, constituting 18.7% (3) of the new units and 15.8% (3110) of newly represented graduate assistants. They also represent two new faculty units that include postdoctoral scholars.[99]

Another factor that explains the growth was the decisions by private universities to not contest the certifications of graduate assistant unions following an NLRB election or to voluntarily recognize a union after a non-NLRB election. Other institutions, such as Yale University, the University of Chicago, and Boston College, strongly resisted graduate assistant unionization based on perennial legal arguments and policy concerns that unionization might be detrimental to the educational goals of institutions and could harm faculty-student relationships.[100] At Columbia University, it took a seven-day strike in 2018 before the university agreed to commence bargaining for first contracts for its student employees and postdoctoral scholars.

Work Stoppages, 2013–2019

There was a total of 52 strikes and one lockout in higher education during the period 2013–2019 among faculty, graduate assistants, and non-academic employees.[101] The largest number of strikes per annum (13) occurred in 2018 and 2019, while the fewest (3) took place in 2014. Figure 7.6 identifies the total number strikes per annum in higher education beginning in 2012.

Close to 27% (14) of the 52 strikes in the period 2013–2019 involved faculty, although faculty strikes have historically been infrequent, particularly since the mid-1980s.[102] Seven of the strikes in 2013–2019 included tenured, tenure

Number of Strikes

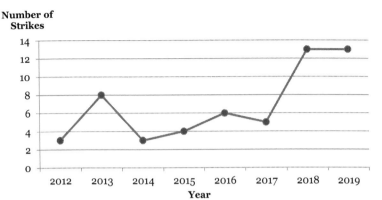

FIGURE 7.6

track, and contingent faculty, six were limited to contingent faculty, and one involved only tenured and tenure track faculty. AAUP and AFT, separately or jointly, were the national affiliates in 50% (7) of the faculty strikes. Although SEIU dominated new contingent faculty representation during the period, it was involved in only one faculty strike. The only faculty strike in 2019 took place at Wright State University, which lasted 20 days and was the longest since 2012.[103] The sole lockout of faculty during in the seven-year period was imposed at Long Island University and it lasted 12 days.[104]

There were 11 strikes by graduate assistants in the seven-year period, 7 at public universities and 4 at private institutions. UAW was the national affiliate in over 63% (7) of the graduate assistant strikes and the AFT was the national affiliate in the other four strikes.

Collective Bargaining and the COVID-19 Pandemic

Collective bargaining relationships have played a role in resolving issues that developed in 2020 from the COVID-19 pandemic. At some institutions, written labor-management agreements were negotiated, which enabled the completion of the Spring semester and the reopening in the Fall semester. On other campuses, informal labor-management structures led to quick distribution of information and resolution of issues.

The most common terms in the approximately 200 written labor-management agreements covered compensation, evaluations, telework, technical training, online instruction, workload, sick leave, and health and safety. Other negotiated subjects included: extensions for tenure, post-tenure, promotion, and probation review; intellectual property; access to campus; availability of protective equipment; health insurance; and modifications to academic calendars and syllabi.

The following are four illustrative examples of negotiated agreements reached during the crisis.

In October 2019, two new faculty bargaining units, represented by United Academics of the University of New Mexico, were certified at the University of New Mexico. Less than a year later, the university and the faculty union were able to reach pandemic related agreements, although they had not yet completed negotiations for first full contracts.

In August 2020, the University of New Mexico and United Academics of the University of New Mexico signed memoranda creating an early retirement incentive program, establishing faculty health and safety protocols, eliminating the use of student evaluations in the Fall semester, permitting a one-year tenure clock extension for certain faculty, and allowing virtual participation in faculty and departmental meetings.[105] In September, the parties issued a joint statement explaining that they wanted to "create a culture of mutual protection" for the reopening in the Fall semester.[106] Among the announced terms was a reduction in the number of full in-person classes, and a series of other health and safety related measures. The following month, they signed another agreement permitting temporary and voluntary work reductions for tenured and tenure track faculty in the Spring 2021 semester to provide "flexibility to dedicate time to family care and other personal responsibilities related to the COVID-19 emergency."[107]

California State University and the California Faculty Association have a much older bargaining relationship, which has included periods of strong disagreements and protests.[108] In response to the pandemic, the university and the union negotiated a series of memoranda in May, June, and August 2020. Those agreements extended their current contract, created voluntary work reduction and early retirement programs, provided additional funding for faculty professional development during the summer, and required consideration of the pandemic's impact when evaluating coaches.[109]

Columbia College Chicago, a private sector institution, and its part-time faculty union negotiated written agreements for the Spring 2020 semester. The agreements focused on issues tied with the transition to remote education during the pandemic. They included terms concerning compensation, intellectual property, performance evaluations, faculty development funding, and limitations on the use of access to online classes by department chairs.[110]

For four decades, the graduate assistants at the Florida State University have been represented by United Faculty Florida-Graduate Assistant Union. During the Spring 2020 semester, the university and union negotiated an agreement for the transition to remote learning. It excluded student evaluations and decreased scholarly productivity from employment evaluations, and provided that the failure to maintain satisfactory student status during the emergency would not be a basis for termination. A second agreement codified terms for the Fall 2020 semester, which included health and safety protocols, telework, and limitations on the use of student evaluations. In the agreement, the university committed that it would not terminate international graduate assistants for performance-related reasons during the pandemic, and it would provide them with assistance in navigating travel and immigration restrictions. Lastly, the agreement created a procedure for graduate assistants to request a funding extension and guaranteed a continuation of their housing benefits.[111]

Final Thoughts

This chapter has demonstrated the scope of unionization growth among faculty, graduate assistants, and postdoctoral scholars in the 2013–2019 period. It placed those increases in the context of historical trends in higher education. For decades, collective bargaining growth was primarily a public sector phenomenon. The recent data shows new significant unionization growth in the private sector among contingent faculty and graduate assistants. Both groups are also central to the documented growth in the public sector.

These trends are the byproducts of various factors: decreased funding for higher education and other external pressures; increased reliance on non-tenure eligible teachers, researchers, and graduate assistants; changes in applicable laws; and the expanded roles of unions like SEIU and UAW in new campus organizing.

The chapter has highlighted how collective bargaining was modeled on republican democracy, outlined the genuine choices university leaders have in responding to unionization efforts, and presented examples of the role collective bargaining played in resolving issues resulting from the COVID-19 pandemic.

There is little question that the pandemic has placed significant financial and operational strains on institutions, faculty, staff, students. In the face of the growing crisis, institutions have started to announce unilateral austerity measures including layoffs, program cuts, closures, and mergers. Collective bargaining can be an important means for administrators and labor to jointly develop timely solutions responsive to the crisis, but it requires creativity, transparency, compromise, and reexamined priorities and modalities. Conversely, the imposition of unilateral measures in responding to the financial turmoil might lead to greater campus conflicts, new unionization efforts and other collective action by faculty and others seeking to preserve their benefits and privileges or to attain a greater voice in decision-making.[112]

The need for labor-management alliances is particularly important at the present time to persuade federal and state policymakers to allocate greater financial support for higher education, and to help stem the growing tide of anti-intellectualism. The absence of effective coalitions will lead to the further diminution and availability of higher education and its mission of encouraging the pursuit of knowledge and understanding. Such an outcome will undermine our society's democratic values and practices which include collective bargaining and shared governance.

Notes

1 Mr. Herbert acknowledges the important contributions of National Center affiliated researchers Jacob Apkarian, Assistant Professor of Sociology, York College, CUNY and Joseph van der Naald, a doctoral student in Sociology at the CUNY Graduate Center. He also acknowledges the assistance of Hunter College student researchers Anna Xia and Sarah Mathai.

2 Kemerer, Frank R. and J. Victor Baldridge. 1976. *Unions on Campus* (San Francisco: Jossey-Bass Publishers), 50–52; Ladd, Jr., Everett Carll, and Seymour Martin Lipset. 1973. *Professors, Unions, and American Higher Education* (Washington, DC: The American Enterprise Institute for Public Policy Research) 41–46. Historically, AFT, NEA, AAUP were not the first unions to negotiate collective bargaining agreements for faculty in higher education. In fact, NEA and AAUP initially resisted the concept of faculty unionization and collective bargaining, viewing it as inconsistent with professional status. Herbert, William A. 2017. "The History Books Tell It? Collective Bargaining in Higher Education in the 1940s," *Journal of Collective Bargaining in the Academy*: Vol. 9, Article 3 22–31, n. 138.
   https://works.bepress.com/william_herbert/34/ [December 10, 2020].

3 The phrase "industrial union" is not used in this chapter to describe these organizations because the term is antiquated, and its use historically inaccurate. Both before and after changing its name from Building Services Employees International Union (BSEIU) in 1968, SEIU has a long history of organizing and negotiating on campus. Herbert, "The History Books Tell It?" 12–14, n. 73; see also, *County of Genesee and Genesee Community College* 7 NY PERB para. 4044 (1974) (SEIU petitioned to represent community college administrators); *Worcester Polytechnic Institute*, 213 NLRB 306 (1974) (SEIU represented college maintenance employees since 1969). Similarly, the UAW has been organizing clerical staff and graduate assistants on campus for close to 50 years. See, *Barnard College*, 204 NLRB 1134 (1973) (excluding graduate assistants from a UAW proposed bargaining that included clerical staff).

4 Jacoby, Susan. 2008. *The Age of American Unreason* (New York, New York: Pantheon Books).

5 Altbach, Phillip, "Harsh Realities: The Professoriate in the Twenty-First Century" in Altbach, Phillip G., Patricia J. Gumport, and Robert O. Berdahl (eds.). 2011. *American Higher Education in the Twenty-First Century: Social, Political, and Economic Challenges*, Third Edition (Baltimore, Maryland: Johns Hopkins University Press), 227–228.

6 Parker, Kim.2019. "The Growing Partisan Divide in Views of Higher Education," (Pew Research Center, August 19) https://www.pewsocialtrends.org/essay/the-growing-partisan-divide-in-views-of-higher-education/ [November 20, 2020].

7 Sandel, Michael. 2020. "Disdain for the Less Educated Is the Last Acceptable Prejudice," *New York Times*, Sept. 20, 2020 < https://www.nytimes.com/2020/09/02/opinion/education-prejudice.html> [December 1, 2020].

8 Hochschild, Arlie Russell. 2020. "Unearned Credit: How our meritocratic system fosters inequality and despair," *New York Times Book Review*, Nov. 22, 2020, 19. https://www.nytimes.com/2020/09/15/books/review/the-tyranny-of-merit-michael-j-sandel.html [December 1, 2020].

9 Herbert, William A., Jacob Apkarian, and Joseph van der Naald. 2020. Supplementary Directory of New Bargaining Agents and Contracts in Institutions of Higher Education, 2013–2019 (New York, New York: National Center for the Study of Collective Bargaining in Higher Education and the Professions).
   http://www.hunter.cuny.edu/ncscbhep/assets/files/SupplementalDirectory-2020-FINAL.pdf [November 25, 2020].

10 Directory of Contracts and Bargaining Agents in Institutions of Higher Education. 1976. (New York New York: National Center for the Study of Collective Bargaining in Higher Education, April) http://www.hunter.cuny.edu/ncscbhep/assets/files/directory%20april%201976. pdf [December 5, 2020]; Douglas, Joel M. with Elisabeth A. Kotch. 1986. *Directory of Faculty Contracts and Bargaining Agents in Institutions of Higher Education and the Professions* (New York, New York: National Center for the Study of Collective Bargaining in Higher Education, January); Hurd, Richard and Amy Foerster with Beth Hillman Johnson, Directory of Faculty Contracts and Bargaining Agents in Institutions of Higher Education in the Professions. 1996. (New York, New York.: National Center for the Study of Collective Bargaining in Higher Education, January); Moriarty, Joan and Michelle Savarese. 2006. *Directory of Faculty Contracts and Bargaining Agents in Institutions of Higher Education and the Professions* (New York, New York: National Center for the Study of Collective Bargaining in Higher Education, January); Berry, Joe and Michelle Savarese. 2012. *Directory of U.S. Faculty Contracts and Bargaining Agents in Institutions of Higher Education* (New York, New York: National Center for the Study of Collective Bargaining in Higher Education and the Professions, September).

11 Herbert, William A. and Jacob Apkarian. 2019. "You've Been with the Professors: An Examination of Higher Education Work Stoppage Data, Past and Present" *Employee Rights and Employment Policy Journal* Vol. 23 Iss. 2, Appendix. 277. http://works.bepress.com/william_herbert/43/; National Center Work Stoppage Data Report for Calendar Year 2019. 2020. National Center E-Note (January) https://myemail.constantcontact.com/January-2020-Newsletter–News–Analysis–and-Updates.html?soid=1102372137664&aid=Rzj0_-PNjz0 [January 2, 2020].

12 Garbarino, Joseph W. 1975. *Faculty Bargaining: Change and Conflict* (New York, New York.: McGraw-Hill) 16–18; Ladd and Lipst, 4; Kemerer and Bladridge. 48–49, 19–20.

13 Wollett, Donald H., "Issues at Stake," in Duryea, E.D., Robert S. Fisk and Associates (ed.). 1973. *Faculty Unions and Collective Bargaining* (London: Jossey-Bass, Inc.) 24 ("Collective bargaining is a system of representative government in which members of a body politic (in labor relations parlance, the groupings of jobs constituting the bargaining unit) participate, through a designated organizational representative, in decision-making which affects their working environment—salaries, terms and conditions of employment, and other matters related to this interests as an occupational group").

14 Quoted in Herbert, William A. and Joseph McCartin. 2019 "Janus's Progeny? A Supreme Court Threat to Majority Rule Looms," *The American Prospect* (March 21) https://prospect.org/labor/janus-s-progeny-supreme-court-threat-majority-rule-looms/ [November 24, 2020].

15 29 U.S.C. 151.

16 *Id.*

17 79 Cong. Rec. 7571 < https://www.govinfo.gov/content/pkg/GPO-CRECB-1935-pt7-v79/pdf/GPO-CRECB-1935-pt7-v79-8.pdf > [November 25, 2020] While most leaders of industry steadfastly opposed the NLRA, other company officials assisted in drafting the legislation. Wartman, Rick. 2017. *The End of Loyalty: The Rise and Fall of Good Jobs in America* (New York, New York: Public Affairs) 33.

18 Herbert, William A. and Jacob Apkarian. 2017. "Everything Passes, Everything Changes: Unionization and Collective Bargaining in Higher Education," *LERA Perspectives on Work,* 30.

19 Under some public sector collective bargaining laws, a labor representative can be certified by a labor relations agency through an alternative procedure known as card check. Under a card check procedure, a representative can be selected when bargaining unit majority shows support for representation through dues deduction

authorization cards or similar written evidence. See, Gely, Rafael and Timothy Chandler. 2011. "Organizing Principles: The Significance of Card-Check Laws," *Saint Louis University Public Law Review*. Vol. 30, No. 2, 475–516.

20   The likelihood of conflicts of interest between full-time and part-time faculty is one reason the NLRB ruled that they should be in separate bargaining units. *New York University*. 221 NLRB 1148 (1975).

21   Lieberwitz, Risa L. 1987. "Due Process and the LMRDA: An Analysis of Democratic Rights in the Union and at the Workplace," 29 *Boston College Law Review* 21 (December). The federal law was enacted in 1959 with bipartisan support following disclosure of corruption and undemocratic practices in certain unions.

22   The availability of alternatives is frequently unknown to university and college leaders because few "have labor relations expertise or decision-making styles conducive to effective institutional responses to union organizing drive." Julius, Daniel J. 2004. "Will Universities Lock Out Students?" *Academe*, Vol. 90, No. 1 (Jan. – Feb.), 36. Nevertheless, the choices made, and the actions taken, will reflect on an institution's priorities, pressures, and values.

23   The United States Supreme Court has recognized that "the economic dependence of the employees on their employer" must be considered in determining the lawfulness of employer speech and conduct concerning a representation effort. *NLRB. v. Gissel Packing Co.*, 395 U.S. 575, 617–18 (1969).

24   Dullea, Henrick N. 2003. How Cornell Beat a Union by Letting TA's Vote. *The Chronicle of Higher Education,* January 17 https://www.chronicle.com/article/how-cornell-beat-a-union-by-letting-tas-vote/ [January 1, 2021].

25   University of Michigan Board of Regents. 2020. "Board Resolution Regarding Employer Neutrality, Cooperative Determination and Recognition of Bargaining Units, and Notification of Agreements" (June 25, 27–33) https://regents.umich.edu/files/meetings/07-20/2020-07-I-1.pdf [November 27, 2020]. Jane McAlevey has identified distinct union strategies and outcomes when facing a practical-pragmatic employer rather than an ideologically anti-union employer. McAlevey, Jane F. 2016. *No Shortcuts: Organizing for Power in the New Gilded Age* (New York, New York: Oxford University Press) 62–66.

26   Herbert, William A. 2017. "The History Books Tell It? Collective Bargaining in Higher Education in the 1940s" *Journal of Collective Bargaining in the Academy*: Vol. 9, Article 3, 4–9 https://works.bepress.com/william_herbert/34/ [December 10, 2020].

27   Herbert, "The History Books Tell It?" 26–36. In comparison, Columbia University thwarted organizing efforts by its non-academic employees in the 1940s and 1950s through successful litigation to have it exempted from state and federal collective bargaining laws. *Trustees of Columbia University,* 295 N.Y. 605 (1945); *The Trustees of Columbia University in the City of New York*, 97 NLRB 424 (1951).

28   Nevada System of Higher Education, Professional Employee Collective Bargaining Regulations, Codification of Board Policy Statements, Chapter 4 http://system.nevada.edu/tasks/sites/Nshe/assets/File/BoardOfRegents/Handbook/T4CH04Pro fessionalStaffCollectiveBargainingRegulations.pdf [November 25, 2020].

29   Herbert, Apkarian, and van der Naald. 2020 Supplementary Directory, Table 5.

30   Logan, John. 2006. "The Union Avoidance Industry in the USA," *British Journal of Industrial Relations*, 44:4 (December) 651–675; Logan, John. 2020. "The labor-busting law firms and consultants that keep Google, Amazon and other workplaces union-free," *The Conversation* (Aug. 24) https://theconversation.com/the-labor-busting-law-firms-and-consultants-that-keep-google-amazon-and-other-workplaces-union-free-144254 [November 29, 2020].

31   Mishel, Lawrence, Lynn Rhinehart, and Lane Windham. 2020. "Explaining the Erosion of Private-Sector Unions" (Washington, D.C. Economic Policy Institute)

https://www.epi.org/unequalpower/publications/private-sector-unions-corporate-legal-erosion/?s=03 [November, 18].

32 Hendrickson, Robert H., Jason E. Lane, James T. Harris, and Richard H. Dorman. 2013. *Academic Leadership and Governance of Higher Education: A Guide for Trustees, Leaders, and Aspiring Leaders of Two- and Four-Year Institutions* (Sterling, Virginia: Stylus Publishing Inc.).

33 McCartin, Joseph A. 2016. "Bargaining for the Common Good," *Dissent* (Spring) https://www.dissentmagazine.org/article/bargaining-common-good-community-union-alignment [December 1, 2020].

34 Julius, Daniel J. and Nicholas DiGiovanni, Jr. 2016. "What Factors Affect the Time It Takes to Negotiate Faculty Collective Bargaining Agreements?" *Journal of Collective Bargaining in the Academy*, Vol. 8, No. 6, 5. https://thekeep.eiu.edu/cgi/viewcontent.cgi?article=1649&context=jcba.

35 Bureau of Labor Statistics, TED: The Economics Daily, Union membership rate 10.5 percent in 2018, down from 20.1 percent in 1983 (Jan. 25, 2019). https://www.bls.gov/opub/ted/2019/union-membership-rate-10-point-5-percent-in-2018-down-from-20-point-1-percent-in-1983.htm [January 1, 2021].

36 Schuster, Jack H. and Martin J. Finkelstein. 2006. *The American Faculty: The Restructuring of Academic Work and Careers* (Baltimore, Maryland. Johns Hopkins University) 40–41, 191; Bowen, William G., and Eugene M. Tobin. 2015. *Locus of Authority: The Evolution of Faculty Roles in the Governance of Higher Education* (Princeton, New Jersey: Princeton University Press) 153. The movement in higher education labor relations toward a two-tiered system with low-wage temporary labor force is not unique. See, Hyman, Louis. 2018. *Temp: The Real Story of What Happened to Your Salary, Benefits, and Job Security* (New York, New York: Viking Press); Wartman, *The End of Loyalty*.

37 Kemerer and Baldridge. 64–67. There are, of course, a multitude of other factors, but wages, benefits and job security are among the most important. Kemerer and Baldridge, pp. 38–69. See also, Ladd and Lipset, 25–46.

38 Garbarino, Faculty Bargaining: 56–57.

39 Directory of Contracts and Bargaining Agents in Institutions of Higher Education. 1976. (New York New York: National Center for the Study of Collective Bargaining in Higher Education, April), 1, Chart 1. http://www.hunter.cuny.edu/ncscbhep/assets/files/directory%20april%201976.pdf [December 5, 2020].

40 Douglas, Joel M. with Elisabeth A. Kotch. 1986. *Directory of Faculty Contracts and Bargaining Agents in Institutions of Higher Education and the Professions* (New York, New York: National Center for the Study of Collective Bargaining in Higher Education, January), 105, Table 4.

41 Hurd, Richard and Amy Foerster with Beth Hillman Johnson. 1996. *Directory of Faculty Contracts and Bargaining Agents in Institutions of Higher Education in the Professions* (New York, New York: National Center for the Study of Collective Bargaining in Higher Education, January), 119, Table One.

42 Moriarty, Joan and Michelle Savarese. 2006. *Directory of Faculty Contracts and Bargaining Agents in Institutions of Higher Education and the Professions* (New York, New York: National Center for the Study of Collective Bargaining in Higher Education, January), 89–90. Table 9a.

43 Moriarty and Savarese, 86–87, Tables 9a and 9b. The study reported nine additional public sector units at higher education institutions with both two and four-year campuses. Table 9a.

44 Berry, Joe and Michelle Savarese. xi. Chart 1a; Herbert, Apkarian, and van der Naald, 14; Table 6.

45 Berry and Savarese, xi. Chart 1a; Herbert, Apkarian, and van der Naald, 14; Table 6.

46 Berry and Savarese, xiv, Chart 9; Herbert, Apkarian, and van der Naald, Table 6.

47 Herbert, William A., and Joseph van der Naald. 2020. "A Different Set of Rules? NLRB Proposed Rule Making and Student Worker Unionization Rights." *Journal of Collective Bargaining in the Academy*, Vol. 11, no. 1, pp. 9–10.

48 Herbert, Apkarian, and van der Naald, 20.

49 Herbert, Apkarian, and van der Naald, Table 4.

50 Julius, Daniel J. and Patricia J. Gumport. 2003. "Graduate Student Unionization: Catalysts and Consequences." *The Review of Higher Education*, Vol. 26, no. 2, pp. 187–216.

51 Berry and Savarese, xii, Chart 8; Herbert, Apkarian, and van der Naald Tables 4 and 6.

52 Ladd, Jr., and Lipset. Professors 16 ("Faculty employed in the lower tier of academe—in terms of scholarly prestige, financial resources, and economic benefits—and those who are in the lower ranks, lack tenure, and who are younger, are much more likely to favor organized collective action"); DeCew, 13; Altbach, 242.

53 McNicolas, Celine, Margaret Poydock, Julia Wolfe, Ben Zipperer, Gordon Lafer, and Lola Loustaunau. 2019. "Unlawful" (Washington, D.C. Economic Policy Institute, December) https://www.epi.org/publication/unlawful-employer-opposition-to-union-election-campaigns/ [December 11, 2020].

54 444 U.S. 672 (1980).

55 DeCew, 44–49.

56 Shaw, Patrick. 2006. "Prospects for Full-Time Faculty Organizing at Private Universities and Colleges," in Ernst Benjamin and Michael Mauer (eds.), *Academic Collective Bargaining* (Washington D.C: American Association of University Professors and Modern Library Association), 78–96; DeCew, 45, 49.

57 National Labor Relations Board Freedom of Information Act Responses, NLRB Case No. LR-2017–0964 (May 11, 2017) and NLRB Case No. 2020–0423 (June 1, 2020) (in possession of author).

58 Shaw, 91.

59 *National Labor Relations Board v. Catholic Bishop of Chicago*, 440 U.S. 490 (1979); *University of Great Falls v. National Labor Relations*, 278 F.3d 1335 (D.C. Cir. 2002).

60 Herbert, Apkarian, and van der Naald, 14, footnote 8.

61 Donn, Clifford B. and Brenda J. Kirby, "Research Panel, An Inside Look at an Adjunct Faculty Unionization Campaign: The Case of Le Moyne," *Journal of Collective Bargaining in the Academy*, (April 2018) Art. 47, 5.

62 Quoted in Herbert and van der Naald, "A Different Set of Rules?" 7.

63 Herbert and van der Naald, "A Different Set of Rules?" 10.

64 Herbert, Apkarian, and van der Naald, 19, Chart 8.

65 Herbert, Apkarian, and van der Naald, 17, Table 3.

66 Herbert, Apkarian, and van der Naald, 17–19, Chart 7.

67 Bowen and Tobin, 152.

68 Schuster and Finkelstein, 40–41; Bowen and Tobin, 153; Kezar and DePaola, "Understanding the Need for Unions: Contingent Faculty Working Conditions and the Relationship to Student Learning," 30; Scott, Daniel and Adrianna J. Kezar. 2019. "Intergroup Solidarity and Collaboration in Higher Education Organizing and Bargaining in the United States," *Academic Labor: Research and Artistry*: Vol. 3, Art. 10, 30.

69 Berry, Joe. 2005. *Reclaiming the Ivory Tower: Organizing Adjuncts to Change Higher Education* (New York, New York.: Monthly Review Press).

70 Herbert, Apkarian, and van der Naald, 15–16, footnotes 10 and 12.

71 AAUP Report, "The Inclusion in Governance of Faculty Members Holding Contingent Appointments" (January 2013) https://www.aaup.org/report/inclusion-governance-faculty-members-holding-contingent-appointments [January 4, 2021].

72 Wertsch, Nicholas M. Wertsch and Joseph A. McCartin. 2018. "A Just Employment Approach to Adjunct Unionization: The Georgetown Model" in Kim Tolley. (ed.) *Professors in the Gig Economy: Unionizing Adjunct Faculty in America* (Baltimore, Maryland: Johns Hopkins University Press) 87–103.

73 Tolley, Kim, Marianne Delaporte, and Lorenzo Giachetti, "Unionizing Adjunct and Tenure-Track Faculty at Notre Dame de Namur University" in Kim Tolley (ed.), 115–116.

74 Herbert, Apkarian, and van der Naald, 14.

75 Beyer, Gerald J. 2021. *Just Universities: Catholic Social Teaching Confronts Corporatized Higher Education* (New York, New York: Fordham University Press), 47–89; Gregory, David L. 2016. Is Religious Liberty the Ultimate Management Prerogative? Some Reflections on Pacific Lutheran University and Service Employees International Union, Local 925, 33 *Hofstra Labor & Emp. Law. Journal* 207 (Spring) 238. *See also,* Gregory, David L. and Charles J. Russo. 1999 "The First Amendment and the Labor Relations of Religiously-Affiliated Employers," 8 Boston University Public Interest Law Journal 449, n. 40 (Spring). The relationship between Catholic social teaching and labor rights was examined in a panel discussion at the National Center's 2021 annual conference with Gerald J. Beyer, Associate Professor of Christian Ethics, Villanova University, Patricia McGuire, President, Trinity Washington University, Mary-Antoinette Smith, Professor, English, and Executive Director, National Association for Women in Catholic Higher Education, Seattle University, Lily Ryan, Organizer, Kalmanovitz Initiative for Labor and the Working Poor, Georgetown University, and Donna Haverty-Stacke, Professor, History, Hunter College, CUNY, Moderator https://www.youtube.com/watch?v=DZ6zeQx56_Q.

76 *Duquesne University of the Holy Spirit v. National Labor Relations Board,* 947 F.3d 824 (D.C. Cir., 2020), *pet for en banc rev denied,* 975 F.3d 13 (2020).

77 The complex issues relating to unionization at religiously affiliated institutions was the subject of a recorded discussion at the National Center's 2015 annual conference. The panel was titled "Impact of Pacific Lutheran on Collective Bargaining at Catholic Colleges and Universities" and the participants were: Nicholas P. Cafardi, Dean Emeritus & Professor of Law, School of Law, Duquesne University, Michael P. Moreland, Vice Dean & Professor of Law, Villanova University School of Law. Maryann Parker, Associate General Counsel, SEIU, Clayton Sinyai, Director, Catholic Employer Project and David L. Gregory, Dorothy Day Professor of Law & Executive Director, Center for Labor & Employment Law, St. John's University School of Law, Moderator http://silo.hunter.cuny.edu/xglL0KRt.

78 Hurd, Richard W. Hurd. Ruth Milkman and Lowell Turner. 2003. "Reviving the American Labour Movement: Institutions and Mobilization," *European Journal of Industrial Relations* 9(1), 99–117.

79 Moriarty and Savarese, 87, Table 7b.

80 Herbert, Apkarian, and van der Naald, 16, 78, Table 6; Berry and Savarese, 11, Table 2.

81 Herbert, Apkarian, and van der Naald, 17, Chart 4.

82 Herbert, Apkarian, and van der Naald, Table 2.

83 DeCew, 18–25.

84 Herbert, Apkarian, and van der Naald, Table 2; Herbert, Apkarian, and van der Naald, 18–19, Chart 7.

85 See, Greenhouse, Steven. 2019. *Beaten Down, Worked Up: The Past, Present, and Future of American Labor* (New York, New York: Anchor Books) 232–252.

86 Herbert, Apkarian, and van der Naald, 20–21, Chart 14, Table 5.

87 Herbert, Apkarian, and van der Naald, 20–21, Chart 14, Table 5a.

88 Herbert, Apkarian, and van der Naald, 20, Tables 2 and 4.

89 Herbert, Apkarian, and van der Naald, 20–24, Tables 4 and 5.

90 Kezar, DePaola, and Scott, 53–67.

91 Kroeger, Teresa, Celine McNicholas, Marni von Wiplert and Julia Wolfe. 2018. *The State of Graduate Student Employee Unions: Momentum to Organize Among Graduate Student Workers Is Growing Despite Opposition.* Washington, D.C.: Economic Policy Institute. https://www.epi.org/publication/graduate-student-emp loyee-unions/ [December 10, 2020].

92 Camacho, Sayil and Robert A. Rhoads, "Breaking the Silence: The Unionization of Postdoctoral Workers at the University of California," *Journal of Higher Education*, Vol. 86, No. 2 (March/April 2015) 299.

93 Herbert, Apkarian, and van der Naald, Table 5. An empirical analysis of the provisions in 42 collective bargaining agreements applicable to student workers at public and private institutions in 2019 is contained in Herbert and van der Naald, "A Different Set of Rules" 20–28.

94 Herbert, Apkarian, and van der Naald, 20, Tables 2 and 4.

95 *The Trustees of Columbia University in the City of New York*, 364 NLRB No. 90 (2016).

96 Berry and Savarese, xii, Charts 7 and 8; Herbert, Apkarian, and van der Naald, Charts 10 and 11.

97 Herbert, Apkarian, and van der Naald, Tables 4 and 5.

98 Herbert, Apkarian, and van der Naald, 20, 22, Tables 4 and 5.

99 Herbert, Apkarian, and van der Naald, 20, 22, Chart 10.

100 *The Trustees of Columbia University*, 9–13. *See also* Julius, "Will Universities Lock Out Students?" 36 ("Institutions have greeted graduate student unionization by seeking legal counsel often familiar with hard-nosed 'no representation' campaigns and lockouts. Not only are decision-making structures inadequate to manage unionization, the arguments used to dampen employee enthusiasm – that unions destroy professionalism, harm teacher-mentor relationships, lead to increased litigation costs, damage learning environments, and result in greater conflict – are also largely unsubstantiated (and not persuasive to state and federal labor boards.") Opposition to graduate assistant unionization can also come from faculty. See, Harvey, Marcus. 2006. "Graduate Employee Organizing and Representation" in Benjamin, Ernst and Michael Mauer, ed., *Academic Collective Bargaining*. Washington D.C. and New York, New York: American Association of University Professors and Modern Language Association, 141("Graduate employee activists can experience profound disillusionment when respected professors, noted liberals and Marxists among them, fall in line with the forces marshalling in opposition to unionization").

101 Herbert and Apkarian. "You've Been with the Professors"; National Center Work Stoppage Data Report for Calendar Year 2019.

102 Herbert and Apkarian. "You've Been with the Professors." 256–260.

103 National Center Work Stoppage Data Report for Calendar Year 2019.

104 Herbert and Apkarian. "You've Been with the Professors." 268–270.

105 University of New Mexico and United Academics of the University of New Mexico. 2020. Memoranda of Understanding (August 19); University of New Mexico and United Academics of the University of New Mexico. 2020. Memorandum of Agreement "Voluntary Retirement Incentive Option-Faculty" (August 19).

106 Holloway, James Paul and United Academics of the University of New Mexico.2020. Covid Joint Communication (September 3) https://provost.unm.edu/faculty-unio nization/docs/joint-comm-docs/covid-joint-communication-09-2020-03.pdf.

107 University of New Mexico and United Academics of the University of New Mexico. 2020. "Temporary and Voluntary Reduction (TVR) in Full-Time Equivalent (FTE) for Spring 2021 for Unit 1 Faculty" (October 21).

108 Hoffman, Elizabeth and John Hess, "Organizing for Equality within the Two-Tier System".2014. Keith Hoeller (ed.), *Equality for Contingent Faculty: Overcoming the Two-Tier System* (Nashville, Tennessee: Vanderbilt University Press) 9–27.

109 California Faculty Association and California State University. 2020. Memorandum "Extension of Current Collective Bargaining Agreement," (May 20); California Faculty Association and California State University. 2020. "Summer 2020 Professional Development and Training for Faculty as a Result of COVID-19" (May 22); California Faculty Association and California State University. 2020. "Impacts related to COVID-19 on Operations" (June 5); California Faculty Association and California State University. 2020. "Impacts related to COVID-19 on Coach Evaluations" (August 4) (in possession of author).

110 Columbia College Chicago and Columbia College Faculty Union.2020. "COVID-19 Pandemic Phase 1" (March 26); Columbia College Chicago and Columbia College Faculty Union,.2012. "COVID-19 Pandemic Phase 2"; Columbia College Chicago and Columbia College Faculty Union. 2020. "Chair Access to Canvas" (April 8).

111 UFF-FSU-GAU and FSU-BOT. 2020. "COVID-19 Health Emergency" (September 28) (in possession of author).

112 Kemerer and Baldridge, 64–67.

8

COLLECTIVE BARGAINING AND SOCIAL JUSTICE IN THE POST-COVID DIGITAL ERA[1]

Daniel J. Julius

Background

This chapter examines social justice and collective bargaining with a focus on higher education. Observations are offered around the following issues: a) a brief history of social justice as it has been conceptualized in labor management relations with a particular focus on unions in higher education; b) identification of collective bargaining scenarios when social justice platforms may have a more salient impact on negotiations; c) actions and strategies the parties might consider to accommodate social justice concerns in the bargaining process; and d) measuring and assessing collective bargaining outcomes. Collective bargaining in post-secondary institutions remains a complex phenomenon where political and legal guidelines are evolving particularly in a post-Covid environment. Accurate assessment of bargaining outcomes presents a variety of methodological challenges some of which are discussed in this chapter.

A Complex Context

The relationship between "social justice" and "collective bargaining," is interwoven, complicated and long standing. Making sense out of what is transpiring on campuses today with respect to these two concepts requires an understanding of the definitions used to characterize these terms, the interpretation of "social justice" over time, the arc of social movements in the U.S., and the nuts and bolts of collective negotiations (which involve table dynamics and the legal and legislative parameters framing labor management interaction). To

DOI: 10.4324/9781003138990-9

complicate matters, these relationships have undergone strain as the pandemic elucidates underlying weaknesses of current operational models and has accelerated trends less visible prior to the pandemic. One observation is increasingly clear; even with state and federal stimulus funds, coupled with an effective Covid vaccine, the post-secondary landscape (with the exception of the largest and wealthiest schools) will probably not look as it did prior to the pandemic. The same may be said of labor management relations, which has seen changes in processes during the rise of the digital university. Many practitioners believe we will not see a return to what was euphemistically referred to as normal for years. Given the above observations, what might we say about the future of social justice and collective bargaining in higher education in the coming years?

Do We Share Common Assumptions?

Whether social justice issues inform collective bargaining processes at all reveals a cacophony of ideas, values, opinions and views, some of which are connected to what actually occurs in collective bargaining negotiations, others not. To be sure, there are many facets of labor management relationships, less ideological in scope, which should not be framed under a social justice banner. These contract discussions, particularly with unions in place for years, may simply involve the give and take over contract reopeners, extensions, or traditional (and narrower) scope of bargaining matters; wages, hours and working conditions. Social justice concerns invariably represent broader societal issues and revolve around the correction of perceived injustices to various social groups.[2] When combined with labor management relations, which revolve around power and influence shaped by legal precedent, legislation, politics, and the "hammer and anvil" of the bargaining process, outcomes are varied and difficult to predict.

Contemporary points of view on the efficacy of social justice reflect differences in opinion over the meaning of social justice, how it impacts collective bargaining, the role of unions, universities and their obligations to society, the rights of those attempting to unionize, the ethics or lack of them inherent in capitalism, Catholic and Protestant social teachings, community organizing, institutionalized racism, diversity, inclusion, and salary equity. Many of these concepts are echoed in the current debate and sometimes find their way into negotiations involving particular employee groups. Moreover, as unionization drives are increasingly successful, particularly for adjuncts, part-time employees and graduate students, social justice concerns may eventually focus on the considerable inequities between working conditions and benefits for full-time faculty with tenure (compensation, teaching loads, etc.) and everyone else at the university save for a handful of senior administrators, many of whom had tenure and full professorships before becoming administrators.

The relationship between issues being discussed in this chapter and negotiations processes is further complicated because "social justice," as mentioned previously, is also raised on campus through student boycotts, legislative lobbying or other forms of advocacy simultaneously with or away from the bargaining process. "Social justice" has also been discussed in the context of other initiatives in higher education normally unrelated to collective bargaining, for example, student success, enhancing graduation and retention rates and the like. Here again, definitions and intent are important. If for example by social justice we mean protecting employees from arbitrary decision making, unfair terminations, equal pay for equal work, or fair and equitable grievance and arbitration provisions, such matters are central to labor management relationships. If, however, by social justice we are referring to more expansive anti-discrimination protections, fair trade policies, anti-poverty initiatives, anti-globalization campaigns, race, gender and human rights issues, these concerns, however important, are not often well accommodated in bargaining. Generally, the further away "social justice" is from the heart of labor management relationships, the more likely these union demands will be found not to be mandatorily negotiable and dropped at the bargaining table, particularly if compensation packages are improved or legal actions taken. The above notwithstanding, with the advent of the Biden administration, calls for reciprocity, fairness, equity and justice might be taken more seriously as constituencies who claim credit for the Biden-Harris ticket ask for what many would characterize as long overdue measures to address social justice concerns.

There is an old adage in labor relations among practitioners that suggests one's point of view is determined by what side of the table one sits. There is another quip about tables and universities applicable here which posits: if we were to construct a table with enough sides for all constituencies with a rightful claim to the university, it would need to be a round table. With these two "table" caveats in mind, this chapter will endeavor to untangle issues followed by recommendations on how the parties could approach collective bargaining from a social justice perspective in the post-Covid digital era.

Labor History and Social Justice Concerns

Many would agree labor unions have historically advanced social justice. From their inception (and here again "inception" depends upon how terms are defined) the earliest attempts in the U.S. to merge social justice and assertion of worker rights dates back to 18th-century New England and the mid-Atlantic region. Industries devoted to rope and barrel making, the construction of canvass sales for ocean-going sailing vessels, and a new textile industry, provide early examples of how these concepts and ideas shaped conflicts over the rights of respective parties: the jurisdictional territories between communities, laborers and owners. Well into the 20th century, powerful elites, the courts and federal legislation defended owners in these conflicts, not workers.[3]

Early in the American labor movement we find a growing divide between those who advocated social reform and workplace democracy versus "business unionism," or what many 19th and 20th century labor leaders referred to as "bread and butter" unionism. These differences in orientations and approaches are evident today as we shall see.

A practical form of collective bargaining has transcended (with a few exceptions) more ideological approaches. This has not been the case in Europe, Latin America or South Africa. In the U.S., "ideology" has been less a factor and, in most jurisdictions, securing higher wages and better working conditions continues to drive bargaining. The old saying, "let's rise above principle and settle this contract" infuses labor management dynamics to this day. However, through the years labor unions have successfully addressed important societal issues such as child labor, the length of a working day, living wages, health and welfare, the environmental safety of workers, parental leave, medical and related benefits, and other concerns (economic prosperity, upward mobility of workers, workplace democracy) that many Americans take for granted. Such gains often came at great personal costs and sacrifices to individuals and communities. While gains made at the bargaining table have ebbed and flowed over time, depending on those who occupy state and federal offices, (did anyone ever expect to witness Michigan or Wisconsin as right-to-work states?) and some argue (with evidence) that the union movement in the private sector has been gutted since the heydays of the 1950s. In the public sector, where the major growth in unions has occurred since the 1960s, the trajectory has been toward what many would characterize as more progressive and equitable policies.

Of course, labor history is never neat and tidy. Organized crime infiltrated some unions. Nor is the record clear whether unions in general have advanced the rights of marginalized populations or women. Well into the 1950s and 1960s, many industrial and craft locals were forced to desegregate; they did not do so willingly. Police and firefighter unions in numerous cities are presently under consent decrees to hire and promote minority candidates. Add to this the perception that some union leaders are thought to exhibit lifestyles more in common with the company CEOs than with rank and file men and women. Even in constituencies where there should be support for unions, they are thought by some, across the political spectrum, to be complicit in the "structural apparatus" working to the disadvantage of marginalized populations and, over time, the entrenched power of union bureaucracies serves to protect the status quo. Of course, the situation is complex, and the dynamics, realities, outcomes and points of view around unions in education as opposed to those in manufacturing or shipping, are different. An argument can also be made when it came to broader political support (perhaps not locally) engagement in the civil rights movement among organized labor, the UAW a good example, has been consistent over many years. There are close ties between civil rights and some unions especially in the public sector (AFSCME in many places) and 1199 in New York City. What we also witnessed in 2020 election is that many white and less educated workers, the traditional base for unionism in midwestern states for example, voted for candidates hostile to collective bargaining. The tectonic plates that underlie support for unions and collective bargaining are changing in ways not entirely clear at this time and attitudes remain polarized: a legacy of the Trump era.

Social justice proponents often using the term "Bargaining for the Common Good," a newer label for social unionism, represent a vigorous faction within the labor movement. They are focused on how to win organizing campaigns, transform union campaigns into broader human rights and community action, help dues paying members connect to their union, and advance union membership for societal gains. No doubt these groups are also part of the broader movement for social justice in society which transcend narrower union issues. These goals can, and do, conflict with the practical business unionism approach of the established union leadership. Here tensions reflected in the labor movement are not unlike those in the Democratic party between those who may identify as more established centrists versus progressive left-leaning advocates. Coalitions unite to oppose a common adversary and fall apart, arguing among themselves, soon after an election.

Academe is not immune from these attitudinal and political crosscurrents and the push for "social justice" in higher education is more readily seen in negotiations involving employees (often newer unions, with less power); graduate assistants; part-time employees, adjuncts, and clerical employees. The impact of social justice concerns is more difficult to discern in negotiations involving full-time faculty, laborers, or craft locals, and the like, where contracts have been in existence 40 or 50 years or longer. Social justice concerns may be on the minds of represented faculty or craft employees, but such concerns are not often realized during negotiations. Contract clauses covering, for example, discrimination, salary distribution or "recognition" are immeasurably harder to amend once in existence for many contractual years. Particularly in the give and take of "trade-offs" involved in negotiations, the notion of "if it ain't broke don't fix it," (which, in negotiations, refers to contract clauses which have not been the subject of grievances, legal challenges or arbitrations), serves as a powerful protector of the contractual status quo.

Collective Bargaining in Higher Education

The union movement in higher education stretches back over 100 years although, in general, negotiations with legally "recognized" faculty unions did not occur until the judicial, legislative and political environments in several regions became more supportive of organizing activities in the 1960s. Unions in academe, however, predate the 1960s. The "Daily Illini" contains news of a union action by Custodians at the University of Illinois in 1917 (asking for an increase of six cents an hour in wages) and faculty locals existed in Montana and South Dakota nearly 100 years ago. No doubt there were many other attempts at organized activities. Following more favorable federal legislative and judicial treatment in the 1930s and 1940s, early craft unions appeared in the Ivy League (for example, painters at Columbia in 1938) and faculty at Howard University, Hampton Institute and the New School for Social Research, organized and were recognized in the latter 1940s.[4] However, it was not until the mid to late 1960s, following the passage of public sector labor legislation (and significant social upheaval on campus with many echoes of social justice we hear today), that unions gained a real foothold in academia commencing in New York, Michigan and Wisconsin. Bargaining for full-time faculty in the private sector also began in this era, particularly in the same states where public employees unionized. Following a Supreme Court decision in 1980 involving Yeshiva University in New York, bargaining in the private sector was curtailed particularly for units trying to gain recognition or negotiate a first-time contract. The decision had a negligible impact on established units in the private sector, for many reasons, and a majority continue to exist. The court found that such employees (but not graduate assistants/students, adjuncts or clerical groups) were generally excluded (because they exercised discretion over so many work-related matters) from coverage of the National Labor Relations Act and hence unable to claim employee status required by law to bargain collectively. Although unionization of part-time, adjunct and graduate student employees has grown considerably in the private sector since the Yeshiva decision, it is the public sector that remains the most robust for faculty where it is estimated over a third are represented, primarily in states (approximately 15) that are, or were, favorably disposed to public sector labor unions.[5] In these locales, unions representing public employees have access to state legislators who not infrequently succumb to union demands. There has been a great deal written about unions in academe, the reasons for their existence, the causes and consequences. For purposes of this chapter, the following information about collective bargaining in higher education is pertinent:

- Institutional and demographic factors shape the process. For example, bargaining with academic-related personnel and faculty is associated with larger institutions and public two-year and four-year systems in the east and mid-west and several (what are considered to be) union-friendly states (with enabling labor legislation) in the far west and Florida. Institutional prestige tends to be inversely related to the presence of unions with respect to four-year faculty (this is not the case for graduate students or assistants or adjunct/part-time faculty, where the elite private sector has become fertile ground for organizing campaigns). Parenthetically, it may not be prestige per se, but the individual and departmental autonomy, lighter workloads, and greater voice in institutional affairs full-time faculty in higher prestige institutions possess, all of which mitigate against needing a union. Such is not the same for faculty in many comprehensive state systems or two-year schools. For example, full-time faculty bargaining units exist in only five member institutions of the Association of American Universities (AAU), an association considered the most exclusive. Even here the demographics are interesting. Of the five, two (SUNY Buffalo and Stony Brook) are part of the huge New York (SUNY) public university system. The University of Oregon and University of Florida, also organized, were, but are no longer, in large state systems. Rutgers University, the other AAU member, is situated in a state with accommodating labor legislation and where all public sector colleges and universities (and most public sector employees) are unionized. The overwhelming majority of organized public sector faculty can be found in comprehensive state college systems in locales where favorable legislation supporting unionization exists or existed, and where the majority of faculty have few opportunities for mobility to other institutional sectors.

- Faculty unionization reflected, from its earliest inception, the desire to gain more control, or safeguard jurisdiction over, decision making in academic matters: the curriculum, and particularly reappointment, promotion, and tenure. Later in the 1960s and 1970s the union movement in academe may have been energized by opposition to the war in Southeast Asia, changing mores in society, permissive attitudes and the like, but I would suggest preserving hard won gains in shared governance and professional autonomy which included promotion and tenure processes were the primary factors. During this era, a rise in student power and student rights sometimes intersected with the rise of faculty unions and at other times did not. Whether or not these two movements reinforced or negated each other is at best speculative. No doubt the reaction to what was perceived as arbitrary decision making and heavy-handed management of university leaders, over teaching schedules and workload, research and other funding priorities spurred organizing activities. These trends emanated, in the eyes of organized labor and many faculty, from the corporatization of academe, the nexus of academic and the military industrial complex, and later, a decline in state and federal support leading to the need for alternative revenue sources, downsizing and the like, in response to fiscal and enrollment-related factors. This was definitely not the view from those leading institutions; their reality was and remains very different; shaped by enrollment, student demand, funding and political factors. The rise of unions in the public sector correlates with favorable legislation incorporating public sector labor boards to oversee unionization. Many unions may have also reached out to new clienteles for dues in the wake of declining traditional employee bases. Faculty in public institutions soon found they were the only groups at state capitals lacking union representation, and because of this, were without concomitant leverage needed to pressure state legislators and other elected officials to assign greater resources to post-secondary education. Deliberative processes associated with senates and shared governance in general (some of which did not even operate in the summer) were not initially able to accommodate themselves to the realities of decision making environments, as internal and external forces buffeted the academy in the 1960s and 1970s. Unions represented a more effective way to assert voice. The desire to preserve professional autonomy, shared decision making and safeguard the status quo were more salient than economic concerns for faculty who sought to unionize in these years. After all, in comparison to many in the labor movement, the vast number of full-time faculty have exceptional working conditions, salaries and benefit packages compared to (with a few notable exceptions in arts, entertainment and professional sports) other unionized workers. The union movement commencing in the 1960s was largely non-ideological and focused on "boiler plate" contract matters. These included; recognition of bargaining agents, preservation of craft-like or professional authority over entrance into and promotion through academic ranks as well as academic freedom, workload, grievance and arbitration provisions, and equitable layoff clauses. What occurred in academe from a labor relations perspective did not mirror collective bargaining in numerous industries. There remain unique aspects of labor agreements, for example, the preservation of academic freedom and "academic judgement" which is normally withheld from arbitral review.[6]

• Non-ideological approaches prevail in more established relationships and unions representing faculty have partnered, and in some cases merged, with other unions regardless of organizational differences or ideology. For example, more full-time faculty are represented by joint affiliations of the AFT, NEA or AAUP then are represented by a single bargaining agent. This has not been the case with graduate students, clerical or adjunct/part-time employees. Here, many of the more established academic unions appeared to be reluctant, for a variety of reasons, to represent units comprised solely of graduate students or assistants, particularly at elite private schools (where faculty were not represented) or in larger state systems.[7] More often than not, bargaining representative for these groups, where their status as employees is often contested, tend to be unions characterized as "industrial unions" (UAW, CWA, UE, SEIU) many in search of new dues paying members. Perhaps, in the case of SEIU, the union may have been approached by employees in need of representation after more traditional education unions failed to accommodate certain groups. In these locales SEIU may have been well organized at the ground level and used a city-based strategy not unlike their geographic labor market strategy used for janitors in the west. Interesting however, that despite a great deal of rhetoric to the contrary, claims by one bargaining agent to be more effective than another agent in advancing the rights and benefits of one or another employee groups are suspect and few, if any, scholarly or objective studies, demonstrate this to be the case.

It is in the organizing and negotiations of "first-time" contracts covering graduate students, part-time, adjunct faculty, clerical employees where the emergence of social justice concerns are most salient. Why is this the case? To begin with, collective bargaining relationships are newer or emerging. Once contracts have been ratified and the parties are living with them, it is much harder to change existing language and, in bargaining "trade-offs," more established unions have dropped "common good" proposals in favor of economic gains. Secondly, social justice has been a potent force for organizing those who may believe themselves to be more marginalized, have fewer, if any, opportunities to exercise influence, and are non-represented. It is not surprising that contract proposals from newly organized groups reflect social justice issues.

When Social Justice Factors Influence Negotiations

The following variables determine whether social justice precepts are introduced during negotiations, possibly shape negotiation discussions, and result in contract clauses which reflect social justice concerns:

- The age of the bargaining relationship and whether the contract represents a successor agreement or first-time contract;
- The definition of the scope of bargaining in federal, state labor statutes, or scope as determined through past practice;
- The type of employee group represented and the extent to which social justice issues were utilized to initially organize them;
- The extent to which a particular faction of employees in a bargaining unit have embraced social justice and have the organizational power to ensure such concerns are acted upon;
- The views, skills, sympathies, and levels of trust between the chief negotiators. Experienced negotiators on both sides of the table find ways to introduce such precepts or, conversely, ensure they will not be advanced during negotiations;
- The primary issues framing bargaining and the extent to which leaders at (or away) from the table, agree with the broader aims of social justice and are in a position to exercise power, or absorb organizational conflict, both of which are invariably required to obtain bargaining objectives;

- The extent to which important constituencies who impact negotiations support social justice concerns/issues during negotiations;
- The agenda of bargaining agents representing employees and whether that agent also represents (and has negotiated contracts with) other employees in the same institution or system that reflect social justice precepts.

Negotiating from a Social Justice Perspective

What follows are observations on how the parties may more effectively accommodate social justice precepts during negotiations. At the outset what is being recommended work well in traditional negotiations, in fact some recommendations have been a feature of labor management relationships for the past 75 years. It may be worth noting as well that negotiating from a social justice perspective may appear superfluous to many union advocates with social justice agendas. However, the points raised here are germane to employer representatives who, in my experience, often interpret "social justice type" proposals in one of four ways: a) as needless and perhaps harmful expansion into the scope of bargaining or arbitral review; b) demands the university (or state) has little, if any, power to effectuate; c) as arguments for higher compensation based meaningful but perhaps somewhat abstract and naive funding principles; or, d) as continuation of political organizing activities by groups who may not be able to arrive at compromises needed for settlement.

Ironically, even if employer advocates sympathize with a number of social justice type proposals (and many do) the folks they report to may not, or economic realities at the present time, do not permit entertainment of demands. Beyond the narrower internal issues, however, in some locales, social justice objectives intersect with roles and responsibilities of colleges and universities in communities where they are located. Resisting proposals can be damaging politically or reputationally. Consequently, the parties may be well served to consider the following recommendations particularly as impact bargaining occurs over loss of revenues in the wake of the pandemic.

Agree Upon Shared Definitions of Social Justice and How These Definitions Apply in the Collective Bargaining Setting

Proposals that seem straightforward to union negotiators may be interpreted as so far out of scope to employers they may be reluctant, for a variety of legal and political reasons, to discuss them. For example, demands to demilitarize or defund campus police departments may be put on the table and no doubt reflect broader societal concerns with police and the rights of marginalized populations. In such cases proposals which may seem morally or ethically sound to one party may be viewed with extreme skepticism by the other, thought to be beyond the scope of bargaining, even the control of one party to address, regardless of what is negotiated. Expansion of the scope of arbitral review for non-mandatory subjects of bargaining may dissuade conversation on matters that appear basic and directly relevant to those with a social justice perspective. Shared definitions and criteria around the scope of bargaining and the costs of proposals may enable the parties to identify other kinds of approaches that will satisfy constituencies who shape bargaining from afar and, more importantly, whose support is necessary to ratify agreements.

Agree Ahead of Time on Shared Methodologies to "Cost-Out" Proposals

This is always an important feature of labor relations but particularly so in this case for several reasons. First, what might seem like a negligible cost to a bargaining agent may in fact appear overwhelmingly costly to the institution.[8]

As one example, take the matter of benefit coverage for transgender operations which may by some be considered a human right and should be included more broadly in all benefit packages. While such procedures may be a negligible expense for employees in one bargaining unit, institutions, should they agree to provide coverage, may be legally obligated to provide such benefits to all employee groups. In such cases costs assume a different proportion, and what may appear to be "fair and equitable" to one party may be unaffordable to the other.

Changing institutional budget and resource priorities in a post-Covid era, when unionized institutions will become more, not less, dependent on state and federal support (and when elected officials will be more concerned with the economy in general) is fraught with pitfalls and may require agreement of important external constituencies and reconsideration of tuition (not always under the control of university officials), revenue streams, deferred maintenance, operating expenditures, and the like. If agreement can be reached beforehand on meaningful institutional "comparators" and costing methodologies, (always important in all negotiations) arguments can be ameliorated to the benefit of the parties. Take the seemingly straightforward issue of a "living wage" which is often predicated on factors associated with the cost of living (COL) in a particular locale. Agreement on a COL cost methodology could advance negotiations and arguments on whether the COL is similar or different in Berkeley, New Haven, Cambridge or Ann Arbor. In fact, such arguments can delay negotiations for months, perhaps to the detriment of all concerned.

Educate All Parties About the Fundamentals of Collective Bargaining and Possibilities Inherent in Established Processes to Address Challenging Social Justice Issues

Unions representing graduate students in particular often appear not to have a firm grasp on or choose to ignore for whatever reasons, many of the essential basics of negotiations in place for nearly a century. For example, appointing "team coordinators" or "revolving negotiators" as chief spokespersons may seem reasonable to some union advocates and ridiculous and non-productive to experienced employer representatives. Better understanding of what constitutes an "unfair labor practice" or an "end run," and how such tactics derail negotiations and destroy trust between the parties (the latter almost always essential for final settlement) will advance discussions. The value of arriving at a "tentative agreement" (and knowing what that means in the bargaining context) is important if bargaining is to be productive. The importance of establishing and adhering to "ground rules," why tweeting or taping bargaining sessions, or viewing compromise as capitulation (the above lead to non-productive outcomes), should be understood. Negotiations will not conclude effectively if viewed as political theater, but operate well when long-standing best practices, procedures and guidelines are employed. For example, employing "side bar" discussions or union-management committees (which are given a defined scope, timelines, and meet away from the table, making recommendations to the parties) constitute an effective approach; one used successfully for the last 75 years to resolve contract disputes. This strategy, recently used by the University of California in negotiations with the UAW proved effective in addressing social justice issues.[9] To complicate matters, the legal environment for labor management relations for some groups (graduate students in the private sector) is still evolving; additional reasons to ensure the parties are cognizant of time-tested methods to resolve disputes.

Social Media and Its Impact on Negotiations

Bargaining with a group more adroit in the use of social media can confound those who may not be as conversant with these communications and organizing strategies. Graduate students or teaching assistants for example, may be less sophisticated (or influential) around reaching settlement at the bargaining table but more effective using social media for leverage, political disruption or continuation of the organizing process. Bargaining reflects the exercise of power and influence. In this respect pitfalls exist for professionals at the bargaining table. For example, a skilled negotiator may not take seriously the political theater unfolding at the table or on campus. However, Presidents and Provosts may be sensitive to legislators and board members who want to know why disruption on campus is occurring. Those in power have adversaries and competitors who skillfully use such scenarios to demonstrate why a particular leader in charge cannot manage the situation (and therefore should not be in charge). Presidents and Provosts may not be familiar with (or may not have time to study) the give and take at the table, the details of proposals and counter-proposals, or legal challenges winding their way through labor boards or courts. Often these individuals have been told by well-meaning experts that there are "ground rules" to prevent social media campaigns, and that theatrics at the table, or "legal challenges" have no merit. While the above may be true, people in charge get concerned when students, alumni, legislators or full-time faculty, may be influenced by social media, and start calling about ongoing conflict involving other groups beyond the union trying to reach agreement. Presidents may be vulnerable if they appear unable to resolve conflict without effectively communicating why. University representatives would do well to prepare for wider social media campaigns that inevitably accompany negotiations. Employer side bargainers, particularly in larger institutions, may be challenged on how to keep senior leaders (often many administrative levels above them) informed. In addition, a number of the union leaders involved are often unfamiliar with post-secondary education cultures and therefore reluctant or unable to exercise authority at the table. Add to this mix, and in my experience, that departmental faculty will be inclined to side with graduate students or research assistants and will exercise real pressure on Deans and others to admit them back into the classroom regardless of the tactics, legal maneuvers, or demands made during negotiations. What may seem like nonsensical or ineffective bargaining to professionals at the table may be taken in a very different light by senior academic leadership or others away from the table. The result will be far less leverage in bargaining than might be suspected by those representing the university (or in some cases the union) unless issues discussed here are planned for in advance.

Measuring and Assessing Collective Bargaining

Attempts to measure and assess collective bargaining in higher education, especially in the areas of social justice, fall into two general categories. The first has to do with research on the impact of bargaining on human resources, institutional autonomy, or decision-making processes in the organized college or university. The second has to do with measuring or assessing the impact of collective bargaining on progress the parties may make toward realizing particular institutional or organizational goals and objectives. With respect to the first area, a considerable degree of research on these matters exists and much of the evidence is inconclusive, which is not surprising considering that bargaining processes and outcomes are very difficult to untangle and separate from other forces buffeting the academy. This is certainly the case with more expansive social justice issues. Moreover, upon closer scrutiny, generalizations are difficult because of the substantive differences in mission, funding formulas, other institutional and demographic variables, between the types of colleges and universities where collective bargaining is found. For example, on the general questions of whether unions are associated with higher salaries for college and university employees, or have benefitted employees from marginalized or underrepresented groups, there is evidence going back 40 years which supports these assertions and evidence that negates them. Collective bargaining itself has not been found for example, to have a deleterious impact on institutional quality, the manner in which curriculum is developed, the student mentor relationship, professionalism of faculty, affirmative action, scholarly productivity, student success or graduation rates and shared governance, most conclude, has by and large coexisted with unions. Whether unions per se protect the jobs of the less competent, those on part-time contracts, curtail academic freedom, or alter existing promotion and tenure processes or standards, is also not found to be the case across the board, although no doubt this has happened on some campuses.

The extent to which social justice concerns are accommodated as a result of bargaining will depend on how focused the parties were on such matters (and how close they were to the scope of bargaining) at the time negotiations commenced. The above also depends on the union or university leadership and how their experiences and perceptions of "history" shape bargaining dynamics.

A number of the earliest predictions made about unions in academe have been difficult to assess because many predictions were based on attitudinal surveys which proved incorrect when it came to predict actual labor management outcomes.[10]

This is not to suggest that bargaining has been without any impact whatsoever. It has, but not in ways envisioned by those studying these processes initially. Bargaining has changed decision making by moving authority upward to legal, labor relations and state offices, codified handbook policies and made them more consistent and subject to grievance procedures ending in arbitral review. The latter giving a final decision-making authority on contractual matters (grieved to arbitrators, not university administrators) and thus representing a real change in control over contractual policies and procedures. Certainly, the type of "old time" administrator who made individual arrangements with faculty (on workload for example) does not often survive in an organized environment. Bargaining imposes new kinds of deadlines and accountability for decision making, provides forums that offer "newer" employee groups formal and consistent input into decision making; those not traditionally included in shared governance forums. In my experience organized faculty may have greater protection and autonomy from decisions they consider unfair or arbitrary. The manner in which conflict is managed and decisions are effectuated in unionized organizations is different than in the non-unionized. It may also be the case that more sophisticated longitudinal approaches are needed to properly discern the full impact of unionization. Non-advocacy research which purports to compare rights, privileges, working conditions, faculty voice and the like, of those in unionized institutions with those in non-unionized locales, is less common, and conducting objective studies are fraught with methodological challenges.

The second area, as stated above, concerns measuring progress the parties make toward realizing organizational objectives through collective bargaining.

In essence utilizing the bargaining process to advance goals rather than, for example, preserving the status quo (which can, in and of itself, be a laudable objective particularly at this time. Depending on which side of the table one is sitting, simply extending the current contract may be a desirable outcome). In conducting negotiations and administering contracts, research exists on best practices. Of course, it is also the case that if either party achieves what it sets out to do initially goals are accomplished (for example, gain recognition or a multi-year settlement, the latter may work to bar union competitors from trying to organize the same unit; often a union goal during the first rounds of bargaining in newer relationships). In these kinds of cases an employer or union can point to, at least for the short term, identifiable measures of success. In my own experience the bargaining process can be used to advance long-term institutional or justice type objectives under the following circumstances; where institutional leaders are supportive and willing to withstand conflict that inevitably accompanies labor management relationships where substantive changes in processes and outcomes is desired, when negotiation parameters are developed inclusively, where the legal environment presents autonomy to the parties, where a significant number of people in the respective bargaining unit may be dissatisfied with the status quo, and where requisite authority is given to and used effectively by the chief negotiators.

Advancing long-term social justice type objectives is far more difficult in politicized larger public institutions/systems where those responsible for major decisions often work in state capitols, negotiators may not be system employees, or in multi-campus systems where university leaders may compete with or distrust each other. Sometimes, the procedures and processes inherent in enabling state labor legislation governing bargaining are less accommodating to those desiring substantive changes through negotiations processes. In these contexts, there are multiple players and constituencies, many with competing agendas, and bargaining more often results in preservation of the status quo. Whether the pandemic will change these observations remains to be seen.

A Final Thought

Bargaining processes are cyclical. They reflect the needs, interests and influence of various employee groups and employers at particular historical times. Newer bargaining relationships are often focused on concerns, many of which were settled long ago in contracts for other employee groups. Once matters are negotiated and codified into collective bargaining agreements, they become, over time, the "status quo," and, as such, are more challenging to change. Tom Mannix, now long retired and one of the early pioneers of labor relations in higher education in New York, Michigan and California, once observed in regard to this matter that codification or maintenance of the status quo represents real advances to some, or a detriment to others, depending on the rights and privileges, or lack of them, the respective parties had prior to bargaining. Over time, if social justice proposals are embraced by the individuals and constituencies (labor or management) who determine bargaining outcomes, such concepts will inevitably be codified into labor agreements and become the "status quo" which will be, as they are now, the subject of debate for a future generation.

Notes

1 An earlier version of this chapter appeared in Adrianna Kezar and Julie Posselt, Eds., *Higher Education Administration for Social Justice and Equity: Critical Perspectives for Leadership*. Routledge, 2020.

2 More recently this has been referred to as Social Movement Unionism (SMU), or Social Unionism, a trend of theory and practice in contemporary trade unionism. SMU is distinct from many other models of trade unionism because it concerns itself with more than organizing workers around workplace issues, pay and terms and conditions. It engages in wider political struggles for human rights, social justice and democracy. SMU grew out of political struggles in developing countries and was theorized as a distinct industrial relations model in the late 1980s and early 1990s. In this model, trade unions are not distinct from social movements and form part of a wider ecosystem of political activism that includes faith groups, civic and residents' organizations and student groups, organized into democratic umbrella organizations and with a manifesto to which affiliates are committed. SMU attempts to integrate workers, trade unions and the labor movement into broader coalitions for social and economic justice. Thus, in theory, unions and other organizations support each other in what are seen as mutually beneficial goals.

3 The influence of the Catholic and Protestant church can be found on both sides of conflicts involving workers and owners. See, David Brody, Ed., *The American Labor Movement*. New York: Harper and Row Publishers, 1971; Lens, Sidney, *Radicalism in America*. New York: Thomas Y. Crowell Company, 1966; Daniel J. Leab, Ed., *The Labor History Reader*. Champaign Urbana: University of Illinois Press, 1985; Foner, Philip S., *History of the Labor Movement in the U.S.* Volume 1. New York: International Publishers, 1982.

4 Timothy R. Cain, "The First Attempts to Unionize the Faculty," *Teachers College Record*, Vol. 112, No. 3, March 2010; "Janitors Union Asks for a Raise" *The Daily Illini*, Vol. 46, No. 91, January 16, 1917, page 1; Julius, D. J. "The Status of Faculty and Staff Unions in Colleges and Universities: 1930s–1990s." In D.J. Julius (Ed.), *Managing the Industrial Labor Relations Process in Higher Education*. Washington, D.C.: College and University Personnel Association, 1993.; Herbert, William A. (2017). "The History Books Tell It? Collective Bargaining in the 1940s," *Journal of Collective Bargaining in the Academy*, Vol 9.

5 Herbert, William, Apkarian, Jake and Joseph van der Naald. 2020. *Supplementary Directory of New Bargaining Agents and Contracts in Institutions of Higher Education*. New York: National Center for the Study of Collective Bargaining in Higher Education and the Professions, Hunter College, CUNY, 2020.

6 It might be of interest to note that arbitrators who work in industry, those who adjudicate disputes in the NFL or NBA, or for unions representing city or state workers, teachers, firefighters, police, ballet dancers, journalists or airline pilots, serve as arbitrators for colleges and universities. Collective bargaining has proved itself to be very elastic and flexible. The industrial labor relations environment has accommodated unionized colleges and universities regardless of how unique faculty or

administrators believe their working arrangements and institutional cultures are. Arguments around "professionalism versus unionism" were brought forward by those scholars who wrote in the 1970s about the emergence of collective bargaining for faculty. These concerns were eventually muted due to a lack of evidence to substantiate such claims and as industrial labor relations processes, precedents and procedures from industry and other public sector jurisdictions, were adopted and adapted in academic organizations. By the early 1990's, none other than Clark Kerr, former President of the University of California, and an industrial labor relations scholar, identified faculty unionization as an extension of shared governance and a formalized assertion of professional rights. A very cogent argument can be made which suggests collective bargaining has preserved professional or craft-like pre-rogatives and rights. Information on the numbers of faculty unionized, their bargaining agents and the like, can be found at the National Center for the Study of Collective Bargaining in Higher Education and the Professions, http://www.hunter.cuny.edu/ncscbhep.

7 In recent years the AFT has been active organizing graduate students at elite institutions (Cornell, Brown, University of Chicago, Georgetown and Pennsylvania among others). It would also appear that social unionism is stronger in graduate student union campaigns.

8 The lack of tax revenue stemming from pandemic-related challenges to the economy will make economic factors far more salient in the future. While the parties may initially delay tough decisions in the hope stimulus funds address shortfalls in state and federal support, it is probably the case that more furloughs and layoffs are on the horizon. Unfortunately, this may occur in more tuition-dependent schools with declining enrolment and at state schools (less in flagship institutions) in larger systems; schools with less political clout, and where identities, missions and outcomes may be less evident to funding authorities.

9 At the University of California the UAW (a union with a social justice agenda) clearly articulated concerns for human rights and discrimination issues and proposed the following; divestment of retirement funds in fossil fuels; demilitarization of the campus police; all-gender restrooms including signage and conversion of single stalls; and sanctuary campus; no cooperation with DHS on immigration issues.

The parties recently settled a four-year contract and agreed to a one-time committee to discuss campus policing, an immigration side letter outlining procedures, and language for all-gender restrooms. The above notwithstanding, which social justice precepts are introduced, or the proclivity to drop social justice language in favor of more acceptable "boiler plate" clauses, is not always clear cut. During negotiations between Tufts University and graduate students represented by SEIU, the union argued to expand the definition of discrimination based on "socio-eco-nomic status". However, the final clause agreed upon by the parties is a standard anti-discrimination clause. Social justice concerns were introduced but for whatever reasons were dropped. Other issues, on many campuses, where social justice issues are raised, include gender equity in pay, Title IX, with respect to sexual assault on campus, and paid family leave. At the University of Vermont, Plymouth State University, Wayne State University, Michigan State University and the University of Florida, unions representing graduate assistants or students proposed lesser overall salary increases in favor of larger increases for lower paid members. Examples of a complex relationship between social justice and business union interests can also be discerned in negotiations over concepts such as "seniority" and "across-the-board" salary increases. Using seniority, for layoffs, economic benefits or other actions (seniority being a very hard won concept for unions), often favors those who have been in the organization the longest and if used to determine benefits or layoff status, employees newly hired (who may be women or those from marginalized groups) can be disadvantaged. Across the board salary percent increases, very common in many negotiations, provide for higher raises to longer serving employees; those who have reached top step salaries (after all, 3% of $70,000 represents a higher amount than 3% of $35,000). Here too, union proposals may conflict with the values of individuals who are more concerned with pay equity or the rights of recently hired employees. The situation becomes more complex when lower paid part-timers and tenured faculty are in the same bargaining unit. Tension also arises when, for example, unions have the right not to represent those who refuse (or cannot afford to pay) union dues.

To be sure, chief negotiators on both sides of the table interested in advancing social justice concerns can have an impact. In my own work, during the 1970s and 1980s at the Vermont State Colleges and University of San Francisco, as chief negotiator I proposed, for adjunct faculty and clerical employees, articles on pay equity, job security and family related leaves (considered very progressive at the time although not called social justice). There are always alternative approaches to addressing recognition, compensation, discrimination, seniority, work–life balance and other contractual matters. In certain jurisdictions and particularly where labor management relationships have remained stable and professionalized, social justice type clauses have been proposed by the administration or union and eventually ratified.

10 Daniel J. Julius and Nicholas DiGiovanni, Jr., "Academic Collective Bargaining: Status, Process, and Prospect." *Academic Labor: Research and Artistry* 3, article 11 (2019): 127 183. https://digitalcommons.humboldt.edu/alra/vol3/iss1/11; Ladd, E. C. & Lipset, S. M. (1973). *Professors, unions and American higher education.* Berkeley, CA: The Carnegie Commission on Higher Education. In this study the authors found that faculty from the highest prestige public institutions, particularly junior faculty, were by and large, the most supportive of collective bargaining. In fact, this is not where unions have gained a foothold and few of these organizations are unionized. On attitudinal studies and collective bargaining see; Rosenfeld, Jake, *What Unions No Longer Do.* Harvard University Press, 2014; Freeman, Richard B., and James L Medoff, *What Do Unions Do?* Basic Books, Inc., Publishers, 1983.

PART II

Case Studies: Select Institutions and Systems

9

CASE STUDY

City University of New York

Pamela S. Silverblatt

Background

This chapter seeks to illuminate the benefits of a positive, collegial labor–management relationship in a higher education setting. With a particular focus on rebuilding the labor-management relationship and modernizing the collective bargaining agreement, I will discuss strategies to build trust and confidence, ultimately promoting bilateral flexibility. Although the exact nature of labor relations at the City University of New York ("CUNY") – the nation's largest urban public university system, with 275,000 degree-seeking students and over 200,000 non-degree-seeking students, 25 schools, and 45,000 employees in what may be the United States' most powerfully unionized city – may not be paralleled at every institution, I hope to provide broadly applicable concepts. I will also explore strategies to promote proactive, organized and cohesive internal management of labor issues within the institution's administration.

Historically, labor relations at CUNY had been combined with human resources, but in 2008 CUNY created a new position for a Vice Chancellor of Labor Relations and I was hired for that new role, having been a practitioner of public sector labor relations since my law school graduation many years before. In 2018, I was promoted to Senior Vice Chancellor of Labor Relations, and from 2018 until 2020, in addition to the labor relations role, I was the University's Interim Senior Vice Chancellor for Legal Affairs and General Counsel.

The primary impetus for creating the separate position of Vice Chancellor for Labor Relations and hiring me in that role was to reboot the relationship between the University and the union representing its faculty and professional

DOI: 10.4324/9781003138990-11

staff, the Professional Staff Congress/CUNY ("PSC"), and to move the University toward a more modern collective bargaining agreement. Rather than have a function that was just one sliver of a larger portfolio, CUNY concertedly focused the attention of the office on labor relations activities and labor-management relationships. Structurally, the office has a few attorneys who work primarily on PSC-related matters; a classified staff function to support the non-PSC unions; and a small labor hearings and appeals unit to administer the Step 2 grievance and disciplinary hearing process, which consists of three steps.

Despite being the management negotiator, I bring a sensitivity to the labor-side impact of collective bargaining issues as the natural result of being raised by a single mother who was a veteran New York City Department of Education schoolteacher. She also happened to be a graduate of Brooklyn College and the first woman in her family to graduate from college. Much of my great affection for CUNY stems from the top-notch education provided to first-generation college attendees and the doors that a CUNY education opens. This interest in labor relations motivated me to attend law school. Prior to joining CUNY, I was appointed as the First Deputy Commissioner for Labor Relations for New York City by two separate Mayors. During my tenure as the City's First Deputy Commissioner, my multilateral orientation and collaborative emphasis was instrumental in maintaining productive and strong relationships between the City and its uniformed service unions in the wake of the 9/11 attacks. Although my only son was born nine days before the attacks, I returned to work to support the City's labor-management relationships almost immediately. At CUNY, I have applied the lessons of cooperation, collaboration and empathy that I learned during the recovery from 9/11 and the subsequent time spent devoted to labor-management relations at the highest levels of City government to steer the University's relationship with the PSC toward a place of mutual understanding. Leaving behind personal grudges and political power plays has been essential in building a strong labor-management relationship; my team is instructed that there is no time to play games.

CUNY receives funding from both the State and City of New York, which each appoint Trustees to the governing Board. PSC, which represents faculty and non-teaching instructional staff (i.e., professional administrative staff) is the largest and most complex of the 14 bargaining units at CUNY. Included under PSC's umbrella are 7,200 full-time tenured and tenure-track faculty; over 12,000 part-time adjunct faculty; counselors; librarians; professional administrative staff; and graduate student assistants. While PSC is the largest and most complex of the bargaining units at CUNY, where all but a very limited number of executives and managers are represented, the unions are varied and diverse. Each of the skilled trades groups of employees – both journeymen and supervisors – are represented by a separate trade or craft union or association; the carpenters, electricians, plumbers and painters, for example, are all separately represented. We have a unit of operating engineers and a separate unit of steamfitters. These unions have their own complicated bargaining relationships with CUNY; their wages and leave benefits are set by the NYC Comptroller – in a process that compares them to their private sector counterparts – pursuant to State statute, but some of their non-economic terms and conditions are bargained with CUNY. The same locals that represent employees at CUNY, represent trade employees in the private sector, including in construction, in New York City. As a result of this structure, CUNY does not control their economic settlements, which are frequently retroactive, giving rise to a lack of predictability.

We have two different IATSE unions representing theatrical and stage employees. There are nurses at some of the college health centers represented by the New York State Nurses Association. Importantly, we also have AFSCME, AFL-CIO-represented employees, such as clerical, custodial, administrative and professional employees, in several different locals within the AFSCME district council. District Council 37 is the same union that represents more than 150,000 City employees, and 50,000 retirees, thus giving them a presence much larger than their representation at CUNY. Our public safety employees are represented by a Teamsters local which similarly represents employees city-wide in other agencies. If these city-wide unions negotiate an enhancement with one of the other employers, they may look to CUNY to follow suit.

Needless to say, the varied interests of PSC's membership heighten the stakes of collective bargaining. At the same time, effective communication and preparation are essential in ensuring alignment among the University, the City and the State. CUNY is a public employer authorized to negotiate and enter into collective bargaining agreements with its constituent unions. At the same time CUNY is required to consult with the Governor's Office of Employee Relations and the City's Office of Labor Relations. The faculty at CUNY has been unionized for five decades. Thus, we have a rich history between organized labor and the administration at the University and a mature collective bargaining agreement – most of the provisions of which are of long standing. Prior to 1972 the faculty were represented by two different groups, the Legislative Congress and the United Federation of College Teachers; the two groups had a complicated history prior to 1972 involving challenges, statutory determinations and elections. In 1972, the two groups merged to form the Professional Staff Congress; the current president has held that position for 20 years and her predecessor was president for 26 years.

Making changes in a collective bargaining agreement of such long-standing involves finding opportunities to leverage, having a willingness to trade, and understanding the union's needs to achieve modifications as well. Conceptualizing what a more modern contract might look like in the face of long-existing contract language and entrenched behavior meant charting out a course for incremental, year-over-year change that would move the needle in a particular direction, at a pace and with a comfort level that would satisfy both the administration and the union.

Preparing for a Round of Collective Bargaining

The preface to any round of bargaining or serious time at the bargaining table is in-depth preparation. I have always believed that every institution – like every family – has its own unique culture and norms. Although resources, both financial and human, vary across institutions, there are some principles and exercises that are common and critical to all. While CUNY is one of the largest university systems in the country – and unusual in that it is composed of the City's community college system, senior colleges and professional and graduate schools – there are collective bargaining lessons relevant and adaptable to institutions of all sizes, urban, suburban and rural.

Gathering Financial Data

How much will it cost? One of the earliest exercises in readying for a round of bargaining involves a detailed undertaking to determine the cost of a 1% increase for the bargaining unit. This involves gathering data by title and separating out wages, fringe benefits, pension costs, and the like across the bargaining unit, so that determinations of the fiscal impact of potential raises can be assessed with precision. This information is equally critical to determining the cost of increasing specific benefits that may only apply to an individual title or subsets of the bargaining unit. For example, if a particular title or subset of the unit has a depressed salary issue that warrants an additional increment but the cost of that increase is going to be spread across the entire unit, you may be able to substantially address that targeted inequity for a modest cost when "amortized" across the entire unit. Without detailed headcount, payroll and budget data, it is impossible to make these assessments and to determine the cost of various bargaining proposals. As these data are developed, we share the relevant information with the union in an effort to reach agreement on the information being used to cost proposals. Having a shared understanding of the financial data is key to ensuring an eventual meeting of the minds on the cost and value of the entirety of an economic settlement.

Development of Bargaining Proposals

While development of the economic data is largely an exercise driven by budget and human resources, development of a bargaining agenda and bargaining proposals crosses several other disciplines. The expertise of a seasoned negotiator to solicit input, synthesize divergent perspectives, and communicate the limitations of bargaining to key constituencies and high-level administrators is critical. Although there is a substantive knowledge and skill-base necessary to practice higher education labor relations, I frequently repeat the adage that "it is more art than science." Shaping a bargaining matrix in a multi-institution, multi-site organization requires soliciting broad input from all relevant constituencies and then streamlining and funneling all of the information received from dozens of people into a workable framework. The complex needs of 25 colleges – each with a president, provost, human resources director, chief labor officer, vice president for finance and administration, and more – must be considered. In addition, input from the multi-tiered, multi-discipline central administration must be garnered and incorporated into the proposals for modifications to an academic collective bargaining agreement.

Consultation

While there may be different ways to structure this process, rather than reinventing the wheel, I have found it beneficial to use the existing long-established standing discipline-based councils as a foundational element to the consultative process. This allows for meetings with all of the college presidents, the college provosts, the human resources directors, and others to educate them about the process, provide information, and answer individual questions, as well as those that are shared by several colleges.

Using the discipline-based meetings begins with a primer on collective bargaining, its role in the public sector in New York and a brief history of the parties' negotiations. In order to put theory into practice, discussion of memoranda of agreement from previous settled contracts assists in clarifying the issues that are frequently addressed and what can be achieved at the bargaining table. After initial discussion, I solicit input from the stakeholders on what they would like to see changed in this current round of bargaining. Although the initial solicitation of ideas may begin as round-table discussions, ultimately, written input is necessary because of the extensive number of stakeholders involved. In order to ensure executive cohesion and buy-in at each of the colleges, ultimately proposals from college-based leaders have to be presented as a unified submission, approved by the college president. Requiring the submission of one unified list of suggestions by a college allows for early identification of local concerns, aggregating patterns across colleges, analyzing relevant information and data, and avoiding too much focus on siloed matters.

Synthesis

Because CUNY has an omnibus collective bargaining agreement that is applicable at all of the colleges, bargaining proposals have to have broad appeal and relevance and transcend individual situations. Reconciling potentially disparate bargaining interests of 25 separate institutions, spread across the City's five boroughs, requires a systematic, multi-layered approach. Select members of my bargaining team and I compile all of the suggestions submitted from the respective colleges and identify potentially viable proposals based upon their broad appeal among the colleges, whether similar issues have been raised in earlier negotiations, and precedents in previous settlements. As a team, we review the college-based proposals with a focus on what we believe are the more promising ideas, co-mingle our own thoughts based upon our varied experiences working with the collective bargaining agreement, and begin to envisage potential goals for the upcoming round of bargaining. In building a preliminary list of management proposals, in general, we look for thoughts related to creating more flexibility, optimizing efficiencies, and better deploying faculty and staff to meet capacity and institutional needs. Once there is a consolidated set of tentative proposals, discussions with senior system-wide leaders – including the Chancellor, University Provost, Chief Operating Officer, Chief Financial Officer, General Counsel and Vice Chancellors – are undertaken to work toward consensus and ultimate approval. The end product of this process is a finalized set of bargaining proposals ready for presentation to the union at one of the first bargaining sessions during a round of negotiations.

Feedback Loop

Invariably, the stakeholders consulted will make suggestions for bargaining proposals to amend items not actually contained within the collective bargaining agreement, but which the colleges find restrictive, nonetheless. A college leader may not be aware that the provisions from which they are seeking relief are not contract provisions; they may mistakenly believe that if an employment rule or practice is restrictive, it must be as a result of the collective bargaining agreement. While moving ahead with the exercise of narrowing bargaining suggestions and preparing a cohesive, comprehensive set of proposals for endorsement by the senior leadership, we also compile the items with which we are not proceeding. At a later point we circle back and have discussions to explain why some of the suggestions – while they may be reflective of areas ripe for change – are not appropriate for the bargaining table. Ensuring support from presidents and provosts is critical and educating them regarding why their ideas are not being advanced is a necessary precursor to ensuring that support. Communicating early in the process that you understand their needs and desire for change while explaining that some matters are not appropriate for bargaining ensures that you build support and understanding. In explaining why something does not belong in bargaining, you should endeavor to propose alternative suggestions on how to address the matter in a way that creates the opportunity to collaborate with the college on a solution.

Time at the Bargaining Table

Frequently, a round of collective bargaining may begin with a flourish leading up to initial bargaining sessions. The union may communicate broadly that negotiations are going to begin, and expectations may be heightened. Some parties start a round of bargaining by taking photos of the full bargaining teams to reflect the opening of the negotiations. Being prepared for what to expect at a first session is critical, as all eyes will be on the negotiators to see what kind of tenor and tone will be set for the process. Having the full team at the table for an opening session conveys the seriousness with which the administration views the negotiations and provides an opportunity for the union's team to meet all of the management representatives, which is beneficial as some team members may be able to attend future bargaining sessions only sporadically, owing to teaching and other responsibilities. On a cautionary note, depending on how quickly the parties are moving, there can be allegations that management has been slow to move ahead. Whether it is or is not true, you may have to manage both the perceptions and the public relations that flow from those assertions.

Ground Rules

Often a discussion of the ground rules for conducting the bargaining sessions and activities related to bargaining will begin at a first session. Items such as the frequency with which the parties will meet, the locations of the sessions, who will attend, statements that the negotiations will be closed to the press and whether interim agreements will be tentatively agreed to subject to an overall agreement are just a few examples of potential ground rules. The parties to any contract tend to have their own history and culture regarding what they specify, the detail with which it is specified, and whether their practice is to reduce ground rules to writing or simply to agree orally. The chief negotiator is charged with determining the parties' practices, whether they are effective, whether there is a desire by one or both sides to update their practices, and setting the tone to credibly manage the bargaining process.

Exchange of Proposals

Whether at a first session or a session shortly thereafter, the parties will exchange proposals; sometimes this is done simultaneously, but it does not have to be done contemporaneously. This begins in earnest the discussions that will ultimately result in a new collective bargaining agreement. As the management negotiator, the proposals you present will be the result of months of work and will demonstrate to the union, for the first time, the roadmap of where you want to take the negotiations. Your team will receive a set of union proposals that will be the result of broad outreach by the union's leadership to ensure that their constituencies' needs have been incorporated. The parties may begin to review their proposals at the same session at which they are exchanged. The first round of review of proposals can take several sessions, depending upon how numerous each side's proposals are and the level of explanation and detail attached to the initial review of proposals.

Working Internally

Receipt of the union's proposals signals the next stage of work to be undertaken as a team and with your principals and other constituencies. With whom do you share the union's proposals? Your president, provost, trustees? What is the process for sharing this information? Hopefully, you will have established these understandings before your first session, so that when you receive the union's proposals, you can share them quickly. It is a good idea to also reiterate for your principals that negotiations are confidential, that it is not for the administration to share the union's proposals, and that bargaining gets done at the bargaining table and not in the press, with distribution of the union's bargaining proposals.

Digesting and explaining the union's demands in a way that allows for meaningful understanding by decision-makers is critical. With respect to the proposals that are purely labor related (e.g., grievance processes, disciplinary rules), the negotiator can prepare explanations; for proposals that are academic in nature (e.g., how faculty will be evaluated), collaboration between the academic representative on the bargaining team and the labor staff may be necessary to understand the proposal. Of course, the finance representative will need to start to assess the costs of proposals. The processes of describing and quantifying proposals will be ongoing over the course of bargaining as proposals get amended and revised throughout the negotiations. As the principals begin to understand the union's demands, they will be in a position to provide feedback regarding areas over which they are prepared to negotiate and those they prefer to avoid.

Signaling Areas of Openness and Unwillingness

Perhaps the longest section of the process in a round of collective bargaining is the middle, which can sometimes feel like the route to crossing an ocean. After each of the parties has the opportunity to thoroughly explain and discuss its proposals, the process of signaling areas over which you are prepared to work together to see if common ground can be found versus those that are of no interest begins in earnest. There are going to be some topics – like wages – which are straightforward and cannot be avoided. But you may be able to avoid discussing other topics, especially if you work within a statutory framework that provides limitations on the matters over which an employer is required to bargain. The art of collective bargaining is continuing to pursue those management items about which the union does not want to bargain, packaging and repackaging them, while narrowing the union's issues and encouraging them to engage on the issues your side finds more acceptable among their many issues.

Staying the Course

It is easy to say all of the above about moving through the vast middle area of a round of bargaining, but that process can take months – sometimes even years – during which there are fits and starts. Emotions can run high, tempers can get frayed, and it may be impossible to see a path to an endgame that will bring you to closure of a successor agreement. Keeping your calm and maintaining open communications while keeping your eye on the prize will get you through what can seem like an endless back-and-forth of exchanging language. Even when you think you are going in circles, as long as you are engaged with the union, you are progressing. I have several mantras that I use to instill an understanding in staff new to this process. "Keep it neutral" – while at times it may feel like the language directed at you is harsh or personal, you are dealing with issues that are very serious and govern peoples' work lives. Losing your cool, engaging in *ad hominem* attacks, or otherwise demeaning the ideas emanating from the other side of the table does not advance your cause. Everyone is well served by maintaining a calm and neutral demeanor and working to put yourself in the shoes of the other.

The need to engage is real. Understanding the union's proposals is not just about understanding the substance of the proposal, it is about understanding what underlies the need – either real or perceived – for the union to be advancing a particular proposal. This means asking questions and giving the union bargaining team ample time and space to elaborate and educate. Cutting short team members across the bargaining table or being presumptuous, assuming that you know what they are trying to communicate, has a chilling effect on the colloquy and, therefore, on your ability to advance your agenda.

Consider thoroughly everything presented to you, be willing to review written materials, studies, articles and the like on any topic, whether your side is predisposed to consider the topic or not. Shutting down proposals without making an effort to understand is devaluing to the other side. While the union's chief negotiator may understand that your unwillingness to extend yourself regarding certain proposals is signaling that they may be non-starters, less seasoned members of the union's bargaining team may not intuit that and may feel disrespected. The bargaining team members are your institution's faculty and staff; they will report their perceptions of the administration's lack of interest or seriousness back to their colleagues.

Getting to Yes

Are there alternatives? It's not hard to say "no." You can send anyone into a room with marching orders to just say "no." Getting to yes is much harder. Your job as the negotiator is finding ways to get to yes on enough items to get you to done. Expand your thinking, be creative, propose options, ask the union to extend itself to consider other possibilities, and work to find a middle ground. All of this means that you have to have a listening ear and an open mind. Humor is a good thing. You do not want to disrespect anyone, but if there are opportunities for a bit of humor, it is okay to inject some. Provided your timing is right! And, then finally be real, be yourself. You are going to spend a lot of time with the union's team; everyone has his/her own style, be comfortable with yours. You will have some sessions that are productive, some that are discouraging – and worse. Bargaining is not like some other kinds of negotiating where you are putting together a business deal and you are never going to see your adversary again. The parties to a collective bargaining agreement have to live with each other. You are going to wake up and go to work the day after you settle an agreement and have to deal with the same people again. The purpose of collective bargaining is not victory at any cost, it is having a meaningful agreement that both sides can live with. The word "no" carries tremendous weight; if overused, it loses its value. Consider unconditional vetoes on union proposals only when they are absolutely unacceptable to your principals.

Another bargaining mantra to live by is "do not make promises that you cannot keep, *ever*." This principle should govern all communications with the union, as well as with fellow stakeholders on management's side. Living by your word is non-negotiable. In order to do so, I have to be honest with the union if a proposal does not make sense, is not feasible, or is appealing but will need further discussion among management. Along those lines, I often repeat the refrain "do not take my silence as assent" during bargaining because, although I will hear any demands out, a lack of a response does not signal a willingness or agreement. Bargaining is a bilateral process to reach consensus, not a unilateral series of declarations. Exercising patience during the process is critical.

Bargaining Is a Team Sport

No matter how good of a negotiator you are, you simply cannot do it alone. Bargaining is a gritty, labor-intensive, long-term project; none of its parts can happen in a silo. Consistent and honest messaging from management is vital to every union, but the level of scrutiny to which management is subject increases when negotiating with a union comprised of university faculty. Therefore, all departments of the University's administration need to be on the same page, and they need to progress in tandem. This high level of collaboration is achieved by including on the bargaining team representatives from the offices of Human Resources, General Counsel, Budget and Finance, and Academic Affairs, in addition to several members of the Office of Labor Relations. In identifying members of the bargaining team, I search for the most collaboration-minded, emotionally intelligent, savvy and astute members of the relevant administrative offices. Flexibility is an essential trait to possess and demonstrate throughout the bargaining process, as settlement always requires compromise, and demands and priorities on both sides of the table can shift in the blink of the eye. In addition to the team members, supplementary expertise may be warranted at times through consultation with, or involvement of, departments or individuals not formally part of the bargaining team. While it is the responsibility of the chief negotiator to set the tone for the bargaining team, plan and develop its strategies and keep its focus, multi-disciplinary expertise supporting the process is mandatory.

Contract Administration

The negotiating and bargaining processes are only a piece of the pie when it comes to promoting and building a strong labor-management relationship in a unionized environment such as CUNY. Despite the media attention, press coverage and photo ops that may be present on the day of a contract settlement, the hard work of labor relations does not end with the celebratory moment. In fact, that is only the beginning.

Timely Implementation

As my son loves to say, a deadline has its name for a reason: "if you don't meet it, you're dead." This principle, albeit extreme, is worthy of some reverence and consideration in collective bargaining. First and foremost, any pay or wage increases, especially if they are retroactive, require urgent action. Immediately after settling a contract, even before the union membership ratifies it and the Board of Trustees approves it, my colleagues in Labor Relations and I shift our focus to informing the University at large, such as the Chancellery, senior administrative leaders and College presidents and vice presidents, of the contractual changes. Again, I use the discipline-based councils as a medium to quickly disseminate information in a discussion-based forum and distribute briefing memoranda describing the salient changes. Labor Relations also ensures that other offices in the administration take steps to implement the necessary provisions. For example, in order to actualize wage increases, we create salary schedules and supporting information for the Human Resources' Payroll division so that it, in tandem with Computer and Information Services, can program the necessary changes. Despite the deceptively simple-sounding nature of this process, enacting payroll changes for over 25,000 employees in a 25-campus university with employees on both the New York State and New York City payrolls is a daunting task. On an ongoing basis, the Office of Labor Relations provides clarification and advisement as the negotiated changes are implemented.

In addition to implementing wage increases, oftentimes funds are earmarked for specific purposes in a collective bargaining agreement. For example, training and education funds, professional development funds, travel funds, and funds for research may be negotiated. Similarly, salary differentials for specific purposes such as for exemplary work or to address equity issues can be established or augmented through collective bargaining. With the creation or restructuring of these special funds comes a responsibility to administer them effectively and properly. To that end, Labor Relations may provide directions and guidance to the offices such as Budget and Finance or Human Resources to ensure that the relevant funds are set aside in the correct amounts and that the steps are taken to correctly implement the negotiated provisions. My colleagues and I also communicate with all of individual colleges and their administrative leaders to explain the purpose of the earmarked funds and the procedures for disbursing them and monitoring their usage.

Grievance Management

Stuff goes wrong, Murphy's Law, as they say. Despite everyone's best intentions toward a shared vision and mutual understandings, it is axiomatic that things will, in fact, go wrong. The parties will disagree over the contract's interpretation and application. In light of that eventuality, effective administration of the contract's provisions should include a grievance and dispute resolution process.

Timely Scheduling and Issuance of Decisions

I advocate for having a strong and clearly defined plan in place for resolving contract disputes before they arise. The existence of robust grievance and arbitration or alternative dispute resolution processes allows for confident and trustworthy resolution of conflicts. The specifics of the grievance process (e.g., the number of steps in the process, the timeframes for appeal from one level to the next, the designees who will review grievances) are less important than the fact that the process is clearly defined, understood, and respected by both of the parties. Sometimes grievances can be university-wide, however, individual employees frequently believe they are aggrieved in the application of a contractual provision. In those cases, the union has to manage the member's expectations through the process, which may include appeal of adverse decisions. Being able to point to a well-regarded structure for the resolution of disputes provides some guardrails in managing expectations. Conversely, there are limitations on what management can do – as circumscribed by collective bargaining agreement's provisions – and it is important for administrators to know that when disputes arise, the disposition of those disputes will be fairly decided.

Consistency of Interpretation and Application

For those responsible for managing the grievance process, taking actions that result in both sides having faith in the process is essential. This begins by timely scheduling matters for discussion and ensuring that witnesses, documents, or other information necessary to have a complete discussion (or hearing if that is what your process entails) are readily available. Dragging your feet, being ill prepared, or not being forthcoming detracts from the credibility of the process. Adherence to timeframes for meetings and outcomes is integral to a robust process and allows the process to move along smoothly.

Our process provides for a university-wide review after the initial step in the grievance process is held locally at the colleges. Being familiar with the contract and the history of the provisions, ensuring orderly proceedings, and allowing both sides to fully present their arguments lends confidence to the process and is incumbent upon the hearing officer. At this stage, in addition to considering the specific facts of the instant matter before him/her, the hearing officer considers the instant matter in a much broader context as well. Critical to the process, and especially at this juncture, is ensuring equity and fair treatment across the institution. Often the decision-maker at the first step will have a narrow focus, in a large system, perhaps only his or her college, but not a system perspective. Once a grievance moves beyond the initial step, the reviewer must consider how other similar situations have been decided or resolved university-wide. Implicit in the grievance process is ensuring an absence of disparate treatment across the institution. When a department or college wants to adhere to a particular interpretation, it is incumbent on the hearing officer to ensure consistency of application with prior similar matters.

The University and its faculty union have a three-step disciplinary process and a long-standing provision in the collective bargaining agreement that mandates that tenured faculty must remain on payroll until the completion of a disciplinary arbitration conducted by a jointly selected neutral arbitrator. In New York, with the most popular arbitrators having calendars that schedule several months in advance, it became apparent several years ago that we could have employees remaining on payroll for months (and sometimes more than a year) while awaiting the outcome of serious charges. Through the bargaining process, we were able to agree on a pilot program to eliminate one step in the disciplinary process thereby moving these matters much more quickly, saving personnel costs and time, and allowing colleges to move forward with greater decisiveness.

Settlement and Dispute Resolution

Often during the grievance process, one of the parties or the hearing officer will suggest settling the matter. This is generally based upon an assessment that the risk of proceeding may result in an adverse decision that is less favorable than what can be achieved in a settlement. Even though the settlement may fall short of everything you wanted, losing in entirety would be worse. Proceeding with a third-party decision-maker (arbitrator or factfinder) is typically an all or nothing proposition. It is generally preferable for the parties to settle grievances; sometimes a neutral or mediator can be a useful to help parties who may have become entrenched in their positions. A mediator can provide an objective assessment of the relative weaknesses and strengths in positions. Passing up a reasonable – albeit compromise – settlement can quickly become a regrettable decision. Of course, settlement is not always possible. In those instances, as the grievance progresses, active partnership between labor relations and the other involved departments is necessary, as they have a shared responsibility to ensure an optimal outcome.

Moving Toward a More Modern Contract

When I arrived at CUNY, the collective bargaining agreement was expired, and although the parties had commenced bargaining, the negotiations were not progressing. Fostering administration support and buy-in for union proposals requires an understanding that collective bargaining is not a zero-sum game, and it is often as much in management's interest to reach a consensus. Once management understood that agreeing to contractual benefit improvements was critical to moving the bargaining forward, the negotiations were able to proceed quickly to a mutually beneficial, successful conclusion. The foundation for the next several years of collaborative work, including complex bargained-for agreements in between rounds of formal contract negotiations was established as a result of the successful contract negotiations that concluded shortly after I joined CUNY.

Paid Parental Leave and Increased Sick Leave

The union had made the establishment of a paid parental leave benefit a centerpiece of the [my first] round of bargaining. While meeting the union's need in total would have been prohibitively expensive, it became quickly obvious that the collective bargaining agreement could nonetheless be made more family-friendly. Solving the paid parental leave issue became critical to advancing the bargaining. Initially, we were able to identify funds to create the benefit only for a few years. Prior to exhausting the funding, but before the next formal round of bargaining, we found ourselves at the bargaining table again, this time successfully working to identify funding so that the paid parental leave benefit could become permanent.

Although the initiative for a paid parental leave benefit originated from the union, the University stood to become an indirect beneficiary; the benefit provided to the faculty and professional staff afforded the University a new, additional tool to aid in recruitment and retention. In addition to the paid parental leave benefit, that round of bargaining was marked by an overall expansion of leave benefits, including establishing a sick leave bank and a dedicated sick leave program that enabled full-time faculty and staff to donate sick leave into a bank or directly to a critically ill colleague who no longer has any available leave.

Enhancing Faculty Recruitment and Supporting Research

After taking stock of critical issues during my first round of bargaining at CUNY, I took note of the importance of a new faculty title that would enable the University to hire experts to expand clinical education and increase the availability of practitioners to teach. The University was also looking to have greater flexibility in already existing positions. Over the course of negotiations, we were able to reach an agreement that both allowed for the establishment of a new non-tenure-bearing title and expanded flexibility.

In addition to the need for a clinical teaching title, a top priority for CUNY during that time period was to hire more full-time faculty. For several years, the University actively sought to significantly increase the full-time faculty ranks through external faculty hiring; between 2000 and 2008 the University had increased the number of full-time faculty by 965 positions and would go on to increase it by a total of 1,773 positions by 2014. The imperative of successfully recruiting and retaining talented, gifted faculty was also supported by expanding bargained-for benefits.

Not long after the bargaining for the first contract ended, the then-Vice Chancellor for Research asked for support to negotiate a restructuring of the faculty research awards program, which because it is delineated in, and funded out of, the collective bargaining agreement had to be negotiated with the union. Her goals were to streamline the review process, reduce the time faulty spent on administrative tasks, optimize the distribution of grants, and create a new higher dollar value grant award. The impetus for modifying the awards program was the Vice Chancellor's, who, although not a formal member of the bargaining team, became a necessary partner, without whose expertise and cooperation the restructuring would have been impossible.

This was an extremely lengthy and uphill difficult negotiation that played out in fits and starts; it was only with the investment of time and reassurances that awards supporting research in the humanities and awards supporting research by untenured faculty would be maintained that we were able to ultimately prevail upon the union to restructure and create a much higher value award. Although we were only able to convince the union to restructure the research awards program on a pilot basis for three years, before the end of the pilot period, we were able to make the program permanent.

Advancing Adjunct Equity

As a result of an ongoing union campaign, we also agreed, through negotiation to the provision of stable quality health insurance to eligible part-time employees at CUNY. In an agreement that the union characterized as "a landmark," the University and the union, by working with the Governor's and Mayor's offices, secured support and additional funding to enable part-time employees who met specific eligibility criteria to participate in the same City Health Benefits program that CUNY's full-time employees are in, along with hundreds of thousands of NYC employees and retirees. In a joint statement at the time, the University's then-Chancellor and the union president, said,

> [t]his accomplishment assures equitable access to health insurance, which will profoundly affect the lives of dedicated adjuncts, many of whom have been teaching core courses for decades. Qualified CUNY adjuncts will now be able to receive their basic health insurance through the City Health Benefits Program, on an equitable basis with full-time CUNY employees.

At the time of my second round of bargaining with PSC, CUNY exclusively employed adjuncts on a semester-by-semester basis with a limited number of two-semester appointments. Recognizing the commitment of many adjuncts to CUNY, and with every intention of providing more stable, predictable employment for longer-serving adjuncts who taught at least two courses every semester, we undertook a pilot program to provide three-year appointments for eligible adjunct faculty. This pilot program continues to the present.

Perhaps most significantly, in the most recent round of collective bargaining, we reshaped the payment and working structure for CUNY's 12,000 adjunct teaching faculty. Over the course of the agreement, adjuncts at the lowest salary level would see substantial increases increase in pay of more than a 70% for a three-credit course. As part of this restructuring, adjuncts would be required to hold mandatory office hours, in general one hour per week for a three-credit course. We expect this to inure to the benefit of students by providing much greater opportunities to meet with faculty and to the benefit of adjunct faculty by affording them paid time for office hours and for professional development.

Expanding Salary Advancement and Professional Development Opportunities

In terms of non-teaching professional staff, in my second round of bargaining for a successor collective bargaining agreement, the parties created a new discretionary salary differential for professional administrative staff in the lower levels in these titles to recognize excellence in performance or increased responsibilities. By collaborating, we were able to carve out funding to address equity issues for this cohort of employees, in particular, those who had been at the top salary step in these non-promotional titles. In our most recent contract, the parties agreed to take money out of the collective bargaining settlement to create a matching fund for colleges that awarded the differential in furtherance of our support for this program. In addition, in order to strengthen the opportunities and show a greater commitment to the affected staff, we set up a more exacting and rigorous timeline for the colleges to follow in reviewing and responding to applications for these differentials.

Among other initiatives, we have continually increased funding to expand and improve professional development opportunities for professional administrative staff and adjunct faculty, among others. We have increased travel funds available for attendance at professional conferences and meetings. We have continued to augment the funds available for the research awards program to support faculty research and scholarship. Most recently, we have agreed to create research accounts to support scholarly and creative activities of department chairs and we enhanced support for graduate assistants through expanded tuition waiver opportunities. These are just a few examples of mutually beneficial initiatives or programs that the parties were able to achieve only as a result of working collaboratively. In each instance, expanding equitable opportunities for employees was paramount.

Measuring Success

How do you measure success in bargaining and in the bargaining relationship? While some would argue for quantifiable metrics, such as employee turnover, savings generated, length of time to complete a round of negotiations, I would posit that they do not tell the whole story and that changes resulting from bargaining and the success of those changes may be equally amenable to qualitative description. One person may think you had ample success while another person thinks you failed. Also, what did you give up to achieve what you got? Perhaps there was a round of bargaining with robust salary increases, so you were able to achieve some sought-after policy changes. Or what about a round of bargaining where the salary increases were modest, so you had to concede on some other items about which you would have preferred to hold the line? Is that round unsuccessful because you had to give up some precious items? Or is it a success because in the face of economic scarcity, you brought home a contract with minimal wage increases?

I prefer to think about the success of the bargaining relationship qualitatively over time. This brings me back to where I started…with a charge to modernize the contact through the bargaining process. By building incrementally in ways that fit within the then-prescribed budget parameters, we have been able to use the bargaining process very effectively. The effective use of the bargaining process has supported a more progressive, family-friendly agenda and greater diversity, equity and inclusion. From my first bargaining session at CUNY, with the union side of the table, filled with mothers – pregnant mothers, nursing mothers, mothers with infants and toddlers – fighting for a paid parental leave benefit, to a contract that now includes many expanded family-friendly benefits; new differentials; substantial increases in funds for professional development and travel to further research and scholarship; and streamlined, restructured and augmented research grants, CUNY and the PSC have demonstrated what can be accomplished through the bargaining process.

Concluding Thoughts

Within higher education, faculty unions and collective bargaining are not universal. For that reason, it may be challenging to conceptualize what a unionized faculty can add to an institution when so many have faculty that are not unionized. Quite possibly, those doubts will gain momentum in the aftermath of the Janus v. AFCSME US Supreme Court decision in 2018, which rendered the collection of mandatory agency shop fees in the public sector unconstitutional. My career at CUNY has given me a glimpse of the ways in which a collectively organized faculty can enhance and benefit an institution of higher education. Such is the case when there is a mutually beneficial, positive working relationship. Achieving that level of trust and cooperation is an ideal to work toward; at the core of any collective bargaining relationship is the push and pull of negotiation, an inherently adversarial process. Forming solid working and interpersonal relationships across the table is an uphill battle, a challenge for any negotiator.

I prefer to focus on the "collective" nature of collective bargaining; it is not a zero-sum game with one winner and one loser. To the contrary, the only possible outcomes following a round of bargaining are either two winners or two losers. With two winners, faculty retention is strong, and attracting topnotch faculty is a shared priority jointly undertaken. With two winners, faculty morale is high, resulting in strong faculty–student collaboration and improved educational outcomes.

Conversely, a labor-management relationship with two losers is detrimental and can be destructive for all parties involved. With two losers, there are extremely costly arbitrations and fact-findings, including additional costs incurred for outside counsels. With two losers, there is recalcitrant positioning, foreclosed communications, and, perhaps even threats of job actions. In those cases, faculty morale is low, retaining and attracting talented faculty may become a challenge, and most importantly, the instructional time available to students may be reduced and not optimized. In such a situation, initiatives that the administration proposes when the labor-management relationship is strained may be met with resistance.

As we sit here today in the middle of a pandemic, it remains to be seen how effective administrations and unions will be in negotiating provisions that are responsive to the needs of students, faculty and staff in the face of COVID-19. When colleges and universities sent their students home last spring and quickly pivoted to remote learning and working from home, I want to believe that everyone put their best feet forward – even those with limited technological abilities – to get students through the semester without loss of credits or academic momentum. Now that we are well into the fall semester, with many colleges still remote, and others having had to send students home after bringing them back to campus, and no end in sight, adjustments that seemed temporary will have to be reexamined. Provisions related to extensions of time to tenure, evaluations and observations in remote mode, office hours in remote mode, access to campus, responsibilities while on campus, to name a few are all ripe for reconsideration. And of course, perhaps the most difficult issue for the foreseeable future will be rebuilding the economy; where and how higher education will fit into that, and what new opportunities will exist for greater funding for higher education, will be a challenge that confronts us all.

There are no rosy, picture-perfect labor-management relationships, even when both sides are doing their respective jobs right. Tension, disagreement and haggling are natural and healthy. The line between positive friction and dangerous acrimony is often thin, if not blurred. What can never be ambiguous, however, is a belief that both the management and labor sides share in the mission and care deeply about the students and faculty of the institution.

10

CASE STUDY

State University of New York

Raymond L. Haines Jr.

Background

I think it helpful in understanding and evaluating this writing to know the vantage point from which these thoughts were formed. What follows is my "opinion" based upon personal experience as an attorney specializing in public sector labor relations during a career that spanned over four decades. It is also important to note that I served exclusively as a management representative for my entire service in higher education administration. After an internship at the New York State Governor's Office of Employee Relations (GOER), my first professional position immediately after graduating law school was as the Assistant to the President for Labor Relations and Legal Affairs at the State University College at Oswego (SUCO). SUCO is one of the State University of New York's (SUNY) largest four-year colleges, and is now a "comprehensive" college granting advanced degrees. I served in this capacity for two different presidents, and in order to be effective I needed to come to a full understanding of virtually all aspects of a collegiate enterprise. This included labor-management, governance, academic, student affairs, affirmative action and legal issues (to name a few) which all intertwine in the operation of a college campus. The SUNY College at Oswego is but one part of a large system with an overlay of State and Federal laws, rules regulations and policies that necessarily must also be considered. This overlay also required developing an understanding of what is referred to in New York as the "control agencies" and the offices within those agencies that essentially determine the direction and outcome of most large issues. Last, but most certainly not least, was appreciating the role of each of the local chapters of the large State bargaining units

DOI: 10.4324/9781003138990-12

and understanding the need to cultivate relationships with the local chapter leaders. That campus experience was truly a primer for my next assignment in the SUNY System Office of Employee Relations where I spent the next 40 years with increasing levels of system-wide labor relations responsibilities.

I joined the SUNY System Office of Employee Relations at a point early in the development of collective bargaining in NY when the unions were weaving their way into the fabric of public sector employment and management was attempting to adopt to a developing concept that work rules could no longer be imposed unilaterally. I decided to retire a few years ago and currently have the title of SUNY Associate Vice Chancellor for Employee Relations, Emeritus. As the Associate Vice Chancellor, I directed a staff of four other attorneys who all had particular expertise in public sector labor law. Together, each serving as a designee of the SUNY Chancellor, we were given the responsibility of handling all matters pertaining to collective bargaining on behalf of the system. In this regard, we were the interface on such matters with GOER, the central office staff of the unions, and administrators at the 29 State-operated campuses (more on that to follow). Our office represented SUNY on the State's bargaining teams and I served as the University Chief Negotiator for bargaining with the SUNY Professional Services Negotiating Unit and the SUNY Graduate Student Negotiating Unit. During my service in this capacity, I authored much of the language appearing in those contracts. Both units will be addressed later in this article. What I hope to provide in this chapter is practical assistance in handling at least some of the myriad of challenges that will arise in the course of interactions between the representatives of labor and management under the umbrella of collective bargaining. I will attempt to identify how these challenges were overcome, thus offering some guidance to readers as to what might be considered when faced with a like situation. While a number of my colleagues like to affix a label to a particular concept as a "best practice", I would argue that it was "best" only for that specific and unique set of facts and circumstance because it yielded a desired result. I will therefore not be referring to anything that follows as a "best practice", but simply something that worked for us in a particular set of circumstances. "Success" in the arena of labor relations is, in my view, the product of creative thinkers coming together with some level of trust to find a mutually acceptable (or at least not mutually repulsive) resolution to the issue they are addressing. In the context of collective bargaining, I would suggest that "success" is measured by the ability of the parties to find creative resolutions to enough issues to make a written compact regarding the rules under which they will co-exist for a specific period of time. While changing external conditions are likely to cause the parties to make some adjustments going forward, the durability of the heart of provisions pertaining to core issues is a good measure of how well the parties have done. In addition to trust and creative thinking, luck, proper timing and access to substantial funding also help, but the latter never seems to be available.

So, after six Governors, about ten or so Chancellors, and multiple shifts in bargaining units and their leadership, I offer the following information.

New York State Public Sector Collective Bargaining

Starting with a bit of history, unionism was introduced to the State of New York in the late 1960s with formal recognition of bargaining units and representatives shortly thereafter. In large measure, the impetus for going in this direction was a crippling transit strike in New York City and the resultant desire for legislation that would prevent the vast majority of State employees from engaging in a work stoppage at any time thereafter. Labor organizers were willing to accept this limitation in order to pursue unionization of the well over 200,000-person State workforce. A key item to be included in the enabling act (generally known as the Taylor Law in reference to the head of the drafting commission) was therefore a prohibition of strikes by State bargaining unit employees accompanied by the disincentives of substantial penalties and forfeitures for engaging in such activities. The regulatory structure for public sector collective bargaining concurrently created an oversight agency, the Public Employment Relations Board (PERB). PERB was charged with ongoing responsibility for:

1. Determining the composition of bargaining units using "community of interest" as the guiding factor (such as clerical duties, law enforcement, etc.).
2. The certification of bargaining units based on a showing of employee interest in having union representation.
3. The certification of specific bargaining agents through an election process.
4. The ongoing monitoring and protection of employee rights specified under the Taylor Law.

Within the structure for determining bargaining units, two fundamental principals were underscored. First, the vast majority of employees of the State should ultimately be placed in a bargaining unit covered by a collective bargaining agreement (Agreement). Such employees would thus, by virtue of their inclusion in a bargaining unit, be prevented from withholding their service to the State. That principle significantly limited the number of employees and titles categorized as "management" who were precluded from participating in a union and are generally terminable at will. The second principle was that a bargaining unit should be as broadly based as possible while still honoring the concept of "community of interest". The interest of State management was to have large bargaining units which would naturally result in a fewer number of bargaining agents with which to bargain. This was clearly an important factor in both limiting the resources management would need to dedicate to the negotiations process and enabling the monitoring and coordination of the rights, benefits and attendant costs attributable to the Agreements. As a practical matter, the type of work performed by State employees is similar in multiple State agencies, thus making State-wide units the most logical structure where the community of interest is broad based. Separate concurrent legislation created the Governor's Office of Employee Relations (GOER). This new agency, which reported directly to the Governor, was given broad statutory authority with regard to all aspects of collective bargaining. It was charged with ongoing oversight responsibility for negotiation and implementation of collective bargaining Agreements with all entities certified to represent State employees. Despite GOER's wide authority with regard to collective bargaining, the financing of associated costs (such as increments, health benefits, and the like) remained subject to the approval of the Division of the Budget and ultimately the Legislature and the Governor.

State University of New York

Next, we will look specifically at SUNY. In this regard, my role in system administration was to serve as its senior representative on all matters pertaining to collective bargaining. SUNY generally employees about 65,000 people of which about 1,600 at any given time are regarded as "management". The remaining 63,000 plus employees are all assigned to one of eight separate bargaining units represented by six different bargaining agents. Each bargaining unit has its own collective bargaining Agreement. SUNY has 29 State-operated campuses spread throughout the State which include large university centers, colleges, specialty schools, medical schools and three major hospitals. In addition to the 29 State-operated campuses that function under the umbrella of the State Agreements, SUNY also has a 35 Community Colleges which are county based. Although organizationally reporting to SUNY's Chancellor and Board of Trustees, Community College employees are not covered by the Agreements applicable to SUNY's other employees. The 29 State-operated campuses function under a uniform regulatory structure, Agreements that have system-wide applicability and report administratively to the Chancellor and the Board of Trustees. Each campus, however, is regarded as an individual agency for budget purposes. The President is appointed by the SUNY Board of Trustees and serves as the sole appointing authority for that campus. Continuing or permanent appointment (Tenure) is campus specific, but may only be granted by the Chancellor upon recommendation by each campus President. Although appointed by the Board of Trustees, the President similarly receives tenure to the faculty separately by grant of the Chancellor. As noted above, certain of the units represent employees in a number of State agencies. Such units would generally be comprised of administrative assistants, clericals, physical plant personnel, guards and others with similar occupational titles. The Agreements with these units are generally bargained at the State level by GOER with participants on the bargaining teams from the larger agencies. Two units, however, are specific only to SUNY. Those being the SUNY Professional Services Negotiating Unit (PSNU) which represents the faculty and professional staff, and the SUNY Graduate Student Negotiating Unit (GSNU), which represents graduate students employed in certain specific titles. I will attempt to address noteworthy items for each unit, starting with the disruption of academic governance resulting from the move into collective bargaining with the PSNU.

Academic Governance

As noted, the SUNY System is a creature of statute created in the late 1940s under the NY State Education Law. The various rules and regulations pertaining to the operational aspects of SUNY were placed in the NY Code of Rules and Regulations (NYCRR) published by the Secretary of State. The NYCRR contained provisions for the administrative structure of system administration, campus administrations, as well as the appointment and termination of those SUNY officers, faculty and professional staff. Also contained in those regulations was an academic governance structure called the Faculty Senate, which was given the responsibilities of both interfacing with campus governance and providing administrative officers with guidance on the development and delivery of academic programs. Each campus had its own local governance structure which functioned under the umbrella of the SUNY Faculty Senate. The campus faculty senates developed local by-laws covering all sorts of matters, including local procedures for appointment, reappointment and non-renewal. Prior to collective bargaining the SUNY Faculty Senate and the local faculty senates were essentially the sole consultative bodies for both the campus and SUNY System administrative offices. The advent of collective bargaining dramatically and permanently reduced the sphere of influence of the senates by drawing legal boundaries around what, and with whom, matters could henceforth be discussed. SUNY administrators at all levels were unavoidably caught in the middle of the predictable tension accompanying this redistribution of authority to the union, a tension exacerbated by the initial lack of clarity on those boundaries.

A fair reading of the rather broad limiting language in the Taylor Law with regard to management's interactions with entities other than the certified bargaining agent leads to the conclusion that it is intended to keep employment-related issues within both the labor-management forum and under PERB's enforcement jurisdiction. PERB's view of a "term or condition of employment" would therefore be determinative of what, if any, role the senates could continue to have. Early on, PERB recognized that the Faculty Senate and the local governance organizations were critical to SUNY's educational mission with regard to matters pertaining directly to the educational programs. PERB balanced the specific need to allow that organizational structure to continue in some form against a clear recognition that the union was henceforth the sole representative of the faculty and professional staff on any and all matters involving "terms and conditions of employment". The latter would wait for clarification as PERB developed case law in responding to charges filed by the various bargaining units during the Taylor Law's infancy. The decision to recognize the Faculty Senate as having a continuing role in SUNY acting on behalf of the faculty on educational matters concurrent with the recognition of a bargaining agent representing this same group for collective bargaining purposes created a challenging dynamic for labor, management and academic governance. There was some fear on the part of some people who had been historically active in faculty governance at the campus or system levels that the first bargaining agent certified by PERB, the Senate Professional Association (SPA), might attempt to dismantle the senates or somehow render them ineffectual. Concurrently, there was some concern that faculty participation in the senates might erode the union's importance to their membership. While skirmishes did arise over the evolving boundaries, labor, management and the leadership of the senates recognized that they needed to co-exist in order to best serve the educational mission of SUNY. It was a fact that the dues-paying SPA membership was relatively small (dues were voluntary at that point) and SPA was actively attempting to improve the level of faculty support. SPA apparently recognized that it would be counterproductive in this effort to overtly attempt to undermine an established faculty-based organization. It would appear that the same rationale was applied to local faculty by-laws, which were excluded from the grievance process and remain so to date. Although the Faculty Senate did not wish to relinquish its former role as the sole consultative body for both the campus and SUNY System administrative offices, it was faced with the fact that the Taylor Law had unilaterally changed that status and it would not be regained. The emerging PERB case law served to better define the role of each organization in litigation, thus adding an element of self interest in avoiding additional risks. In addition to the PERB determinations, a contributing factor to a reduction in the union's concern with its status with the faculty in relation to that of the Faculty Senate was the substantial increase in union membership and the arrival of agency shop dues deductions. SPA's successor in interest, United University Professions (UUP) achieved a massive increase in membership and enjoyed an affiliation with the politically powerful New York State United Teachers (NYSUT) and its affiliate, the American Federation of Teachers (AFT). With UUP secure in its representation status and PERB's case law guidance firmly in place, campus and system administration could communicate separately with the Senate and UUP on matters appropriate to each, while respecting their particular roles with SUNY.

It would seem that the old adage that "necessity is the mother of invention" is applicable to the co-existence of both the bargaining agent and the Faculty Senate and must certainly be regarded as a success as now having survived decades.

Evolution

As noted earlier, PERB was liberal with the concept of "community of interest" in order to create large bargaining units. It therefore determined that those employees unique to SUNY would be housed in a single bargaining unit. As a consequence, there are blocks of employees within this single bargaining unit whose common responsibilities ultimately needed to be addressed separately. The SUNY teaching faculty came under the umbrella of collective bargaining with the concepts of tenure (referred to as "continuing appointment") and promotion well established for the profession. While some procedural adjustments and clarifications have been made over time, those concepts were essentially left undisturbed going forward. This block of employees is referred to as the SUNY academic employees. Academic employee titles appear in the SUNY Policies of the Board of Trustees, also published in the NYCRR. Within the unit is another block of employees who provide technical and administrative support for the educational enterprise. This group has a wide range of responsibilities distinct from the teaching faculty and is referred to as the SUNY "professional employees".

Professional Employees

The responsibilities of the academic employees are primarily teaching, research and publication. While professional employees (generally numbering over 18,000) may also engage in limited teaching, research and publication, the primary components of their professional obligation are focused on other types of service. These responsibilities can range from the provision of various administrative services (such as student services, fund raising and counseling) to classroom support in the form of audiovisual, laboratory equipment and others. While the faculty had an established system of solidifying their employment relationship through tenure, a similar structure did not exist for professional employees. It is important to note that for many years prior to collective bargaining, NY had in place a statutory system for the "classified service" administered by the Department of Civil Service pertaining to State employment that provided for permanent appointment (tenure) after six months to a year of acceptable service. This system did not apply to the State University Professional Service, which was defined by law and regulation. Other than management, the SUNY professional employees were therefore in the unique and unenviable position when compared to the rest of the State workforce in not having a means to obtain permanency of employment.

The union was, at this time, attempting to increase its membership. The bargaining agent therefore had an immediate opportunity to demonstrably represent this block of employees by pursuing a solution to an obvious and undeniable inequity in the lack of job security. The problem simply could not be ignored by SUNY as the system was concurrently attempting to expand. The acceptance of the concept of tenure for the professional employees (termed "permanent appointment") brought with it the need to establish procedures by which such decisions would be reached. Continuing appointment was achieved after seven consecutive years of service. The union sought a shorter period of service for professional employees. The jockeying for representation among the bargaining agents apparently made it strategically unwise to argue any analogy with the classified service and the parties agreed to a seven-year system similar to faculty. The campus by-laws, which were pretty much left undisturbed, had a structure by which recommendations on reappointment, promotion and continuing appointment flowed from the departments up the administrative chain to the President. The next challenge was to develop a system for the same transactions pertaining to professional employees. The organizational structure most similar to the academic departments were professional programs. Each, such as Student Affairs, had a person in charge of the program with subordinates who supervised others responsible for component parts. Analogizing to the faculty model, the parties structured a system that began with an evaluation and recommendation by the immediate supervisor which moved upward through the program and the rest of the organizational structure until reaching the President. The collective bargaining Agreements generally ran for four years and the parties recognized that a new system for the evaluation and promotion of professional employees might need to be adjusted by mutual agreement during the contract period. In order to allow for such changes, the systems for the evaluation and promotion of professional employees were put into Memorandums of Understanding. Although there have been minor changes implemented as changing conditions warranted, these systems have remained largely unaltered for more than four decades. One could consider that durability a measure of success.

Librarians

The role of librarians has evolved significantly over the years. The antiquated stereotype of a person who helped patrons find materials and put them away is simply gone. That, however, was not the case when this unit was certified. As a consequence, the librarians (generally numbering about 300) were treated as professional employees under the various procedures noted above. The evolution of the profession had commenced and early on it became clear that the change in identity would need to be addressed. Technology obviously changed the responsibilities of librarians as materials and collections could be searched electronically and shifted between campuses. Library administration recognized that the librarians would need to provide instruction and assistance to students and campus staff on the availability and use of these new and developing tools. This was clearly a departure from, and an increase in, the historic job responsibilities. These changes precipitated a shift from fixed hours of work to a more flexible arrangement needed to provide these services to the various segments of the campus community as their schedules permitted.

These changes made the appointment and review system designed for the professional employees increasingly difficult for the administration to make work for the librarians, and therefore equally challenging for the union to assist their members. The situation was aggravated by two additional factors. While some may disagree, there has long been a "perception" of increased status for members of the teaching faculty. Perhaps more importantly, there is limited opportunity for local administration to unilaterally award meaningful salary increases, and there are SUNY salary schedules (which are periodically adjusted to reflect the negotiated increases) specific to the academic employee titles and the professional employee titles. The collaborative solution for labor and management was to agree to designate the librarians as academic employees. This required mutual agreement on modifications to the Agreement as well as the Policies of the Board of Trustees and the NYCRR. This shift moved the librarians out from coverage of the Memorandums of Understanding for the Evaluation and Promotion of Professional Employees and into the campus procedures for academic employees. The librarian titles were added to the salary schedule for academic employees.

Although this shift helped the parties reconcile a number of issues that had arisen with the evolving role of the librarians, there are lingering considerations that are being addressed through the campus governance process as time passes. One of the most challenging of these considerations is determining equity in the standards used at the campus level for the promotion and tenure (continuing appointment) of the teaching faculty versus those for librarians.

Clinical Practice

SUNY operates three hospitals (Stony Brook, Downstate and Syracuse) and has affiliation Agreements between SUNY Buffalo Health Sciences and hospitals in the Buffalo area as part of the medical education programs offered at each of those locations. The physicians (generally numbering about 2,500) are an integral component of any medical education program as medical students learn through a combination of instruction and observation. The physicians have academic titles and are in the bargaining unit. As a condition precedent to being on staff, each physician must obtain and maintain the appropriate licenses, certifications and hospital admitting privileges required by the State of New York to engage in the practice of medicine. The earning capacity of physicians in NY clearly exceeds the level of compensation SUNY is able to provide through salary. Although a relatively modest portion of the 35,000-person PSNU unit, the physicians have been successful at identifying their unique concerns and speaking with a single voice. As a group, they are not unexpectedly the highest earners in SUNY and therefore pay a substantial amount to UUP in dues. The physicians were therefore of great importance to SUNY's medical education programs and a very valuable block of members for the union.

The manner in which SUNY was able to recruit and maintain physicians was to allow physicians to augment their salaries by billing for their medical services. Although this arrangement had existed for many years unchallenged, it was arguably in direct contradiction to a State prohibition of private entrepreneurialism on State property. At a point in time after a change in State leadership, with SUNY expressing concern with the sufficiency of its budget, there was a determination by the administration that SUNY needed to (a) exercise greater control over the income derived from medical services provided in its facilities (or through the affiliations in Buffalo) and (b) receive some portion of those monies for its own programmatic needs. In assessing the challenges the parties faced, it must be noted that NY has a rather broad indemnification statute covering State employees for damages resulting from acts performed within their scope of employment, as long as such acts were not performed in a manner that is "willful wanton or malicious". The State specifically excluded the SUNY physicians from such indemnification while performing medical services. As a result, the medical departments organized concurrently as corporations in order to obtain malpractice insurance.

The solution to this rather complicated situation was to focus on the underlying issue: money management. Recognizing that the corporations needed to continue, the parties had to structure an umbrella under which the clinical practice revenue stream would be made visible in a coordinated fashion without disrupting their operations. While SUNY needed to acquire a "slice of the pie", the parties recognized that any monies taken from that revenue stream would need to be directed back into the campus medical education program in order to be acceptable. With these fundamental mutual understandings, the parties were able to formulate what became the "Plan for Management of Clinical Practice Income". This structure was incorporated into the SUNY Policies of the Board of Trustees and the NYCRR. Overseen by a Governing Board comprised of representatives from the departments with input from the campus President, the "Plan" lays out an order of distribution of such revenues within the departments with a small percentage dedicated specifically to educational program enhancements. The collaboration between the parties enabled the creation of a system that seemed to satisfy all of the differing interests, yet not do damage to the efficiency by which these departments/corporations had successfully operated for many years.

Observations

The three topics discussed above, professional employees, librarians and clinical practice, were selected as illustrative of difficult situations confronting the parties that were precipitated by events external to the bargaining process. The parties each recognized that finding a mutually acceptable resolution to each of these situations was an imperative that could not be avoided. Of singular importance is the mutual recognition of the specific problem the parties are trying to solve, separate from other issues that will impact the solution. For the "professional employee" matter, it was creating systems for evaluation and promotion. With regard to the librarians, it was resolving a disconnect that had developed over time between the systems for evaluation and promotion that were based upon a set of norms for the professional obligation of professional employees and the actual professional obligation of the librarians. For the physicians, it was creating a mechanism for the oversight and accountability for private income derived from billings for medical services performed by State employees. Each of these "problems" had accompanying issues of concern to labor and management. In order to find a common ground, the parties each had to determine what core issues would have to be addressed. This is the point where the "wish" list becomes a very realistic "have to have" list. That determination, for both sides, will necessarily involve an evaluation of "what won't hurt" rather than "what do we want". It is important in this regard to recognize that negotiations are an ongoing process that simply stop for a brief period during the term of the Agreement. The parties will meet again in subsequent rounds where items will be revisited after being tested in practice.

In the author's view, the parties must develop a level of trust that allows for a communication or signaling of these core issues if the process is to move to a conclusion. For example, labor obviously wanted evaluation and promotion systems for the professional employees that were reasonably straightforward and provided enforceable procedural protections for fair treatment of its members. Management's primary concerns were the preservation of its right to determine the elements of the professional obligation consistent with operational needs, and protection of its decision-making authority. The relationship of the parties eventually allowed for identification of these core issues for inclusion in the systems ultimately accepted by the parties. A similar process occurred with the librarian and physician matters which both yielded mutually acceptable solutions. As noted above, all three arrangements have been in place, with minor adjustments, for a number of years. A measure of success for negotiations is most certainly reflected in the durability of the item agreed upon.

Unionization of the SUNY Graduate Student Employees

The Graduate Student Employee Union (GSEU) is comprised of all SUNY non-medical students enrolled in a graduate degree program who have the title "Graduate Assistant" or "Teaching Assistant" and receive a stipend from a SUNY State-operated campus. The substantial majority of the GSEU's members are employed at SUNY's University Centers (which are doctoral degree-granting institutions) with a significantly lesser number of members employed at the Comprehensive Colleges. As mentioned earlier with regard to the College at Oswego, the latter are four-year Colleges that subsequently expanded their educational programs to include a limited number of advanced degrees. SUNY and the State did oppose unionization of the graduate students based upon the then widely held beliefs by SUNY administration and faculty that such a change would wholly disrupt the educational process for advanced degrees and that there was only limited interest in unionization on the part of the graduate student employees. The option of voluntary recognition was therefore declined. PERB determined that the community of interest for this block of employees extended across the SUNY System. PERB therefore required a showing of interest for unionization by graduate student employees from each campus where they were employed. After several failed attempts at obtaining the requisite level of support from graduate student employees across the SUNY System, the GSEU organizing effort (supported by its parent affiliate, the Communication Workers of America (CWA)) was finally successful in 1992. The GSEU and its bargaining agent were certified by PERB and bargaining commenced in 1993. In more recent years, the GSEU has maintained its affiliation with CWA as a local, but now has a great deal more autonomy than in the early years. The GSEU generally has 4,000 plus members, each of whom is an employee of the campus where they are pursuing their degree. It is most important to note that each student must remain in good academic standing and meet the academic progress requirements for his/her specific degree program to remain concurrently employed at that campus. The failure to maintain a student status results in an automatic termination of employment as a graduate student employee. A SUNY policy, which long proceeded collective bargaining, also limits the work obligation of a graduate student employee to 20 hours per week. The import of that policy, which is rooted in SUNY's education mission, means this is a unit of half-time-or-less employees when compared to the work obligation of other State employees.

Preparation for Bargaining with the SUNY GSEU

Bargaining with this unit has necessarily evolved over the subsequent years, but many of the initial challenges remain instructive. SUNY was established legislatively in 1948 and expanded rapidly during the late 1960s and early 1970s. The graduate student programs therefore had a long history and well-established local practices and protocols at each campus well prior to the certification of the GSEU in 1993. Both academic administration and the teaching faculty generally viewed graduate students as exactly that...graduate students. Collective bargaining suddenly gave all of these graduate students a new identity as "employees" with specific rights, thus placing new obligations on campus administration as well as the faculty. An early challenge for management in preparation for bargaining was simply gathering accurate information on the unit, as this category of "employees" had never before existed in the in the States' organized work force. At most campuses, the interaction with the SUNY System Office of Employee Relations generally occurred at the local senior human resource management level. We anticipated that having to address new matters in the bargaining process that were unique to the blending of employment and academic issues would be beyond the experience and expertise of our usual contacts. Assistance in understanding the student academic part of such issues would necessarily have to come from within the educational program side of campus administration, which was normally only on the periphery of the negotiation process with other units. It was also clear that the implementation of any change in local practice, policy or procedure necessitated by the terms of a system-wide Agreement would require the cooperation of the campus provosts, academic vice presidents, deans, department chairs and faculty. We therefore depended on the ranking academic officers at each campus to provide input regarding their administrative issues as well as provide reaction to the proposals we received. For these purposes, a standing committee of such academic officers was formed for the duration of the negotiations. In addition to creating this new system-wide communication network, we invited a limited number of ranking academic officers from the University Centers to participate on the State's bargaining team and provide us with immediate insights. We found that participation from the academic side of SUNY was later very valuable in getting some "buy in" at the campus level. These administrators were also relied upon to convey a significant message that needed to be understood at each campus: the treatment of graduate student employees as "employees" was now a matter of law.

Challenges in Bargaining with the SUNY GSEU

We next move to the negotiations with GSEU. It has long been my opinion (which I believe is shared by many in the negotiating business) that trust between the team leaders is an absolutely essential element of reaching an Agreement. Trust develops over time and is the foundation for a working relationship built on mutual honesty and integrity. Both sides must view the negotiation process as a joint effort to find acceptable common ground on core issues, understanding that those matters on the periphery are likely to ultimately go unaddressed at that time. Unfortunately, that is not a scenario that generally exists with a new bargaining unit such as the GSEU. A new unit, like the GSEU, tends to come to the table expecting to receive much the same in their first contract as other units achieved through many years of negotiations. The initial rounds of bargaining with GSEU were, not unexpectedly, particularly difficult. Among a variety of factors, the following items seem to be the most noteworthy of the many impediments needed to be overcome in order to reaching Agreements:

1. The GSEU team was led by its President (at that time, simply another graduate student elected to that position) rather than an experienced negotiator. The GSEU bargaining team was comprised of graduate students selected by their peers at each campus. The entire team was therefore inexperienced with the collective bargaining process.
2. There was a lack of familiarity with, and understanding of, much of the State and SUNY laws, rules, regulations and policies that affect all SUNY employees, and therefore impact bargaining.
3. The GSEU came with expectations for health coverage and salaries that mirrored those provided to full time employees in other units. This was most unrealistic in light of the fact that, as noted above, the work obligation of GSEU unit member was half-time or less when compared to the work obligation of State employees in other units.
4. The lack of trust of the State and SUNY representatives on the part of the GSEU resulted in an inability to develop any type of working relationship between parties.
5. The transient nature of both the members' employment with SUNY and their personal participation in the bargaining process.

Particularly in the first round of negotiations, an inordinate amount of time was dedicated to attempting to educate the GSEU bargainers to the external limitations on SUNY and the State with regard a number of their bargaining proposals. The three GSEU proposals that seemed to dominate the table discussions early on pertained to health insurance, salary and a grievance process. These proposals unrealistically sought to track benefits, salaries and procedures provided to full-time employees in other units that were achieved through the give and take of many rounds of bargaining. In this regard, it is always necessary for the management team to be aware of the fact that each of the bargaining units in the State monitor the contents of the Agreements reached with the other units and expect some level of parity on common items such as benefits and salaries. The outcome of the negotiations with the GSEU could therefore impact the negotiations with other State bargaining units. The GSEU was also either unaware or insensitive to the insurmountable limitations imposed by both the State and SUNY budgets. A persistent problem in identifying and understanding the GSEU's core issues was attributable to the ever-present air of distrust of the SUNY and State representatives and resultant reluctance to prioritize their issues. Nonetheless, the State and SUNY offered compromises on what was believed to be the union's essential interests. The first Agreements were ultimately reached with professional assistance furnished by CWA. The GSEU subsequently obtained substantial administrative independence from

CWA, thus ending what had been valuable assistance to the parties in reaching prior Agreements. The GSEU's continued resistance to using the services of labor relations professionals offered by CWA has contributed to perpetuating the difficulties in working with this unit. The GSEU now has paid positions for representatives assigned to specific campuses and a salaried (but still elected) President. It remains to be seen whether or not the advent of these positions and recurrent interactions by the GSEU representatives with both campus and external administrative offices will eventually help to achieve a more regularized relationship with SUNY and the State. On a positive note, after 26 years of negotiations, there does seem to be the beginnings of a somewhat better understanding of management's limitations in a State-wide multiple bargaining unit negotiating arena. That being said, it is unfortunately anticipated that due to the transient nature of the unit members, turnover of bargaining team members and recurrent changes in their leadership, the GSEU will continue to foster unrealistic expectations for the membership for the immediate future.

Noteworthy SUNY GSEU Bargaining Issues and Solutions

Notwithstanding this somewhat challenging relationship, the collective bargaining process did provide a forum for successfully examining matters that prior circumstances had prevented from being addressed effectively in the past. A selective list of these matters, not offered in order of importance, and their current status is as follows:

1. Health Benefits: This was mostly a matter that had to be addressed by either coverage under the students' parents' family health insurance or use of the campus Student Health Center Services. Family health insurance policies frequently have age limitations and the cost of individual health insurance policies are most often beyond the economic reach of most graduate student employees. Thus, the burden of providing care for mental or physical health issues generally fell upon the campus Student Health Center.

2. Employment Issues: Various problems could generally be brought to local student judiciary or academic committees operating with procedures that were simply not designed for examining employment issues. Other State and Federal avenues are available to seek redress for very specific employment issues pertaining to safety and discrimination. Those forums were often not applicable to the student employment matters at issue and costly for the employer to respond to and defend the accusations raised therein.

3. Support for travel, educational or professional conferences, or other such professional development endeavors: access to such support was historically a completely local matter. Determinations were made at the department or

division levels and funds drawn from very limited general purpose department and/or division accounts. Budget limitations were routinely a significant obstacle for approving, in whole or in part, any such requests.

4. Recruitment and Retention: The additional costs associated with the
    recruitment and retention of particularly talented graduate student employees
    were necessarily drawn from campus funds. Divisions and departments within
    those divisions often competed against each other for limited monies. Com-
    petition within the SUNY System for such students would therefore often be
    determined simply by the annual campus budget allocations.

As is readily apparent, virtually all of the items mentioned above are attributable to having encompassed the graduate student employees within the
various local policies and procedures heretofore applicable to students in general. For matters involving cost, individual campus decisions were intended to
best advantage their own educational programs and the entirety of their student
population. The overall economic parameters, as noted, were largely dependent
upon budgetary factors. The shift into collective bargaining eventually forced
the GSEU to recognize that the potential contract solutions to a number of
their issues needed to be flexible enough to be responsive to differing student
interests at dissimilar campuses. This recognition provided the impetus for the
GSEU bargainers to consider management's more creative proposals. During
the preparation for bargaining and during the course of negotiations, the concern most voiced by campus administration was that the final Agreement would
contain unfunded mandates that the campus budgets could not absorb. With
regard to these "creative" offerings, it is important to first understand that the
funding of the SUNY as a State agency and the distribution of funding by
SUNY to each of its campuses are matters separate and apart from the State
funding of cost items in the State's collective bargaining Agreements with the
individual bargaining units. These funding decisions and allocations take place
at different times, each through a specific legislative process. An external source
of funding obviously offers a means to overcome campus opposition to various
items where such opposition is based primarily on financial concerns. While
collective bargaining for this group of employees has most certainly posed its
challenges for SUNY and campus administrations in certain areas, it was concurrently a "game changer" on other matters.

Looking first at health benefits, NY determined many years ago that there
was an economic advantage to developing and managing State-wide contracts
with the health benefits providers. With some individual program tailoring and
an array of options, the State has successfully, and cost effectively, managed
programs across the agencies and for multiple bargaining units. A program tailored to their lesser work obligation was put in place for the GSEU-represented
employees and funded by the State as part of the collective bargaining process.
The result was a uniform health benefits program for all graduate student

employees at no cost to the individual campuses, while concurrently relieving some amount of pressure on campus Student Health Centers. The State has also had a Work/Life Services Committee (formerly the Employee Assistance Program) which crossed bargaining units and assisted State employees in obtaining mental health and substance abuse services. The GSEU became a participant in this State-funded program, therefore rounding out benefits to their members at no additional cost to each members' campus.

Early on, the State experimented with using Joint Labor-Management Committees (JLMC) to address matters raised during the course of negotiations where such matters were thought to require attention spread over the term of the Agreement. The JLMC concept was to establish a central committee comprised of representatives from labor and management that would manage programs having bargaining unit-wide application. The costs associated with JLMC items would then be included in the State funding of the Agreements. The historic success of the JLMCs for other bargaining units made this mechanism a viable solution for addressing a number of the GSEU issues in a mutual gains fashion. The initial resistance to moving forward in this regard was largely due a combination of unfamiliarity with the JLMC concept and the distrust mentioned earlier. This initial resistance was overcome by the demonstrable popularity and success of the JLMCs with other State bargaining units. JLMCs subsequently became a most valuable tool for resolving issues with this unit going forward. One of the first uses of this structure was the creation of a JLMC with funding for individual graduate student employee professional development. This program provided an external source of monies for conference attendance, research projects and other related activities that would otherwise been dependent solely on limited campus resources. This mechanism was subsequently used to allocate negotiated funds to a JLMC for distribution to the campuses to be used as stipends for the purposes of recruitment and retention of graduate student employees at the Comprehensive Colleges and University Centers. While the specific campus allocations and distribution protocols were determined by the JLMC, the selection of awardees at each campus was done by academic administration. Additional mandatory student fees were put in place to offset the cost of such things as athletics, technology, and other items not directly associated with degree programs that were draining the static (and in some years reduced) campus budgets. The cost of these items has continued to rise, with such costs being passed on to the students. Concurrently, although still a bargain in the realm of higher education, SUNY's tuition has seen modest increases for several years in a row. Using the JLMC concept to help reduce some of the increasing financial burden on the graduate student employees, the parties put in place a JLMC for "fee mitigation". The committee was charged determining a methodology for the distribution of negotiated funds to the campuses for the purpose of offsetting some portion of the mandated student fees that would otherwise be the responsibility of each member. The result was to ensure campus receipt of the necessary funding while largely taking that cost burden off of the shoulders of the graduate student employees.

Grievance Procedures and Contract Language Generally

The final item for discussion pertaining to this bargaining unit is the grievance process. Before turning to the specifics for the GSEU, some general observations are in order. Grievance procedures are a critical, and perhaps the most critical, component of any collective bargaining Agreement. These procedures serve as the "gatekeeper" for funneling conflicts over specific terms and conditions of employment identified in the Agreement into a formal process for review and potential remediation. They also provide a means by which a union can, in a very visible way, provide direct service to individual unit members. Although sometimes overlooked, they also serve as a means by which management can monitor the relative success or failure of contract administration at the local level. Most grievance procedures have several steps which culminate in the submission of the claimed contract violation to a third-party neutral for a final determination and the award of an appropriate remedy. The early steps of the grievance procedures are therefore of great significance in allowing the parties to retain control of outcomes by reaching a mutually acceptable accord to resolve grievance claims before such matters go to an external decision maker. When collective bargaining first appeared in higher education, the parties had little or no experience in either the negotiating process or the drafting of contract language. Precise language for identifying what constituted a grieveable claim and what would be the permissible remedy were many times overlooked in these early Agreements. These deficiencies generally resulted in a barrage of grievance claims filed by fledgling unions attempting to enthusiastically serve the membership. Equally lacking in many instances was precise language pertaining to the negotiated contract entitlements. This initial failure on the part of both parties to anticipate controversy over ambiguous terminology ultimately led to arbitrators deciding the terms under which the parties would live until the next round of negotiations. "Imposed" contract terms are many times found unsatisfactory by both parties, but generally do lead to a much higher level of care in drafting contract language thereafter.

That being said, it is of obvious importance that all the terms of an Agreement be written (to the extent possible) in clear language that reflects "the meeting of the minds" of the negotiators and leaves as little room as possible for alternative interpretations. It is simply a reality that the language written by the negotiators at a specific point in time after lengthy discussions will inevitably be read and interpreted later on under different circumstances by others not having the benefit of background information and perhaps with different agendas. Any lack of clarity in the language is therefore very likely to result in controversy down the road. It is also necessary to understand that whatever appears in a first Agreement, whether procedural or substantive, will be regarded by the bargaining agent as a starting point upon which to build and expand. That pattern will exist with regard to every Agreement thereafter and can present significant long term difficulties if either or both the description of a permissible grievance claim and/or the permissible remedy are loosely written. There is an old saying that "not every itch needs to be scratched", and that statement is particularly applicable to labor Agreements. It is clearly the responsibility of a union to vigorously represent its membership. If there is an argument to be made on behalf of a member, and a forum in which it can be delivered; then such argument must be offered. To believe otherwise is unrealistic and fails to recognize a union's unavoidable obligation to basically "scratch every itch" unless procedurally barred from doing so. The only real control mechanism for the flow of matters into the grievance arena is very tightly drafted language limiting the specific claims eligible for review. Equally important is the need to avoid an outcome whereby, unbeknownst to the decision maker, his/her award has the impact of also significantly changing the meaning and intent of an established contract provision. The only real control over this matter is tightly drafted language as to what specific remedy or remedies are available should the grievance claim have merit, thereby carefully circumscribing the authority of the decision maker.

The SUNY GSEU Grievance Procedure: Novel and Effective

Fashioning the Agreement with the GSEU presented an opportunity to create a unique grievance procedure incorporating the concepts noted above and the lessons learned refining such procedures in other unit Agreements. As noted, the GSEU has a regular turnover in membership unlike any other State unit. With completion of the graduate student employee's degree program, he or she graduates and ceases to be a graduate student employee. While the aggregate GSEU unit membership numbers are relatively consistent from year to year, the membership numbers at a specific campus may be affected by program availability and enrollment. Those potential shifts in the membership at different campuses adds yet another level of instability to contract administration for the GSEU negotiating unit. The fact that unit members are only employed for a finite period created an imperative for a grievance procedure that would provide a review and final determination within a relatively narrow time frame. The efficiency of a grievance process is often dependent on how readily the actual grievance claim can be identified, as well as the expectation of the grievant as to what he or she expects to receive. Both of these items therefore need to be addressed in the body of the grievance procedures. Another important consideration in this development process was the likelihood that representation, different from the other State units, would not be provided by experienced labor relations professionals. The grievance procedures therefore needed to be easy to understand and follow with minimal procedural requirements. Recognizing the unavoidable grievance processing delays attendant to off-campus reviews, another consideration was to provide ample opportunities and direction for local resolution of all grievance claims. The parties ultimately agreed that identifying specific claims subject to review in the grievance forum and attaching a specific remedy to such claims would enable those at the campus level to readily recognize management's contractual obligation and the prescribed outcome of a proven contract violation. The initial activity in coming to this arrangement was for the parties to agree to a list of unambiguous graduate student employee entitlements by contract article and subsection. An example would be the payment of a specific salary increase on a date certain. Next, was to mutually agree to what specific action was appropriate for remediation of a proven failure to provide each of these specified entitlements. A grievance form was designed that provided a list of grieveable claims with an accompanying box to check off which claims were being submitted for review. The Agreement specified the sole remedy for each such claim. Those initial lists have been expanded over the years, but the structure of identifying the claim for review and its attendant remedy has remained in place as a mutually acceptable and efficient mechanism for contract administration and enforcement at the campus level. Since the implementation of these grievance review procedures in 1994, less than a half dozen matters have been appealed off campus to SUNY System Administration. No data was available regarding the number of grievances that were filed and ended at the campus level.

The State-GSEU Agreement and this unique grievance procedure can be viewed in their entirety at either the SUNY Graduate Student Employee Negotiating Unit section of the NYS Governor's Office of Employee Relations contract website https://goer.ny.gov/state-university-graduate-student-negotia ting-unit-gsnu28 or the SUNY System Administration Office of Employee Relations website https://www.suny.edu/hr/contracts/.

Closing Comments

Although the above discussions dealt with specific topics, it is hoped that they provide some insight as to methodologies that have a wide application. A comparison of efficiencies of problem resolution between SUNY and the PSNU and as between SUNY and the GSNU reveals a stark contrast. Rather than having some level of cooperation in moving toward a common goal, the negotiations with the GSEU have generally been characterized by a prolonged effort to determine and respond to undefined core issues. That is not to imply that the relationship between SUNY and UUP has at all times been serendipitous. To the contrary, there have been pitched battles in the past and there will be some in the future. A significant difference is that the SUNY Office of Employee Relations has been in daily contact with UUP's central office and field staff for a number of years attempting to resolve the myriad of issues and/

or concerns that arise with such a large and diverse unit, whereas the contacts with GSEU representatives are sporadic and generally in concert with collective bargaining. As mentioned above, this has enabled SUNY and UUP to develop a working relationship that does not yet exist with the GSEU.

While this discussion has attempted to address the importance of collaboration between the parties on specific issues and how such collaborations have affected the efficiency of the bargaining process, there is no specific reference as to how that process has impacted matters of "social Justice". NY is a most progressive State with a long history of recognizing such issues through broad-based legislative or Executive action. Examples would include matters pertaining to discrimination (such as on the basis of race, gender, religion and sexual orientation) that are covered by State law and policy. Health benefits for domestic partners has been in the State-wide programs for both labor and management many years. A State-wide labor-management committee that receives contributions through the collective bargaining process has also been in place for many years, but was preceded by legislative funding specific to day care for the children of SUNY employees and students. It has long been the State's position that individual Agreements are not the appropriate mechanism for addressing broad issues that in fact pertain to the citizens at large. Given the State's activism in this area and its policy regarding such matters, the collective bargaining arena has historically not been the forum in which matters of social justice were addressed.

As a final note, it is most important for both labor and management to always have the correct people and personalities at the table present to address issues and think creatively. Speaking from a management perspective, the persons most knowledgeable about the implementation of labor contract provisions and the interconnectivity of a labor contract and its related statutory and regulatory overlay are clearly those given responsibility for day-to-day contract administration and interaction with the unions. These are the individuals best equipped to respond and debate proposals at the table pertaining to operational matters. Unless intimately familiar with such workings, the most skilled of negotiators may unknowingly offer comments or statements that modify something important in the bargaining history, or entertain proposals that unintentionally impact other parts of the Agreement. It is therefore an imperative that the Employee Relations Representatives having direct responsibility for the unit be actively engaged in the table discussions, decision-making, and preparation/review of language submitted as proposals or for the final Agreement. To do otherwise with regard to operational items is simply an invitation to mistakes that will be most difficult to correct going forward. That is not to say that other offices should not have an equally active role with regard to specific non-operational areas of the Agreement. For NY, two examples would be the benefits programs that have provisions common to multiple units and cost items (such as salary increases) that are dependent on State funding and may also be considered as precedential for other units.

11

CASE STUDY

University of California

Nadine Baron Fishel

Former University of California President Clark Kerr once said "The United States has, overall, the most effective system of higher education the world has ever known. It is our responsibility to make students safe for ideas, not ideas safe for students." Couple that with first American Federation of Labor President Samuel Gompers: "to be free, the workers must have choice. To have choice, they must retain in their own hands the right to determine under what conditions they will work." Herein lies the great balancing act of collective bargaining in higher education.

Background

On March 23, 1868, the University of California (UC) was founded at the original Berkeley campus as a land grant institution. In subsequent years, Davis served as the Farm School (1908) for agricultural research and San Francisco (1873) developed a medical school to augment the University, though all three were considered the University of California, not separate locations. San Francisco remained dedicated to health care with an established medical school – Parnassus Hospital opened in 1907 and a nursing school in 1941 – yet became its own sovereign campus separate from Berkeley in 1958, along with UC Santa Barbara. In 1927, the University expanded and built the Los Angeles campus in Westwood. Davis, while retaining its agriculture roots then as well as now, transformed into a full independent campus in 1959, the same year of the establishment of UC Riverside.

In 1960, California created the Master Plan, expanding the system even further and granting the university the "sole authority" to award doctorate degrees

DOI: 10.4324/9781003138990-13

in public education. Additionally, the University of California had "exclusive jurisdiction" to provide training in law, medicine, dentistry and veterinary medicine as well as becoming the primary state-supported institution for research. New campuses were born established in Santa Cruz (1965), Irvine (1965), and San Diego (1964). In 2005, Merced opened to provide access to UC in the Central Valley, the heart and soul of California's agriculture base. The story wouldn't be complete without mentioning the growth of this system to be one of the top systems in the world with an explosion of academic programs that today includes five medical schools, requisite health systems and other professional health-related schools (nursing, dentistry, optometry, pharmacy), five law schools including the independent UC Hastings in San Francisco, five business schools, and the Lawrence Berkeley National Laboratory funded by the Department of Energy.

The UC system created a unique academic governance structure as well, with the Senate Faculty (tenure track) governing the academic organization. There is a President of the system and chancellors at each campus location. Between faculty, staff and students, the University of California's population totals 300,000, the second largest employer within California, with only the State of California exceeding the University in size.

Unlike many public state universities, the University of California is not governed by the state. While the Governor sits on the Board of Regents and the state provides the University with an allocation of funding, it is the Board of Regents who set the tuition rates. The mission of the University of California is to teach, research and engage in service, all of which require hiring qualified and talented academic employees, with five academic bargaining units to date.

Collective Bargaining

The Higher Employer-Employee Relations Act (HEERA) went into effect on July 1, 1979. Organized labor represented traditional staff jobs such as custodial, clerical and healthcare back to the early 1980s. With "fair share" provisions allowing for public employee unions to charge an agency fee for all covered employees in the bargaining unit, union power changed radically. Fair share legislation boomed public sector unionism in the State of California with growing organizing efforts at the University. The increase in financial support to the current unions and the newcomers alike gave them a presence with resources to challenge the University, who had been conducting business as a benevolent parent. The University currently has 14 systemwide units, skilled crafts local units at every campus, and recently added medical residents and interns at the five medical school locations. The UC Santa Cruz campus has a Senate Faculty unit, though they are the only campus with such a unit.

On the academic side, there are five academic bargaining units in addition to the local medical interns and residents. There is an **Instructional Unit** including lecturers, demonstration teachers, supervisors of teacher education, and educators in three K-12 University-run schools (4,000). The graduate students who teach are **Academic Student Employees (ASEs)** and represent Teaching Assistants, Readers and Tutors (13,000) at all locations with undergraduate students. The **Librarians** have a small unit of 400, which is shrinking given the nature of online library services. The **Postdoctoral Scholars** including fellows and paid directs became represented in 2008 (6,000). Most recently, in 2018, the **Academic Researchers** (4,000) joined the unionized workforce. The University Council of American Federation of Teachers (UC-AFT) represents the Instructional Unit and the librarians' unit and the United Automobile Workers (UAW) represents the ASEs, postdoctoral scholars and the Academic Researchers. The UAW sought to represent all graduate students including the graduate student researchers, but the court ruled against them, providing the following premise: 1) employment had to be contingent on student status; and 2) services rendered were unrelated to educational objectives or 3) if educational objectives were subordinate to services performed. This ruling held until 2018 when the UAW successfully moved the state legislature to change the language in the Higher Education Employer-Employee Relations Act to accept premise 1 only (above) to allow for all graduate student employees to be represented.

University Systems in California

Unlike other states, California has two distinct public university systems: University of California, which is an RO1 research university, in addition to issuing degrees, and the California State University (CSU) system, which is primarily an educational institution. UC has 10 campuses and CSU has 23 campuses. While California is the most populous state in America, the number of public options for students is immense. Both systems depend in part on state funding but to very different degrees. CSU is far more dependent on state support than UC. However, CSU has much greater central control over the system than UC. At UC, campus autonomy holds great weight. Additionally, HEERA covers both state systems, though there are special provisions specifically for UC. At CSU, faculty are covered in a bargaining unit and at UC, only the Santa Cruz campus has such a unit. Also, UC has two distinct levels of faculty: senate faculty (tenure track) and lecturers (non-tenure track). There are also adjuncts, professors of practice, lecturers with security of employment, though they are not captured in either of the two main categories. The UC-AFT has attempted to change on multiple occasions.

Bargaining Process

As a large system, the University of California has many layers of consultation for collective bargaining. Ultimately, the President provides the guidance, based on direction from executive vice chancellors and vice provosts. The formulation of bargaining objectives comes through academic personnel and labor relations at each campus location as well as a review of the key issues that reached the arbitration stage over the life of the current agreement. At the campus level, administrators survey departments with large populations of the bargaining unit prior to attendance at the first preparation session. With academic bargaining units, the campus consultation usually includes ladder-ranked faculty, deans and chairs. The Office of the President has directed each campus to develop consultation teams, composed of key leaders who serve as sounding boards for sharing union and management proposals during the bargaining process.

Economic parameters are set by the council of executive vice chancellors. While parameters usually change an average of three times over the course of collective bargaining (initial, mid-way, final), negotiators develop parameters carefully. Models are presented strategically with the ultimate interest in solving the problems raised at the table, while balancing the economic implications and maintaining academic judgment and integrity.

In California, there is a requirement to "sunshine" the topics and issues each party plans to present in bargaining as part of public notice. The sunshine process takes about three weeks. Although it is legally management's responsibility, the union also participates in the scheduled public notice meetings. The process is included in the Duration article of each agreement.

Once complete, the parties schedule meetings (face to face) at mutually agreed upon locations. As a statewide university, spanning over 500 miles from the Northernmost campus (Davis) to the Southernmost campus (San Diego), the parties must plan in advance to have appropriate space for full bargaining teams to attend a two- to three-day session.

Beginning with each party making an opening statement and a brief summary of its proposals with reasonable explanations, the process is underway. Full language proposals are presented with commentary about objectives. The unions take great pride in bringing members in to provide testimonials from the grassroots; management rarely brings guests, unless they are subject matter experts (health and safety or parking directors). Advanced agendas guide the process but are loosely followed and not binding. Counterproposals follow proposals with caucus time in between sessions. Typically, the parties are together for two hours with caucus time and a meal break in between and then back for another two-hour session later in the day.

Unlike many negotiations, the University of California passes full language proposals. While it is more cumbersome than bullet points or conceptual proposals, when tentative agreements are reached, the language is already set in stone, eliminating the number of arbitrations on contract interpretation or messy interactions after settlement of first constructing language. Although contract interpretation cases are part of contract administration during the life of the agreement, passing full language leads to fewer controversies. Bargaining history remains the critical component for such hearings, as the arbitrator either chooses 1) the plain language interpretation of what the language means or 2) reliance on the actual words the parties "said" to each other at the bargaining table on the intent of the meaning of the language. This is the reason a note taker is used (bargaining is typically not recorded), with each party keeping their own notes of each and every session.

At some point, either a settlement is reached, or the parties reach impasse. The University has passed package proposals with positions on all outstanding issues as a "last, best and final offer." At times, last, best and final offers result in an agreement; in other instances, they are the last step prior to impasse.

In California, the parties file for impasse (either unilaterally or jointly) with the Public Employment Relations Board, who determines whether there is an impasse. If so, the parties must go through 1) mediation with a state mediator, and, if not resolved in mediation, 2) fact-finding hearing. The fact-finding process involves a tripartite panel: a neutral arbitrator, a university official and a union official (with the authority to make binding agreements). During the hearing, the parties present key proposals and factual evidence supporting positions. The tripartite panel may meet in closed session, with the goal of finding a strategy to settle the impasse. If the panel is unsuccessful, the neutral writes a decision and the two partisan members may concur or dissent. There is a "quiet period" before the decision is released publicly for the parties to use it and get back to the bargaining table, once again with the goal of settling the unresolved issues. Once impasse procedures have completed, if a dispute remains, the University has the right to implement portions of its last, best and final offer and the union has the right to engage in a strike.

While the University of California has worked tirelessly with its unions on the academic side to reach agreement, it has endured impasses and strikes. Leaders must decide whether a strike is worthwhile, given the stakes. There is no right answer. At times, the union muscles its collective strength and the University finds a way to resolve the issues; at other times, the union falls short and, without the required might, the University is able to hold the line.

Academic Student Employees

Every time a University representative mentions that the UAW represents graduate student employees, researchers and postdocs, the guaranteed look of surprise and confusion appears: "The UAW? Don't they make cars? What are they doing representing academic employees?"

The UAW, like the Steelworkers, wisely looked for new terrain as the traditional industries upon which these labor unions were built began to shrink. The UAW searched for a growth industry and found their way into the academic setting. The University of California graduate students were one of the first of the UAW's organizing drives at an academic institution, though UC did not voluntarily recognize the UAW and a long and bitter litigation embroiled the parties for close to a decade. In 1999, when the court allowed for recognition, the University forced the UAW to organize separate bargaining units at each campus. Although the University anticipated very unique outcomes based on the diverse political leanings on campuses across the state, the UAW did in fact organize each campus and prevail as the exclusive representative for all local units. Bargaining a first contract proved to be a difficult task. Even with local units, the Office of the President took the lead and bargained global provisions for a new collective bargaining agreement. Given the need to balance the issues handled at a system wide level with those left to each campus to bargain locally, the process proved divergent. Critical to the UAW was salary equality, meaning a Teaching Assistant in Davis would be paid the same salary as a Teaching Assistant in Riverside. Given tuition was set statewide, the campuses acquiesced to a statewide salary provision. For UC, market-based autonomy for salaries is common for staff and faculty, so salary equity was unique to the ASE unit.

During the first year of the contract, the number of grievances filed exceeded those filed in the remaining two years of the three-year agreement. The UAW challenged each provision to ensure the new language was adhered to and conditions changed. There was a lot of educating to do both in training faculty and administrators to understand the unionized environment as well as to alter practices no longer allowed by the terms of the collective bargaining agreement.

Balancing the student status and the employment status proved to be delicate business and remains so even to this day. Benefits, a traditional subject of collective bargaining, had to be merged with existing student programs. The end result was a remission program, where the University covers the student health insurance and partial tuition when the graduate student is working in a covered title. When a graduate student is out of the bargaining unit, they are responsible for paying tuition and health insurance premiums, unless they are researchers or have fellowship funds. There are many difficult issues with graduate students who are employed. The University requires them to be students, as the work is part of their ability to support themselves through graduate school. The University essentially has a "closed shop," meaning only students may be employed in these titles. The University also prohibits them from working more than 50% time, another factor thrusting their student status as the first and foremost reason for participation. And yet, Teaching Assistants are salaried employees. The 50% rule has been the source of many workload grievances, one of the articles that has had multiple iterations to solve with an obligation to report early to academic supervision if working over the expected number of hours. If the matter cannot be solved, there is an expedited arbitration process. While collective bargaining provides four corners, graduate students are not traditional employees hired for career performance. They are essentially temporary workers, who are also gaining teaching experience for their academic careers, while receiving compensation as support.

Another issue requiring balance is pedagogical training and providing credit for teaching rather than compensation. This provision continues to be one where the University works through each case to ensure pedagogical credit is limited and while it may be given concurrently, it may not be given exclusively in lieu of employment for more than one term under certain circumstances. Academic Student Employees play two unique and distinct, albeit intertwined, roles during their time in graduate student programs. Many controversial issues arise based on which hat the ASE is wearing at the time.

Social Justice

The ASEs have been the movers and shakers on forcing issues of social justice to be rectified at the bargaining table. They pursued using neutral pronouns in the agreement long before it was adopted by most institutions. They presented a strong agenda with respect to all-gender restrooms, clearly articulating that gender equity was more than male and female in the early days of trans recognition. Their language became part of the institutional fabric and they convinced the University to seek changes at local governmental levels in order to ensure Building and Safety ordinances reflected the proper number of fixtures to ensure restrooms could be converted. While the University was instituting family single stall restrooms in new buildings and retrofitted buildings, the UAW accelerated this program to ensure adherence to the contractual provision on providing an all-gender restroom near each requesting ASE's work location.

Dealing with the possible repeal of Deferred Action for Childhood Arrivals (DACA), the ASEs fought to have a process to grant those graduate students who did not have the right to work opportunities to provide instruction and be on the same footing as American graduate students or foreign students with the right to work in the United States. The importance of this social justice provision was equality of access. The University and the UAW created a joint labor management committee and developed the program from that platform under a closed contract. Further, although campuses already had Dreamer offices, they primarily supported undergraduates. The Office of the President created a fund to support undocumented students, which for the first time, truly recognized undocumented students at the graduate level.

The UAW also fought for student parents. The University already had programs to support affordable childcare, and the collective bargaining agreement had a provision for a reimbursement subsidy for each term of ASE employment, but the UAW took it one step further to secure space, refrigeration and privacy for nursing mothers to pump. The issue was entirely different for ASEs who had no private offices or home base while on campus. The idea of lactation stations seems commonplace today, but when this issue of gender equality and opportunity was raised, it was presented as a real problem for this population.

Two more issues of distinction on the social justice agenda must be raised: university policing and affordable housing. Policing is both controversial and necessary. These discussions are sure to permeate the next round of bargaining. The controversy over affordable housing, however, manifested during a closed agreement, resulting in a wildcat strike. UC campuses are fortunate to be in beautiful areas, near the coast, the bay and on hillsides, which lead to market driven prices for housing. At UC Santa Cruz, a campus nestled between the mountains and the coastline in Northern California, housing costs are high and there is limited on campus graduate student housing available. And so, a movement began. UC Santa Cruz ASEs engaged in a wildcat strike in December 2019 to get the University to reopen a closed agreement and provide additional support. Housing is not normally seen as a term and condition of employment, with the exception of the Residents and Interns, where living close to the hospital is considered part of the job.

As we go to press, the University and the UAW are engaged in settlement talks around the unfair practice charges each party filed against the other. If the settlement talks fall apart, a six-day hearing is scheduled for early 2021.

With the exception of the wildcat action, the University and the UAW have been successful to resolve issues at the bargaining table or in subsequent joint labor management committees, a tool often used to handle issues once the contract is ratified.

Organizing Efforts

In 2000, the Public Employment Relations Board (PERB) adopted a card check system upon the passing of state legislation for organizing. Under California's card check system, unions may organize new employees and have them sign a membership card, which is essentially their vote in favor of the union. Card check requires 50% +1 of the eligible employees (covered under the titles listed in the petition for recognition) to be submitted in order for PERB to recognize the petition as a valid new unit and forego an actual election. The card check system has been used in multiple organizing efforts to develop new bargaining units, some of which will be discussed in this section.

Postdoctoral Scholars

When the UAW organized the postdocs in 2006, they used the card check system and confused many, including foreign postdocs who went to PERB and successfully got the representation petition revoked on the basis that the union did not have the majority. But the UAW persisted and two years later they filed a new petition with the requisite number of cards to demonstrate a clear majority. The University had initially objected to union membership of post-doctoral fellows and paid directs, however, it decided to add them to the bargaining unit with the strategy that they wouldn't sign cards. But, alas, they did, and the unit grew by an additional 30% for the initial recognition.

The postdoctoral scholars proved to be a difficult bargaining unit to manage at the table because of the internship-type nature and short-term positions. In addition to traditional bread and butter issues regarding salary and benefits, the postdocs pushed for reform particularly in the arena of sexual harassment. The first round of bargaining in 2009 predated the slew of cases against faculty across the nation. Postdocs were the most vulnerable population at the university, given the Principal Investigator (PI) held the Postdoc's career in their hands. Postdocs needed to publish in the research world to move into faculty positions and make academic standing for themselves.

Because of the nature of research, PIs had autonomy over grant funds and research which included staffing with a wide array of researchers. The nature of research made employees feel vulnerable, leading to massive organizing efforts.

Academic Researchers

The newest of the academic bargaining units, the UAW organized the researchers (academic specialists, project scientists and professional researchers) in 2018. There is a tremendous difference between an academic specialist at the lower end of research and a project scientist or professional researcher who have PhDs and usually have completed a postdoctoral scholar appointment (1–5 years).

Given the UAW's interest in getting a contract in place, the negotiations took less than six months. Timing was a combination of getting dues in place and keeping confidence in the union after the University and the union fought over the petition to represent for nine months before recognition was achieved.

Critical terms for this new unit was to receive regular increases including academic merit increases, which UC could have been more diligent on keeping the review processes moving on a timely basis. Also, researchers fought for greater job security, a theme in research, as appointments matched grant funding, an often-uncertain income stream.

The first agreement resulted in increasing the terms of appointment, while holding fast to strong layoff language, given the tenuous nature of grants. An alignment of the salary scales and processes ensured timely reviews and smoothed scales to provide equitable increases. This also assists the university in competitive recruitment for these coveted positions.

Academic Judgment

A critical component for any university is to maintain academic judgment and protect it as a management right. Academic judgment involves educational programming, appropriate staffing, determining enrollments, deciding on the way departments, programs and units will operate. This should never be encroached upon in any negotiated terms, though unions will continue to propose language to do just that. In addition to traditional management rights, language specifically addressing academic rights must be included:

> Decisions regarding who is taught, what is taught, how it is taught and who does the teaching involve academic judgment and shall be made at the sole discretion of the University.

The University must retain the right to hire, layoff, determine qualifications, conduct academic merit reviews, determine research programs, make changes to projects, investigate misconduct and handle many other key managerial duties. Agreements must prohibit the grievability and arbitrability of management and academic rights. Language such as "the sole, non-grievable right" should routinely be asserted in language to preserve ultimate management control of its mission.

Lecturers

The system at UC for instruction depends on lecturers hired solely to teach undergraduates. Although senate faculty teach, the hiring of lecturers provides senate faculty with the ability to focus on research and publishing. Lecturers are represented and are appointed annually, some term by term, for the first six years. At the end of six years, provided the department continues to have a need long term, the lecturer undergoes a major excellence review to determine if the University should retain. If the lecturer passes the excellence review, they gain full appointment job security and one-year notice or pay in lieu of layoff, should it be necessary.

When the lecturer system started, the University used them to fill in as temporary teachers. Over time, the dependence on lecturers for writing programs, foreign languages, and large introductory courses has broadened. While the University is unlikely to give up its academic control over determining its staffing needs based on programmatic decisions, the pressure for job stability during the first six years is mounting and a current issue at the bargaining table.

Measuring Success

"No news is good news" may be the simplest measurement of success after bargaining a new collective bargaining agreement. When the parties finish the process, implement changes without a great deal of need for further interaction, the agreement has achieved its purpose. If only it were that simple.

One measure of a successful agreement is that both parties walk away from the bargaining table mildly satisfied, having achieved many bargaining goals, but not all of them. A compromise is always the best success. However, to fully understand this measurement, it is necessary to examine the vote of the ratification. If the union overwhelmingly voted to ratify the new terms, then there is a likelihood of apparent success. If, on the other hand, the union ratification snuck through by a narrow margin, keep an eye on the emotion of the bargaining unit. The current UAW 2865 agreement for the Academic Student Employees passed a narrow margin and, while the union uses an aggregate vote total, it failed at two campus locations. One of those locations, UC Santa Cruz, had a wildcat strike, built on unrest from housing issues. Serving as a barometer, the ratification vote measures satisfaction with the agreement.

Grievances are not a good measurement, since many cases hinge on individual employee experiences such as discipline and other alleged violations of the agreement. Contract interpretation cases serve as a better measure, though they can also be case specific and, at times, the union's attempt to get issues resolved through an arbitrator it failed to get resolved at the bargaining table.

Lastly, the best measure of success is the relationship itself. The nature of the ongoing relationship generally promotes fair dealing as both parties will continue to work together long after the new agreement is in place. The tenor of talks about problem solving, working through joint solutions and entering into settlement agreements may serve as solid evidence of measuring success. When the parties can work effectively together to ensure the terms and conditions specified in the collective bargaining agreement rule the relationship, labor relations success measures high.

Lessons Learned

Understand the Issues Before the Union Organizes Employees

When employees are happy and well cared for, they don't look to outside organizations to assist them. The larger the University, however, the more distant employees feel they are from the decision-making process. Perform checkups on employees to understand brewing issues and solve them before they organize. These issues could be economic or equity issues or simply treatment and respect. When management is in tune with the issues and works to resolve, there is no need for them to organize.

When the Union Does Begin to Talk to Employees, Use It as a "Head's Up"

Unions are usually successful in organizing. They are skilled professionals who know how to find the problems and make promises ensuring representation will solve the problems, since the employees will have a voice at the bargaining table. Management needs to be proactive and progressive enough to recognize the signposts and work to solving the problems.

If the Union Does Organize and File a Petition to Represent, Do Not Immediately Voluntarily Recognize the Union

The determination of the bargaining unit is unlikely to change. The initial recognition stage is the time to challenge the inclusion of titles that do not belong, because once they are in, it is unlikely they will be deleted from the unit. On the other hand, management shouldn't be overly litigious at this stage. A relationship with the union needs to be built. Neither party is going anywhere. Once the determination is finalized, through voluntary recognition after being presented with a clear majority or through election process, it is time to build the relationship and get to the bargaining table.

Generally, First Contracts Take More Time to Negotiate

Often, the parties do not know each other and there is a period of gaining some modicum of trust. The union comes to the table with all sorts of bargaining promises from the organizing campaign which they now have to deliver on, realistic or not. The university is reluctant to alter practices or relinquish control over many subjects which have been management rights.

Organize Campus Teams of Key Faculty and Administrators to Provide Feedback to the Bargaining Process

Stakeholder involvement must be considered on each pertinent issue at the table, although there are many ultimate reasons not all objectives can be achieved. Still and all, sending guidance on bargaining goals to the academic team shapes the ultimate language, protecting critical elements and procedures from union encroachment.

Train Administrators and Faculty Supervisors on the Terms of the Agreement

Good training prevents grievances. Administrators and faculty supervisors need to alter "the way we've always done it" and conform to the new contractual provisions. Training in the terms as well as providing sample documents, such as a toolkit, is critical for success.

Expect a Slew of Grievances in the First Year to Test the New Language

Especially in the post-Janus world where unions must prove their worth to convince represented employees in the bargaining unit to become or remain members, grievances are the main methodology for challenging university decisions. Every test of the language is a gamble for both sides as it is precedent setting for future decisions and interpretations. The union often grieves issues to attempt to attain through a grievance gains unachieved at the bargaining table.

Ensure Central Control of Resolutions Beyond the Department Level

While it is always best to resolve cases at the lowest level, employers must have some central control to guide the process. Unions love to "whipsaw" departments and campuses by getting one to respond favorably and then sell that resolution, even though it was not intended to go beyond the instant situation. Central control assists in preventing the whipsaw and regularizing grievance outcomes.

Resolve What Is Fair; Challenge What Should Not Be Settled

Fairness and equity must remain drivers of ultimate outcomes. Whenever cases arise which can be resolved on this basis, they should be resolved. However, when the union is pushing for resolutions that involve unearned money and benefits, be careful to stand ground. It is worth going to arbitration over cases that will change the landscape of the employment relationship.

Past Practices May Continue – Unless Defunct – Based on New Language

After a new agreement is reached, past practices are not automatically halted. Unless the language specifically articulates changes, past practices may continue. If the university wants to alter them, however, they must provide advanced notice and bargain over the change. An example of a past practice is that appointment letters are always issued no later than a month before the term begins. The new language guarantees appointment letters shall be issued by July 1, unless they are last-minute replacements. The former practice is now defunct.

Engage in Joint Labor Management Committees to Resolve Difficult Issues

Labor-management committees offer the parties a way to collaborate and find solutions to problems outside of engaging in mandatory collective bargaining. Recognizing that joint committees are intended to be problem solving, resolutions result in achieving goals of both sides while continuing to accomplish the university's mission.

Embrace the Union as Partners

So often management takes an adversarial view of the labor-management relationship and misses the overall objective of the university's goals to teach, to research and to provide service. While each party has its own objectives, commonality lies in the cross section that creates satisfied employees who perform well and proud management who carry the university's reputation to the highest levels of greatness.

Summary

Unions are here to stay. Academic management must engage with them as partners in solving problems, yet not allow the union to run the university. This can be a delicate balance, a dance that continues to evolve. Stay solution focused, keep equity and fairness in mind, and good academic labor relations will be achieved over the long term.

12

CASE STUDY

Northern Michigan University

Dale Kapla

Introduction

This chapter discusses contingent faculty in higher education and their impact on administrators in the academy. It is no secret that the sheer number of contingent faculty members throughout higher education has increased dramatically over the past several years. They have become so prevalent that, in fact, many of these individuals have come to rely on their teaching as the sole source of income. This poses challenges for administrators, as they will need to work with an ever-shrinking full-time tenured faculty and an ever-increasing part-time contingent faculty whose presence and voice in higher education is becoming the majority. No longer does the part-time adjunct drive to campus after their workday once or twice a week to teach a night class. Indeed, the 'job' of being a contingent faculty member is – or already has – evolved into career.

Just as many of these faculty have come to rely on the institution for their livelihood, so has an institution's reliance on them to keep the institution viable in many ways. The tangible benefits afforded to a university employing contingent faculty are many, and include a varied workforce, temporary or short-term employment commitment not present in tenured employees and lower instructional costs. On its face, the surge of contingent faculty throughout the academy seems like a positive trend for both the institution and the faculty member, and for the most part, this is true. However, there are bumps in the road. These bumps are not necessarily too large to be insurmountable, but they do present challenging obstacles to higher education institutions, and more specifically, the administrators responsible for managing contingent faculty.

DOI: 10.4324/9781003138990-14

This chapter proceeds in three parts. The first discusses the varied definitions of contingent faculty and how there is really no agreed upon description of what it means to teach on a contingent status in higher education. The second discusses the surge in the employment level of contingent faculty and the ramifications of that fact, both for the individual and the institution. Part Two introduces a discussion of how rising numbers in contingent faculty ranks carries with it a need to anticipate an inevitable rise in the level of unionization for that group and how that is impacting the 'profession', higher education and the administrators working is such a framework. This chapter ends with Part Three, which focuses on a case study illustrating the dynamic changing nature of organized, contingent faculty who unionized at a mid-sized Midwestern, comprehensive university, and the challenges for administrators this new represented group presents. That section begins with the process of accretion and how the part-time faculty became unionized. Discussed next is a detailed view of the major issues discussed at the first negotiations and what was and was not collectively agreed to. An update of those major issues is also provided, reflecting changes – if any – to successor agreements post-accretion.

Part One

Defining Contingent Faculty

Although contingent faculty holding academic teaching positions in higher education is hardly a new phenomenon, and their prevalence in the academy had grown significantly, it appears that settling on a clear definition of who contingent faculty are has not been clearly determined. This is a bit odd because for decades, classifying faculty in higher education has been fairly straightforward and well established, as a faculty member was either full-time or they were part-time. The former was either a tenure-earning, tenured or limited-time (sometimes called term) faculty, and the latter was simply called an adjunct. However, it appears that defining and distinguishing among part-time faculty to fit them into a specific, one-size-fits-all definition of contingent faculty is proving to be a bit more complicated. Knowing this is important to institutions and administrators as such a diverse definition can and does pose significant problems in the delivery of the curriculum, discussed later in this chapter.

Part-Time Faculty – Adjuncts

Adjunct faculty in higher education are ubiquitous; every college and university has them. Their utility is quite well-known and they have been a godsend to administrators for many years and for several reasons. These reasons include the low cost of employing an adjunct, as their salary does not generally come close to even a fraction of a full-time faculty member's. This low cost has also contributed to the fact that adjuncts do not normally receive any type of fringe benefits, such as employee sponsored health care, or paid time off such as vacation and sick leave. And retirement plans are simply not an option for adjuncts. Finally, and certainly not any less important, is that this group is not generally unionized, nor do they expect to be represented by a union once employed. They are, as most of the part-time workforce, 'at-will' employees.

Given these characteristics, why would anyone want to be adjunct, and why would institutions not want to employ them at high rates? First, those in the traditional adjunct pool of most colleges and universities have not earned the terminal degree in their respective discipline. This is because the academy is not their first career choice, and most have earned at least a bachelor's degree, with many of those possessing a master's. This degree attainment, coupled with the practical experience possessed by most adjuncts, make them attractive instructors. Indeed, often the main reason to hire an adjunct is for the practical skill and knowledge set each of them have in a given discipline. This not only brings up-to-date content to students, but may sometimes fill a void in the curriculum or help to comply with accreditation requirements. Thus, it makes complete sense for institutions to hire adjuncts, and hire them often and consistently.

Part-Time Faculty – Introducing Contingents

Peruse any higher education website of unions who represent part-time faculty and you will see the word contingent. You will also see on that same website how that particular union defines contingent. In fact, you will not only see a definition applying to one classification of employees, but applying to many classifications, not just simply part-time.

For instance, the American Association of University Professors (AAUP) is one of the largest parent unions in the U.S. representing both full-time and part-time faculty. This organization defines contingent faculty as any instructor in an adjunct, postdoc, teaching assistants, lecturer, clinical faculty, non-tenure earning or non-senate faculty (https://www.aaup.org/issues/contingency). To most administrators this is confusing, as higher education institutions have not often referred to students, for example, as faculty. Is a full-time non-tenure earning faculty member considered contingent? Is an adjunct? What is going on here? Taking a deeper look into their definition, one starts to see that a contingent faculty member, according to the AAUP, is any class of instructor in higher education that is not tenured or on a tenure-track to earn tenure. A broad definition to be sure, but one that makes complete sense, as unions are almost exclusively focused on membership and strength in numbers, and the inclusion of every instructor (student or not) with the exception of tenured or earning tenure with the contingent framework is understandable.

The AAUP is not the only higher education parent union with such a definition. Indeed, their definition is somewhat consistent with the American

Federation of Teachers (AFT), who define contingent faculty as adjuncts, non-tenure track, lecturers and graduate employees (http://seiufacultyforward.org/faculty/our-impact/). Here again, we see the definition including adjunct and full-time non-tenure track instructors. And we see students who teach being classified as contingent faculty, even though they are in fact graduate students. Once again, is it probably safe to assume that the same membership drive is at play here, and the definition of contingent faculty has captured all classifications of higher education instructors other than tenured and tenure-earning.

Part Two

Characteristics of Contingent Faculty

Who Are They and How Many?

There is no doubt that the traditional characterization of professors in higher education as portrayed in the media and in everyday conversation is one of high status and respect and belief that all possess a doctorate. This makes them more educated than 95% of the rest of the population (Census.gov). Given this, most students (and prospective students) and parents assume that the delivery of the curriculum is in the hands of professors holding the necessary doctorate with an expertise in the subject matter. However, much of what a student will hear in a classroom is professed by a contingent faculty member holding an academic credential less than a doctorate. Indeed, nearly half of all the curriculum in the U.S. is taught by contingent faculty (https://www.insidehighered.com/news/2019/11/27/federal-data-show-proportion-instructors-who-work-full-time-rising).

Reasons for this are well-known, and most commonly include a slow decline in state appropriations toward higher education over the past 20 years. Such decline in the level of funding has forced institutions to rely almost entirely on tuition dollars for their expenses. So, it naturally follows that the number of more expensive long-term full-time faculty are in decline. Consequently, since state appropriations continue to decline, and the number of college-aged young adults decline, it seems as though this trend will continue for the foreseeable future.

While respect is high for higher education professors with Ph.Ds., we do not know what the level of respect is for contingent faculty. Although difficult to ascertain, respect for part-time faculty seems to be high on the agenda for unions representing them. For instance, the SEIU (Service Employees International Union), with a fairly large presence in higher education, notes that just by simply being associated with the union garners them instant respect. Although this may or may not be true, given who is being included in the contingent ranks, they certainly have become or are becoming a real force in higher education. For instance, the estimated number of non-tenured or tenure-track faculty delivering higher education curriculum in the U.S. is about 75%. Two decades ago, that percentage was flipped, with the majority of the academy consisting of tenured or tenure-earning faculty.

Level of Education

Since the definition of contingent faculty varies and encompasses a variety of employee classifications, it follows that their level of education would vary as well. While higher educational professor positions classified as tenure-track require a terminal degree; the non-tenure track faculty do not (Higheredjobs. com). Thus, contingent faculty can vary in their degree attainment, from a bachelor's degree (sometimes an associate degree in community college), to the Ph.D. level, with half holding a master's degree (CUPA.org).

Level of Unionization

As previously noted, unions representing contingent faculty have made efforts to include every non-tenured or tenure-earning faculty member – including students – in their definition of a contingent faculty member. This obviously increases the likelihood of contingent faculty organizing with one of the parent unions commonly representing such faculty (e.g. SEIU). To contingents, their low-pay, no benefits, no longevity job looks bleak as a career, so the opportunity to be represented and garner more 'respect' through membership in a union seems quite appealing. While this is true, there is no clear data on the level of unionization for contingent faculty. Yet, if the success of the SEIU in organizing graduate students is any indication (see below), the level is quite high and is rising. Such level of unionization is certainly something administrators need to be aware of, as organizing means that periodic mandatory bargaining with labor groups becomes part of the fabric of the university and subsequently a large part of an administrator's duties.

Contingent Bargaining

What to Expect

Since unions have defined what a contingent faculty is and what characteristics they possess, we can assume that there will be (and are) several potential bargaining units the administration of any institution must bargain with on a periodic basis. Specifically, graduate students generally organize separately as one unit. Non-student, part-time contingents organize similarly into part-time-only units (PTOs), and non-tenure earning in another; often called lecturers. Obviously, given the ever-changing nature of the labor force in higher education, there can be several amalgamations of these units. This may include the part-time faculty being accreted into the full-time faculty. Or, the lecturers may be accreted into the full-time, or any combination of the two. Whatever the case, it is likely that any higher education institution has a least one – if not multiple – faculty units to bargain with. Each have their own set of challenges (or advantages), and one would be well served knowing at least some of the issues that may be facing administrators.

Graduate Students

Although bargaining with graduate students is covered in another section of this book, it is worth noting a few things administrators need to be made aware of. First, roughly three years ago, four labor organizations and numerous graduate students banded together to push for unionization for private university faculty resulting in the successful unionization of students (https://uaw.org/graduate-wor kers-four-major-unions-launch-unprecedented-national-campaign-bring-private-universities-bargaining-table/amp/). This continues today, and those institutions with any number of graduate students not already organized, can probably count on at least being contacted, or having a discussion with a union.

Part-Time Faculty

Non-student part-time faculty teaching just a few credits each semester poses their own set of challenges when bargaining. Most often, the faculty bargaining team consists of those individuals who are working toward making part-time teaching a career and focus their proposals as such. This simply means that the team puts forth proposals that tend to be very similar to full-time proposals. But not all are teaching as their primary source of income, and many are simply teaching because they enjoy being part of a university. Yet because the part-time faculty member wishing to teach at a college or university as a chosen career is becoming more prevalent, the issues they focus on and the benefits they strive for are looking more and more like full-time faculty benefits, including such obvious benefits as healthcare and retirement.

This trend for part-time faculty to 'look' like full-time faculty is beginning to be something more commonly referred to. A perfect example of this is the AAUP, who believes that both part and full-time faculty cannot be classified into either contingent or not. Specifically, the AAUP posits that because part-time faculty sometimes teach the same or even more courses than full-time faculty, one cannot classify them as part or full-time. Rather, each classification is best defined by being compensated by class or credit, or being salaried (http s://www.aaup.org/report/contingent-appointments-and-academic-profession). This can and does have a profound impact on how the union may approach the bargaining table when representing part-time faculty.

Salary

Undoubtedly, the unionization of part-time faculty is in large part fueled by the promise of increases in pay and benefits. For many part-time instructors, their teaching salary is their main source of income. Whereas a little as a decade ago teaching part-time at an institution of higher learning was just simply *part-time*, not even close to a main source of income, and often engaged in because the person thoroughly enjoyed it or had a penchant for being affiliated with such an institution. However, as the number of tenure-track faculty decreased, part-time instructors increased, naturally increasing the level of part-time unionization.

As part-time representation by a union increased, so did the pay calculation. For instance, instead of the traditional per-credit wage, unions have pushed for a *per-course* wage based on a full-time salaried professor. Another is cancelled course fees, or 'prep' fees, which are when a course is scheduled to be taught, but cancelled within a certain timeframe prior to the course beginning.

Non-Salary Benefits

Traditional full-time work quite often comes with common fringe benefits such as medical insurance for the employee and their family, sick and vacation leave and some type of retirement. These benefits have not often been afforded to part-time employees, who were historically not afforded any at all.

Just like salaries, the increased unionization of part-time instructors has been quite positive for the benefits becoming available to such instructors. Many institutions are now offering their medical plans to contingent faculty, although most require that the employee pay the cost of the premium. Other sources of non-salary benefits include tuition waivers (or discounts) for the employee, and in some case, their families. Some institutions offer the tuition benefit only to the employee and only during the semester or term when the contingent is actively teaching a course. Still others offer it to the employee and their dependents.

Job security is also a primary concern for contingents, as by definition, they teach 'as needed'. This is considered a significant issue for contingent faculty. Not knowing from semester or term to semester or term whether you will have employment is particularly concerning. However, part-time unionized faculty have usually negotiated some sort of seniority rights for contingent faculty. This often takes the form of first right of refusal for those courses they are qualified to teach. Since many institutions use contingent faculty at high rates, this is almost always a guarantee of continued employment albeit not a promise of a course. Some institutions have processes that permit the contingent faculty to 'be on the books' as an employee for a specified period of time – say two or three years. Some may even offer a full-time position after a specified period of time, although those instances are rare.

Bargaining Issues for Contingents

Contingents without union representation do not necessarily have a formal, regular avenue to bargain over wages and working conditions. However, they can – and still do – bargain with management informally. Essentially, informal bargaining would consist of the contingent speaking with their immediate supervisor about any or all of those items above. In this instance, the employee would be bargaining for themselves, not for the good of the unit.

Another advantage to the unrepresented employee is that they do not have to wait until the regular negotiation or reopener, which can sometimes be years, to bargain for increased wages and benefits. They can simply schedule an appointment with their supervisor and have that discussion.

On the con side, being an unrepresented contingent provides little, formal protection from the whims of administration, who can reduce pay and benefits essentially at will, and in fact, end the contingent's employment at will. Additionally, the pros of negotiating alone may result in a simple 'no', leaving the contingent with little avenue to pursue better wages and working conditions.

Finally, often, institutions without a collective bargaining agreement for contingents do not have specific performance evaluation policies and procedures for instructors, as they quite often only exist in the Human Resource area and do not apply to instructional staff. Unionized contingents normally have a formal evaluation process which may mirror that of full-time instructional staff, although not necessarily containing the same evaluative criteria. This is a definite advantage as this forms a consistent history of evaluations and is commonly accepted as the norm in higher education.

Part Three

Case Study

Accretion of Contingent Faculty

The following is a case study involving the accretion of contingent faculty into a full-time faculty AAUP union at a small, upper-Midwest, master's level regional comprehensive university, Northern Michigan University (NMU). Covered below is first a brief history of how the existing full-time faculty union and administration worked together to develop the characteristics and attributes of part-time faculty that eventually made them eligible for union status. Discussed second is the detailed 'benefits' afforded to contingent faculty as a result of regular negotiations with the full-time faculty. Next is a discussion of implementation issues – both negative and positive – and how the accretion affected administration and faculty. Finally, a summary of how well the accretion is working eight years later and what may be in store as negotiations approach.

NMU

Northern Michigan University is nestled on the south shore of Lake Superior in Michigan's Upper Peninsula. With an enrollment of just over 7,000 students and a 100-year history, for decades NMU has been the producer of most nurses, police and correctional officers and teachers who work in the Upper Peninsula. Unionization is prevalent, not only at NMU but in the greater Upper Peninsula. Those police and nurses trained at NMU are now part of unions, as are correctional officers and teachers. Other unions include local construction and electrical workers, and iron ore miners.

NMU has seven employee unions representing about 900 employees, with parent representation coming from AFSCME, UAW, AAUP and the Michigan Education Association (MEA). Faculty unions at NMU have been in existence for decades and consist of the AAUP chapter, which is the largest on campus with about 300 eligible members.[1] Faculty in this union are the non-career and technical education (vocational) instructors, and consist largely of baccalaureate and master's programs. The other faculty union is the NMUFA (Northern Michigan University Faculty Union), which consists of about 22 eligible members, not including part-time.[2] This faculty is the vocational and career technical instructors. Both faculty contract durations are staggered to facilitate bargaining with Academic Affairs, as there is no separate academic personnel office, and the administration's chief negotiator is the associate provost, who has other academic affairs duties. Generally, agreements are bargained for three-year periods, until 2015 where a five-year agreement was negotiated for both unions.

Part-Time Accretion

As mentioned, part-time faculty at any institution of higher education have proliferated over the last few decades because of various reasons, most of which are financial – for both the faculty member and the administration. The latter has hired more part-time faculty almost out of necessity, as financial models for university and college budgets have necessitated more of a reliance on tuition rather than state dollars, making steady and certain revenues tenuous at best. The former saw this rise in numbers as a percentage of total share in teaching across the university and felt the time had come to work toward equity in pay and benefits. Indeed, as full to part-time ratios changed, so did the awareness of part-time faculty of their wages and working conditions. This increase has no doubt given rise to pooling resources and human capital to work toward a collective action; which is what occurred at NMU, and specifically with the AAUP chapter. Although part-time faculty exist in the NMUFA, the union have not yet taken steps to start the conversation about part-time accretion.

In 2011, the AAUP approached the administration at NMU to discuss accreting the part-time faculty, or adjuncts. Subsequently, a petition was submitted to the

Michigan Employment Relations Commission (MERC) to change the makeup of the current chapter. Interestingly, there was no discussion or hint of the part-time faculty forming their own PTO (part-time-only) union, however, there was some internal, non-public discussion that did not materialize. Apparently, there is strength in numbers, as there existed about 70 or so adjuncts at the time, and most felt in necessary to be part of the larger organization. This decision may have also been based on deferring to experience and possibly the greater likelihood of more similar full-time benefits. Still another reason may be that those adjuncts most vocal about organizing were in the minority of the 70, so a PTO may not have been feasible.

Nonetheless, a component of the MERC petition for accretion was a definition – or a characteristic of – who would be accreted in the bargaining unit. Was it the number of courses taught? Over what time period? Or was is the number of credits taught? And again, if so, what time period? Or was it simply seniority? For how long? These questions and more were asked over a several month span, and after much deliberation, it was decided that the number of credits taught over a specific timeframe would define eligibility for bargaining unit status. However, there was disagreement on this as the administration thought that four credits (generally one class) in one year made an adjunct eligible, but the AAUP thought eight credits in one year did. Despite this disagreement, MERC made the final decision and ruled that an adjunct who taught at least eight credits in one calendar year is eligible for bargaining unit status. MERC also defined adjunct eligible for union status Contingent Faculty. Thus, another classification of part-time faculty was created. The actual MERC definition is currently in the AAUP Agreement:

> *1.1.4.2 "Contingent faculty member" shall mean a bargaining unit member who has been employed to teach a minimum of eight credit hours over the previous three consecutive academic sessions defined as the fall session, the winter session, or either of the two summer sessions and who are assigned less than a 12 (twelve) credit load in the current semester.*

It should be noted that MERC's original definition did not include part-time librarians or counselors, as they do not teach courses as part of their assigned responsibilities. That language above was added in 2020.

Inclusion of Part-Time Faculty in a Full-Time Bargaining Unit

The timing of the MERC definition was somewhat serendipitous for the AAUP as a negotiation year (2012) was fast approaching. Bargaining proposal on both sides were being prepared, and included the usual mandatory subjects of bargaining like wages, benefits and job security. In preparation, the AAUP formed a part-time faculty committee to look at bargaining proposals and sought to include a part-time faculty member on their negotiating team. Bargaining commenced in the spring of 2012.

It was clear from the beginning of negotiations that part-time faculty interests are not much different than that of full-time faculty. This came as no surprise, as traditional bargaining issues for contingent faculty ranged from an assurance from administration and contract language that contingent faculty would in fact be considered faculty, to healthcare and retirement benefits. These issues would be essentially discussed concurrently with full-time faculty issues, which made for an odd, if not awkward, bargaining process. For instance, full-time faculty felt that the traditional research and service accomplishments they needed to achieve to achieve rank must be preserved and applied to anyone teaching in the academy – including part-time, contingent faculty. The contingents, however, felt the mirroring of those accomplishments with full-time faculty was a stretch too far, as opportunities (not to mention most have had little or no training in the scientific method) were fewer at the part-time level, and therefore the ability to achieve advanced rank was virtually non-existent for most contingents. In the end, full-time faculty prevailed.

Many of the issues or benefits proposed for contingent faculty seemed to follow this type of scrutiny by the full-time faculty. It almost seemed to the administration team that there was a bit of strife between full-time and part-time, or that accretion was not as popular as union leadership portrayed it to be. Nonetheless, both sides soldiered on, and the first combined part and full-time agreement was ratified.

Implementation

As with any newly agreed upon labor contract, there are always issues that arise that no one foresees, and this agreement was no exception. Those issues – and their solutions – are discussed briefly below, but first, the major themes associated with the accretion are discussed. Below are the most salient issues discussed at the 'accretion negotiations', followed be a brief explanation of their specifics and how they are faring eight years on.

Contingent Attributes

Contingent Rank

Traditional rank structure for faculty in higher education include the customary Instructor, Assistant, Associate and Professor. Existing in the Agreement before accretion was a fourth – Special Instructor. This classification is reserved for instructors not possessing a graduate degree, but those that have special and significant applied experience that could be substituted for education. This is important, as the university does not make a habit of hiring such a classification of faculty, but nonetheless, if they do, they are always part-time and now could become a member of the bargaining unit.

The initial discussions on contingent rank first centered around newly appointed contingent faculty and the minimum criteria for their rank. It then moved to how an existing contingent faculty member would or could earn promotion. It was decided that designation of rank for new contingent faculty be predicated on one factor: degree attainment. Since most current contingents lacked the terminal degree for their discipline but possessed an earned master's degree, they were assigned the rank of Contingent Instructor. However, some existing contingent faculty did in fact possess the terminal degree for their discipline (e.g. MFA in English), so were assigned the rank of Contingent Assistant Professor. Below are the current categories and criteria for the achievement of contingent rank, which were the original criteria at the time of accretion.

> *Contingent Special Instructor: An appointment reserved for individuals who do not meet minimum criteria for other ranks but who have special attainments, skills, or experience and for those rare positions in which it is difficult or impossible to find individuals with master's or doctoral degrees.*
>
> *Contingent Instructor: An earned master's degree from an accredited institution.*
>
> *Contingent Assistant Professor: An earned doctorate from an accredited institution or other terminal qualifications appropriate to the position subject to the review and approval of the appropriate dean and the Provost & Vice President for Academic Affairs (PVPAA).*
>
> *Contingent Associate Professor: An earned doctorate from an accredited institution or other terminal qualifications appropriate to the position subject to the review and approval of the appropriate dean and the PVPAA; normally six (6) years of full- or part-time higher education experience at the rank of instructor or above and evidence of teaching excellence.*
>
> *Contingent Professor: An earned doctorate from an accredited institution or other terminal qualifications for the position subject to the review and approval of the appropriate dean and the PVPAA; normally, twelve (12) years of full-or part-time higher education experience at the rank of instructor or above and evidence of teaching excellence.*

Next, the teams addressed how a current contingent faculty member would achieve promotion. This proved to be a more difficult discussion, as the full-time faculty on the bargaining team were adamant about preserving the integrity of the achievement of ranks in the academy, and therefore pushed for parity in the contingent promotion process. This was not the sentiment of the contingent faculty, however, as they felt the bar was set too high. For the administration's part, parity seemed to be the most likely method of contingent faculty promotion criteria. Thus, parity and the mirroring of accomplishments became language.

Updated Language

During the five-year life of the contract, there were several discussions between administration and the union regarding contingent faculty promotion. The main issues centered around contingent faculty not being well-versed in the scientific method, and therefore not able to produce peer-reviewed research required of full-time faculty promotion. So, in the 2020 negotiations, both sides agreed to remove the parity language and focus primarily on the quality of contingent faculty teaching, and their sustained overall performance. Below is the current [partial] language:

> *Contingent faculty may submit a letter requesting a higher rank as part of their annual evaluation (due February 1). Supporting evidence will include: 1) current CV, 2) annual evaluations, 3) student ratings, and 4) peer reviews.*

This language is proving to be welcome news to deans and departments, as the vagueness of the original language left too much open for interpretation. This attempt at clarification is obviously more detailed and less open to criticism.

Faculty Governance

An undeniable tenant of the AAUP (or most any faculty union) is the ability to participate in university decision-making. Most union committees were created and designed for just that purpose. It is important to understand, however, that this participation only amounts to recommendations for final decisions, not the decisions themselves. Most often called 'shared governance' or 'faculty governance', such governance can take on several forms. These can include the aforementioned union or university committees, union leadership and administration holding regular meetings or faculty presence on university executive search committees.

Prior to ratification of the 2012 Agreement, such shared governance was the sole purview of full-time faculty, with no part-time faculty allowed. However, during the 2012 negotiations, things changed. The union's bargaining team, with part-time faculty representation, insisted that contingent faculty join forces with the full-time faculty and have a role in shared governance. Not having too many compelling reasons to oppose this, the administration team agreed.

However, how to implement – or describe – what that meant by true shared governance by both full- and part-time faculty in the Agreement proved a bit difficult. All committees? Can contingent faculty be part of a tenure-earning search committee? What about full-time promotion and tenure applications? Many more questions were asked and discussed, and the teams came up with an agreeable solution; everywhere in the Agreement where the word 'faculty' appears would apply to contingent faculty, and where the words 'full-time faculty' appear would exclude contingents. Thus, this not only clearly defines who faculty are and what they do, it made editing the Agreement very easy.

One caveat, however. As noted in two of the above questions regarding promotion, tenure and hiring, the union negotiating team did not feel that contingents should be part of those processes. And by doing so effectively removed contingent faculty from most subcommittees that departments have. Here are two excerpts noting such an exclusion for contingent faculty:

> All department faculty will have a voice in departmental affairs, including the right to vote on all matters brought to the department faculty at meetings that would reasonably be construed as a meeting of the whole.

Notice the 'meeting of the whole' reference. This simply refers to regular department faculty meetings, as most promotion, tenure, evaluation and search committees are subcommittees. Another partial excerpt is below:

> Evaluation for other than promotion or tenure review or continuing contract review shall be conducted in accordance with the following schedule:
> February 1: The faculty member submits the evaluation to the departmental evaluation committee.

Further notice the reference to 'departmental evaluation committee', as this is not the committee as a whole. Obviously, most departments vote on matters such as this during a meeting as a whole, but overwhelmingly defer to the subcommittee's recommendation, which, by definition, does not include part-time contingent faculty.

Benefits

Pay

Up until the accretion, part-time faculty pay was determined by the university, and more specifically, in consultation with the provost and deans. Of course, accretion changed that, as pay for contingent faculty was now a mandatory subject of bargaining. During initial discussions in negotiations, the union insisted that contingent pay was quite low and needed some serious adjustment. The union also insisted that whatever across the board percentage raise the full-time faculty received, it would apply to contingent faculty. The administration agreed to both of these concepts, but then both sides needed to determine what the contingent faculty adjustment would consist of and later, the full-time across the board percentage raises.

Both teams started the specific discussions about contingent faculty pay by determining how much of an adjustment contingent faculty would receive.

Since adjunct pay was per credit, it was agreed that the practice would continue. The current per-credit rate at the time was consistently about $800 as there did not exist a salary rank structure for adjunct faculty. This led both sides settle on a starting point for each credit taught at $900 for a Contingent Instructor and $1,000 for Contingent Assistant Professor. Minimum salary tables were then decided upon, and the final rank increments were determined. In the end, each rank increment essentially amounted to about a 2% increase in salary. These increases seemed small, however, the percentage increases were initially 4% for those adjuncts eligible to become contingent faculty. And later in negotiations, both sides agreed to a 2.5% across the board increase for full-time faculty, making the total pay increase for contingent faculty 6.5% – quite significant during most times.

Additionally, although adjunct pay was not part of the discussion for obvious reasons, the administration sought to adjust their per-credit pay commensurate with the agreed upon rates for contingent faculty. This was done to simplify things from an academic personnel perspective and from a payroll standpoint.

Updated Language

Subsequent agreements have not addressed the pay concepts for contingent faculty, as both sides seem fairly satisfied with how the processes work. Although there is no language that requires the administration to pay across the board full-time faculty raises, it is a practice that continues.

Sick Leave

While the aforementioned issues for contingent faculty dominated the accretion negotiations, the full-time faculty felt that they did not do enough for the newly accreted contingents. Thus, they pressed the administration to consider at least a few 'traditional benefits' often associated with full-time faculty to be offered to contingent faculty. One of these included paid time off for illness of a contingent faculty member. Since most contingent faculty only teach a class or two each semester (two days a week in the classroom, generally) and are not required to conduct research, the discussion centered around sick time for class periods, instead of hours or days of leave. At first, the administration adamantly opposed such a concept; part-time faculty are just that – part-time. Sick leave is a full-time faculty benefit. However, as negotiations wore on, the administration softened and compromised with the union and settled on language that was fairly generic, but did address sick time off:

> *Reasonable accommodations will be made for contingent faculty who are unable to work because of personal illness.*

So, what are reasonable accommodations? Both sides could not decide, but did agree that each case is different and would be handled on a case-by-case basis. Also notice that inclusion of 'personal', as this pertains only to the contingent faculty member, not dependents, or family sick leave.

As the new agreement was implemented and contingent faculty did in fact need to utilize the reasonable accommodations clause, and it became to mean two class periods, or for most, one week. Even though this was not codified in the Agreement or in a Memorandum of Understanding, it worked quite well.

Updated Language

Although the language worked quite well for almost all of the five years, there were some hiccups. Even though it was rare, some contingent faculty needed to be away from teaching for longer than a week and the class periods needed to be covered by another faculty member. Often this resulted in a full-time faculty member substituting until the contingent faculty member returned. Or until the end of the semester is rare instances. Several issues arose from this, including how much to pay the full-time replacement, and whether or not the contingent faculty member should be paid; or more specifically, should the latter's pay be stopped at all.

Two solutions were decided upon. First, if the contingent faculty member was away because of sick leave for more than a week, they would be paid for the week away, but then their pay would be reduced by any additional weeks they were away. This was not welcomed by the union, however, they understood that the sick leave benefit afforded to contingent faculty is much different than full-time, salaried faculty.

The second solution involved the contingent's replacement, and how that person would be paid. For this, both sides decided it would be better for there to be a formal agreement in the form of a Memorandum of Understanding (MOU). After several iterations, a deal was struck, which both sides thought was quite innovative. The solution simply consisted of a formula that included the amount of class periods left to teach and the load credits of the course based on the person's salary. A partial excerpt from the MOU is below:

> When the instructor of record vacates a course after the start of any semester (including each summer session) the respective department head shall staff the vacancy consistent with the provisions of 9.1.4 and subsections of the Master Agreement. The new instructor's teaching load shall reflect a prorated amount of credits according to the guidelines below:
> (Number of class meetings remaining/total number of class meetings) x number of load credits for the entire course.
> Number of load credits for the course shall be defined by the department's load calculation document as required by Master Agreement 6.1.1.1. The proration value shall be rounded to the nearest half (0.5) credit of teaching load.

This has worked very well, and both sides continue to see no reason to change it. However, in a subsequent negotiation in 2020, the original contingent faculty sick leave language was amended to:

> *Reasonable accommodations will be made for contingent faculty who are unable to work because of personal illness, injury, disability, pregnancy, or childbirth.*

Notice that injury, disability, pregnancy or childbirth were added. It is interesting to note that the reasonable accommodations clause was used at least once for each of the new added words during the initial Agreement. However, this troubled the union, as they do not believe that any of these should be called leave for being 'sick', and used the example that pregnancy is not a sickness. The administration could not disagree, and therefore agreed to the new wording.

HealthCare

Full-time employees at NMU, their spouse dependents and Qualified Household Member (partner benefits) are covered by a health, dental and vision plan, but the part-time employees are not. Like many institutions of higher education, NMU's healthcare expenses are self-funded, which opens the university to fiscal liability should (unfortunately) several employees have catastrophic events. Stop Loss insurance is purchased to minimize such events; however, the limit is set high to keep premiums down. To date, the university has not had to rely on Stop Loss, and yearly costs have remained relatively steady for many years. Additionally, the university is part of a healthcare consortium with other universities in the state which helps keep insurance management fees in check.

Furthermore, the university is fortunate to have its own on-campus health center with two physicians, nurses, Nurse Practitioners from the School of Nursing and a pharmacy. This is a great benefit to the campus community, as full-time employees, students and retirees can utilize the services. Such care and services are covered by the university self-funded plan, and are supplemented by co-pays from full-time employees and a student fee. This meant that no part-time employees were eligible to visit the health center or use the pharmacy services.

Nonetheless, since the administration rejected a full healthcare plan for contingent faculty, it seemed appropriate to offer, at the table, some access to the health center for contingent faculty. In the end, both sides decided that part-time faculty can be eligible for healthcare services at the center for a $20 co-pay per visit.

Updated Language

While access and relatively small co-pay were not what the union initially wanted, they understood that it was a rather large step forward for part-time faculty. Statistics are kept on health center visits by employees, and during the life of the agreement, contingent visits held steady at around one-third of total eligible part-time faculty.

Since this was not a huge expense for the university, during the 2015 negotiations it was decided that the contingent faculty could access the health center free of charge. This too was a large step forward, and worked well. Although it did not increase the number of visits by contingent faculty (and in turn, did not increase university expenses), another, unintended consequence arose from its implementation.

Implementing the free visits was easy since it did not require any type of co-pay at the health center or premium charged to a contingent's account. However, while their visits may be free for them, the university incurs a cost. This cost, therefore, is born solely by the full-time employees of the university since, as mentioned above, a portion of full-time employees' premiums are allocated for health center operations. Thus, contingent faculty have totally free healthcare, while full-time employees do not. The administration continues with this practice, as they deem it the right thing to do. This fact is often presented to the union to illustrate that the contingent faculty with little income at least have some access to health care.

Tuition Waiver

Similar to healthcare, full-time employees, their spouses, dependents and Household Member can receive a tuition waiver benefit. By most standards, this benefit is quite generous, as it is a full waiver for all of the aforementioned categories for both graduate and undergraduate courses. As also with healthcare, this benefit is only offered to full-time employees, not part-time. Given this, it follows that contingent faculty propose such a benefit for themselves, and so they did.

However, the administration disagreed, citing that the benefit is certainly something they want to continue for the groups already covered, but the benefit does have an impact on revenue. This impact is mostly in form of missed revenue, and the administration was not interested in reducing that even more.

Updated Language

After the accretion agreement was implemented, the frequency of contingents taking advantage of the waiver during the semester they were teaching remained fairly steady. During the 2015 negotiations, the union proposed an enhancement to the current benefit, which added language permitting waivers to dependents of contingent faculty, if the credits were taken during the same semester in which the contingent was teaching. No increase to the amount of credits was proposed, meaning the waiver needed to equal the credits that the contingent was teaching. Since utilization was low, the administration agreed on the following language:

> *Contingent faculty may enroll in classes, including for-credit courses offered by continuing education, up to the number of credit hours they are teaching in the semester (e.g., if teaching four (4) credits in winter semester, may take four (4) credits in winter semester at no charge). These credits may be transferred to a contingent faculty member's dependents as defined in 9.2.7.1 during that semester. NMU will abide by state and federal laws regarding the taxability of benefits.*

Other Contingent Benefits

Just a couple of additional benefits currently afforded to part-time employees were proposed for contingent faculty during the accretion negotiations. First was a free parking pass, which does cut into university revenues, albeit the loss is not significant. And since NMU does not have extensive parking issues on campus, this benefit seems quite reasonable, and was therefore agreed to.

Second, no-cost access or membership to the university's physical education center was also proposed. Given this too was a full-time benefit and only slightly cut into university revenues, the administration agreed.

Conclusion

There is very little argument among university administrations that part-time faculty play a valuable role in higher education, both in terms of what individual faculty offer the curriculum and their relatively low cost. These facts alone have contributed to the proliferation of part-time faculty in the academy, and coupled with the ubiquitous reduced federal and state funding for higher education, the U.S. is now experiencing record-high levels of part-time faculty. And although the definition of part-time faculty is not necessarily agreed upon, what is for sure is that part-time teachers in higher education is certainly a powerful group, as evidenced by the increased union representation of part-time faculty.

It is therefore incumbent upon university administrators to be as knowledgeable as possible about the issues surrounding part-time faculty, as they may well be faced with sitting at the negotiation table in the very near future. When that occurs, being informed with those salient issues surrounding part-time faculty can assist with an oftentimes difficult (but sometimes rewarding) process. Such issues quite often mirror full-time faculty issues and include healthcare, paid time off, promotion and of course, parity in salary.

This chapter was an attempt to assist the administrator with the dynamics of part-time faculty, by briefly reviewing the current state of part-time faculty in higher education and its level of unionization. After nearly a decade of part-time accretion, the case study detailed above is illustrative of part-time faculty issues, and may assist those administrators currently facing, or those who will soon face, accretion or the creation of new part-time-only unions.

Notes

1 Michigan became a right-to-work state in 2014, and the Janis decision solidified union due paying as an option. Most of the 300 eligible faculty – which includes part-time pay dues voluntarily, the number of which had remained fairly steady since 2014.
2 The NMUFA dues paying members have dwindled to 15; a decrease of about 25%.

13

CASE STUDY

University of Delaware

Matthew J. Kinservik

Background

The first time I encountered the collective bargaining agreement (CBA) between the University of Delaware (UD) and the campus chapter of the Association of American University Professors (UD-AAUP) was a few days before I became the Chair of the Department of English. I had been a faculty member at UD for 12 years and had been a dues-paying member of the bargaining unit from day one. For the previous four years, I had served in an administrative role as the Director of Graduate Studies in English. But never once had I picked up, let alone paged through, the CBA. My introduction to it was not auspicious. The departing chair handed a copy of the CBA to me and said, "Here you go—you better hope you never need this." This did not inspire confidence. Nor did it motivate me to open up the document and get familiar with it. Instead, I did what I suspect many administrators do: I put it in a desk drawer and hoped I'd never need it.

So far as I knew at that time, the CBA existed for one purpose only, and that was to empower disgruntled faculty members to persecute department chairs and other administrators by filing grievances. To my mind, having a grievance filed against you was like being made to wear a scarlet letter. Since that time, I've served as Associate Dean for the Humanities and I am now in my seventh year as Vice Provost for Faculty Affairs. In both roles, I have learned to embrace the CBA, not fear it. Instead of regarding it as the source of the dreaded grievance process, I have come to see it as an indispensable resource for administration, offering guidance for how to go about our business within the framework of shared governance. Yes,

DOI: 10.4324/9781003138990-15

you will find the grievance process laid out in the CBA, but it is much more than that.

If used properly, the CBA will help any administrator to do their job better and to greatly reduce the likelihood of being the subject of a grievance. Here are some of the things a typical CBA can tell an administrator:

- How faculty performance appraisals should be conducted.
- How faculty workload assignments are to be made.
- What the salary parameters and benefits are in a given year.
- What academic freedom protections faculty enjoy.

And here are some of the corresponding questions they can answer:

- Can I put an underperforming faculty member on a personal improvement plan?
- What is the maximum (or minimum) teaching load I can assign a faculty member?
- How much discretion do I have to award raises to individual faculty members?
- How can I defend a faculty member who is under assault for the nature of their research or public statements?

As any administrator knows, managing faculty is exceptionally challenging. What too few know is that a union contract is a critical tool for administration. As the lists above show, CBAs contain essential information for proper administrative action.

In my seven years as Vice Provost for Faculty Affairs, I may not have seen it all, but I have seen plenty, and precious little has had to do with conflict that leads to formal grievances. Rather, the existence of a faculty union and its attendant CBA has not fomented conflict but has provided all parties with the means to avoid or resolve disputes. After all, conflict is inevitable. This is particularly true in academia, which trains faculty members to be disputatious in their disciplines, promoting skills that are transferrable to other domains, such as issues of shared governance and contract interpretation. Smart people who are conditioned to be critical and argumentative are bound on occasion to, well, argue. And the shared governance model that defines the faculty as both laborers and partners in management empowers faculty members to assert their opinions freely and often with gusto. There is nothing wrong with that, and an awful lot that is right with it. Regarded properly, the CBA with a faculty union is a job aid for any administrator who wants to lead productive change and who, therefore, is likely to encounter some conflict and resistance.

What I hope to show in the coming pages is that conflict and resistance from a faculty union can be productive and salutary things. Too often, I hear my colleagues in administration dismissing faculty unions as serving only to resist change and shield underperforming faculty members from accountability. Those opinions have their corollaries, of course, among many faculty members, who feel that all administrators are overpaid careerists bent on destroying venerable academic traditions in an effort to make universities more "corporate." Caricatures like these can be comforting, but they're seldom accurate. In a unionized environment, lasting progress can only come from respectful engagement between the administration and the union. Of course, respect and harmony are not synonymous, and by the same token, respect and conflict are not mutually exclusive.

The greatest achievement in the domain of Faculty Affairs that I've seen during my time at the University of Delaware has been the development of a career model for full-time, non-tenure line faculty that I believe is without parallel in American higher education. It has transformed the make-up of our faculty and it came about as a result of productive, respectful (although not always harmonious) engagement between the administration and the UD-AAUP. It took years to develop and has required a great deal of dialogue, education, and policy revision along the way, but the result is that today roughly 25 percent of the full-time faculty at the University of Delaware are on "Continuing Track" appointments (full-time, non-tenure) and 75 percent are on tenured/tenure-track appointments. How did we get to this point? What are the benefits of this model for faculty and students? How have we maintained—even increased—high standards of achievement in promotion and tenure decisions while developing a sizeable non-tenure line faculty? And what can the story of this process tell administrators about the value of collective bargaining in an academic setting?

"Continuing Track" Faculty: The Delaware Model

Before describing the process of engagement between the administration and the union that led to UD's Continuing Track (CT) faculty, a definition of that model is helpful. The CT role at the University of Delaware is based upon principles of equity, academic rigor, and unity among the faculty. The key features include:

- A unique, long-term contract structure that parallels the career progression of a TT (Tenure Track) faculty member.
- Parity in pay and benefits with TT faculty.
- The same professorial titles as TT faculty.
- Opportunity for promotion in rank to Associate Professor, Professor, and even Named Professor.
- Sabbaticals, earned on the same schedule as TT faculty.

- The right to participate in most Departmental, College, and University governance.
- Membership in the same bargaining unit as TT faculty.

Many colleges and universities have recently developed a full-time, non-tenure line faculty with some of the elements in this list, but none has done so as early and as comprehensively as the University of Delaware.

Perhaps the most distinctive feature on this list is the contract structure. CT faculty first serve under a series of three, 2-year contracts, each of which requires a peer review for renewal. After a successful sixth-year peer review, CT faculty are awarded a 3-year contract and a pay increase equivalent to that awarded to TT faculty promoted to Associate Professor with tenure. At the end of the 3-year contract, CT faculty are reviewed by the chair and dean and move onto a 4-year contract. After that contract (now the thirteenth year of service), another full peer review occurs, followed by the awarding of a "rolling" 5-year contract and a pay increase equivalent to that awarded to TT faculty when promoted to Full Professor. In summary, the contract terms are: 2, 2, 2, 3, 4, and "rolling" 5.

A CT faculty member may move through each of these contracts—and earn the two big salary increases—without ever seeking promotion in rank. The pay increments awarded at years 6 and 13 come as a function of contract progression, not promotion in rank. However, as members of the academy, CT faculty at Delaware know that titles matter. Therefore, a CT faculty member with a terminal degree is titled Assistant Professor—not "Lecturer," "Assistant Teaching Professor," or "Assistant Professor of Instruction." All Delaware academic departments are required to establish criteria for rank promotion specific to the teaching- and service-intensive roles of CT faculty. In most cases, these documents specifically acknowledge the teaching- or service-intensive nature of the CT faculty role. In order to be promoted, CT faculty document teaching excellence, pedagogical leadership, research, or service excellence, according to their typical workload. CT dossiers are usually reviewed externally by teaching- or service-oriented scholars. External letters and dossiers are evaluated by the same departmental, college, and university promotion committees that review TT candidates.

Our principles of equity, rigor, and unity extend to faculty governance and scholarly achievement. Most CT faculty can vote on departmental curricular and (sometimes) hiring issues. They have held campus roles such as College Senate President, Associate Department Chair, and AAUP Officer. Such service ensures that they are integrated into the life of the university through shared governance. In addition, most CT faculty members are engaged scholars in their respective disciplines; therefore, a part of their annual workload is dedicated to scholarship. In these ways, many CT faculty engage in the same activities as TT faculty, yet in different proportions.

In sum, at Delaware, CT and TT comprise a unified faculty working under the same Faculty Handbook, same title structure, equivalent salary structures, and similar contract and sabbatical schedules. No other U.S. faculty model comes as close to the ideals proposed by higher education writers Michael Berube and Jennifer Ruth (in *The Humanities, Higher Education, and Academic Freedom*) or those outlined by Adrianna Kezar, Daniel Scott, and Hannah Yang (*Delphi Project on the Changing Faculty and Student Success*). The University of Delaware faculty and administration regard the blend of TT and CT faculty to be the key to maintaining our deep commitment to undergraduate education while also greatly expanding the research profile of our faculty over the past 25 years.

Promoting Equity and Academic Rigor

The story of how the CT faculty role developed at Delaware has been told by one of its architects, Gerry Turkel, Professor Emeritus of Sociology and the long-time Contract Maintenance Officer of the UD-AAUP. For the purposes of this essay, a briefer overview of what Turkel covers in greater detail will suffice. It is a story worth telling because it powerfully exemplifies the fundamental concerns that some academic administrators have about a unionized faculty: that promoting equity in faculty wages, benefits, and working conditions will come at the cost of academic rigor. On the one hand, there was the UD-AAUP and non-tenure track faculty members, advocating for a policy that would provide long-term contracts, better pay and benefits, and fuller participation in shared governance. On the other hand, there were some administrators and TT faculty members who worried that empowering non-tenure track faculty in these ways would diminish the quality of the faculty, lower the expected standards of achievement, and alter institutional priorities for the worse. In short, equity concerns were sometimes seen to be at odds with academic norms and standards.

In response to the sizeable growth of the undergraduate student population in the 1990s, the University of Delaware developed policies creating what was then called the "Continuing Non-Tenure Track" (CNTT) role. More students meant greater instructional demands, but institutional budgets and policies provided only for traditional TT faculty roles and a variety of less stable, contingent roles. These included full-time non-tenure faculty on one-year contracts, adjunct faculty teaching on a course-by-course basis, and professional staff positions with instructional responsibilities. In 1996, the UD-AAUP and a new Provost worked together to create the CNTT faculty policy. The union's goals were to achieve better job stability, academic freedom protections, and greater gender equity (since women made up a high proportion of the contingent academic workforce). The administration sought to ensure that the undergraduate teaching mission was valued and supported even as strategic goals around graduate education and research productivity were being stepped up. The work between the union and the administration was supported by the fundamental belief that, with the right faculty structure, UD could excel in both teaching and research. That meant relying less on precarious contingent labor to provide undergraduate instruction and developing a non-tenure track faculty model focused on teaching and service activities.

The policy creating the CNTT faculty model was approved by the University Faculty Senate in 1996, but the Senate was not a key player in developing it. And attitudes toward the CNTT faculty role varied greatly between different academic departments. Some had no CNTT faculty at all while others (English, Math, Foreign Languages and Literatures) had a large number. The establishment of the policy meant that some individuals in professional staff positions who had significant teaching responsibilities were converted to CNTT faculty lines. Long-serving adjunct and temporary faculty were also converted to CNTT lines. These changes had a great impact on those departments that suddenly found themselves with a large number of CNTT faculty members. A number of important questions immediately arose. To what extent should CNTT faculty members participate in departmental governance, including voting privileges and participation on promotion and tenure committees? Should CNTT faculty be involved in discussion and votes on hiring priorities and should they serve on faculty search committees? How should the heavy teaching and service workloads of CNTT faculty members be reviewed, and what are the appropriate standards for promotion in academic rank? The union's chief concerns were with wages, benefits, and conditions of employment (including academic freedom protections, a necessary condition for participation in shared governance). The policy addressed these concerns, but it left the thornier questions to be settled by the various academic departments, resulting in a greatly uneven landscape for CNTT faculty.

In the late 1990s and early 2000s, the university continued to add CNTT faculty positions, filling them by means of national searches. Meanwhile, individual departments wrestled with the governance and academic quality questions. In my home department of English, a dividing line was quickly drawn between tenured literary scholars and non-tenured instructors of composition. Led by an equity-minded department chair, the English faculty addressed important questions about shared governance and promotion standards, often landing on the side of inclusion and equity. But the debates were fierce and many of the tenured literature faculty members were convinced that the CNTT faculty would vote as a bloc to change departmental priorities, alter the nature of the faculty through the hiring process, devalue literary study, and (worst of all) erode the justification for tenure by their very presence. If the meetings were sometimes unpleasant, the outcomes for CNTT faculty in English were almost always positive. But in other departments, like Math, the opposite was true. For a variety of reasons, the gulf between the TT and CNTT faculty in that department was deep and wide. The upshot was that the CNTT policy promoted equity in important ways, but what Turkel calls the "states' rights" approach to issues of shared governance and promotion led to greatly differential treatment. The TT and CNTT faculty might have been unified in the CBA, but they often were not unified in the monthly faculty meeting.

In 2012–2013, the Interim Provost worked with some Faculty Senate leaders in an attempt to impose university-wide uniformity on key issues regarding CNTT appointments, including participation on promotion and tenure committees, academic titles, and promotion standards. As Turkel explains, these proposals were motivated by concerns that the growing number of CNTT faculty was "diluting the quality" of the university. The remedy was a series of proposals that many felt would have diminished the CNTT faculty role and marked them as second-class citizens among the faculty. In response, the CNTT faculty established a formal caucus to advocate for its members. And that spring, the UD-AAUP and University administration bargained over a new contract. Central to that effort was a discussion relating to the conditions of employment for CNTT faculty, resulting in a revision of article 3.3 of the CBA that stipulated that any future changes to the CNTT policy would require the approval of the Provost and the UD-AAUP. The policy proposals under consideration at the Faculty Senate that spring failed to pass, resulting in a victory for CNTT faculty and their allies, but without resolving the concerns that motivated those proposals or providing university-wide consistency in the CNTT faculty experience. Nevertheless, the collective bargaining process, particularly the revision of article 3.3, laid the groundwork for the ultimate resolution of these issues.

The "Kerfuffle" Over Modified Titles

Less than a year after the new CBA took effect, issues relating to the conditions of employment for CNTT faculty once again fueled conflict. In April, 2014, a new Provost announced that all new CNTT faculty hires would carry modified titles in order to distinguish them from TT faculty. For example, a CNTT hire in the English Department would be called "Assistant Professor of Instruction" instead of "Assistant Professor." Modified titles of this sort had become common in the academy by 2014, so the proposal was not an innovation. Nevertheless, it met with strong opposition from the CT Caucus and the UD-AAUP, who regarded the imposition of modified titles without the approval of the union as a violation of article 3.3. The union contended that academic titles are no trifling matter and that titles constitute an important condition of employment, especially for non-tenure track faculty. And unlike the previous year, the Faculty Senate leadership was not aligned with the Office of the Provost on the matter. I watched this dispute unfold with special interest because just as it was happening, I had accepted the offer to become Vice Provost for Faculty Affairs, a new position at the University of Delaware. It was clear that the controversy over CNTT titles would be a focus of my work in the new role.

One of the key moments in this story was a memorable Faculty Senate Open Hearing on the modified titles, during which members of the CNTT Caucus gave voice to their concerns that modified titles were the first step in a process that would diminish and devalue their contributions to the University. Recalling the proposals from the previous year that failed to pass in the Faculty Senate, CNTT faculty feared that, beginning with titles, those proposals were now going to be enacted by administrative fiat. And they were especially provoked by the Provost's dismissal of their objections as a "kerfuffle," a word that now has a special resonance among the University of Delaware community. To the CNTT faculty, the modified titles were not a trivial matter because the effect of them was to distinguish CNTT from the "real" faculty, their TT counterparts. If the titles change, then one can imagine other changes, such as the elimination of sabbaticals, the abridging of academic freedom protections, and the like. They reasoned that it was better to stand and fight this first step than to allow it and hope the others don't follow. In fairness to the Provost, there was no plan to follow the titling decision with other actions that undermined the CNTT model. The goal was simply to find a way to publicly represent the composition of the faculty in a manner consistent with other research universities. But recent history made CNTT faculty suspicious of the Provost's intentions, and the contentious Senate Open Hearing turned up the temperature on the matter.

As the new Vice Provost for Faculty Affairs, I served as the chief administrative liaison to the UD-AAUP. One of my first meetings, held shortly after the Open Hearing, was a discussion between the union leadership and representatives from the Office of the Provost concerning the titling controversy. The union was threatening to file a grievance against the Provost for violating article 3.3, which read, "Any proposed change to the policy governing the conditions of employment for CNTT faculty that are approved by the Provost during the term of this contract must also be approved by the AAUP before taking effect." As is often the case, the union's foothold on the issue was with the process: because the Provost had not secured AAUP approval, the declaration of modified titles violated the CBA. This was the very reason that article 3.3 was amended the previous year. Having seen the Interim Provost bypass the union and work with Faculty Senate leaders on the CNTT policy proposals the year before, the union negotiators successfully altered the CBA to require not just consultation with, but approval from the UD-AAUP before changes could be made to the CNTT policy. Faced with a brewing revolt from the CNTT Caucus, a lack of support among the Senate leadership, and the threat of a grievance from the union, the decision was made to take a step back from this escalating confrontation. The union agreed to hold off on filing a grievance (which would only have addressed the titling issue) and instead supported the creation of a Provost's Commission on CNTT Faculty, which was charged with and undertaking a comprehensive review of the CNTT faculty role and making recommendations for policy changes, including, but certainly not limited to, titling. With the creation of this commission, the stage was set for addressing the issues around promotion standards and participation shared governance that called for a university-wide solution.

The commission was chaired by the Dean of the College of Arts and Sciences, the largest college at UD, home to nearly half of the faculty and the lion's share of CNTT faculty. I served as an ex officio, non-voting member, representing the Office of the Provost, and there were eight faculty members, evenly split between TT and CNTT. One member was an officer in the UD-AAUP and another was Vice President of the Faculty Senate. The stated intention of the chair was that the group would work to achieve a consensus report and that parochial interests could be set aside. In order to help bring this about, the commission began its work not by debating the merits of modified academic titles, but by taking a step back from that controversy and carefully reviewing the CNTT policy, which was found in multiple sections of the Faculty Handbook and the relevant sections of the CBA. The commission also developed a survey of faculty attitudes toward the CNTT faculty role. Beginning with the review of policies was a crucial decision because it brought every member of the commission up to speed, leveling the playing field for discussion, and because it raised questions and concerns that had not been raised before. But the biggest benefit was that it fostered a discussion among faculty, administration, union, and Senate representatives about what the CNTT role is versus what it ought to be. And by means of the survey and focus group discussions, we learned about the great variety of CNTT faculty types and their attendant workload variations in the three major categories of teaching, research, and service. Several members, myself included, assumed that we knew the policies and had a good sense of the nature of CNTT work, but we quickly came to realize that there was a great deal we didn't know.

Humbled by what we learned from our initial work, it became clear that although the University had developed a unique and robust model of non-tenure track full-time faculty, and despite the fact that CNTT faculty comprised more than one-fifth of all full-time faculty at UD, little thought had been given to questions of career progression, equity, and academic standards for these faculty members. Wages, benefits, and working conditions (including academic freedom protections) were covered by the CBA, but the academic policies that comprise the Faculty Handbook at UD had not kept pace with the hiring of so many CNTT faculty in many ways. The issue of modified titles might have been the catalyst, but it was not the most significant one that needed to be addressed. The most important concerns had to do with establishing a promotion path for CNTT faculty that was based upon the nature of their work and how it differed from a standard TT faculty member's work.

The fundamental inequity that had developed over nearly 20 years of hiring CNTT faculty was that their TT counterparts could be promoted in rank but CNTT faculty were mostly stuck at the rank of Assistant Professor. Why? Because the promotion and tenure criteria were created for TT roles, not CNTT. For example, an Assistant Professor of English is typically expected to publish a book to earn tenure and promotion. This is a reasonable expectation if the teaching load is 2/2. But many CNTT faculty shouldered teaching loads of 3/4 or even 4/4, which presents a barrier to achieving the same quantity and quality of scholarship relative to their TT peers. And yet that was the reality. In order to earn promotion in rank, CNTT faculty had to do significantly more work than a TT faculty member in the same department. This fundamental inequity arose partly from benign neglect and perhaps partly form a concern that allowing for different promotion standards for TT and CNTT faculty would be tantamount to "lowering standards." Without campus-wide guidance, departments were left to address or ignore this problem. In tackling the issue, the commission turned to article 11.4 in the CBA that read:

> An individual's workload shall be assigned with the expectation that the faculty member will have the opportunity to meet the criteria for promotion and satisfactory peer review. An individual's assigned workload shall be considered in the promotion and tenure and peer review process in a manner consistent with the promotion and tenure and peer review criteria written by each department to fit its particular circumstances and needs.

The principle stated in the first sentence is clear enough. But what to do with the second sentence? It's all well and good to consider workload in relation to promotion and tenure criteria, but if the criteria for rank promotion do not, in turn, recognize the different workload associated with CNTT faculty roles, nothing changes. Unless departmental promotion and tenure standards were revised to establish a separate set of criteria for CNTT faculty promotion, these two sentences could never be reconciled.

Reconciling Equity and Institutional Achievement

The key to resolving this basic inequity of having CNTT faculty judged by TT criteria was not to lower standards for promotion, but to recognize that workload variation was a key framework for judging any promotion case and, further, to recognize that the CNTT faculty role and the TT faculty role were different. CNTT faculty were not lesser versions of their TT counterparts, and providing a path for rank promotion to them would not diminish the University's reputation or inhibit the success of the research enterprise. Quite the opposite. The work that CNTT faculty performed helped to meet our instructional and service missions, freeing up their TT colleagues to focus more on the research mission. Each mission is critical to the institution, and the entire point of developing a full-time, non-tenure line faculty was to pursue each mission with fully enfranchised, fully benefited, full-time faculty members, reducing the University's reliance on more precarious contingent labor. In other words, TT and CNTT faculty were meant to work in a symbiotic way, not a competitive or adversarial one. Recognizing this, the recommendations of the Commission on CNTT faculty included specific guidance on titles and on promotion standards.

The controversy over modified titles catalyzed the campus-wide discussion on CNTT faculty, leading to the forming of the commission. The ultimate recommendation on titles was very different. The commission called for changing the name of Continuing Non-Tenure Track faculty to "Continuing Track." This was important because the name CNTT emphasized tenure-track faculty as a prevailing norm that other full-time faculty needed to be defined against, and *non-tenure track* was, therefore, a fundamentally pejorative description. We defined these faculty by what they were not, rather than emphasizing what they were. This hurt us in recruitment efforts because we were advertising positions characterized by their difference from a norm (who is eager to be hired as "non" something?). And it hurt us in morale because the very name emphasized the negative instead of the positive. As a result of the commission's work, the name has since changed to Continuing Track faculty. As for the modified titles, the recommendation was to employ them narrowly and only when appropriate to the discipline and nature of the faculty work (e.g., clinical professors and for professors of the practice). But a title like Assistant Professor of Instruction was not recommended. Therefore, the vast majority of CT faculty bear unmodified professorial titles. This recommendation reflected the opinions of strong majorities of TT and CT faculty, who responded to a survey question by opposing the modified titles. Focus group discussions and other input showed that faculty of all sorts regarded the modified titles and unconducive to collegiality and faculty cohesion.

The other major recommendation was that every department must have clearly defined promotion criteria at all ranks for CT faculty as part of their units' approved P&T document. In addition, it called for clear criteria for CT faculty promotion to be included in all college and University P&T documents. Specifically, the commission recommended that promotion of CT faculty was to be based on excellence in one role, aligned with preponderance of assigned workload. CT faculty would need to demonstrate high quality performance in other roles represented in their workloads (e.g., excellence in teaching and high quality in service and scholarship). This was how University promotion standards and practices would become responsive to differential workloads between TT and CT appointments. It also resolved the contradictions in the workload article of the CBA because it provided the academic policy guidance that could ensure that an "individual's workload shall be assigned with the expectation that the faculty member will have the opportunity to meet the criteria for promotion and satisfactory peer review." This was later bolstered by an addition to the University P&T policy in the Faculty Handbook that reads:

> Workload shall be assigned with the expectation that the faculty member will have the opportunity to meet the criteria for satisfactory peer review, contract renewal, and promotion and/or tenure. An individual's assigned workload during the review period shall be considered in the promotion and/or tenure and peer review process in a manner consistent with the approved promotion and/or tenure and peer review criteria written by each department. Candidates for promotion and/or tenure are required to report their assigned workload as part of their dossier so that all reviewers—including external reviewers—have a clear sense of their workload in the various areas of their effort and can judge their achievements fairly.

With these policy changes, CT faculty now were no longer defined by their difference from the TT norm (*non-tenure track*) and they were no longer reviewed for promotion by TT criteria. As one might expect, the ensuing years have seen a great number of CT faculty applying for promotion in rank. The process for review is identical to that for TT faculty, but the departmental criteria distinguishes the expectations of TT from those of CT faculty.

Providing equity for CT faculty has not diminished institutional achievement or standards of quality; rather, the standards of achievement for both TT and CT faculty have increased. Promotion rates are roughly commensurate for TT and CT faculty, and both research standards and productivity have been raised. For instance, along with establishing promotion standards for CT faculty, departments were also required to strengthen the standards for research achievement for TT faculty, requiring excellence in research as a condition for promotion and the award of tenure. Since these policy changes took effect in 2015, sponsored research expenditures have increased 25 percent, rising from $137,402,359 to $171,533,306. Additionally, UD ranks among the top 100 institutions for federal science and engineering obligations, and ranks eighty-sixth nationally in total R&D expenditures (excluding medical school expenditures), ahead of a dozen AAU institutions including Rice University, Stony Brook University, the University of Chicago, and the University of Rochester. And contrary to the fears of some, improving equity for CT faculty has not led to an erosion of tenure. The proportion of TT to CT faculty has not changed notably, with three-quarters of the faculty in TT/tenured and one-quarter CT. All faculty members are expected to uphold the University's reputation for excellent teaching, but CT faculty, in particular, are expected to be pedagogical leaders on campus, a role they have embraced in a number of ways, including directing major programs of study, such as the first-year writing program; leading new student support initiatives, like the Mathematical Sciences Learning

Laboratory; and developing a researched-based cohort program for the peer observation of teaching.

These outcomes have been achieved in the context of the policy decisions and changes that first created and then improved the CT faculty role at the University of Delaware. None of it happened by union action alone, but it's likely that none of it would have happened at all without the engagement of the UD-AAUP at the outset and throughout the process. Notably, the development of the CT faculty role and the important steps taken to realize greater equity between TT and CT faculty never occasioned a formal grievance (although one was threatened). Instead, dialogue between the administration and the union, both within the context of collective bargaining and between contract negotiations, was the key. At crucial moments, progress was facilitated by turning to specific articles in the CBA relating to policy changes for CT faculty and the relation between workload and promotion standards. There were periods of close collaboration between the union and the Office of the Provost, as well as times of sharp disagreement. Looking back on this process, Turkel, the former Contract Maintenance Officer, concludes,

> due to its mix of union representation and sometimes conflicting but generally supportive initiatives by the university faculty senate and administrators, conditions of employment for these faculty members are quite favorable. The exercise of academic freedom, especially in institutional policy making regarding these faculty members, has been robust.
>
> *(Turkel, 16)*

In the best spirit of shared governance, working with open minds and engaged in open dialogue, the University and the union found a way to reconcile issues of equity and institutional goals for achievement.

14

CASE STUDY

University of Florida

William W. Connellan

Background

I joined the University of Florida (UF) in March 2012 as assistant provost with responsibility for academic collective bargaining.

The University of Florida is the flagship campus in the 12-university system in the state. The university has 16 colleges, a large hospital system, more than 100 undergraduate majors, and 200 graduate degree programs. The university also is the designated state leader in online education student population is 50,000, with 13,000 graduate students.

What I endeavor to show in this chapter are some of the differences and the similarities in collective bargaining at Oakland University and the University of Florida.

The University of Florida has moved into the top ten public research universities in the country and currently is ranked number six. the University of Florida is the flagship campus in the 12-university system in the state. The university has 16 colleges, a large hospital system, more than 100 undergraduate majors, and 200 graduate degree programs. The university also is the designated state leader in online education student population is 50,000, with 13,000 graduate students.

The rankings are done annually by US News and World Report. There are specific criteria that US News measures. University of Florida aspires to become a top-five public research university. The university generates $900 million in funded research activities.

The two institutions are very different in size, scope, and impact in the state. For example, in Michigan I had direct contract with the Board of Trustees. In Florida I deal with my provost and occasionally with the president.

DOI: 10.4324/9781003138990-16

University of Florida Setting

There are two academic collective bargaining units – the faculty and the graduate assistants. The United Faculty of Florida represents both the faculty and grad assistants. The union is affiliated with several national unions: the Florida Education Association (FEA), the National Education Association (NEA), the American Federation of Teachings (AFT), and the American Federation of Labor and Congress of Industrial Organizations (AFL-CIO).

Because of the significant increase in faculty positions, and the large number of teaching assistants, there is only a limited number of adjunct faculty.

The University of Florida has a rather unique situation with respect to collective bargaining. At Florida, the law school, medicine, nursing, public health, and others are not in the bargaining unit. The result is that two-thirds of the faculty are not in bargaining unit. That presents some interesting challenges. The university cannot stray too far from the campus norms. For example, the faculty union has pushed hard to increase the percent the university contributes to the pension program, wanting to go from 9% to 15%. There were years in which they might have been possible or last a movement up from 9% in exchange for a lower raise. But the cost to the university would have been prohibitive if extended to faculty not represented by a bargaining unit.

Like many universities, Florida has a number of non-faculty bargaining units. There needs to be consistency between the units, particularly in the benefits area.

The graduate assistant union (GAU) has 4,000 members and represents both teaching assistants and research assistants. Unlike the faculty union, the GAU represents all units on campus save for professional degree programs. The university recently invested $14 million in graduate assistant pay so has to become competitive with the best universities in the country. Units benchmarked their pay with peers across the country. One unique aspect of the graduate assistant union is that we provide health care through the university rather than buy commercial insurance. Because we have a large hospital system, we have that ability. Our own Gator Grad Care is very competitive nationally and graduate assistants only pay $12 a month to fund it. That lets the university tailor the program to fit its needs, but it also is challenging us because, rather than select options from an outside vendor, the university bargains all provisions of the Gator Grad Care program.

Former governor Jeb Bush dissolved the old Board of Regents in 2000. Prior to that, all universities were in a single bargaining unit. With the change, each university inherited its own collective bargaining unit. The faculty collective bargaining agreement contract that came with the disbanding of the Board of Regents did not fit University of Florida well. The old contract spanned everything from small institutions with limited graduate programs to places like Florida State University and University of Florida that are large research-intensive enterprises. The University of Florida negotiated its first independent collective bargaining agreement with its local union starting in 2005.

Coming to UF in 2012

My boss was candid about the frayed relationship with the union. My job, he said, was to fix the relationship and he gave me great latitude as to how I would go about that.

Re-shaping the collective bargaining agreement to meet our needs was a huge task. It took the university and the union five years to negotiate the first contract following the end of the Board of Regents.

It took several years just to cleanse the contract of duplicative provisions up the contract. Because it took so long to negotiate the first contract, duplicate provisions were common. We also tightened the language, eliminating 40% of the words without changing anything substantive.

Collective bargaining agreements (CBAs) can, on occasion, be a stumbling block to university goals. My mission always is to have the CBA be one of the tools to help the university achieve its goals. Getting the union to appreciate the importance of that took some time. In the end, both sides agreed that if the university prospered then so did the faculty.

Many perceive collective bargaining as an impediment to university aspirations. I do not. Collective bargaining can be a very powerful tool for helping the university to achieve its goals. We try to couch our bargaining proposals in terms of university goals. There is academic reasoning behind our proposals. One example in recent years involved our k-12 developmental research school. We wanted the school to expand its research impact and paid them to spend four hours a week in research. That resulted in the school having a teaching and research effort, not just a teaching role.

Oakland University

Oakland was one of the first public universities to have faculty collective bargaining and the first to have a strike in the 1960s. The school came into being in 1959 and was affiliated with Michigan State University until 1970. It was, when I was there, primarily an undergraduate institution with 7,000 students. Our first chief bargainer's approach to bargaining was very standard: only he talked for the university, he would put full proposals on the table without prior discussion with the union, and he viewed the union as adversaries. The union responded in kind. I was on his team one year, and then took over in the following negotiations.

The union tried to frustrate him at the table in diabolical ways. For example, one of the members would try to engage others of us in conversation. One particular example was telling. I had been a student at Oakland before joining the staff, so I knew the faculty members at the table well. The union had put on the table a phased retirement program. One of their members, a political scientist, outlined the virtues of the proposal and then teased us by saying that the university would benefit because most faculty members had only two good courses in them. He turned to me and said, "Isn't that right, Bill?"

I could not resist and broke our protocol and shot right back at him. "Yes, and I had both of them from you". One of their team members asked how many. I had taken from him. "Four." That broke the ice and we ended up with a good program that benefited both sides. Most faculty in the phased retirement program did not go the full three years. They were comfortable with the change in pace. The benefit to the university was the ability to plan for replacements and also to save money with the new hires.

Humor plays a vital role in bargaining; personal relationships across the table are critical. That story is reflective of best practices in bargaining. The very conservative approach to bargaining, at least in Michigan, was flawed.

Three years later, I was the rookie chief bargainer and made my share of mistakes, but we survived despite a three-day strike.

It was very disappointing when the faculty announced they were going on strike. The union's attorney walked out to the car with me and said "there is no reason for this strike," and gave me a hint as how to resolve it quickly. The lesson learned was: listen to the union, regardless of who in the union is sending you messages. In this message, the bargaining team could not deliver that message.

One year we went to impasse before a strike and the State Employment Relations Board assigned a fact finder. The fact finder's job is to determine a solution, which either side could reject, or a strike could ensue. If a strike followed, the courts would likely end the strike because of the involvement of a fact finder.

The fact finder met with both sides together, laid out data he wanted, and gave us a strict deadline to produce the information. I discussed our options with university leadership and found a potential solution. I called the fact finder to see if he could play mediator instead. He joined us that evening and we settled.

I always had a good working relationship with the union chief bargainer. It was good enough that it was easy to tell him that we understood why they had a proposal on the table: that is, to send a message to the administration. He knew from our informal conversations that it would disappear when we got to crunch time.

There are also times when it is important to call the union bluff (or for them to call ours). One year the faculty turned down a contract that the team had negotiated. The president of the union thought his team had given away everything. It was an unprecedented move and created a rift within the bargaining unit.

Union bylaws mandated a new bargaining team. We started negotiating in January. We knew that we would not move much, if at all, from what the original agreement was because both the board and senior administration were determined not to reward the faculty for the fall strike.

The union was in a tough spot. It knew that once a semester started, faculty would not support a strike. Before classes a strike was not a problem, and the Oakland union used that weapon frequently over the years.

That was my first year on the team. We were meeting one Wednesday night in early February and we had our outside counsel with us. The space was cramped, deliberately so. The union's chief negotiator pounded the table and said if we do not have a contract by Friday we are going on strike. As he said it, he looked not at our chief bargainer, but at me, knowing the underlying message would be understood.

His threat had the intended impact on our team. We clearly were rattled, and we took a quick caucus. Once in the caucus room my first words were "let them go on strike." My team looked at me horrified, as we were under strict orders to settle without a strike.

Next week was spring break, so it would be a "phantom" strike. I knew they would cave if necessary because they had no choice. We went back into the bargaining room and simply said let us recess and bargain again tomorrow.

There was one simple fix that would work to the benefit of both the faculty and the university: If the university received "x" amount of funding from the state, we would give the faculty a slightly bigger raise. It was a tough time financially for the university because of an automotive-driven recession.

The president bought into our suggestion, the union worked back channels, and we had a contract. In the end, the union got a larger raise, but it was a gamble. Had we not settled, it would be a long, bitter struggle to get back to the good relationship we had with the union.

We also had our experiment with interest-based bargaining one year. Interest-based bargaining is the ultimate in collaboration. Rather than simply put proposals on the table, the teams identify issues and see if there is common interest that can lead to a proposal acceptable to both sides.

The Oakland experiment went extremely well. We did not sit across the table from each other, we had one set of minutes, and we shared financial data easily. We even traded turns in providing food. The success at the bargaining table set the stage for the university to change its approach to general academic operations, but we failed to take advantage of that. That failure was a huge missed opportunity.

I also had one case where my president intervened in the bargaining process without my knowledge. He had lunch with the union president and chief bargainer and offered them a package. They turned it down because they were angry with him. We settled later that night at less than the president had offered them.

External factors often impact bargaining. They can be political, or economic, what is happening at other universities, or what is happening in industry or other government areas. For example, the faculty were pressing us to provide health care coverage to same-sex couples. It was the union's social justice issue. Our bargaining team was receptive, but we could not show that at the table because of our Board of Trustees. The trustees were concerned about potential costs, but the primary reason was philosophical. Ford, GM, and Chrysler announced in June that they would begin offering same-sex health care coverage. That same day we were meeting with the board. Our board members threw up their hands and said give it to the union, but try to extract a price.

Oakland did one of the early market equity studies. It was a crude one by today's standards. We narrowed the focus to gender equity. The numbers were so stunning that we clearly had to make some significant adjustments in salaries for women faculty.

The request to look at the salaries of women came from the union. Everything was done informally, not at the bargaining table.

Today's market equity studies are much more sophisticated. They are expensive to do because they look at multiple variables such as salary compression, gender equity, and disciplinary differences. They also are incredibly expensive to implement.

I left administration in 2000 and spent my remaining time at Oakland teaching journalism. When I retired in 2008, the new provost prevailed upon me to do an "encore" round of bargaining.

We always met with the Board of Trustees prior to bargaining to get our marching orders and to let the board know of expected issues at the bargaining table. That list of issues included anticipated faculty proposals and needs that we perceived to be important from the university's perspective.

In that initial session with the board, the board chair. He then asked for any initial observations since I had been away from the table for 9 years. "I read through the most recent contracts to see what had changed and I was startled by one thing. There is a fine line between a mature contract and a creaky one." The board chair asked for an explanation. I said that some language was outdated, some provisions were made for a specific case that no longer pertained, and frankly wondered what idiot had written certain provisions. I confessed that the idiot was me, which prompted some chuckles. That round of bargaining also proved that despite best intentions, collaboration does not always work.

External factors can impede collaboration, such as a recession or a pandemic. External political factors can impact collaboration; as can fear of difference with similar institutions. In other words, a continuous environmental scan is important.

In Oakland's case, the university was in the process of establishing a medical school, and the president and general counsel wanted to barrel ahead and implement it without bargaining. I told them that was not possible, and they relented, but said if we accomplished nothing else that contract had to get the medical school faculty out of the bargaining unit. We succeeded, but it left some bitter feelings among faculty, most of whom did not want a medical school and wanted to use bargaining as a tool to block it. I refused to let the union bargain on academic issues. In my mind, academic governance had no place in a bargaining context.

In the end, the union decided that having the medical school faculty out of the bargaining unit would be a good thing for a variety of reasons, so we accomplished the university's main goal.

That round of bargaining was very difficult. It was also a difficult bargaining session because I was constrained by the president and the general counsel. Rather than let me pick my bargaining team in consultation with the provost, they told me who my team was. They often dictated what we should put on the table, and when. Neither had experience at the bargaining table. My final lesson learned at Oakland was to let the chief bargainer do his or her job.

Bargaining at Florida

The bargaining processes at the two universities are generally similar. For example, I work hard at developing a good working relationship with the chief bargainer for the union. I often will have lunch with him once a month during bargaining. We have to be careful not to bargain away from the table, but the lunches provided an opportunity to find out what some of their concerns are and how we might be able to provide the union with information it needs.

The same applies at the table. Either the union bargainer or I will have a sidebar. A sidebar is a conversation between the two chief bargainers away from the table. We cannot bargain away from the table, but we can deliver messages. One such example several years ago was telling the chief bargainer away from the table that we were going to declare impasse. We had discussed the possibility of impasse at the table. We wanted him to know we were going to impasse. When we went back to the table, we announced we were going to impasse, but the sidebar gave him a chance to prepare his team before the bombshell. This move gave the union chief bargainer the opportunity to prepare his team for what was forthcoming.

In my mind, impasse is a failure. We were not able to be collaborative at the table, and no one wins in an impasse. In Florida, impasse situations require a representative from the Public Employees Relations Commission to make a recommendation. If both sides agree, the issue is resolved. If they disagree the University Board of Trustees makes the decision. It is good for only one year, and then we are bargaining again. One could argue that there was at least a temporary winner because that team's position prevailed. The truth is that both sides lose because of the damaged relationship between the university and the union. It can take years to recover.

One item is obvious in a bargaining relationship. Each chief bargainer has multiple bargaining sessions going on. One, of course, is across the table. But I also am bargaining with my team, with my provost, and with the deans. That requires extensive work. With the deans, it is seeking out what their needs are before bargaining begins. When I arrived in Florida, I asked the provost to set up a policy committee to give me advice. It includes one associate provost, the chief financial officer, the president's chief of staff, and the vice president for human resources. That requires another set of bargaining as that group has different perspectives.

During negotiations, we meet monthly with the associate deans to keep them apprised of progress at the table and to seek input.

It is important to remember that the chief bargainer for the union has a similar task, perhaps more challenging than mine. It is more challenging because a dean speaks for his or her college. The union bargainer has 2000 free agents. That includes people who are against the union, those who are high powered researchers, and those whose primary focus is teaching. Naturally there are some different needs for faculty at different stages in their careers. A new untenured faculty member and a lecturer with nothing more a one-year contract likely have much different needs than a mid-career faculty does, and those approaching retirement have other needs. The academic discipline of the faculty member also has a marked impact on his or her approach to bargaining.

One of my colleagues in the provost's office, whom I turn to for advice or to vent, reminded me one day that they are our faculty. "In the heat of negotiations we sometimes forget that," he said. "They are our faculty and we want them to succeed."

We occasionally fail at the bargaining table – either to be collaborative or to achieve some particular goal. We also get some wins. This year, in particular, we succeeded with respect to paid parental leave and personal time off. Our previous contracts had parental leave, but the university advanced the time and faculty had to pay the time back over several years. With the new contract, we are implementing an eight-week paid parental leave.

We also had a traditional vacation and sick leave policy. We replaced it with a paid time off program, which is much more flexible. Sick leave and vacation were merged into the paid time off (PTO). The last piece was a paid medical leave program for faculty to take care of themselves or family members who are ill.

The union's initial focus was paid parental leave and it requested a full semester of paid parental leave. We signaled an interest in paid parental leave, but also said the faculty proposal was too rich.

In the meantime, our human resources team was putting together its comprehensive proposal noted above. It was a complicated effort. In addition, the entire leave article was riddled with antiquated and likely not permissible provisions, so it required a complete overhaul. I met regularly with the human resources team as it was designing the program. One human resources person eventually joined the bargaining team and she was a terrific team member. As is traditional at the bargaining table, we do not bargain money issues until all other language items are agreed to. Paid parental leave clearly had cost implications.

It was important to keep lines of communication open with the union on this one. It also took several sessions for the union to understand the concept of PTO (paid time off) and the paid medical leave and how they dovetailed with paid parental leave.

The result was a huge win for the university and the faculty. We now have a model program that will serve us well in the years ahead.

We already have invitations to present at conferences. Being in the national spotlight will make the faculty happy that they fashioned the program at the bargaining table. It will bode well for future negotiations as the union will see that major change can be accomplished at the bargaining table.

We had another win-win situation this year, albeit not quite as spectacular as the paid parental leave program. We had in place a "term professorship" program in which certain faculty members received a special stipend over a three-year period. When we implemented the term professorship program in a previous contract, the union leadership reluctantly agreed to it. The union did not like the concept, but knew that if it did not agree to it all the awards would go to areas of the campus not represented by the union.

We wanted to end the program this year so that we could invest the money budgeted for this program in the 100 new faculty positions for a new AI initiative. It was not a hard sell at the bargaining table. Again, both sides came out winners.

We also had a case a couple of years ago that provided some positive responses. Our contract has a provision called "administrative discretionary increases" (ADI). It permits the university to give some raises without bargaining, but there is an annual cap on how much we can award via ADI.

We wanted to exceed the cap one year so we could put an extra 2% into funding ADI raises. Our stipulation was that such raises would go to outstanding performers whose salary was below the norm for that discipline. After some discussion, the union agreed. The deans made the decision as to who would get the raises and how much the raises would be. The result: women were the big winners.

Thus far, this part of the chapter has focused on the bargaining process. Collaboration with the union is important in other ways. I talk regularly with grievance representatives, and they do not hesitate to call with questions or suggestions on how to solve a problem without a grievance. I even have had a grievance officer walk into a grievance hearing and give me a hug. We have a relatively small number of grievances each year, on the order of half a dozen bargaining unit faculty, and perhaps one a year from graduate assistants.

Of course, when we get to arbitrations, it becomes adversarial. Even in these situations, there is some give and take, and arbitrators often will work with both sides to fashion a solution. Our CBA provides a mechanism for selecting our arbitration panel. We never have had to use that mechanism. We simply talk with the union and agree upon the panel.

External forces also impact the bargaining relationship. The COVID-19 crisis is one example. It has upended the university, as it has done across the country. We shifted to mostly online instruction, and many are working from home at least part of the time. The impact on the university budget is going to be severe. We are exploring some alternatives now. For example, our collective bargaining agreement provides for layoffs, but not furloughs. We are now proposing to the union that we add furlough language to the contract to ease the impact on employees.

The current situation also has the union, and others on campus, worried about a variety of issues, including measures to assure safety. As a result, we are having bi-weekly sessions with union leadership to consult about such matters. Normally, we have such consultation sessions once or twice a year.

One last comment on faculty before turning to graduate assistants. Some administrative colleagues occasionally complain about union leadership because those individuals often have run afoul of the administration in the past. In my opinion, that often makes them more effective union leaders, particularly in grievance situations. I would much rather have strong union leaders representing their colleagues than weak ones.

As noted earlier, graduate assistants are represented by the same union as the faculty. We try to have the same collaborative relationship with them. One of the challenges we face with that union is the turnover because of graduations, and therefore we constantly have newcomers at the table. This, of course, is their first experience with bargaining. The union tends to have large teams, which makes bargaining unwieldy at times.

One of the interesting observations is that the chief bargainers for the graduate union often end up not in faculty positions when they graduate, but they become union organizers or manage faculty negotiations.

Part of that is due to the lack of faculty positions, but part is also that they find their calling through their experience at the bargaining table. Several former graduate assistant leaders at Florida have done so and they stay in touch.

As noted earlier in this chapter, we invested $14 million increasing stipends for graduate assistants. We are in year three of a four-year rollout. Initially, it caused severe challenges for the union. The dollars were reserved for new hires and were limited to doctoral students. We also insisted that those eligible had to be at .5 FTE. Prior to that, units often spread out their assistantships to cover more students. The .5 requirement has helped speed up degree completion.

The new program has several positive benefits. In the first year of the new program our acceptance rate from those offered assistantships jumped from 60%

to 82%. Units reported that they were getting much better students and reported significant gains in diversity. The improved status of graduate students can help in recruiting faculty, because the prospective faculty can attract better graduate assistants.

This chapter has focused on academic labor relations, but we do not operate in a vacuum. The University of Florida is a massive enterprise with some 28,000 employees. Its impact on the Gainesville community is enormous. Remembering the context in which collective bargaining operates is critical to our success, or in some cases, failure.

Recap and Advice

My 50 years of bargaining roles at Oakland and Florida have given me some insights that point to best practices. Times have changed substantially, but some basics still apply.

- In recent years, the trend has been to hire outside attorneys to negotiate contracts. That has some advantages. A knowledge of labor law is useful, and an outside person can distance him or herself from the institution between negotiations. On the other hand, it may be more expensive. Even with outside attorneys as negotiators, institutions need to buttress the team with inside academics.
- I am a firm believer that the provost's office should be the driver. It is important to include human resources in some fashion, either as team members or as backup. We have been lucky to have superb HR representatives at the table.
- Keep your bargaining team small and encourage the union to do the same. It is much more efficient at the table.
- Trust your chief negotiator. He or she needs to be confident that the university supports the chief and his or her team. Regardless of his/her regular role at the university, during bargaining time recognize that this is a full-time effort.
- Give your chief negotiator room to grow and prosper as an academic – teaching, publishing, consulting.
- Recognize that your institution's collective bargaining may impact other institutions in the state. It does not mean you should be bashful. Rather, it can be an opportunity to lead the state, as we did this year with the paid parental leave program.
- Do not let external problems get the better of you.
- Keep academic governance and bargaining separate. At UF, the union leaders have also been governance leaders. Academic issues belong in the colleges and not at the table. We need to trust faculty to do the right thing in governance matters.

- Most important, as my friend said, they are our faculty and we want them to succeed.
- In every action we take, we embrace equity whenever we can. Several examples of that are delineated in this chapter.

Each of the above are examples of best practices that other institutions can emulate.

Summary

I believe that this chapter shows how interwoven everything is in collective bargaining. Collaboration is critical, but cannot be achieved without substantial ground work. Equity is imbedded in many decisions we make, sometimes as a by-product, sometimes by intent. We do not necessarily achieve what we want, but the effort is there. Continuous environmental scanning impacts how we approach bargaining, and external factors drive many decisions we make.

I realize that my particular situation is rather unique because I have been involved for 50 years and at two public institutions: one that matured over time and one that is a flagship campus. I had many different roles, including serving as interim provost at Oakland for two years, and being in the bargaining unit after I left administration.

The academic world, despite our problems, is a great place. I look forward to continuing to learn and contribute.

15

CASE STUDY

Portland State University/Oregon Employment Relations Board

Shelly Chabon, Janet Gillman and Leanne Serbulo

Perspectives on the Transformational Potential of an Interest-Based Orientation

Background

Portland State University (PSU) is an urban, access-oriented institution that serves over 26,000 students and has more than 6300 employees (Facts: PSU by the Numbers). The PSU chapter of the American Association of University Professors (AAUP) was founded in 1978 and represents over 1100 tenure-track and non-tenure track faculty, researchers, academic professionals, and librarians (About PSU AAUP). In 2014, contract negotiations broke down, and the union voted overwhelmingly to strike. This would have been the first ever faculty work stoppage in Oregon. The state mediator was brought in and a settlement was reached just days before the union was scheduled to walk out. Since negotiations had taken so long, the parties soon returned to the table to begin discussions about the next contract. This time, the University and the union agreed to use Interest-Based Bargaining (IBB).

Three Perspectives

This chapter is written from the perspectives of the labor negotiator, management negotiator, and the neutral party to provide our individual and integrated accounts of the use of IBB at PSU, as well as our ongoing and critical assessment of its virtues and shortcomings. This enabled us to explore and be inclusive of different ways of discovering and interpreting our histories with the IBB

DOI: 10.4324/9781003138990-17

process, how each of us internalized it, as well as how it was experienced by the other team members and our stakeholders. Indeed, as Fisher et al. (2011) recount: "as useful as looking for objective reality can be, it is ultimately the reality as each side sees it that constitutes the problem in a negotiation and opens the way to a solution" (p. 25).

We offer an overview of IBB as implemented at PSU; posit the role of IBB in the adoption or assimilation of an Interest-Based (IB) Orientation; discuss IBB's potential to transform the cultures of the University and the labor/management relationship; and share our perspectives about the benefits and challenges of engaging in IBB. In doing so, we advance an IBB framework that retains similar stages and steps as others previously used to describe the IBB process but also attends to the phases prior to, during, and after bargaining and considers their interconnections. We use the terms union/labor/faculty and administration/management interchangeably.

We hope this chapter provides readers with a deeper understanding of the content and meaning of IBB and its potential to take the negotiation process to a new level of significance. As the title suggests, when IBB is used effectively, it cannot only change our approach to bargaining and labor-management relations; it can lead to a shift in our way of thinking about the 'other' and support post-negotiation cultures that encourage reflection on equity, justice, and collaboration and rely on and reward different perspectives.

Toward a More Comprehensive IBB Framework

IBB is a collaborative approach to negotiation in which parties work together to create and reach mutually beneficial, consensus-based agreements. Interest-based approaches to labor negotiation have been in existence for decades. Various models, under different names (integrative, principled, mutual gains, win-win), have been developed, studied, and practiced in a number of dispute resolution contexts. Walton and McKersie (1991, originally published 1965) promoted a model of integrative bargaining in their classic work, *Behavioral Theory of Labor Negotiations*. Contributions of others who have observed and analyzed integrative bargaining processes date back to the 1940s and 1950s (Walton & McKersie, 1991). Fisher and Ury introduced the concept of principled negotiation in the groundbreaking, *Getting to Yes* in 1981, and shortly after co-founded the Program on Negotiation that propelled further study and development of collaborative bargaining models and practices. It is clear that labor and management have been engaged in various forms of interest-based bargaining for the better part of the last century.

The literature on IBB focuses almost exclusively on what occurs during negotiations and to a much lesser extent, pre-bargaining activities (Barrett and O'Dowd, 2011, Tremblay, 2016, Budd, 2021). Interestingly, the engagement that occurs after the contract is ratified, or, the post-bargaining phase, is largely overlooked. We believe this misses IBB's transformative potential and central

importance in prioritizing collaboration and structural equality at the cultural
level. We therefore contemplate its value not only in reaching a successful
contract, but also as a means for examining how the parties—as members of the
same macro-community while also representing distinct organizations or sub-
cultures—view themselves and their future work.

Taking a more holistic view of effective IBB practice, we advance a framework that considers best practices in three phases of a contract cycle: 1) preparation for bargaining, 2) contract negotiation, and 3) post-bargaining
engagement (preserving and building on negotiated gains between bargaining
cycles). We see the IBB framework as a continuous cycle of preparation,
engagement, reflection, and maintenance. Our experience leads us to the sup-
position that when IBB principles and practices are applied in each of these
phases, an interest-based orientation is fostered. This orientation informs all
aspects of the labor-management relationship and promotes organizational cultures that value and maintain collaboration and partnership.

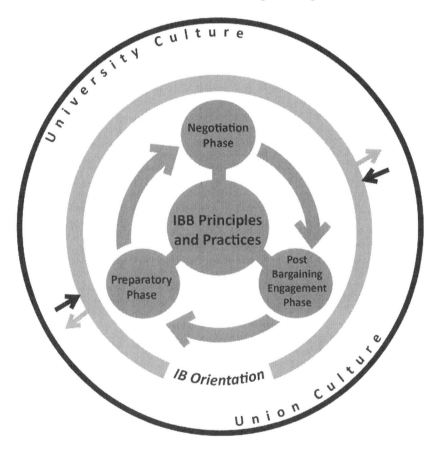

FIGURE 15.1 IBB Framework

Phase I: Preparation for Bargaining

The Decision to Pursue IBB

When the state mediator stepped in to assist with talks between PSU and AAUP in 2014, the stress, anger, frustration, and unease within both parties' caucus rooms was palpable. The tell-tale signs of resolution-resistant conflict were evident: the problems the parties were struggling to resolve were long-standing and complex; they lacked a shared understanding of the facts and underlying concerns regarding many of the issues before them; trust was low to non-existent, and it was unlikely that in a week's time, there would be meaningful, long term resolution to many of the issues they were grappling with. The mediator's task was to help the parties bridge enough of their divide to avert a strike. If this experience led to a reconsideration of how the parties engaged in collective bargaining the next time around, all the better.

Looking for an alternative bargaining approach after the near strike, the parties contacted the State Conciliator for help in evaluating the feasibility of using IBB.

It is not unusual for significant changes in labor relations to follow a period of crisis. Walton and McKersie (1991) wrote that

> a type of unfreezing occurs because of the trauma and catharsis associated with the strike [or other period of crisis] and because it brings the parties to a new realization of the costs of deficiencies associated with the previous pattern.

(p. 200)

A meeting of the teams was convened to provide information about IBB, and to bring their questions, concerns, and needs to the fore. Difficult topics were broached, and challenging, but constructive, conversations were had. As Mary Parker Follett observed so many years ago (1942), "The first step towards integration is to bring the differences into the open" (Walton & McKersie, 1991, p. 148). By doing so, the parties took a first bold step toward a new approach to their labor relations, although the dust and debris from their conflict was far from settled.

Administration broached the possibility of IBB with a combination of hope, commitment, and trepidation. After the contentiousness of the previous contract negotiation, there was little appetite among the administration for another strike threat, and a strong desire for a fresh start. Despite outward expressions of support for the IBB process, there remained a sense among some administrators that they gave too much during the last contract negotiations and that the university needed to stand its ground. Being soft on the people and hard on the issues (Fisher, et al., 2011) was not necessarily understood as advantageous.

Some of the directions to the management team from leadership suggested a lack of consensus about whether firmness and flexibility could coexist and a propensity to scapegoat the other party for past challenges and current difficulties. Authority and control can be important interests for administrators, especially those who have been distant from or less familiar with the bargaining process.

AAUP was highly skeptical when the PSU Administration first suggested using the IBB process. The negotiations leading up to the strike vote had been so acrimonious that the union was mistrustful of administration's motives for using a more collaborative bargaining model. Labor negotiators tend to be more hesitant than management about engaging in IBB. Surveys of union and management representatives consistently show that management has a stronger preference for and greater satisfaction with the IBB process than labor does (Cutcher-Gershenfeld et al., 2001, Cutcher-Gershenfeld, 2018), a cynicism grounded in its perceived emphasis on the labor/management relationship over contract gains and outcomes (Miller et al., 2010).

Although an agreement was reached at Portland State in 2014, and a strike was averted, the resulting contract failed to fully address many of the union's longstanding issues. The union was committed to making gains in the next contract cycle and worried that IBB was simply a management ploy to quell potential labor unrest without making any substantive changes to working conditions.

Despite their reservations, both parties agreed to give IBB a try. We concurred that IBB may be particularly suitable for the University setting even if the reasons that drove our choice of this process might have differed. Colleges and universities have a rich tradition of deliberation and collaborative decision-making through shared governance structures, which provides a useful basis for the parties to build upon at the negotiating table (Dennison et al., 1997). Administrators usually come from faculty ranks, and some will return to the faculty when their administrative service ends. The more permeable boundaries between faculty and administrators make it easier for the two sides to understand each other's perspectives. Further, faculty, staff, and administrators share a commitment to the delivery of high-quality education and to providing support for the generation of research and knowledge. While labor and management may have fundamental disagreements over how the mission of the university should be executed, their mutual dedication to public service creates opportunities to find common ground.

Preparing for IBB

Preparation for bargaining, regardless of approach, involves a number of decisions and actions. In the following section, we discuss some important considerations in the pre-bargaining phase of IBB, including team composition, training, establishment of ground rules, and preparing constituents for the road ahead.

IBB Teams and Subcommittees

Composition of IBB teams is important because of the substantive role that team members play in the process. Rather than relying on chief spokespeople to control and direct communication, interest-based problem-solving calls for full participation of all bargaining team members. When team members are selected based on their expertise, experience, and proximity to workplace issues and organizational solutions, and at the same time, granted the opportunity to openly and freely contribute information and perspectives at the bargaining table, a more effective and efficient IB process is realized.

IBB teams may also make use of technical specialists and subcommittees to assist with data gathering and analysis, and in some cases, to offer options and recommended solutions to the teams. Subcommittees also have the potential to increase and decentralize constituent involvement which expands organizational knowledge and exposure to the principles and practices of IBB. Parties ideally establish clear ground rules for subcommittees to provide direction on the approach to problem solving, decision-making authority, and how and when they are expected to coordinate with the full bargaining team.

IBB Training

Training and facilitation are critical to the success of IBB. The bargaining teams engage in IBB training provided by mediators at Oregon Employment Relations Board (ERB) at the outset of each bargaining cycle. Participants are introduced to the principles and methods of IBB and encouraged to develop individual and group problem solving and communication skills. Participants engage in negotiation role-plays, applying the steps of the problem-solving process to hypothetical bargaining issues. Parties reverse roles for the exercise—the administration team takes the role of the union team and vice versa to give them an early experience with seeing problems from the other's vantage point.

Through this multi-day training, negotiators deepen their understanding and appreciation for one another, not only as bargaining representatives and colleagues but, as human beings with lives and interests outside of the bargaining process, and they begin, in sometimes significant ways, to address issues of trust.

Establishing Ground Rules and Expectations: Bargaining about How to Bargain

While it is broadly accepted that training is a prerequisite for effective engagement in IBB, the aim of training is not wholesale acceptance of a predetermined methodology or course of action. It is important that parties are given an opportunity to jointly reflect on what they gained from the training and tailor bargaining methods and procedures to their needs through process agreements or ground rules. Cutcher-Gershenfeld (1994) termed this process, "bargaining over how to bargain," and explained that

> too often training in IBB has tended to substitute a new iron cage in the place of the traditional constraints. A third alternative would encourage negotiators to fashion their own case and to empower them to continue to modify it so that the bargaining process best matches the interests that are at play. In other words, negotiators should undertake nothing less than interest-based bargaining about the interest-based process.

In the ERB training model, ground rules are developed using the IBB process in the last phase of training, with the support and guidance of the mediator/trainer.

When contemplating ground rules, parties cannot predict or anticipate every bargaining challenge or all of the ways in which agreed upon methods or processes will be tested. The ground rules developed through the IBB process may require revision throughout the course of the negotiations. An important step in pre-bargaining is for parties to acknowledge that IBB will not end all conflict between them, that the process does not promise a clear path at every turn, and that they will invariably need to grant each other some level of latitude when conflict surfaces. What is important in the pre-bargaining phase is that the parties discuss the inherent nature of conflict in labor-management relations and acknowledge the importance of communicating concerns when they perceive themselves or others to be operating outside of the lanes of their process agreements.

Cutcher-Gershenfeld (1994) offered that

> the interests of labor and management will always involve conflict and that there will always be areas of common interest. Such an assumption points toward a bargaining process that is explicitly designed to surface and resolve points of conflict and identify and pursue points of common concern.
>
> *(p. 329)*

Normalizing conflict through some advance discussion in the pre-bargaining phase will increase the likelihood that parties will respond constructively and avoid derailment when conflict occurs.

Preparing Constituents for the Road Ahead

Negotiating teams are representative of and accountable to their constituents. Regardless of the framework used, negotiations can only be successful if each side's stakeholders are satisfied with the process and outcome. Agreements made at the table must be ratified by union members and approved by management decision-makers. Therefore, constituent involvement at the pre-bargaining phase is crucial.

It is particularly important for labor constituents to be actively involved in preparation for IBB. Because the IBB process deliberately blurs the lines between labor and management, union stakeholders may view the process itself as an attempt to undercut labor's power at the table (Miller, et al., 2010). Before making the decision to participate in IBB in 2015, the AAUP bargaining team and executive leadership read *Getting to Yes* (Fisher et al., 2011) and the critiques of the process in the labor relations literature. The team also reached out to other local unions who had used IBB. After learning more about the process, the bargaining team and executive council deliberated before they agreed to accept Administration's invitation to use IBB in their upcoming negotiations.

Adopting IBB necessitated a new approach to preparation for bargaining. Instead of holding mass member meetings and conducting a survey to determine bargaining priorities, AAUP decided to hold listening sessions in individual departments across campus. These open-ended unit-based sessions allowed the bargaining team to explore members' issues in-depth, capture the nuance of how issues played out in different areas, and gather stories and testimony that could be used at the table. Significantly, these listening sessions were two-way conversations. Constituents could ask questions about the IBB process, and bargaining team members could honestly share their hopes and concerns about using an interest-based framework.

AAUP member participation did not end once bargaining commenced. All bargaining sessions were open to member observers. Union members and administrators regularly attended sessions, which allowed them to witness the process first-hand.

Phase II: IBB Negotiation

The Oregon ERB approach to IBB, established in 1991, is rooted in the Integrative Process Model advanced by Walton and McKersie (1991) and shaped by the negotiating principles introduced by Fisher and Ury in 1981. The model involves seven steps that are performed during the three stages of the negotiation: learning, creating, and deciding.

Stages and steps are elaborated below.

The Learning Stage

A commitment to developing a shared understanding of problems before attempting to address them is at the center of most successful interest-based

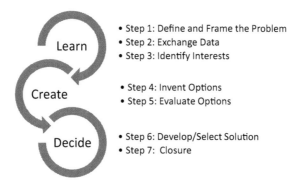

FIGURE 15.2 IBB Process: Stages and Steps

problem-solving processes. In this early phase, negotiators commit to learning about organizational issues and problems from the perspectives of their counterparts. Negotiators pose questions that illuminate how their colleagues see problems and factors that shape their experiences. As negotiators describe the issues from their unique organizational vantage points, others listen empathetically. Effective engagement in perspective sharing requires a commitment to active listening and a willingness to hear stories, examples, and experiences that may challenge or stand in contrast to one's own beliefs and views about how things are or "should be." Effective interest-based negotiators resist the urge to oppose or fix problems, and instead maintain focus on dialogue aimed at broadening and deepening understanding of how issues play out and are experienced across multiple organizational dimensions. Creating an atmosphere where all experiences and points of view are explored and where data and information are openly shared is key to an effective IBB process.

At the outset of the negotiation, each party identifies their selected topics for bargaining and presents them—not as demands, solutions, or contract proposals, but as issues to be addressed or problems to be solved. They describe each issue, from their perspective, the current state or situation, why it is viewed as a problem, and what needs to be addressed. Parties take care to avoid advancing positions in these initial presentations, as it is understood that the problem definition is still being formed and that solutions require an understanding of the interests of both parties, which have not yet been identified.

Parties are encouraged to start with issues that have the greatest integrative potential, meaning that the nature of the problem lends itself to solutions that are likely to benefit both parties, with little to no compromise required. Sequencing issues in this way helps parties achieve early success, which in turn builds trust, boosts confidence in the process, and motivates the parties to continue with the collaborative approach. Economic issues, which often have the least integrative potential, are typically bargained last.

Step 1: Define and Frame the Issue

The objective of the first step is to develop a deeper understanding of the issue to be bargained, building on what was learned in the opening presentation. The parties jointly create one or more framing questions to guide the problem-solving process. The early joint decision on a framing question gives the parties their first experience reaching consensus and helps create joint ownership of the problem.

Step 2: Exchange Data

A critical component of the learning stage is joint fact finding and compilation of data that serve to accurately explain, define, and describe issues and shed light on potential avenues to resolution. Interest-based negotiators engage in joint inquiry, asking what is known and/or needs to be known about the problem to fully and efficiently solve it, and avoid drawing conclusions based on speculation, incomplete information, or misinformation. A willingness to jointly share, gather, and consider a variety of data is critical to forming the requisite levels of understanding needed to effectively engage in interest-based negotiation.

Data is driven by what the parties determine is needed. While some data may be costly and time consuming to gather, it is imperative that parties maintain a problem-solving orientation when discussing data needs and impediments to meeting those needs. Data collection costs and other potential barriers are discussed and weighed against the value the data will add to the negotiators' understanding of the issues. Parties are encouraged to consider alternate means of producing the desired information. Bargaining teams may convene joint data subcommittees to allow for more extensive research and analysis and to harness the expertise of technical specialists and/or those most closely involved or affected by problems and the consequences of alternative solutions.

Step 3: Identify Interests

Interests are the parties' underlying concerns, needs, and motivators, and are used to guide negotiators in developing and evaluating options for settlement. Because of the critical role that interests play, it is essential to allow ample time for identifying, explaining, and learning about interests in the early phase of bargaining. Interests provide negotiators with a critical roadmap for devising mutually beneficial, "yesable" solutions. Effective negotiators avoid viewing interests as right or wrong, true or false, but rather as reflections of the central needs and intangible motivations of the parties. The essential challenge is not to oppose or refute interests, but rather uncover, understand, and be guided by them.

The Creating Stage

Once a joint understanding of the issues has been achieved, the parties enter the creative stage of the negotiation. This stage involves generating options for solving problems through group processes such as brainstorming. Options are then weighed against the interests in the evaluation step.

Step 4: Invent Options

In this step, negotiators generate options to resolve the problem and satisfy as many of the high priority interests of both parties as possible. Teams proceed with the understanding that all options are non-binding, and that they are not committing to any particular solution during this phase of the negotiation. A common protocol during this step is to suspend evaluation of the options. Establishment of an 'evaluation-free zone' during option generation helps promote creativity, build trust, encourage participant engagement and protect the collaborative devising process from devolving into a competitive debate about the merits of the newly developed ideas, which may prematurely restrict or halt the search for options.

Step 5: Evaluate Options

After generating an initial set of ideas, the parties begin to systematically discuss how options meet or fail to meet their stated interests. During this step, interests function as standards upon which options are evaluated and may require further elaboration and explanation as options are tested. Additional data may also be gathered to provide information about the impacts of the options under consideration. Focus is on giving and receiving feedback and staying grounded in the creative problem-solving process. Parties must resist getting polarized around their preferred solutions and stay open to learning about one another's interests and how options may need to be modified, or even redrawn, to satisfy the most salient and pressing collective needs.

The Deciding Stage

In the final stage of the negotiation, parties build on what they learned throughout the bargaining process and reach toward a final, consensus-based agreement.

Step 6: Develop/Select Solution

In developing and selecting a final solution, parties build on the most highly rated options generated in Steps 4 and 5. Negotiators may discover that they are on track to quickly reach a mutually beneficial resolution at this step, or it may become evident that some additional rounds of devising and evaluating are still required. After further evaluative discussion and additional modifications to the solution set, the parties are ready to test their final solution for consensus. Consensus in the IBB context means that all participants agree to accept and support the solution. To reach this conclusion, each participant must feel that all points of view have been heard and understood, that the decision was reached fairly and openly, and that it represents the best solution the parties could reach at the time.

If consensus agreement cannot be reached, because one or more participants cannot support a solution, they are asked to explain why and identify which interests are not fully satisfied. Even at this late stage, it is sometimes necessary and useful to return to a discussion of data and interests and listen for unstated concerns to unblock or shed greater light on the path to resolution.

Agreements that must satisfy conflicting interests often take more time and effort to construct and may put significant strain on the negotiators and the bargaining process. Adherence to the principles of collaborative problem solving, anchored in behavior that reinforces trust, is key to maintaining a principled and interest-based approach down the final stretch of the bargaining process.

Step 7: Closure

If a consensus agreement is reached, the final step in the process involves deciding how the solution will be converted into contract language and what, if any, process is needed for final review before a full tentative agreement is achieved. If the parties are unable to reach consensus, the final step may include arriving at some agreement about how and when the parties will return to problem solving and what steps may be helpful in preparing for that eventuality.

Reflections on Applying the Model

While the model is described as a set of steps, it is not a strict, linear system. The steps follow a sequence, but like most forms of negotiation, IBB is a largely iterative process, where negotiated agreements are achieved through repeated cycles of trial and error. IBB involves successive rounds of learning, inventing, and evaluating.

The steps of the IBB process are known to promote constructive engagement; however, we do not advocate for employing more process than needed. If, for example, problems and interests are well understood and a preferred position is tested and rated highly by both teams early in the problem-solving process, parties may bypass steps and proceed to closure.

We recognize that actions and behaviors that facilitate successful IBB are not exclusive to this approach. Skilled negotiators who engage in distributive or mixed forms of negotiation may utilize a number of the skills and steps we have discussed in the IBB model. Likewise, when problems with limited integrative potential are presented in an IBB context, interest-based negotiators must adapt their approach, especially in the latter stages of the process. We believe it is possible to engage in mixed bargaining approaches, while maintaining respectful and direct communication, providing full access to data and information, and working earnestly to satisfy as many high priority interests as possible.

In situations where the relationship is fraught, reaching smaller agreements can help improve the level of trust between the parties, which makes a mutually agreeable solution on tough issues more likely. Successful IBB requires trust and vulnerability, especially during the brainstorming and option generating steps in the creation stage (Cutcher-Gershenfeld, 2018). If participants are afraid to suggest an option or to reveal a potential barrier to considering an option, the parties will remain stuck within a very narrow range of compromises between two opposing positions, rather than engaging in true integrative bargaining, which involves creating something new beyond the two positional poles (Walton and McKersie, 1991).

While IBB provides a framework to work through seemingly insurmountable conflicts, the process can also be manipulated to prevent resolution and gain advantage. It can be easy to slip into a positional orientation during any of the steps. Interests can be stated in a way that provokes a defensive reaction by the other team and results in an escalating interest-generation war. Options that reflect one team's position but will get no traction by the other side can be suggested with no serious attempts to find a mutually agreeable solution. Arguments can emerge over the need for data, the speed by which data is being gathered, or the analysis and interpretation of that data. During the 2015/2016 negotiations, we became embroiled in a number of heated arguments over esoteric budget details and policy decisions. We spent entire sessions arguing about details that were tangentially related to the issues or options under consideration. None of these conflicts got resolved nor were they necessary for fully processing the issue that was on the table.

The facilitator can intervene in these situations and will often redirect the parties to an IBB framework to try to resolve the conflict. However, the framework itself doesn't provide an easy pathway to de-escalate tensions at the table if one team or individuals on a team insist on continuing the conflict. In a framework that relies upon collaboration to get results, conflict can be means to gain positional advantage at the table or to simply stall the process. In these situations, negotiators need to be willing to recognize when a conflict is productive and when it is merely a distraction. This may require calling a caucus to engage in some "intra-organizational bargaining" (Walton and McKersie, 1991).

The IBB framework does not erase the differences between labor and management, nor is it designed to do so. AAUP's active member engagement and organizing campaigns that continued throughout the negotiations provoked some of the most difficult to resolve conflicts at the negotiating table. AAUP members routinely attended bargaining sessions, and the union continued to hold rallies and other contract actions that occasionally targeted decision-makers away from the table. The actions that targeted administrators who were not present at the table blindsided administrative team members and, subsequently, stymied negotiations. At the heart of these conflicts was the tension between the use of labor tactics that are nearly always viewed as disruptive and the fragile collaboration between the teams at the table.

Entering into the IBB process does not mean that labor gives up its right to organize a contract campaign. Administration also engages in actions outside of the bargaining room. Management advocacy is not always perceived as such because it does not cause the same level of disruption that labor actions do. For example, a message from upper administration may go out across campus warning about the need for budget cuts. Since this type of messaging is considered routine, it may not be viewed as tied to bargaining, even if it is timed to coincide with economic negotiations.

Having an IB orientation does not mean that advocacy actions will disappear. On the contrary, keeping constituents involved in the bargaining process is important and will contribute to the teams' success and help alleviate the need for "intra-organizational bargaining" when tough issues are on the table (Walton and McKersie, 1991, Cutcher-Gershenfeld, 2018). Since IBB negotiations look and feel so different from typical positional bargaining, it is particularly important for union members to have opportunities to observe how the process works. Some IBB practitioners emphasize the need to create closed spaces where the two parties can freely share their interests and consider all potential options; however, the use of closed sessions can contribute to union members' perceptions that IBB facilitates co-optation (McKersie et al., 2008).

Finding the balance between maintaining the parties' right to continue to self-advocate and preserving the collaborative working relationship at the table can be difficult. There will be missteps from both sides. While conversations about those missteps can be difficult, they do help the parties gain a better understanding of each other's perspectives.

Phase III: Post-Bargaining Engagement: Practice of an Interest-Based (IB) Orientation

Based on our experiences, we present a third phase we perceive to be critical in maintaining a post-bargaining relationship when implemented with thought and care. This Post-Bargaining Engagement Phase (PBEP) provides the opportunity to continue to plan for, process, assess, and build on the gains made during formal contract negotiations. Because this phase follows months together at the bargaining table, it affords additional time and space to collectively interpret and implement the written agreement. On a practical level, we have more to hear, more to see, and more to learn about each other and those we represent. While remaining committed to our organizations, we are also members of the same university community and have a shared understanding that effort should continue to be invested to maintain progress and good will.

Walton and McKersie (1991), Eaton, Fonstad, and McKersie (2004) in Leavy (2015) refer to the relationship building that occurs during collective bargaining as attitudinal structuring and view negotiators as relationship shapers,

> who will be able to influence the labor-management relationship not only at the bargaining table, but also after the contract is ratified. All too frequently, the collective bargaining process is viewed as existing in a bubble, completely isolated from any actions or relationships that take place or exist before or after negotiations happen. However, the relationships developed during collective bargaining will have an effect on the day-to-day labor management relationships.
>
> *(p. 2)*

Consistent with this view is the proposition that relations between labor and management are interdependent and do not end with ratification of the contract.

Brown's study, which assesses how IBB shaped the relationship between faculty and administration in a community college district, provides clear support for the notion that the impact of IBB extends beyond reaching a successful contract and leads to changes in the relationship between labor and management as well as in campus culture. Brown (2015) writes,

> the outcomes of collective bargaining include more than just the accords in the collective bargaining agreement. One outcome, that is not explicitly negotiated are the social contracts and interpersonal components of organizational relationships. Given the nature of the social contract, it is a bi-product of the process.
>
> *(p. 4)*

This notion of a social contract is derived from the work of Walton et al., (2000, originally published 1994). Brown (2015) asserts that although scholars have considered the substantive terms within the actual collective bargaining agreement, little attention is paid to the social contracts that outline the nature and scope of the relationship between parties. Walton and his colleagues, in their seminal work on the *Behavioral Theory of Labor Negotiations* (1965), maintain that negotiations may result in substantive agreements, the written settlement, and social contracts or implicit rules that guide interactions (p. 43). In our view, the post-bargaining phase strengthens the 'social contract'.

Based on the results of her research, Brown (2015) concludes that "IBB has an impact on many components of both the social contract and the substantive contract such as; sustaining improved relationships, open honest communication, building trust, substantive cultural outcomes, and advancing complex issues" (p. 74). Thus, IBB may contribute to the creation of bonds between and among participants and these interpersonal connections are influenced by the amount of time spent together as well as the focus, tone, and nature of the dialogue at the table. In turn, these shared experiences may contribute to lasting cultural changes in communication, trust, mutual respect, and camaraderie on campus.

In *Interest-based Bargaining in Education*, Klingel (2003) asserts that "the level of commitment by key individuals to invest in changes in behavior and process in IBB can have a strong effect on whether bargaining teams are able to make use of IBB's potential" (p. 26). This is never more apparent or important than during the continuous engagement between parties that occurs in the PBEP.

Over the course of two IBB contract cycles, the labor/management relationship at PSU moved along the continuum from being highly adversarial to becoming more cooperative. Walton and McKersie (1991) observed that when the relationship between labor and management is cooperative,

> there is … full respect for the other – its organization and officials. The union accepts managerial success as being of concern to labor; management recognizes its stake in stable, effective unionism. Inasmuch as each has found areas in which the other can be instrumental to its own objectives, it is likely to act in such a way as to strengthen the other organization or its leaders.
>
> *(p. 188)*

This cooperative orientation, while still developing, is especially evident in the PBEP.

An effective PBEP is critical for guaranteeing the contract's success. An integrative solution requires that both parties be engaged in the implementation and monitoring of the agreement. By maintaining open and honest communication and instituting joint implementation strategies, we can more easily troubleshoot problems that were overlooked in the agreement and resolve them in a mutually beneficial manner. Our post-tenure review process was a major achievement for the campus. However, upon implementation we identified several ambiguities, and overlapping deadlines. Working in concert, we identified the issues, presented alternative or new language, consulted with our stakeholders, and proposed modifications.

The PBEP is the locus of the labor-management relationship in which to assess the relevance of the knowledge and experience acquired during negotiations and to engage in further self-directed practice. It requires constant monitoring, refining, stabilizing, and at times, returning to a ritualized bargaining mode. The PBEP is not guided by a set series of steps or procedures, but rather it is the operationalization of an IB orientation. This orientation is reflected in the everyday conscious and deliberate practices the two parties engage in after the contract is ratified.

The following are examples of how we maintain and reinforce an IB orientation once contract negotiation ceases. They provide evidence that long after the contract is ratified, the parties remain active participants within the IBB framework.

Contract Training

The first and also an ongoing step is education and training on the provisions within the new contract. Even after an agreement has been reached, each party's constituents have to be satisfied with the outcome (Leavy, 2015). Klingel (2003) cites Friedman, 1992; Suskind and Landry, 1991; and Hecksher and Hall, 1994 in naming the value of educating stakeholders about the new contract. She asserts that "post-bargaining training for constituents in implementation of the contract and use of IBB techniques in contract administration to institutionalize both the agreements and the problem solving process" supports the success of IBB (p. 14).

At PSU we have conducted contract implementation training jointly, such as for the new post-tenure review process, the establishment of the sick leave bank, and the temporary COVID-19 furlough program; however, we have more often provided separate training sessions to afford our constituencies a safe space to be candid about their concerns and to ask questions without fear of reprisal. In these sessions, we apply an IB orientation, by not only offering an interpretation of the contract language but also explaining how all interests were satisfied and how value accrued for everyone involved. The interests represented in the agreement are no longer management or labor interests, but rather, shared interests. We understand our roles in this process to both teach about and advocate for the contract.

Joint Creation of Contract Templates

Labor and management work together to develop templates for department chairs and committees charged with updating their unit's bylaws and promotion and tenure guidelines. These templates result in improved clarity and consistency in the governance documents. Typically, they include language that is obligatory and must be added verbatim, language that can be tailored to reflect the unique elements of the departments and language that is permissible and may or may not be included. The creation of these jointly generated templates communicates to the campus our continued commitment to working together in overseeing adherence to the terms of the contract.

Labor-Management (L/M) Committees

The use of L/M committees is vital to the sustenance of an IBB culture. In our case, we meet weekly. An agenda is co-created; however, these meetings are often informal, held at a coffee hour in a neutral location. This allows for both personal and professional check-ins. L/M is an opportunity to prevent formal grievances by alerting the other party to an issue with the goal of intervening before it escalates. We often confer on language ambiguities within the contract and inevitably agree to a clear and mutually acceptable interpretation. It is not unusual for one of the participants to reference IBB, especially when the other party may be evidencing behavior inconsistent with the IBB principles.

Stakeholder Communications

Both the union and the administration continue to keep their constituencies informed about pressing labor/management issues. The union does this through their blogs, coalitions with other unions on campus, and through meetings with membership. Administration provides regular updates through their website and reports at administrative stakeholder meetings (department chairs, academic leadership teams).

Union Leadership Coalition Meetings

This chapter was written during the COVID-19 crisis. In Spring 2020, in an attempt to address the need for ongoing communication and transparency in the university's response to this situation, administration initiated weekly meetings with all three of the academic unions on campus, including AAUP. The union leaders raised questions, identified interests and provided direct input to key decision-makers, some of whom they might not have been able to otherwise access. Some of the issues that were presented, such as the disarming of campus police, could not be addressed by the teams but could be discussed in an open manner with management outside of the bargaining relationship. These meetings provided an opportunity to engage and practice an IB orientation. Our dialogues helped shape several COVID-19 policies and agreements and contributed to the University's COVID-19 response. Over time, these meetings were moved to a monthly schedule and they continue to this day as a space for crossover between union leadership and management.

Data Sharing

IBB is data driven and as such, establishes the centrality of evidence in guiding decision-making related to the environmental, economic, and social impacts of policies and practices. IBB can therefore have a profound and affirmative effect on the daily interactions between labor and management in the academic environment and can also lead to open dialogue, joint problem solving, and just outcomes for all stakeholders.

The accuracy and completeness of the data sets can either bolster or damage trust between the parties. As new issues evolve after the contract is signed, it is critical that data is used cooperatively not coercively. Teams rely on multiple sources to provide and analyze data requests and are not always successful in acquiring or assuring the validity of the information provided to the satisfaction of the parties. When data is being used as part of the contract implementation process, the parties often work together to resolve data inconsistencies.

Use of Neutral Party

As difficult issues emerge, we have agreed to reengage with a neutral party. This is not a sign that the relationship is broken but speaks to our commitment to ensuring that it is protected in the face of highly charged issues. The neutral party can help to resolve particularly challenging or complicated issues, ensure accountability, review of IBB principles, and prevent or reduce the extent of damage to the relationships.

Monthly Presidents Meetings

The President of the AAUP meets with the President of the University and the Provost on a monthly basis. This direct engagement provides each party the opportunity to exchange interests and priorities. Although compliance is not always successful, we ask that the representatives refrain from addressing mandatory subjects of bargaining and topics currently being discussed by the teams.

Meet and Greet with All New Executive Leaders

We have initiated social gatherings with all new executive leaders and others in positions that regularly interact with union leaders. Some of these individuals come from non-unionized campuses and others may have had negative experiences with unions at their former institutions. This meeting reduces the tendency to demonize the other party and creates an opportunity to build positive relationships.

Addressing Interim Bargaining Issues

Issues that the parties have a statutory obligation to bargain continue to arise between contract cycles. We incorporate IBB principles into these negotiations even when we use a more traditional bargaining framework. The relationships we developed during the bargaining process carry over into the interim period.

The trust we built-up allows us to more easily address and resolve emerging issues. This was especially evident during the pandemic. Indeed, the Executive Director of AAUP recently boasted that PSU had more COVID-19 related Memorandums of Understanding (MOUs) than any other chapter. The use of these memoranda may not be met with uniform excitement, but they do represent our ongoing and successful negotiations.

Task Forces

It is not uncommon for the Collective Bargaining Agreement (CBA) to mandate the formation of task forces comprised of representatives from both management and labor, and at times, with other groups such as the Faculty Senate. This allows the teams to conduct additional research and develop or complete new processes and broadly relies on an IB orientation for success.

Notices on All University Communications and on Any Policy/Practice Revision

Even when viewed to have a minimal impact, management has committed to providing the unions with early notice of campus wide communications and policy changes. At times, this has led to a demand-to-bargain. More often, it results in a request to address and resolve questions and reduce confusion about either intent or impact. Importantly, it serves to keep the union leadership informed.

Participation on Search Committees

Labor representatives are now routinely included on search committees for executive leaders and other relevant key campus positions. This represents the university's acknowledgement of the union's role as a partner and participant in shared governance.

Engagement on Committees and Councils

Labor representatives are commonly called upon to suggest representatives to serve on university committees and task forces. This evidences the institution's recognition that inclusion of the labor perspective and an informed and involved union membership will result in mutual gains for both parties.

Benevolent Assumptions

Giving the other party the benefit of the doubt is the aspiration and inspiration of an IB orientation. It stands in contrast to assumptions of malice that characterize adversarial relationships. At times, it represents an understanding between the parties that seemingly contradictory beliefs can be true and that one does not cancel out the other. A product of the time and intensity of IBB is that it requires participants to sit together and be present for each other even when our views are different. This carries forth in our interactions following negotiations. Although challenges are inevitable, we remind ourselves that we can work through conflicts and create positive changes based on common interests.

Our experiences have taught us that the PBEP is not a panacea. We are constantly managing our relationships and keeping an eye on the climate and our fingers on the pulse of the communities we serve. We have created and found numerous occasions to engage the other party in communication with a variety of constituents and to embrace the power of ongoing dialogue between labor and management. Frazier Hediger (2020) in recounting Lederach's 2014 description of the development of change processes states that, "the mechanisms of this process may appear complicated, but it operates on deceptively simple philosophical principles: equity of communication, capacity, and accountability between parties and maximization of their agency and autonomy in reconciling their past, present and future" (p. 60). This is equally descriptive of the post-bargaining engagement phase.

Final Reflections

Over the years, IBB has been characterized as a strategy, technique, approach, formula, method, tactic, and tool (Shorrock, 2007, Duvall, 2009, Barrett and O'Dowd, 2011, Fitzgerald, 2013 DiGiovanni, 2012). This seems to confine its use to the bargaining table and aligns its utility with a single event: contract negotiations. If one instead, considers IBB to be a shared mindset or philosophical orientation (Brown, 2015), an ideology (Walton et al., 2000), lens (Lederach, 2015, originally published 2003), or conceptual framework for exploring cultural change, its power increases exponentially. It is true that IBB can influence the climate during negotiations. More importantly however, IBB has the potential to result in the transformation of the overall workplace culture by clarifying and codifying values, and rules of engagement. In our view, this transformation is rooted in the content, context and structure of the interactions and relationships (Lederach, 2015) that emerge during bargaining and on our conscious application of what we experience together after the contract is closed.

Brown (1998, originally published 1995) describes organizational culture as "the pattern of beliefs, values and learned ways of coping with experience that have developed during the course of an organization's history, and which tend to be manifested in its material arrangements and in the behaviors of its members" (pp. 33, 176). The administration and the union coexist with one another but are also members of their own cultures. The culturally specific norms, values, beliefs, expectations, and understandings of each team become apparent as bargaining-related actions play out (e.g., what certain parties advocate for, how they approach the very act of bargaining, etc.). If the two entities' cultures are quite different, it can make bargaining quite difficult. The outcomes of bargaining send messages to organizational members that can in turn shape the broader organizational culture because these outcomes signify what the organization values (2020 personal communication, Tierney, P.)

We contend that the transformation of institutional culture depends largely on the parties' motivation for and skill in consciously applying what they have learned and experienced after negotiations have ended. This ability to reflect on, plan, monitor and adjust personal and relational behaviors in different contexts represents a form of metacognition, or reflective practice. We further maintain that IBB's intentional and explicit development of questions, interests, and options increases the potential for active participants to become cognitively active users of IBB, especially when the conditions that led to this change in mindset continue to be present. In our view, Brown's reference to "living the process" (p. 121) captures the essence of this PBEP phase.

"Living the process" involves more than just applying the IBB framework during the PBEP or to issues that arise in ongoing labor/management discussions. A true IB orientation means that both parties view the resulting contract as a shared solution to their shared issues. The agreements they made are no longer labor or management options or labor or management issues, and both parties have an equal interest in ensuring that the new contract provisions they created are successful. This means that parties will jointly implement these solutions, monitor them, raise issues that emerge and attempt to resolve them in a way that meets both parties' interests.

We hope that this discussion will encourage readers to think beyond the mechanics of IBB and its characterization as a method for contract negotiations. We make the case that IBB is not just a tool, it is an orientation that informs our thinking about why tools are used; that IBB is not just an approach, it is an orientation that underscores why issues are approachable; that IBB is not just a strategy or tactic, it is an orientation that raises conscious awareness about the intent and impact of actions; and, that IBB is not just about knowing how, it is about knowing why. IBB is a driving force in the ongoing relationship between faculty and administration. The environment and culture in which bargaining occurs can both influence and be influenced by the outcomes of negotiations as well as by the perspectives of the negotiators. IBB's transformational character is best tested, and most valued, after contract negotiations have ended. The degree and depth of that transformation is the responsibility of those engaged in the work. If they do not believe in it and are not committed to it, IBB will remain performative and lose some of its transformative promise. In this chapter we propose that it may be time to reframe the conceptualization of IBB and harness the extraordinary potential of an IB orientation.

References

Barrett, J. T. & O'Dowd, J. (2011). *Interest-based bargaining*. Trafford Publishing.

Brown, A. C. (2015). *The impact of interest-based bargaining on community college faculty and administrative relationships* (Doctoral dissertation, Northern Arizona University). ProQuest LLC.

Brown, A. D. (1998). *Organisational culture*. Pitman Publishing. (Original work published in 1995).

Budd, J. W. (2021). *Labor relations striking a balance* (6th ed.). McGraw Hill.

Cutcher-Gershenfeld, J. (1994). Bargaining over how to bargain in labor-management negotiations. *Negotiation Journal*, 10(4), 323–335.

Cutcher-Gershenfeld, J. (2018). How process matters: A five-phase model for examining interest-based bargaining. *Negotiations and Change: From the Workplace to Society* (pp. 141–160). Cornell University ILR Press. (Originally published in 2003)

Cutcher-Gershenfeld, J., Kochan, T., & Calhoun Wells, J. (2001). In whose interest? A first look at national survey data on interest-based bargaining in labor relations. *Industrial Relations: A Journal of Economy and Society*, 40(1), 1–21.

Dennison, G.M., Drummond, M.E., & Hobgood, W. P. (1997). Collaborative Bargaining in Public Universities. *Negotiation Journal, 13(1)*, 61–81.

DiGiovanni, N. (2012). This much I know is true: The five intangible influences on collective bargaining. *Journal of Collective Bargaining in the Academy*, 3(5).

Duvall, C. (2009). Making friends of foes: Bringing labor and management together through integrative bargaining. *Journal of Dispute Resolution* (1), 197–212.

Eaton,S.C., Fonstad, N. O., & McKersie,R. B. (2004). Interest-Based Negotiations in a Transformed Labor-Management Setting. *Negotiation Journal 20(1)*, 5–11.

Fisher, R., Ury, W. L., & Patton, B. (2011). *Getting to yes: Negotiating agreement without giving in*. Penguin Group. (Original work published in 1981).

Fitzgerald, T. (2013). Workshop: Interest-based bargaining. *Journal of Collective Bargaining in the Academy*, 0(18).

Hediger, S. F. (2020). *Trailblazing transformation: Pioneering transformative peacebuilding in academic labor conflicts*. (Master's thesis, Portland State University) PDXScholar.

Klingel, S. (2003). *Interest-based bargaining in education*. National Education Association.

Leavy, Z. (2015). Interest-based bargainings' impact on collective bargaining outcomes. *Seminar Research Paper Series*.

Lederach, J. (2015). *Little book of conflict transformation: Clear articulation of the guiding principles by a pioneer in the field*. Good Books. (Original work published in 2003).

McKersie, R. B., Sharpe, T., Kochan, T. A., Eaton, A. E., Strauss, G., & Morgenstern, M. (2008). Bargaining theory meets interest-based negotiations: A case study. *Industrial Relations: A Journal of Economy and Society*, 47(1), 66–96.

Miller, J. K., Farmer, K. P., Miller, D. J., & Peters, L. M. (2010). Panacea or snake oil? Interest-based bargaining in the US airline and rail industries. *Negotiation Journal*, 26 (2), 177–201.

Shorrock, W. (2007). Panel: Negotiating strategies for university administrators an alternative strategy: Interest-based bargaining. *Journal of Collective Bargaining in the Academy*, 0(26).

Tremblay, J. F. (2016). From principled negotiation to interest-based bargaining. *Universal Journal of Industrial and Business Management*, 4(2), 71–79.

Walton, R. E., Cutcher-Gershenfeld, J. E., & McKersie, R. B. (2000). *Strategic negotiations: A theory of change in labor-management relations.* Cornell University ILR Press. (Original work published 1994).

Walton, R. E., & McKersie, R. B. (1991). *A behavioral theory of labor negotiations: An analysis of a social interaction system* (2nd ed.). Cornell University ILR Press. (Original work published in 1965).

PART III

Reflections: Scholars, Practitioners, Advocates

This section of the book is separated into three groups, all containing "reflections" from distinguished scholars, experienced practitioners and advocates, and institutional leaders. Some of those represented here were university leaders or faculty advocates in the 1960s, and intimately involved during an era when collective bargaining gained a major foothold in US Colleges and Universities. A number of these individuals eventually became, or remain as, University Presidents, Chancellors, Deans or Provosts, or the heads of Faculty Unions or Associations. Some remain at the bargaining table, others have not been for many years. There are authors here who also represent newer voices, bringing different perspectives. An effort was made to invite some of the most distinguished industrial relations/labor management/employment scholars, as well as institutional, employee advocates and neutrals, from the US and Canada, representing diverse backgrounds and perspectives. All authors graciously agreed to offer reflections on the matters which inform this volume.

The questions asked of those writing reflections (and, in fact, asked of many of the authors who contributed to this book) were framed as follows:

How can the parties to labor agreements covering academic employees in colleges and universities encourage better collaboration, equity and social justice through the collective bargaining process?

Based on your experience, what general advice would you offer to those who oversee (Boards, Chancellors, Presidents, Governor's Office Staff) labor management processes in higher education. What do these people need to think about, and maybe act upon, vis-à-vis collective bargaining, and the

DOI: 10.4324/9781003138990-18

internal and external factors that determine operational realities in post-secondary institutions or systems?

What would you advise the parties from your vantage point, as they look into the future about where higher education may be headed (programs, finances, student success, inclusion and equity, productively, quality and excellence and the like) if the parties hope to make collective bargaining more proactive, collaborative, and equitable for all concerned?

How does what occurs at the bargaining table, and what may end up in a final agreement or contract, impact the ability of leaders to manage and work in their particular roles?

What do the parties who conduct negotiations – those who negotiate on behalf of labor or management – need to be aware of as they contemplate negotiations process and their impact on university governance, student affairs and working conditions in general?

How can we better measure and assess collective bargaining outcomes?

Responses to these questions were sorted into three groups. First, those who wrote primarily from the perspective of full-time faculty scholars; second, those who were or are primarily institutional leaders (Presidents, Provosts, Deans) and, third, those whose perspectives represented employee advocates (union or association leaders or representatives). These three groups are not entirely clear cut and other ways to combine or sort these reflections were certainly possible. For example, many of scholars represented here may have been Senior Directors, managing large departments and budgets, or Deans, or have served as third party neutrals or advisors to senior governmental leaders or institutional presidents in other settings. Many in the institutional leader category are also scholars and, at one time, held full-time faculty positions. Those in the category representing employee advocates have also, during their careers and currently, produced scholarly work and are, or held, tenured positions at distinguished institutions. Others offering reflections may have had experience in all three groups.

Putting aside the question of sorting responses into neat and tidy groups, which do not entirely fit, these reflections represent some of the most intelligent thinking about labor relations in higher education (and other sectors), found anywhere in the literature to date. Said plainly and simply, the points of view expressed here come from people who really know what they are talking about. They reflect a variety of views, backgrounds, and experiences that will move the debate about collective bargaining in higher education forward, keeping in mind the overarching questions which framed this book.

16

REFLECTIONS FROM FACULTY/SCHOLARS

James N. Baron, Joel Cutcher-Gershenfeld, Paula Knopf, Thomas A. Kochan, David Lewin, Risa L. Lieberwitz and Daphne Taras

James N. Baron

Numerous commentators have observed that higher education in the United States is at a crossroads. The challenges are immense. Enrollments, especially from abroad, are in jeopardy. New technologies are disrupting the sector. Funding from Federal and state governments is precarious. Some segments are witnessing new or intensified efforts at unionization. And so on. Against that backdrop, it seems highly unlikely that the human resource and labor relations models and practices that have served higher education well in the past will prove sustainable into the future.

Of course, American higher education is hardly alone in experiencing such dramatic transformations. Industry after industry and company after company has experienced disruption to established business models, necessitating fundamental shifts in strategies and practices. While many justifiably decry the "corporatization" of higher education, I nonetheless believe there are some potential lessons from the business sector for those who lead educational institutions and those who lead education unions.

Perhaps the most profound lesson is that line employees must be deeply engaged in helping their organizations chart and implement a new path forward. As educational institutions contemplate furloughs, transformations of their core technologies, and other deep-seated changes, employee and union involvement are essential in determining new strategies and tactics for implementation. Faculty and staff have immense local knowledge which administrators often lack. Moreover, there is the obvious point that implementing any fundamental organizational changes will likely prove less daunting when employees and unions have played a significant role in helping formulate the new model.

DOI: 10.4324/9781003138990-19

There are examples from the private sector where unions have played a vital role in helping management adapt to dramatic changes in the environment by assisting in both the formulation of new strategies and the implementation of new tactics. For instance, the AFL-CIO website proudly proclaims how partnerships between the United Auto Workers and Ford and GM "drive innovation in labor-management relations, improve the lives of union members, and propel the auto industry into a pattern of profitable growth for the 21st century." Similarly, partnerships between health care provider Kaiser Permanente and their 28 local unions are viewed by the company as "a joint strategy to lead organizational change, create an environment of continuous learning and improvement, and involve the workforce in decision making," intended to "improve the quality of health care, make Kaiser Permanente a better place to work, enhance Kaiser Permanente's competitive performance, provide employees with employment and income security and expand Kaiser Permanente's membership." Importantly, Kaiser Permanente identifies as one of the pillars of its cooperative partnership with its unions that they "involve unions and individual workers in workplace decisions". Similarly, facing the prospect of layoffs recently, Dan Price, CEO of (nonunion) Gravity Payments—a processor of credit card transactions—enlisted the involvement of his entire workforce in identifying alternative approaches (including pay cuts) that would revamp the cost structure of the business and better position the enterprise for sustained success going forward.

Of course, educational institutions are hardly known for the breakneck pace at which they implement organizational changes. Yet the current pandemic has provided rather compelling evidence of the extent and pace of change that educational institutions can achieve, as well as the unanimity among stakeholders that can be mobilized, when the stakes are high enough and rapid responses are required. We have seen higher education enterprises pivot dramatically and transform their core technologies, budgets, and human resource policies. Many unions have been invaluable partners in achieving these changes, providing evidence that collaborative solutions to existential threats can be architected when the meaningful involvement of line workers is solicited and attended to.

For those who lead institutions of higher education, this implies a posture toward unions and collective bargaining that is less adversarial, more collaborative, and more focused on long-term strategic objectives rather than merely short-term financial considerations. Symbolism is important here. Who is responsible for negotiating labor agreements and what is their background, familiarity, and experience with unions, and organizational location and reporting relationship? How much (and what kinds of) attention do unions receive from the most senior levels of leadership within the institution? What mechanisms—formal or informal—exist to enable unions to participate in formulating strategies and tactics for educational institutions to respond to the myriad challenges they are facing, including during this current pandemic?

How long are contracts negotiated for and what does this imply about the level of trust between the parties to collective bargaining? How explicit and shared are the principles that guide collective bargaining? In business organizations that exhibit robust management–labor partnerships, such as the Kaiser Permanente example cited above, there is usually a shared (and widely disseminated) statement of the general principles or precepts that are to guide the parties in their deliberations and that provide guard rails for what is to be negotiated and how.

For those who lead unions in higher education, I think there are also some valuable lessons to be learned. First, in light of recent events and the adverse publicity some police unions have experienced around issues of racial inclusion and equity, it behooves educational unions to intensify a "social justice" agenda governing who and how they organize, moving beyond a purely "bread and butter" version of unionism. Like corporations, labor unions (including in higher education) will almost certainly receive increasing attention and scrutiny regarding their role in perpetuating versus eradicating historical disadvantages among underrepresented social groups. As Julius notes, "the push for 'social justice' in higher education is more readily seen in negotiations involving employees new (and with less power) to collective bargaining: graduate assistants; part-time employees, adjuncts, and clerical employees." My suspicion is that inertial forces notwithstanding, a similar push will increasingly be felt by unions representing faculty, craft workers, and other occupational groups with long-standing representation. Such social justice concerns as discrimination and systemic racism (including the role of seniority-based practices), the equity of salary distributions and benefits coverage (e.g., health care and retirement), supervisory demeanor and discretion, managing the distributional consequences of furloughs and layoffs, the uses of new technologies, human rights (especially pertaining to privacy), sustainability and environmental justice, work–life balance, employee recognition, and "non-promotable" work are likely to loom larger in importance to higher education employees who are either represented by a union or contemplating joining one.

More broadly, as educational institutions and their unions strive to become more inclusive and demographically diverse, both are likely to be well served by job descriptions and work arrangements that are less "one size fits all" and more tailored to the distinctive abilities, aspirations, and attributes of incumbents. Unions have traditionally favored uniformity of treatment among the members of a given bargaining unit and/or job classification. Yet recent research suggests that "job crafting," which allows individuals to tailor their duties and responsibilities to their unique talents and motivations, has beneficial outcomes for both employees and employers. Especially as educational institutions strive to adapt to the profound challenges they presently face, human resource practices that permit more "mass customization" of circumstances are likely not only to foster greater diversity and inclusion but superior outcomes for employees and employers alike.

Along these lines, I cannot resist noting that the one-size-fits-all approach to human resource management is nowhere on greater display than when it comes to college and university faculty. Implicitly, the mix of duties and responsibilities is assumed not only to be essentially the same across all individuals but across all stages of the academic career, which can easily span four or five decades. Exacerbating this is the absence of any post-tenure performance management or career development regime in most instances. It is difficult to think of other high human capital occupations in which there is essentially no systematic performance management or career planning done after an individual has been on the job for seven to ten years. Many business organizations have recently adopted less formulaic and more developmental approaches to performance management, including extensive reliance on 360-degree feedback, particularly with regard to their professional workforces. I believe both educational administrators and union leaders would be well advised to consider advocating and implementing similar practices. Adapting to the technological, demographic, and financial challenges facing higher education will demand massive organizational change, which is unlikely to materialize magically without more explicit attention to issues of performance management, including among faculty.

Joel Cutcher-Gershenfeld

Aligning Assumptions so that Higher Education Collective Bargaining can be an Engine of Innovation

Collective bargaining in higher education (and more broadly in society) has the potential to serve two functions, one of which is common and one that is all too rare. The common function is setting wages, hours, and working conditions, which is specified in relevant federal and state laws. The less common, but crucial function is to codify past innovations in employment relations and to set the stage for future innovations. The thesis of this article is that the capacity of collective bargaining to be an engine for innovation can only be realized by surfacing and engaging deeply embedded assumptions in the culture and function of universities and colleges.

The first higher education collective bargaining agreements in the United States date back to the 1940s, through voluntary agreements (Herbert and Apkarian, 2017). In the years since, jurisdiction for higher education collective bargaining has come under a mix of state laws, for public institutions in states with public sector statutes, and federal law, for certain private institutions. Collective bargaining agreements may cover faculty, staff, security officers, food service workers, graduate teaching assistants, and others. The interests of these groups are diverse and the substance of collective bargaining needs to reflect this diversity. There is less need for variation in the processes of collective bargaining, yet there is diversity here as well. Behind an observed mix of resistance and embrace of collective bargaining relationships are underlying assumptions that are often incompletely surfaced and discussed. One goal of this article is to foster dialogue on these underlying assumptions, particularly since resistance by management and contentious actions by labor are more common (Ehrenberg, Klaff, Kezsbom, and Nagowski, 2004).

The need to transform collective bargaining in higher education is a product of fundamental challenges to higher education, many of which have been accelerated by the COVID-19 pandemic. These challenges include the burden of student debt, the emergence of competing certification options in society, the erosion of tenure track positions, the financial frailty of many lower and middle tier universities, and complex disparities on campus (adjunct faculty, first generation students, racial and ethnic minorities, international students, and others). At stake is whether collective bargaining is just a forum to adjust wages, hours, and working conditions at a time of great stress or if collective bargaining is also a forum driving innovation.

Examples of issues – beyond traditional wages, hours, and working conditions – that might be addressed through collective bargaining innovations include work/life balance, campus culture, mental health services on campus, anti-racism initiatives, anti-bullying initiatives, campus policing practices, wellness programs, life-long learning programs, professional development initiatives, the rising cost of tuition, social impacts of research, town/gown relations, community green energy, community youth STEM programs, and more. None of these issues are mandatory subjects of bargaining and representatives of labor or management might see certain issues as encroaching on their prerogatives in one way or another. The key question is whether labor and management representatives together, with inputs from others, might be able to accomplish more on these matters than they could do separately. That is a key assumption being raised by this article.

Surfacing Underlying Assumptions in Higher Education Collective Bargaining

Any focus on assumptions in collective bargaining begins with two core assumptions about people in organizations, as identified by Douglas McGregor (1960, annotated edition 2006). McGregor identified one set of assumptions that he termed "Theory X," centering on the view that people need to be monitored and controlled in the workplace, with the assumption that they would not otherwise work as expected. He contrasted Theory X with "Theory Y" assumptions that people need to be provided resources and support, with the assumption that people have an intrinsic desire to do a good job. He famously stated: "The next time you attend a … meeting, … [t]une your ear, to listen for assumptions about human behavior, whether they relate to an individual, a particular group, or people in general." McGregor knew that you would quickly know whether Theory X or Theory Y assumptions were being made and, once you knew that, you would know what else would follows.

In higher education collective bargaining, it is important to "tune your ear" for the underlying assumptions. Table 16.1 lists examples of one set of assumptions that center on the need to contain or counter the other side, with an underlying expectation that failure to do so will result in an erosion of authority and limited results (Ehrenberg, Klaff, Kezsbom, and Nagowski, 2004). This is contrasted in Table 16.1 with a second set of assumptions centering on each side seeking to engage the other. Here there is the underlying assumption that constructive engagement will increase the capability to generate mutual gains in bargaining.

TABLE 16.1 Selected Contrasting Assumptions Driving Collective Bargaining

	Containment Approach	Engagement Approach
Assumptions about the scope of collective bargaining	Collective bargaining is limited to mandatory subjects of bargaining – pay, benefits, and working conditions.	Collective bargaining serves as a forum for labor and management to address mandatory and permissive subjects of bargaining, with the potential to achieve separate and mutual gains.
Assumptions on why higher education unions are formed	Faculty, staff and graduate students form unions in order to increase pay, benefits, and working conditions.	Faculty, staff, and graduate students form unions in order to ensure dignity, respect, and professionalism (as well as pay, benefits, and working conditions).
Assumptions about who should be "at the table"	Only designated bargaining representatives should be "at the table" for collective bargaining.	In addition to designated bargaining representatives, subject matter experts and other stakeholder representatives can add value by being "at the table."
Assumptions about management rights	Management rights need to be protected by management in higher education collective bargaining.	What are termed management rights are matters of mutual interest and shared responsibility.
Assumptions about collective action	Progress for union members is only possible with collective action and concerted pressure.	Progress for union members depends on a mix of collective action/concerted pressure and surfacing/advancing mutual interests around research, education, culture, and related matters.
Assumptions about the impacts of collective bargaining	Impacts are anticipated around pay, benefits, and working conditions.	Impacts include pay, benefits, and working conditions, as well as all other matters of mutual interest.

Surfacing these deeply embedded assumptions is key to understanding and, where appropriate, changing organizational culture (Schein, 1985). This is precisely the challenge suggested here for collective bargaining in higher education. As Schein notes, the espoused values of the organization, as well as the stated policies and procedures, are not necessarily how things actually work in daily relations. The action is at the level of the actual assumptions that guide people in their interactions. These have been termed "operating assumptions" in the context of labor-management relations and high-performance work systems. Changing operating assumptions represents a pivotal event in a relationship (Cutcher-Gershenfeld, Brooks, and Mulloy, 2015). Some pivotal events arise in a crisis, while others can be planned. Both drivers are relevant here.

In recent years, in contexts outside of collective bargaining, I have been facilitating workshops on what I term "assumption wrangling" (Cutcher-Gershenfeld, 2018) – a planned way of fostering a pivot around new operating assumptions. The process begins with participants identifying "from" and "to" assumptions, representing the current state and the desired state. Then we identify "driving and restraining forces" relevant to efforts to shift the assumptions, followed but specification of "indicators" that would represent shifts in the assumptions. Finally, we identify "action implications" for the individuals personally and for broader parts of the relevant ecosystems. Should parties engage in this sort of dialogue, which I am encouraging, they will find that the sample assumptions listed in Table 16.1 are just the tip of an iceberg of assumptions that sit under the surface of regular interactions. While this can be done separately be either the union or management, it is most powerful when done jointly.

Following dialogue on the underlying assumptions and, in effect, the culture of the labor-management relationship, the next challenge is aligning the collective bargaining process with the desired assumptions. This is a likely "action implication" from assumption wrangling. There are transformational models of collective bargaining that will be a helpful reference if the desired assumptions point to a more collaborative, problem-solving approach – engagement rather than containment. Certainly, an engagement approach is more consistent with the espoused values of most higher education institutions.

Aligning the Bargaining Process with the Underlying Assumption

Most collective bargaining negotiations proceed through phases of preparation, opening statements, bargaining, and agreements. Often, the way bargaining happens is unquestioned – rooted in tradition or based on guidance from attorneys, human resource professionals, or central union representatives. There may be early discussions of groundrules and scheduling logistics, but to realign the bargaining process something more is needed – a process of "bargaining over how to bargain" (Cutcher-Gershenfeld, 1994). Table 16.2 lists many of

TABLE 16.2 Contrasting Collective Bargaining Processes

	Traditional Process	Transformational Process
Preparation for collective bargaining	Constituent demands are prioritized to be presented as firm demands.	Constituent demands are reframed around underlying interests and additional stakeholder interests are identified.
Bargaining over how to bargain	Basic groundrules and timing are discussed in advance of negotiations.	In addition to groundrules and timing, there is advance discussion of utilizing a problem-solving approach, subcommittees, and other process matters.
Opening statements	Each side has a single spokesperson who presents firm opening demands.	In addition to a spokesperson, each side has subject matter experts who also contribute to opening statements that identify problems to be addresses and who signal underlying interests that are "at stake" for all stakeholders.
Subcommittees	All discussions are channeled through the spokesperson to ensure control over the agenda.	Subcommittees are established on relevant topics, with subject matter experts collecting data and identifying options.
Stakeholder interests	The focus is on the positions and interests of labor and management.	In addition to labor and management interests, other stakeholders are considered, including students, campus culture, and public goods/societal interests.
Agreements	The wording of agreements is sufficiently precise to avoid future disagreements.	The wording of agreements is sufficiently precise to avoid future disagreements, with additional open-ended language supporting future experiments and innovation.
Implementation	Separate and some joint implementation discussions happen after ratification.	Implementation plans are developed as part of the collective bargaining process to anticipate collaboration during the term of the agreement.

the matters that will be surfaced in a "bargaining over how to bargain" conversation. The discussion of these and other relevant elements is all about developing a bargaining process that is matched to the desired assumptions identified by the parties.

There are many examples of parties who have adjusted their bargaining process to match elements in the "transformational" column of Table 16.2 in health care (Kochan, Eaton, McKersie, and Adler, 2009), manufacturing (Gershenfeld, Brooks, and Mulloy, 2015), and other sectors. There are some documented examples of collaborative bargaining processes from conference presentations in higher education (Sell and Sowulewski, 2007; Curry, 2009; Horsch, 2013; Gilman, 2017), but most higher education collective bargaining scholarship is focused on the impact of collective bargaining on salaries (Hedrick, Henson, Krieg, and Wassell, 2011), governance (Ehrenberg, Klaff, Kezsbom, and Nagowski, 2004), and other matters separate from a collaborative bargaining process.

A collaborative process does not mean that it is free from disagreements and competing interests. Even the most collaborative labor-management relationships have a mixture of forcing and fostering when they engage in collective bargaining (Walton, Cutcher-Gershenfeld, and McKersie, 1994). The point here is to maximize the degree to which common interests are advanced and to ensure constructive engagement of conflicting interests.

Changing the culture and the "rules of the game" in any institutional arrangement is challenging. It is more often that such changes are made in order to mitigate harm, such as after relations have spun out of control. It is harder to mobilize support to change the rules of the game in order to add value, such as by advancing mutual gains (Cutcher-Gershenfeld and Isaac, 2018). This poses a fundamental challenge for collective bargaining in higher education. It will take leadership from many relevant stakeholders to align collective bargaining processes with aspirational operating assumptions so that innovation is not limited to parties recovering from having hit rock bottom. Otherwise, collective bargaining will not be able to fully deliver on its potential to do more than set wages, hours, and working conditions in higher education.

For collective bargaining to serve as a forum for codifying past innovations and setting the stage for future innovations, core assumptions will need to be engaged and bargaining processes will need to be adjusted so that the process matches the desired aims. Figuring out how to expand the process to include subject-matter experts and additional stakeholders on a broader array of issues will be challenging for many. Invariably, implementation will require ongoing committees and collaborative forums, each of which will need a clear charter and leadership. Challenging as these and other changes will be, the potential is there for generating mutual gains and having a broader impact as an institution.

Conclusion

Just after World War II, George Taylor, advisor to five U.S. Presidents on labor policy, observed that collective bargaining would only develop as "a socially desirable institution" if "union and the management voluntarily [gave] reasonable weight to the broad public interest" (Taylor, 1951). By the mid-1980s, the role of collective bargaining in society had deteriorated and there was a call for a transformation of American industrial relations, centered on alignment at the workplace, collective bargaining, and strategic levels of interaction (Kochan, Katz, and McKersie, 1986). Today, there are isolated cases of transformation, but the institution of collective bargaining in higher education, and more broadly in society, has not achieved widely accepted status as a socially desirable institution. The aim of this article has been to outline the elements of change needed to realize this potential.

Collective bargaining in higher education can be an engine of innovation at a time of fundamental challenge. It will take representatives of faculty, staff, campus security, food service workers, graduate teaching assistants, and other represented groups on campuses working with administration representatives to develop shared visions of success, with operating assumptions surfaced "wrangled" to match the visions, and bargaining processes aligned with the assumptions. Then it will be possible to deliver on matters of mutual interest, including matters that are in the wider public interest.

Too often in society, we are captive to inherited institutional arrangements. When it comes to collective bargaining in higher education, we need not be bound by a limited scope of bargaining, addressed with an adversarial approach. Parties experimenting with the process may need to take small steps initially, with sufficient "bargaining over how to bargain" dialogue to ensure that representatives, constituents, and other stakeholders are all on the same page. Imagine the impact, however, were collective bargaining and additional collaborative forums to be widely valued for having delivered results on the challenges of new educational models, growing student debt, rising tuition, social disparities, and more. Rather than being limited and constraining, collective bargaining has the potential to be agile and adaptive – serving labor, management, and society.

References

Curry, T. 2009. "Michigan State University's Collaborative Approach to Contain Health Care Costs", *Journal of Collective Bargaining in the Academy*: Vol. 0, Article 13. Available at: https://thekeep.eiu.edu/jcba/vol0/iss4/13.

Cutcher-Gershenfeld, J. 1994. "Bargaining Over How to Bargain in Labor-Management Negotiations," *Negotiations Journal*, Vol. 10(4) (October: 323–335).

Cutcher-Gershenfeld, J. 2018. "Assumption Wrangling: An Experiment in Culture Change," *Perspectives: Heller Magazine* (34–37).

Cutcher-Gershenfeld, J., D. Brooks, and M. Mulloy. 2015. *Inside the Ford-UAW Transformation: Pivotal Events in Valuing Work and Delivering Results.* Cambridge, MA: MIT Press (1–379).

Cutcher-Gershenfeld, J., and J. Isaac. 2018. "Creating Value and Mitigating Harm: Assessing Institutional Objectives in Australian Industrial Relations," *Economic & Labour Relations Review*, April, 1–26. doi:10.1177/1035304618767263.

Ehrenberg, R.G., D.B. Klaff, A.T. Kezsbom, and M.P. Nagowski. 2004. Collective Bargaining in American Higher Education, in *Governing Academia: Who is in Charge at the Modern University*, R.G. Ehrenberg, ed. Ithaca, NY: Cornell University Press.

Gilman, J. 2017. *Workshop: Training on Interest Based Bargaining in Higher Education,"* *Journal of Collective Bargaining in the Academy*. Vol. 0, Article 2. Available at: http://thekeep.eiu.edu/jcba/vol0/iss12/2.

Hedrick, D.W., S.E. Henson, J.M. Krieg, and C.S. Wassell. 2011. "Is There Really a Faculty Union Salary Premium?" *ILR Review*. Vol. 64(3): 558–575. https://doi.org/10.1177/001979391106400307.

Herbert, W.A., and J. Apkarian. 2017. *Everything Passes, Everything Changes: Unionization and Collective Bargaining in Higher Education*. Perspectives on Work, Labor and Employment Relations Association.

Horsch, E. 2013. "Post-Confrontational Collective Bargaining Models Successful Negotiations," *Journal of Collective Bargaining in the Academy*. Vol. 0, proceedings Article 11. Available at: https://thekeep.eiu.edu/jcba/vol0/iss8/11.

Kochan, T.A., A.E. Eaton, R.B., McKersie, and P.S. Adler. 2009. *Healing Together: The Labor-Management Partnership at Kaiser Permanente*. New York: ILR Press/Cornell University Press.

Kochan, T. A., H.C. Katz, and R.B. McKersie. 1986. *The Transformation of American Industrial Relations*. New York: Basic Books.

McGregor, D. 2006. *The Human Side of Enterprise, Annotated Edition*. Joel Cutcher-Gershenfeld, ed. (with new introduction and annotated text). New York: McGraw Hill (1–423).

Schein, E. 1985. *Organizational Culture and Leadership*. San Francisco: Jossey-Bass.

Sell, L. and S. Sowulewski. 2007. "An Evolution to Collaborative Labor Relations," *Journal of Collective Bargaining in the Academy*. Vol. 0, Article 35. Available at: https://thekeep.eiu.edu/jcba/vol0/iss2/35.

Taylor, George. 1951. "National Labor Policy," *Annals of the American Academy of Political and Social Science*, Vol. 247 (March): 185–194.

Walton, R., J. Cutcher-Gershenfeld, and R. McKersie. 1994. *Strategic Negotiations: A Theory of Change in Labor-Management Relations*. Boston: Harvard Business School Press.

Paula Knopf

Why Are Academic Arbitrations Different from All Other Arbitrations?

During the celebration of Passover, the youngest child in a Jewish family is called upon to ask four questions. The first question is always "Why is this night different from all other nights?" It is a profound question that opens the door for an explanation of the roots of Jewish history, tradition and belief. Asking what makes anything unique is an important question. For this book, the question therefore becomes, "Why are academic arbitrations different from all other arbitrations?"

To begin, it is important to understand the essential purpose of an arbitration. Arbitration is a process that empowers an independent person (or persons) to bring a final and binding resolution to a conflict. Arbitration is an alternative to litigation in the court system. Arbitration was designed to offer an expert and effective way of resolving disputes in ways that the courts could never provide. Arbitrations occur in all manner of disputes, ranging from labour, employment, commercial, matrimonial, intellectual property, family and international issues. In the labour relations context, the authority of the arbitrator extends over the interpretation, application, administration and violation of a collective agreement, as well as to questions of whether the issue(s) are arbitrable. The scope of an arbitrator's jurisdiction can be broadened or narrowed by the parties' collective agreement or by different jurisdictions' statutory schemes.

Labour arbitration is perfectly suited to the academic world. An arbitration provides a peaceful way of airing and resolving disputes during the life of a collective agreement, instead of having issues fester over time and/or erupt into strike action. The process was intended to be quick, efficient and devoid of the technicalities, delays and costs of litigation in the courts. Arbitrators can be selected by mutual consent, chosen on the basis of their reputation for fairness, impartiality and their expertise with the process, the particular issues and/or the sector. Mutual consent to the appointment of the arbitrator helps to ensure that both parties will be better able to accept and implement the final and binding decision that is rendered at the end of the process.

Labour arbitration is a system that evolved from industrialization. Labour historians have tracked the unhealthy and unsafe working conditions that triggered the creation of protective labour standards by governments and prompted workers to join trade unions. These factors led workers to engage in collective bargaining as a means of achieving more effective economic and social goals.

Hopefully, we should be hard pressed to compare a modern university or college with the environment of Dickensian factories and sweatshops. Nevertheless, faulty associations have emerged on many campuses for a variety of reasons. Collective bargaining is now a common reality in the academic world. In Canada, the right to associate and to bargain collectively is a recognized and protected right under the Canadian Charter of Rights and Freedoms. As a result, arbitrators are empowered to resolve all disputes arising out of the collective agreements and to apply employment-related statutes, including violations of Human Rights and Health and Safety legislation. In other jurisdictions, arbitrators may not have the same range of powers when it comes to employment-related legislation. However, the unifying factor for all jurisdictions that allows for collective bargaining is the arbitrators' authority over the working conditions set out in the collective agreements. The collective agreements achieved in bargaining are the responsibilities of the parties to apply and respect. It is then the responsibility and power of the arbitrator to resolve the disputes that arise under those contracts when the parties have been unable or unwilling to resolve them on their own.

As a result, arbitrators have significant power over the careers of employees and over many management or governance functions. If a collective agreement has been misapplied or improperly administered, interpreted or violated, an arbitrator can overturn a management policy or decision. As a result, an arbitrator can overturn or uphold a decision of a tenure committee, a Dean or a board of governors. An arbitrator can overturn or uphold a decision to promote or fire a faculty member. An arbitration decision can determine or affect salaries, vacations, working conditions and overturn or uphold discipline. In short, every aspect of employment covered by the collective agreement can be adjudicated upon and determined by an arbitrator. This may have an impact on an individual, a department, the entire bargaining unit and/or the university as a whole. This process has proven to work because the arbitrators' neutrality and expertise enable him/her to analyze the evidence and arrive at an objective conclusion. The arbitrators' unbiased perspective allows for insight into solutions that the parties could not adopt or craft on their own.

Having stressed how wide an arbitrator's powers can be, it is also important to stress the limits of an arbitrator's authority. An arbitration decision cannot remedy departmental dysfunctionality, heal broken relationships, erase emotional traumas or undo personality conflicts. Nor can arbitrators impose their own opinions about organizational structures or methodologies. Arbitrators can only rule on contractual and statutory rights.

Therefore, the limits of what can be achieved at arbitration are important to keep in mind. It is important to recognize that arbitrators are called upon to make decisions that will have enormous impact without them knowing the full history behind the dispute or the effect of his/her decision once the hearing concludes. This is because the rules of "due process" demand that an arbitrator can only base his/her decision on the evidence presented at the hearing. These rules ensure that both sides have had the opportunity to hear and deal with the evidence that is legally relevant to the issues in dispute. That is the only way to guarantee a fair and manageable hearing. However, this results in a decision that is based only on the evidence presented, nothing else. Therefore, the nature and the quality of the evidence presented will determine the result, not any theoretical notion of "justice".

Time has proven that arbitration can be effective as a dispute resolution system in an academic setting. The prospect of arbitral review or scrutiny serves as a significant protection against actual bias in decision making, particularly in areas of hiring, discharge, tenure and promotion. The right to an arbitration hearing offers an objective way to determine whether or not there is any basis for a perception of bias. The prospect of an arbitration award ensures that there are enforceable consequences when there have been violations of contractual or statutory rights. Arbitration stands as a deterrent to abuse because no person and no institution will want a decision that exposes wrongdoing. Arbitration also offers an objective way to validate appropriate management decisions and policies. The parties' ability to select arbitrators with knowledge and experience in the university sector and/or a particular discipline promises appropriate resolutions. It is also highly significant to note that arbitration brings finality to disputes that could not be solved internally.

Arbitration is especially well suited for the handling of disputes in universities. By its very essence, arbitration is a dispute mechanism designed by the parties, for the parties. A university and a faculty association can determine the scope of arbitral jurisdiction and they can design their own arbitration process. Most importantly, they can choose who will arbitrate their disputes. The ability to choose a decision maker is unique to arbitration. Litigants in the courts or other tribunals do not have the opportunity to select who will hear and determine their cases. Parties to a collective agreement have the capacity to choose their decision maker. That enables them to find an independent, third party who is particularly suited to each dispute. Many arbitrators come from academic backgrounds themselves. Parties can select an arbitrator with specific expertise and experience in areas such as tenure, academic freedom and intellectual property. There are other arbitrators with outstanding reputations in the areas of contract interpretation, discipline, accommodations, harassment and human rights. Many arbitrators are experienced in all or most of these fields. The benefit of arbitration in the academic sector is that the parties can select an arbitrator who is particularly suited to each case. If the parties cannot agree on the arbitrator, different jurisdictions have methods of appointing appropriate people with the necessary expertise and familiarity to handle each dispute.

Having outlined the virtues of arbitration, it must be stressed that in ideal circumstances, arbitration should never be needed, especially on a university campus. Universities should be paragons of harmonious labour relations. University administrators and faculty associations should share a collective will to create a positive atmosphere for scholarship and creativity. Associations can champion their members by protecting contractual rights without undermining responsible governance. All enlightened institutions of learning should have policies, managers and administrators who are able to identify, diffuse and/or resolve conflicts as soon as they arise. All faculty associations should be able to represent their members in ways that enhance their members' wellbeing while they cultivate the success of the students. All managerial personnel should exercise their authority with wisdom and provide leadership that fosters creativity and scholarship. Further, everyone should function in a collegial manner to enhance student learning and to promote research and innovation. When all those factors are in place, disputes can be resolved collaboratively, in a timely and dignified way. Failing that, many universities have Ombuds offices that can often help to resolve issues. If all these ideals were met, there would be no need for arbitrations.

However, conflict inevitably arises. Academics are under huge pressure to research, teach and publish while they are in competition with their colleagues for professional advancement or even struggling to hold onto positions. Departments are places where professional rivalries and personality clashes thrive. Financial pressures on many institutions also result in challenging staffing models and threats to programs and/or courses. That may be why academic arbitrations will continue to occur regularly. Even in the best-run institutions, the interaction of human beings and differing agendas often lead to conflicts that are difficult to resolve internally. Decision makers become invested in their decisions, are protective of their authority and may be unwilling to back down for fear of "losing face". People who feel aggrieved will want to have their complaints aired and will want to seek "justice". Respondents will want vindication. Reputations will need to be protected. When there are allegations of bias, prejudice, favouritism or harassment, it is often necessary to have an independent assessment of the situation to bring the conflict to a close. When careers, reputations and programs are in jeopardy, it is important to have a mechanism to determine whether critical decisions were made in accordance with the procedural and substantive terms of the collective agreement.

Arbitration is also needed in areas of contractual interpretation. In those situations, the role of the arbitrator is to give effect to the language of the collective agreement. The arbitrator's task is to discern the mutual intent of the parties. Therein lies an irony. If there had been an actual "meeting of minds" or mutual understanding about what the parties intended, there should be no dispute about their contract's interpretation or application. However, disputes arise because the wording may have been drafted by people who are no longer responsible for the administration of the contract. Often, the implications of the language may not have been foreseeable at the time the contractual terms were drafted. Different circumstances may arise that no one could have contemplated when the clause was put into place. These are situations when the application of the rules of contractual interpretation provide an objective way to resolve the dispute.

However, there are disputes about the interpretation of a contractual term when one side or the other may wish to call evidence from the negotiators to reveal what transpired during bargaining or to assert that promises were made about how the language would be applied. This kind of evidence is very problematic. First, the basic rule of contract interpretation is to assume that the parties meant what they said. Therefore, negotiating history is presumptively inadmissible. The exceptions to that rule are narrow. Accordingly, there are very limited circumstances when such evidence is even admissible. When and if the negotiating history or circumstances are admitted, such evidence is rarely helpful or determinative. This is because there is a myriad of difficulties that arise from this kind of evidence. It is far too common for each side to walk away from negotiations with different views about what the language meant or was intended to achieve. Further, the passage of time may mean that new personnel may have different views about how the contract should or could be applied. Often, the people who crafted the language are no longer even working at or for the university. Even if they are available to testify, their memories may have faded, or their allegiances may have changed. It is not uncommon for a chief negotiator for a faculty association to be found a few years later sitting on the management side of the table. In those circumstances, everyone is put in an awkward situation if there is desire to call evidence about negotiations where s/he was involved. Further, what is agreed upon in the final hours of any negotiation is frequently a compromise achieved, late at night, to avoid a strike, leaving little time to think about all the possible implications of the language. Accordingly, this kind of evidence rarely reveals a shared understanding or even similar recollections of what was intended. When there is conflicting evidence, an arbitrator may be required to choose between the credibility of one witness over another, resulting in long lasting and negative effects upon individuals' reputations and greater strains on labour relations. In those situations, the fallout of the hearing may go far beyond the dispute itself. The worst thing about this kind of evidence is that it often leads to the revelation that there never was any "shared intent" about the meaning of the contract. That takes the arbitrator back to the exercise of deciphering the meaning of the contract based solely upon the rules of contract interpretation. The result is that a great deal of money, time and stress were created from the airing of the extrinsic evidence that produced no clarity. Instead, the process can create further stressors between a university's management team and its faculty association.

Although arbitration can be more expeditious and efficient than the courts, academic arbitrations are anecdotally infamous for their length and cost inefficiencies. Lengthy hearings are not consistent with the design and goals of arbitration. Far too often these hearings are scheduled to be heard months or years after the events giving rise to the disputes. Far too often, the hearings extend for months, or even years. Far too often the hearings involve issues of minute significance, yet they generate enormous expenditures of human and financial resources. Most importantly, it must be acknowledged that too many cases can involve issues that should have been resolved without the need for an arbitration.

One of the things that make academic arbitrations infamous in the arbitral community is the fact that cases often end up in arbitration about matters that should have been resolved long before the date of the hearing or that should never have been allowed to fester. When a harassment claim comes to arbitration involving allegations that date back years, one has to wonder why it was not addressed long before a grievance was filed. When an allegation of a denial of academic freedom turns out to be a complaint about the size or location of office space, an arbitrator has to wonder whether the hearing is a quest for justice or a battle of egos. When thousands of dollars are spent to prepare and litigate a claim for the accommodation of a disability when the university and the association have never met to discuss options before the hearing, one has to wonder why the parties did not find a way to collaboratively resolve such a dispute. Arbitration should be used only as a last resort.

I would not continue to practice as an arbitrator if I did not believe in this process. However, I take no pleasure in earning money from these hearing when the funds could be better spent on students' successes. Therefore, I urge arbitrators and the parties to use arbitration more wisely. It should be used only as a last resort. It is the responsibility of the arbitrator to manage a hearing and ensure that the evidence being received is only relevant to the issue(s) to be determined. At the same time, it is the responsibility of the parties to focus their cases. Arbitrations in the private sector are usually quick and efficient. The parties to those cases think carefully before spending money and they use hearing time sparingly. In contrast, universities and their employee associations often seem to lose sight of the cost of this process. Arbitrations should not be invoked to attempt to replicate public inquiries or to launch a quest for "social justice". As mentioned above, arbitrators can only deal with contractual and statutory issues. Accordingly, the parties and arbitrators should work diligently to ensure that hearings remain focused, cost effective and invoked only as a last resort.

There are various ways to streamline and improve the arbitration system. However, that is not the theme or purpose of this chapter. Suffice to say, it is in the parties' interests to ensure that hearings are focused and efficient. Arbitrators can and should insist that the hearings are no more lengthy or complicated than necessary.

There is one other aspect of arbitration that can and should become a feature in the resolution of academic disputes. The purpose of a hearing is to resolve problems. Arbitrators are problem solvers. Many arbitrators have the skills and capacity to mediate disputes. Mediation is a way for the parties to explore different options for the resolution of a grievance, without compromising their rights. A mediated resolution is not constrained by the boundaries of a contract. Mediated agreements can be creative, flexible and designed to fit individual or systemic circumstances. Mediated agreements can be confidential and can have limited application. In contrast, arbitration awards are public (in some jurisdictions) and can affect the rights of the parties for as long as the contractual language remains the same. Most significantly, mediation is the most efficient way to bring a final and lasting end to a dispute. Mediation is not constrained by the formality of the hearing process. A mediation session can resolve even a complex dispute in one day. Further, when a party or a person agrees to a mediated resolution, they have had direct input into the terms of the agreement and thereby become invested in the solution. This makes them more accepting of the result than if it had been imposed upon them. In addition, mediated resolutions can be confidential. In all Canadian and many American jurisdictions, arbitral awards are public. In contrast, mediated settlements are most often drafted to be confidential. Affording a private resolution to a conflict can have the remedial effect of preventing parties from claiming victory or suffering the humiliation of defeat. Most importantly, a private settlement document ensures that the conflict is put to bed. Finally, if mediation does not achieve an agreement, the parties are free to pursue arbitration, without concern that the mediation process has compromised their rights. Many arbitrators have the skills to both mediate and arbitrate. Some parties choose to have one person as their mediator and another as their arbitrator. Other parties entrust one neutral to serve as both their mediator and their arbitrator. The choice can depend on the conventions of the jurisdiction, the skill-sets of the arbitrators and advocates or the circumstances of each case. Whatever the choice is, the parties and individuals involved in any grievance can be well served by the mediation process.

In conclusion, I return to the original question: Why are academic arbitrations different from all other arbitrations? On a negative note, they are notoriously longer than in other sectors, they too often deal with trivial issues and they are frequently triggered by disputes that should have been resolved collaboratively, long before the first day of the arbitration hearing. On a positive note, academic arbitrations are different from all others in that they can involve very important issues that are unique to academe: tenure, university governance, intellectual property and academic freedom are just a few examples. Therefore, the academic arbitrations benefit by the parties' ability to choose arbitrators who are particularly suited to each individual case. On the other hand, academic arbitrations are similar to all other arbitrations in that they involve the enforcement of contractual provisions that the parties have crafted together. A balanced and responsible collective agreement enshrines the interests of both management and its employees. Arbitration and/or mediation remain the best methods yet devised to ensure that the rights and responsibilities in those contracts can be protected and enforced.

Thomas A. Kochan

Voice, Representation, and Governance in an Era of Campus Restructuring

This volume is appearing in an era of significant restructuring of higher education. Small colleges are struggling to survive as independent institutions and all colleges and universities are reviewing their staffing, scheduling, and work practices as they cope with the COVID pandemic and look to a post COVID future. The silver lining is that this crisis offers an opportunity for rethinking and changing the traditional structures and processes governing how the different stakeholders on campuses work with each other and find their voice. In this brief comment I will pose a range of options that I would like to see on the table for discussion, experimentation, and innovation.

The various chapters and comments in this volume do an excellent job of discussing how union-management relationships and collective bargaining for faculty and non-faculty staff have evolved, operate today, and could be improved without modifying the existing legal structures governing these processes. I endorse ideas offered in the chapters and comments that call for key stakeholders to respect the rights of faculty and non-faculty employees to organize and join a union and efforts to improve problem solving in bargaining and in day-to-day relationships. But I want to take calls for improvement a step further by suggesting it is time to open up traditional bargaining and governance structures to address the broader set of issues on the table as colleges and universities restructure operations, explore new staffing and work arrangements, and address the challenges and opportunities underway in the modes of delivering education.

The Limits of the Conventional Model

Collective bargaining in higher education mirrors the conventional model authorized under private and public sector collective bargaining statutes. Described in its simplest form this model enables collective bargaining over wages, hours, and working conditions for specified units of employees (e.g. faculty members, service employees, research staff, etc.) if a majority of such employees vote for or otherwise achieve exclusive representation rights. All too often this form of representation is hotly contested—resisted by university administrators and oversight governing boards and organized by employee groups around campaigns that focus on the sources of greatest dissatisfaction among the most disenchanted subset of the employee group. Legal advisors to each party often add fuel to the fire of the contest with the end result (often after a long drawn out contest) either starting a bargaining relationship off with an adversarial history, or if defeated, deepening frustrations among dissatisfied employees. With time and effort this adversarial legacy can and often is overcome by using the tools and processes discussed in other chapters and comments in this volume, but sometimes the adversarial beginnings get molded into ongoing, suboptimal relationships. Moreover, the model fragments the university community into different groups, and gives license to university administrators to differentiate benefits and limit opportunities for broader community-wide engagement on key issues facing the institution. The limited scope of bargaining—on wages, hours, and working conditions—makes it all the more difficult for members of these bargaining units and their representatives to engage top-level college and university leaders on the broad strategic choices facing the institution.

Contrast this model with the nature of college and university work. The range of education, research, and service work performed and the mix of faculty, student, administrative, and governance overseers involved makes them, as David Lewin notes "multilateral," and as Joel Cutcher-Gershenfeld notes, "multi-stakeholder," institutions. Breaking the stakeholders into narrowly defined bargaining units, limiting the topics the parties are legally required to discuss, and trying to limit them to bilateral negotiations processes does not contribute to shared governance processes that encourage joint efforts to pursue the organization's missions.

This critique could have been made with equal validity pre-COVID. The restructuring of education delivery was already well underway with the growth of online learning technologies and programs, competition from various for profit and nonprofit education platforms, rising costs of college education and increased burdens of student debt, and the growing proportion of non-tenure and often part-time or adjunct personnel delivering courses. The COVID pandemic has served to intensify the economic pressures and expanded experiences with alternative in-person and remote models for delivering education, experiences that will inform how education is delivered when the pandemic subsides. Note, I do not say when things return to some "normal." I believe few colleges or universities will return exactly to their past patterns of practice for pursuing their missions.

This does not imply that I favor disbanding bargaining relationships where they already exist or resisting organizing efforts where this option is the one available and preferred by campus faculty and staff. Rights to representation should be honored in principle and in practice.

Complementary Processes for Voice and Representation

But consider how this standard model can be put to best use *and* integrated with complementary voice processes that better reflect the shared missions of higher education. To do so I will draw directly on my experience in serving as the elected Chair of the MIT faculty for two years. I recognize MIT has a number of unique features and norms, but I believe the points I will make here are generic to all institutions of higher education.

Higher education is a team sport. It requires coordination and cooperation of talented, empowered, and respected contributors across the full spectrum of jobs and occupational groups found on college and university campuses. At MIT we have a phrase that we aspire to make real in the governance and relationships at the Institute: "One MIT." By this we mean that all who contribute to the delivery of our mission are important and deserve mutual respect, fair treatment, and a voice on issues of concern to them and to the future of the institution. One of the lasting lessons I took away from my term as Faculty Chair was how important are the contributions the staff at MIT make to the success of our enterprise. Time and again I saw how the good work of administrative, technical, and service staff supported the faculty and administrative leadership. But they often needed greater recognition for their contributions and stronger representation in decision making. One example was when the MIT Corporation (the Institute's governing body) was considering breaking a longstanding tradition of offering the same fringe benefit package to faculty and staff—a break I informed MIT leaders would result in a revolt by the faculty in support of the staff. The idea was dropped. This little example illustrates the value of a governance arrangement that was not constrained by formal lines of demarcation nor by formal scope of bargaining rules. Simply sharing information about how the faculty and staff on campus would coalesce in opposition to an idea under consideration by MIT's governing body was enough to bring their voice into the process before any strategic decision was made. But wouldn't it have been better to have an advisory body composed of this broader coalition to consult on issues like this as a matter of course?

Beware of Adverse Selection of Representatives. Formal election of faculty members into bodies such as Faculty Senates can serve as an option for addressing issues outside the scope of traditional collective bargaining. The challenge in making a Faculty Senate structure work lies in avoiding an adverse selection problem: Faculty members who are most disenchanted with campus leadership and/or with their professional lives are most likely to invest the time and effort to achieve election to a Senate. MIT's governance process recognizes this issue. Instead of a Senate there are over a dozen standing committees of faculty and students, each with an experienced staff member providing support. The various committees deal with curriculum, discipline, financial aid, and other student and faculty affairs. Committee members are nominated by a Faculty Nominations' Committee and voted on at an Institute Faculty meeting. The committees report up to a Faculty Policy Committee (FPC) that has representation from each of the schools, along with student representation. The FPC is chaired by the Faculty Chair and supported by a full-time administrative staff member. The FPC reviews proposals from the various faculty committees and, where appropriate, puts them on the agenda of the monthly faculty meeting for a vote. (The agenda of the faculty meetings is decided jointly by the MIT President and other top officers and Faculty Chair.)

The Faculty Chair sits as a voting member of the MIT Academic Council along with the university officers (Provost, Chancellor, etc.), and deans of each of the schools. This body approves (or rejects) all faculty promotion and tenure decisions of the departments and schools, reviews university finances, and discusses strategic issues as they arise.

This is not a perfect solution to the multi-stakeholder/multilateral nature of colleges and universities but just one alternative way of supplementing bilateral processes. Indeed, staff voices need to be strengthened in various ways if they don't have formal bargaining representation. This is especially important for staff (and faculty) groups that seek to organize and have a voice based on their social or occupational identities: LBGTQ groups, women's groups, groups based on racial identities, post-docs, etc.

These groups need two things to be effective. First, they need support from other stakeholders. Top college/university leaders need to commit their support and have open channels for listening and responding to issues raised by these informal groups. Other groups, including unions with formal bargaining rights, need to support these groups, even those (as most do) that include members that span across occupational and hierarchical levels.

Second, these groups need strong, formal, and enforceable channels for elevating their issues to organizational (faculty and administrative and governance/oversight) bodies and equally strong and enforceable guarantees against retaliation for raising concerns.

An issue I encountered on the second day of my term as Faculty chair illustrates the importance of these features. On that day I was "visited" by a group of very distinguished and angry faculty colleagues who informed me that a highly respected staff member in the student services office had been summarily terminated and escorted out of the office by security (as is sometime the case in private business settings but totally inconsistent with the culture and norms of MIT and most other universities). The beloved staff member (the go-to person for faculty noticing they have a student experiencing potentially serious emotional problems) had challenged her supervisor dean over a key policy decision and he had her fired. The campus uproar this caused led me as Faculty Chair to work with the President and Chancellor to set up two faculty-administrator committees to investigate the handling of this discharge and to offer recommendations for equity for the individual and any administrative changes that the case suggested would be needed to ensure this never happened again. Six months later, an equitable settlement was negotiated with the individual, the unit involved was transferred out from under the dean involved, and the faculty, student body, and other interested campus groups were satisfied with the process and outcome. I use this case to illustrate how a governance process that provides an open-ended portfolio (it was not clear the Faculty Chair had any authority to speak to this issue since it was purely an administrative action) can provide a channel for speaking truth to power without breaking the trust that is essential to making this governance process work.

Shaping the Future of Higher Education Through Multilateral and Multi-Stakeholder Processes

Looking to the future, the revamping of how people work as the pandemic subsides will amplify the need for flexible, multilateral/multi-stakeholder structures and processes on college campuses. The pandemic has opened up new channels for working, teaching, and doing research remotely. I do not expect many (if any) people to work 100 percent remotely in the future but clearly the pandemic has, by necessity, spawned widespread experimentation with flexible places, processes, and times to work that better fit with one's personal and family needs. Working through the new mix of place, process, and time for working will be at the top of the agenda in universities and colleges going forward. Once again working through the equity issues associated with new ways of working for staff and faculty (rather than just allowing faculty with the privilege of working from home) will be an agenda issue that will require ongoing multi-stakeholder dialogue and coordination. These discussions will require lateral (peer-to peer) as well as vertical (hierarchical) coordination.

If my prediction is accurate that the era of restructuring of higher education will continue for the foreseeable future, colleges and universities will need multiple channels and processes to ensure all the key stakeholders' voices are heard and incorporated into the change processes. Key questions about who has access to the institution's courses and seminars will be on the table. Will it just be students on campus that come to the institution through the normal processes of admission and complete their education in a pre-specified period of time and/or perhaps a larger and broader array of students who access online courses, webinars, and specialized programs from whatever part of the world they are located? What will be the mix of full-time tenure track faculty and other educators? Will tenure as we know it continue? What differences in compensation will be appropriate for people in these different categories? These are all issues that cut across bargaining unit boundaries, include but also go beyond mandatory scope of issues in collective bargaining, and do not fall neatly into faculty versus administration, or staff versus administration categories. Nor can they be left to governing bodies that oversee private or public colleges and universities.

In summary, unions and collective bargaining will need to be open to complementary voice and representation processes better suited to the changing economics, changing technologies of teaching and learning, and to the complex mix of stakeholders that make up the college and university workforce. And administrative staff and faculty leaders will need to build and put to work the skills of multi-stakeholder and multilateral bargaining and problem solving.

David Lewin

Observations About Unionism and Collective Bargaining in Higher Education

I have been asked by the editor of this book to address certain questions pertaining to unionism, collective bargaining and labor-management relations more broadly in higher education institutions, that is, colleges and universities. In doing so, I draw on my experience as a faculty member at two institutions, namely, Columbia University and UCLA, my experience as a consultant to unions and management, and the research literature regarding this topic.

Question #1: How does what occurs at the bargaining table impact the ability of university officials to lead and manage their roles?

It is important to understand that among all industries, higher education is one of the most highly unionized. It is estimated that 40 percent of academic-related employees – e.g., full- and part-time faculty, research assistants, librarians – of higher education institutions are unionized, and the percentage appears to be even higher among other employees of these institutions – e.g., professional and administrative staff, health care workers, maintenance workers and security personnel. When college and university employees are unionized, collective bargaining agreements typically result from negotiations between union representatives and college/university officials. Such agreements specify certain terms and conditions of employment, in particular, work schedules, pay rates for specific positions, and changes in pay rates during multi-year agreements. These agreements also contain multi-step grievance procedures that are intended to resolve employment-related disputes that arise during the life of the agreements. As in other unionized industries, the grievance procedure is a key feature of collective bargaining agreements in higher education. Taken together, union representation and grievance procedures constitute the main channels of employee voice.

Does the availability and use of employee voice impact the ability of university officials to lead and manage their institutions? My answer to this question is "only marginally." Without unions and collective bargaining, university officials can unilaterally set work schedules, pay rates, and changes in pay rates. With unions and collective bargaining, they have to do so bilaterally. But collective bargaining agreements in higher education typically do not limit university officials in deciding the specific degree programs offered, the size of entering classes, requirements for student admission, student financial support, and many other related matters. Stated differently, the union impact on management control in higher education is relatively limited.

However, such impact may be expanded depending upon the scope of matters/issues that the parties determine should be negotiable. Typically, management attempts to limit the scope of bargaining whereas unionized employees attempt to broaden the scope of bargaining. For example, university leaders and unionized faculty may decide to negotiate over budget allocations to particular schools and departments within the university. This is not a typical subject of bargaining in higher education, but there is nothing that prevents the parties from including it as a subject of bargaining. More will be said below (in response to question #3) about the scope of collective bargaining in higher education.

Question #2: What do the parties to a labor-management relationship, including those who negotiate collective bargaining agreements, need to know about academic affairs in a university, department or school?

Probably the single most important thing that these parties need to know is that unlike in most other industries, shared governance is a long-standing principle and practice in higher education institutions. In a typical higher education institution, there exists a faculty senate of which all faculty are members or eligible to be members. University officials together with the faculty senate exercise joint governance over many key decisions, including about which degree programs to offer, degree program requirements, faculty staffing of degree (and non-degree) programs, and much more. These areas of decision making are outside of – beyond – the scope of areas traditionally covered in collective bargaining. However, similar to collective bargaining, a faculty senate limits the control that a university's leadership can exercise over its institution. Consequently, where a faculty senate and unions/collective bargaining exist in a university, there is a tripartite form of governance in which some decisions are made solely by the university's leadership, other decisions are made jointly by that leadership and an academic senate, and still other decisions are made jointly by that leadership and unionized employees.

Another way of characterizing tripartite governance of a university is "multilateral bargaining," a phrase first coined in studies of public sector labor-management relations. To illustrate, in a municipal/city government with unionized teachers the parties to bargaining may include a mayor, city council members, school district officials, teacher representatives, state government officials (because state governments often provide certain funding to local school districts), and even community organizations (that may include parents of students). Hence, both conceptually and in practice, multilateral bargaining means that more than two parties are involved in such bargaining, which contrasts with two-party, bilateral bargaining. A university whose leaders negotiate/share governance with a faculty senate and unionized faculty (and also with unionized non-faculty personnel) thus engages in multilateral bargaining.

Question #3: What would you advise the parties about the future of higher education with respect to making collective bargaining more proactive, collaborative and equitable?

Traditionally, collective bargaining is a reactive process in which a relatively narrow set of items or issues – e.g., pay, work schedules, discipline – are negotiated. Yet the scope of bargaining is up to the parties to decide and can be as narrow or expansive as they choose. To illustrate, university officials and unionized faculty representatives could negotiate over the criteria by which faculty job performance is evaluated. Again, traditionally, such criteria include research, teaching and service, but these criteria are typically specified by university officials in conjunction with academic senates. However, there is no conceptual or empirically based reason why these criteria could not be subjects of collective bargaining.

To illustrate, the quality of faculty research can be measured by the quantity of publications and the quality of outlets – journals and others – in which the publications appear. Such quantitative and qualitative measures could be the subjects of collective bargaining. Similarly, quantitative and qualitative measures of teaching effectiveness could be the subjects of collective bargaining. Again similarly, quantitative and qualitative measures of service – both internal and external – could be the subjects of collective bargaining. Including any or all of these subjects in collective bargaining would render the bargaining process more collaborative and equitable than it has been heretofore.

Regarding making the collective bargaining process in higher education more proactive, the parties to bargaining – university officials and unionized faculty representatives – could establish one or more joint labor-management committees to explore and advise about key issues. One such issue is the financial condition/status of colleges and universities, especially in light of the COVID-19 pandemic. The costs of responding to this pandemic, including converting most teaching from in-person on campus to remote online off campus are substantial and were not included in pre-pandemic college and university budgets. Regarding revenue, there is an emerging challenge to colleges and university from students and perhaps especially the parents of students who advocate lower tuitions and lower room and board expenses based on the shift from on-campus to remote online courses and instruction. This pervasive challenge could be addressed in collective bargaining between university officials and unionized faculty by establishing joint committees to study and offer recommendations for dealing with it.

Similarly, the widespread movement to enhance diversity, equity and inclusion (DEI) in colleges and universities could be a subject of collective bargaining in which joint labor-management committees are established to analyze and offer recommendations about how to best implement DEI. Initiatives to do so should include both academic and non-academic employees. Consider that if DEI is a strategic objective of colleges and universities, it pertains as much to their professional and administrative staff, health care workers, maintenance workers and security personnel as it does to their faculty personnel. This recommendation, together with the aforementioned recommendations regarding joint committees to study and advise about college and university revenues and costs, constitutes a substantial expansion of the scope of collective bargaining in higher education. Such expansion, in turn, will make collective bargaining more proactive, collaborative and equitable.

Question #4: What general advice would you give to those – e.g., presidents, boards of trustees, public officials – who oversee the labor management process in higher education?

Most higher education leaders have risen through faculty ranks to become deans, provosts, presidents and the like. Stated differently, such leaders have been promoted via internal labor markets that operate in colleges and universities. Therefore, they are quite familiar with the research, teaching and service activities that constitute the main duties and responsibilities of higher education faculty. The same cannot necessarily be said of college and university boards of trustees or overseers, who for the most part have not risen through faculty ranks. It also cannot necessarily be said of elected and appointed government officials who may have strong influence and decision-making power over higher education institutions – especially, but not exclusively, public colleges and universities. Therefore, giving advice to those who oversee the labor-management process in higher education poses a considerable challenge.

Nonetheless, my main advice to these various leaders is to approach higher education labor-management relations from a cooperative rather than an adversarial perspective. This is easier said than done, however, because collective bargaining between organized labor and management is typically portrayed as a win-lose, fixed-sum, distributive game. From this perspective, the bargaining process basically amounts to dividing a financial pie between two parties. By contrast, a cooperative or integrative perspective on bargaining allows for and may enable both parties (or multiple parties) to jointly benefit, i.e., "win."

As an example, consider the fact that during the last quarter-century or so the proportion of full-time college and university faculty has substantially declined whereas the proportion of part-time faculty (typically titled adjunct or lecturer) has substantially increased. Recent data indicate that the majority of undergraduate degree program courses in college and universities are staffed/taught by part-time faculty. A main "driver" of this trend is that part-time faculty cost far less than full-time faculty – between 50 percent and 75 percent less. A related implication of this trend is that higher education institutions are increasingly developing a two-tiered faculty in which one tier, the upper tier, conducts research and does some teaching and another tier, the lower tier, is exclusively engaged in teaching. This staffing pattern has not traditionally been a subject of collective bargaining (or, for that matter, a subject taken up by an academic senate). Instead, it had been decided and controlled by university leaders. But does this have to continue to be the case? An alternative approach is to have this type of staffing pattern be a subject of collective bargaining so that both higher education faculty and higher education leaders have a voice in determining the balance among these two tiers.

Question #5: How can collaboration, equity and social justice through collective bargaining best be encouraged?

Based on my answers to prior questions, collaboration among higher education leaders and unionized faculty can be better achieved by expanding the scope of bargaining to include, as examples, such matters as institution-wide and school/department budgets, degree program offerings, student admission requirements, and faculty performance evaluation criteria. Doing so will reduce the extent of (single party) management control of key policies and decisions of higher education institutions and thereby also enhance organizational equity.

Whether and to what extent collective bargaining in higher education institutions can address the matter of social justice is both an easier and a tougher call. An example of an easier call is for higher education institutions to allow all ranks of faculty and perhaps even students to be represented in collective bargaining. A tougher call is for higher education institutions to determine whether "under-represented" students should become more fully admitted to – represented in – their degree programs and, relatedly, the extent to which students should receive financial support. Traditionally, these matters have not been determined through collective bargaining. Yet there is no conceptual or empirical basis for limiting collective bargaining in this way. In sum, collective bargaining in higher education can be used to address social justice if the parties to bargaining are willing to do so.

Risa L. Lieberwitz

Reflections on Collective Bargaining in Higher Education

Collective bargaining for faculty in higher education is intertwined with the distinctive nature of faculty work and the societal role of the university. The terms and conditions in current collective bargaining agreements reflect the same collective interests that faculty raised when they organized in 1915 to form the American Association of University Professors (AAUP). Then, as now, faculty made collective demands for employment conditions that would enable them to carry out the public mission of the university. For faculty, this means that "bread and butter" issues include not only salaries and benefits, but also academic freedom in teaching, research, and extramural speech. To protect academic freedom, the AAUP 1915 Declaration of Principles on Academic Freedom and Tenure called for the strong job security of tenure. The importance of these conditions of employment was reiterated in the AAUP 1940 Statement of Principles on Academic Freedom and Tenure, this time jointly formulated with the Association of Colleges and Universities. As in the 1915 Declaration, the 1940 Statement ties academic freedom and tenure to the university's distinctive mission of serving the common good. For the university to serve the public interest, faculty must exercise independence and autonomy in their work, free from the economic or political conflicts of interest that could result from constraints or interference by the university administration, financial donors, or the government. Moreover, such autonomy is essential for both the individual faculty member and the communal nature of academic work, through which faculty contribute to and build on scholarship in the public domain. Further, faculty express their collective interests through shared governance over academic curricula, programs, and related matters.

The 1940 Statement has been endorsed over subsequent decades by more than 250 higher education organizations and scholarly societies. Universities have incorporated AAUP principles into their institutional policies and practices, protecting academic freedom, tenure, and shared governance in peer review hiring and promotions processes and in developing academic programs. Thus, in many ways, unionization can be seen as a continuation of faculty collective action that began in the late 19th and early 20th centuries. Although the AAUP engaged in intense debate over this question, in 1973, the AAUP adopted its Statement on Collective Bargaining supporting collective bargaining for faculty, other academic professionals, and graduate students "as a means to enhance the goals of the organization." The Statement addresses the positive relationship between unionization and shared governance, finding that "collective bargaining can be used to increase the effectiveness of those institutions by extending their areas of competence, defining their authority, and strengthening their voice in areas of shared authority and responsibility."

At the heart of faculty collective demands, whether through shared governance or unionization, are democratic principles. Academic freedom is based on the democratic norms of debate, freedom of thought, and the ability to challenge the status quo. This is not a free for all, as professional standards are used in peer review to evaluate faculty teaching, research, and extramural speech. However, academic norms recognize that broad academic freedom is at the core of faculty work to serve the public interest, which expresses the democratic function of higher education, whether through public or private nonprofit universities. Shared governance and unionization are democratic participative processes that protect academic freedom, academic due process, and other academic professional norms.

The advent of faculty unionization in the 1960s did not replace shared governance, but rather evolved into the coexistence of collective bargaining and shared governance. While this can create tensions between the two, the dual system can strengthen both shared governance and collective bargaining where faculty build alliances between governance bodies and unions. Doing this well, though, requires clarity about the inherent conflict of interests between faculty and the administration. While faculty may find areas for cooperation with the administration, there are issues on which shared governance bodies and unions must be ready to oppose the administration and fight for faculty interests. This has always been the case, but has become even more apparent since the 1980s, as privatization and public funding cuts have led to institutional changes in university goals, functions, and policies. In embracing an identity as market actors, university administrations have adopted corporate labor models at odds with fundamental professional norms of academic freedom and job security. Between the years of 1976 and 2015, the number of full-time executives and managers grew by 140 percent, while full-time faculty grew by 86 percent. The national rate of tenure-track/tenured faculty positions has plummeted from 78 percent in 1969 to the current level of 30 percent. These are structural changes that reinforce the class divisions between the administration and faculty and increase stratification in the faculty workforce.

Non-tenure-track positions range from the most precarious and low-wage teaching on a course-by-course basis to more stable renewable multi-year contracts. The second-class status of non-tenure-track faculty is reinforced by their job duties, which are usually restricted to either teaching or research, and their limited role in shared governance. This employment model also has serious gender and racial impacts, creating institutional obstacles to hiring and promoting women and people of color into faculty positions with the job security of tenure.

The massive increase of non-tenure-track faculty positions breaks the link between academic freedom and the protections of job security. Precarious employment undermines faculty's ability to exercise the independence and autonomy needed to fulfill the university's public mission. Shared governance bodies and unions have a common interest in opposing and reversing these developments. Both can work to strengthen academic freedom and academic due process in university policies and in collective bargaining agreements. Further, shared governance bodies can stand in solidarity with unions that bargain for expanding tenure and job security for all faculty members, including those currently in non-tenure-track positions.

What do these institutional changes mean for university administrations' role in collective bargaining? This question takes on even more gravity at the present moment of the COVID-19 pandemic, as universities have made severe cuts in faculty lines. In unionized institutions, administrations have used *force majeure* and financial exigency clauses to lay off tenure-track, tenured and non-tenure-track faculty. Even in the face of the immediacy of a public health crisis, though, university actions should be evaluated in a historical context. Since the 1980s, public and private universities have responded to the neoliberal agenda of public funding cuts and privatization by increasing universities' market activities and seeking closer relationships with private corporate donors, commercializing research, and undermining the tenure system. At the same time, even as unionization increased in public universities under state collective bargaining laws, private universities have actively opposed the rights to unionize by faculty and graduate teaching and research assistants (GAs). In 1980, Yeshiva University won its arguments that most tenure-track and tenured faculty are managerial employees excluded from the rights to unionize and collectively bargain under the National Labor Relations Act (NLRA), putting the kibosh on faculty unionization in private universities. Even as they reduce tenure-track lines, private universities argue that non-tenure-track faculty are managerial if they participate in any shared governance. Private universities have shown this same hostility to GA unionization and have opposed the National Labor Relations Board's *Columbia University* decision that GAs are employees under the NLRA. In public universities, unions face the ongoing problems of long and arduous collective bargaining process, attacks from state legislative restrictions on rights to unionize, expanded "right to work" laws, and the US Supreme Court's *Janus* decision holding that union security clauses are unconstitutional in public sector bargaining.

Even in the context of university "corporatization" and hostility toward unions, unionization will continue, as will collective bargaining. Faculty unions and university administrations can still enter good collective bargaining agreements with significant gains for faculty. However, collective bargaining in universities can do more. Collective bargaining can build positive relationships between the union and the administration, increase academic freedom and the strong job security of tenure, and contribute to the flourishing of the university. This will take more than rhetoric about cooperation. It will take a commitment by public and private universities to the fundamental principles of serving the public interest through teaching and research. As has always been true, this requires strong and resilient institutional structures grounded in democratic values, including faculty academic freedom protected through the job security of tenure. In collective bargaining, faculty unions and the administration can negotiate for a broad scope of academic freedom, increased tenure-track lines, extension of equivalent strong job security to faculty currently in non-tenure-track positions, and due process systems that cover all faculty. Building positive relationships should not and need not deny that faculty and the administration have conflicting interests based on their different institutional positions. However, reaching agreement to serve the public interest through strong faculty academic freedom and job security will create more common ground for negotiations. This can also lead to better relationships between the administration and shared governance bodies, as well as mutual support between unions and shared governance bodies. Further, common ground on basic principles of the university's public mission can create alliances between university administrations, unions, and shared governance bodies, to develop advocacy and lobbying strategies to increase public funding to support university programs, faculty employment, and low tuition rates.

Thus, revitalizing the university's public mission goes hand in hand with building constructive collective bargaining relationships. Revitalizing the university's public mission also goes hand in hand with reversing private universities' active opposition to faculty and GA rights to unionize. Just as the university's public mission is grounded in democratic values, so is academic freedom, shared governance, and unionization and collective bargaining. In the process of "corporatization," universities have embraced market values and practices that have restricted academic freedom, increased faculty employment insecurity, and weakened shared governance. Reversing these trends is necessary to strengthen the democratic academic norms and values of the university. Returning to first principles of serving the public interest should also move the university toward respecting faculty rights to participate in shared governance and collective bargaining.

Daphne Taras

A Contrarian View from the Trenches

All the advice to strive for harmonious labor relations, in a spirit of mutual respect and collaboration, is nice. The path to achieving that vision is not clear to me. Other authors have written about how the collective bargaining model might be improved. I have chosen, instead, to focus on the impediments to making improvements, and how the day-to-day challenges facing universities in the post-COVID world are likely to foster adversarialism. I'm going out on a limb.

Why am I a contrarian? We all are embedded in our lived experiences. Currently, I am dean of Canada's largest business school. With almost 13,000 students and 300 faculty, we flipped to virtual on Friday 13, March and we will remain that way through the 2020–21 academic year. My country's universities are heavily unionized. Faculty, staff, graduate assistants, and so on. Public sector unionization in Canada is about three times higher than in the US.

My university's faculty union is militant in bargaining and aggressive in grievance-filing. There is low trust between the parties, and many years of hostile relations. We have not been able to conclude a collective agreement through bargaining for many rounds. There is almost pathological reliance on interest arbitration by both sides. The faculty union has not had a strike (yet) but has recently hinted that it might be ready to take on the administration during the pandemic recovery due to increases in workload caused by the pivot to virtual, as well as other nagging issues.

My academic field is labor relations, and so I was never caught off guard by having to manage a large professoriate while being scrutinized by an often-hostile union. Although I have a casual style of interacting, I always assume that every email I send, every conversation I have, and every decision I make might appear in a grievance or at arbitration. When I first arrived to my second deanship – already a seasoned dean – I met with the union and asked that we not play "gotcha" on each other, but rather work together to solve issues. It should not have to be said – but I must say it regardless – that the union is legitimate, the exclusive bargaining representative for our professors, and that I support the collective bargaining system wholeheartedly. But I suffered hubris: my capacity to achieve a rapprochement has not reached fruition. Indeed, quite the opposite.

I decided to capture a few of the many friction points in faculty-university labor relations, with the following brief illustrations.

Academic Freedom, Tenure, and Misconduct: Managerial Traps

Academic freedom and the granting of tenure have become entangled corner-stones of higher education. The years leading from appointment to a tenure-track position to the awarding of tenure are the longest job probationary period of any occupation. What academics know, and the public often fails to appreciate, is that the result of a failed bid for tenure is job loss, often with catastrophic consequences to the professor and their family. Canada, which has most of its arbitration awards publicly available, lists over 200 cases involving academic freedom and tenure, arising within virtually every university in the country.

In 1958, the issues came to the forefront with the firing of tenured associate professor Harry Crowe by United College (now University of Winnipeg). Professor Crowe had sent a private letter to his colleague, expressing anti-clerical concerns about the environment at the College and the impact of an upcoming election on the political timbre. The letter became public, and Crowe was fired, basically for disloyalty, by the College's Board of Regents. In an unprecedented and astonishing show of solidarity, 16 professors resigned from their positions. The case caused investigations, reports, and a very concerted examination of the importance of tenure and academic freedom. In an unrelated case, the Supreme Court of Canada affirmed that tenure is "fundamental to the preservation of academic freedom."

I just hired 38 professors in a two-year period. Each newly hired professor is a significant investment. The net present value of the future income stream of each hire is in the millions of dollars. But tenure is rarely viewed this way. Instead, it is thought of as a job right. The very long probationary period can become a problem when a tenure-track member is deeply embedded into friendship networks in the department. Résumés are padded by helpful colleagues who generously try to provide co-authorships. Friends have trouble voting their friends off the island. I am a fan of tenure, but I do believe it is awarded without sufficient rigor. In my mind then, the number one priority is to hire well, right from the get-go. Selection is everything.

Because of COVID, there will be increased pressures to liberalize tenure standards and protect forms of non-performance. Many universities have added a year to the tenure clock. Others are anticipating a lowering of the tenure bar. I anticipate some ugly battles ahead, because some new scholars are performing very capably, while others are rendered virtually paralytic often by circumstances beyond the professors' control.

There is little debate over the need to protect the iconoclastic professor, the heretic, the brave, and the curmudgeonly. Advances in knowledge do not favour the timid. But here is the problem: when confronted by alleged misconduct, professors and their unions wrap themselves in the protections of tenure. In many cases, the freedoms being enjoyed are not academic at all. Examples from case law include the following scenarios:

- Professors who love their students (too much).
- Professors who poison the work environments of their colleagues as a form of blood sport, often through unlawful defamation.
- Professors who form voting blocs, allowing improper considerations to enter decisions, similar to figure skating judging scandals, contrary to principles of fairness.
- Professors who insult distinguished guests, donors, and are rude to administrators and disruptive of meetings.
- Professors who humiliate students, disparage groups, or create hostile classrooms.

Each of these examples above – based on real cases of course – has the ability to polarize sentiments and cause exceedingly hard feelings, whether between union and management, or within the union itself. And top university leaders are no angels either; there are ample examples of misbehaviour in those ranks.

Where there are humans, there are tensions. And these natural tensions are exacerbated when each party feels themselves to be abnormally bright, accomplished, and protected. Universities are hothouses within which feuds can flourish. I very much doubt that a mutual gains approach will achieve much traction in the battle for tenure and in the expression of academic freedoms.

Entrance of a New Regime. Individual Rights. Cancel Culture. Social Media

On top of the natural battles over job rights, there is a new phenomenon at play. Universities are replicating the individual rights regime with internal policies and dispute resolution mechanisms. Students are complaining directly about violations to university policies, e.g. sexual harassment, racism, violence, and human rights matters. They go to offices that exist quite apart from labor relations. Individual professors and staff members also avail themselves of the individual rights regime, and can bypass the university policies to go directly to government offices. Psychological harassment and its ill effects can be investigated by Occupational Health and Safety inspectors. Racism complaints can go directly to Human Rights offices for investigation and then a tribunal. I see quite clearly that we have multiple layers now, well beyond the conventional issues of the collegium and governing board and the faculty unions.

As dean, it is rare that a month goes by during which I am approached by students running a Twitter, or Reddit, or email campaign to expel an alleged wrongdoer without any access to natural justice or due process. He is a rapist! She is a racist! My inbox fills with dozens of distraught emails. Perhaps only one of them is from the alleged victim, and the remainder are due to a social media campaign and dependent on the zeitgeist of the times.

I would estimate that half my personnel issues arise from the exercise of individual rights and the other half go to labor relations resolutions. This is non-trivial in my world. While there are the usual contract interpretation and disciplinary grievances, I also am dealing with about half a dozen human rights or harassment investigations at any time.

Here is an example of a recent situation. In the autumn of 2020, a part-time University of Ottawa professor used the "N" word in class. She used the word as an example of how groups "re-appropriate" words previously used to disparage or oppress. Vilified by students, her phone number and home address were posted on social media, and she feared for her personal safety. She was suspended, and later reinstated after making a fulsome apology. During the height of tensions, the President of that University issued an "appeal for calm and reflection" that simultaneously refused to discuss details, condemned racism, upheld academic freedom, made glowing statements about dignity, and ended with his "profound commitment ... to the promotion of critical discourse on campus." In my view, it was a carefully worded message that said everything and said nothing at all.

There are abundant examples of activism that uses new channels of communication, entirely unregulated by labor or employment laws.

Neither university officials nor the unions have any idea of how to handle such actors. They exist outside the usual collective bargaining setting, but their activities infringe on the rights and duties of faculty and staff within the quite-ritualized setting of labor relations. My point is that there is a parallel system of rights, activities, and tribunals that is rapidly developing alongside the regime being examined in this book. It is challenging to all parties in the university setting.

Ownership of the Classroom, the Office, and the Curriculum, and the Job

The collegium has exceptionally strong interests in the tools, the setting, the duties, and the allocations of rewards. In most respects, it is the apotheosis of self-management. Issues involving the allocation of resources are found in almost 90 arbitrations and court cases in Canada.

Here COVID likely will produce its greatest stressors, for three reasons. First, there will be financial pressures. Advanced education budgets throughout the US system have been weaned from government funding for well over a decade. The need to increase tuition, or recruit international students who pay higher tuition, or solicit funds from donors is a survival imperative for most universities. In Canada, by contrast, there is still heavy reliance on government transfers, for about half of operating needs. Domestic tuition, on average, is under $8,000 (CDN) and student tuition accounts for only one-fourth of total income. The remainder is from private sources or grants.

As governments in both countries are going deeply into the red to pay COVID costs, the post-pandemic recovery is likely to prioritize health care. Or paying down debt. Or investing in struggling industrial sectors. There will be strong cost-cutting imperatives. Universities may have to fend for themselves.

Second, the opening and closing of the sluice gates for international student enrollment has been shown to be less predictable than we had anticipated. The pandemic certainly created disproportionate and catastrophic effects on universities that developed an addiction to international student tuition dollars. Some Australian universities are gutted and laying off faculty. It should also be noted that the Clinton to Trump to Biden election uncertainties have created new patterns in registrations. For example, US business MBA programs' international enrollments declined during the Trump years, but Canadian MBAs grew quite discernibly. International students who wanted the "American" experience perceived a friendlier welcome from Canada. This can change quickly, and planning is difficult.

Third, student numbers and flows into different majors are disrupted, perhaps for quite some time. For example, I have an outstanding School of Hospitality and Tourism Management, soon to be the top-ranked school in Canada in this discipline. I have Retail Management. Both sectors of the global economy have been crushed. Student numbers have declined to a trickle. But my large Information Technology and Big Data Department is flourishing, and attracting thousands of students. Might circumstances force me to contemplate restructuring my big business school? If so, am I to face an ugly uphill battle with my faculty union? Yes, and yes.

Any type of nimble response to the pandemic will require different ways of delivering education to students. We will be negotiating for some time with the union, as I see the following types of issues now arising:

- If professors can work from home, and indeed, opt to spend a significant amount of their working time away from the university, why do they need dedicated offices? Allocation of office space is a big issue. If they work from home, what compensation will be required for the expense of home offices?
- Certain courses might be cancelled, others started. Professors are likely to respond with hostility to large-scale curricular disruption. It is human nature to accept that change is necessary, while hoping to remain personally unscathed by change.
- Course delivery: is it to be synchronous, asynchronous, hybrid, blended, or flipped, or multi-flex? The smorgasbord of choice is exploding.
- If there are serious budget pressures, we might have to increase teaching loads. Should that be across-the-board, or only for non-research-active faculty?
- Most universities are multi-billion-dollar investments in buildings and infrastructure. They should be operating year round, not basing themselves on a calendar that starts in September and ends in May.

Examine these issues in the context of our current collective agreements. The provision of private offices: are these an implied term in the contract? Do faculty have an inherent right to decline certain types of teaching based not on academic expertise, but the affinity, or lack thereof, of technological savvy? The manner in which collective bargaining happens is to engage in trades, presuming a stable equilibrium has been reached around the deal as a whole, e.g., we will give you more of this for less of that. For many years, we have been negotiating only at the edges, because the basic deal is sacrosanct. But the basic deal might well be changing.

At my University, we are contemplating "agile." We are the largest commuter university in Canada, located at the epicenter of downtown Toronto, surrounded by some of the most expensive real estate in the world. Faculty, staff, and students travel up to three hours a day to be with us. A truly agile workforce will cause a rupture in current collective agreements. Tinkering with the wording of all our clauses will not achieve much except grievances. I hope we have the wherewithal to renegotiate and write new understandings that embrace a rights and responsibilities framework.

This is where labor relations will flourish or fail us. Will new techniques of identifying and solving issues help guide us, or will we default back to adversarialism?

Concluding Thoughts

I want to emerge from this accursed pandemic with the hope of a more collaborative and equitable relationship with all parties. My reality though, is that all my efforts will be directed towards recovering a semblance of normalcy while retaining the positive elements of our heroic pivot to virtual. From my vantage point, as the equivalent of the CEO of a large subsidiary, my priority is to lead, listen, and manage. Labor relations is a constant background noise, sometimes melodic and sometimes discordant. It is not the tail that wags the dog.

Every day, I try to spend at least one hour with a newly hired faculty member. There are moments during which I can discern a rupture between the interests of the faculty union leaders, and their new membership. The new professors tell me they would like the agile workplace, to be given flexibility in delivery styles of teaching. They would really appreciate the chance to determine their own menu at the smorgasbord. Some of them long to be back in the conventional classroom. Others tell me they want to be asynchronous teachers of undergraduates, but highly involved in their research with graduate students. A sizable number, perhaps half, say they are doing really well, and hope they will be able to continue teaching from home, as long as they can still meet students sometimes, and their colleagues for companionship and idea-generation. Why can we not honor preferences, as long as the work is being done effectively?

My advice to all parties is to allow innovation to flourish in a more random and organic way. Universities and unions tend to want predictability and clear understandings. I know that for my faculty, I could work together with my department heads, associate deans, talented staff, and all the members of my team to create something unique and fun and respectful of differences. My fear is that the central administration will try to bureaucratize this wonderful spirit that I sense is developing within my faculty, and squelch it.

This is not a time in the life of advanced education to have uniformity, centralization, or bureaucratic rules. Rather, first-movers should be allowed the freedom to move quickly. Others will catch up, or not. There will be experiments that fail, and there should not be punishments for taking chances.

17

REFLECTIONS FROM INSTITUTIONAL/ADMINISTRATIVE LEADERS

Matthew M. Bodah, Neil S. Bucklew, Jeffrey F. Cross, James M. Glaser, Joseph Glover, James R. Johnsen, Jason E. Lane, Barbara A. Lee, Terrence MacTaggart, Tracy Bigney and Patricia A. Prelock

Matthew M. Bodah

In offering my reflections on collective bargaining in higher education, a few biographical and organizational notes are in order. I have been a vice provost at the University of Rhode Island (URI) since May 2017, engaged in both contract negotiations and contract administration with full-time and per-course faculty unions, a graduate assistants' union, and several staff unions. Prior to becoming a vice provost, I served for 25 years as a professor of industrial relations at the university, including six years as chair of the economics department. I also maintained a practice as a labor arbitrator and mediator, which is currently set aside.

December 21, 2021 is the fiftieth anniversary of the certification of the URI chapter of the American Association of University Professors as the bargaining agent for full-time faculty. Graduate assistants unionized in 2002 and per-course faculty in 2007. Today, nearly all instructional personnel at the university belong to one of the aforementioned units. Most researchers, with the exception of post-doctoral fellows and a very small group of marine research scientists, are represented by either the faculty, graduate assistant, or professional staff unions.

For the most part, labor relations at the university have been peaceful and constructive. With the exception of a brief faculty strike in 1979, nearly all contracts have been settled without incident and with little third-party intervention. In recent years, grievances have been infrequent and arbitration decisions rare. Similarly, there has been little labor relations litigation in the courts and very few cases before the state labor relations board.

DOI: 10.4324/9781003138990-20

Despite several legislated changes in the university's governing board, there has been remarkable stability in university and union leadership. In my nearly 30 years at the university there have been only two presidents and two provosts, and the full-time faculty union has had only three executive directors. In the 50 years since the start of collective bargaining, I am only the third person to occupy my position. There has been similar longevity in the leadership of the human resource department. This stability has allowed relationships to mature and strengthen. And, importantly, the administration has never sought to attack faculty tenure, collective bargaining rights, or infringe on academic freedom. With only one or two exceptions, union leadership—both elected and staff—has been cooperative and collegial. These good relations proved particularly important when we addressed the recent challenges of the COVID-19 pandemic.

Meanwhile, the university has continued to grow and improve in a very difficult environment and with modest state financial support. Applications and enrollments have increased despite unfavorable regional trends, retention and graduation rates have improved, research funding is historically high, and student and faculty diversity have increased. Between 2015 and 2019, a new faculty hiring initiative expanded the size the full-time faculty by nearly 60 and a similar effort is currently underway to increase the number of graduate teaching assistants. More than 50 percent of full-time faculty have been hired during the past ten years. As well, the physical plant of the university is much improved with hundreds of millions of dollars in new construction during the past decade and more planned. Whether these trends continue when the COVID-19 pandemic ends depends mainly on maintaining enrollment and on no major cuts in the state appropriation. Nonetheless, there has been much cause for optimism during the past several years.

I relay these details because the following reflections are, no doubt, colored by my personal and professional commitment to constructive labor relations and the generally positive history of collective bargaining at my institution.

Reflections on Important Current Issues

In reflecting on important issues, I will focus on three areas that I believe are particularly important: enhancing the careers of full-time, nontenure-track faculty; addressing the faculty's quality of work-life; and using student feedback on courses and teaching appropriately in the performance appraisal process. I will give examples from my own experiences in collective bargaining during the past few years and attempt to generalize to other settings. I will integrate some thoughts on bargaining processes and will end with how I think these several issues belong in a broader social justice agenda.

Enhancing the Careers of Full-Time, Nontenure-Track Faculty

The University of Rhode Island has not increased the size of its per-course faculty during the past decade. In fact, the pre-COVID-19 trend suggests the opposite: the new faculty hiring initiative mentioned above actually decreased reliance on per-course faculty. But like many institutions, the number of full-time, but nontenure-track, faculty has increased. Improving the career prospects of this group and more fully integrating them into core governance structures have been priorities of the administration, faculty union, and faculty senate.

Prior to the 2014–2018 collective bargaining agreement, lecturers at the university had no career path. They received one-year appointments with no chance of advancement and, therefore, could count on a career of relatively low compensation, receiving only modest across-the-board increases of rarely more, and often less, than three percent per year. Some remember the time in the 1990s when nearly all lecturers were not renewed in order to balance the budget.

In 2014, however, the parties agreed to add promotional steps with pay raises to the lecturer track. Now, continuing lecturers may advance to senior lecturer after four years and to teaching professor after eight years. To advance, lecturers must go through a promotional process. A terminal degree is required for advancement to teaching professor. In the lowest salary tier, lecturers receive an approximately 13 percent increase with promotion to senior lecturer and an approximately 17 percent increase with promotion from senior lecturer to teaching professor. Lump sum increases are given to lecturers whose current salaries are above the promotional step increase. In the 2018–2021 agreement, the period of appointment for senior lecturers was increased to three years and teaching professors to five. In addition, eligibility for sabbatical leave was extended to nontenure-track clinical faculty at the full professor level and access to faculty development funds was granted to nearly all nontenure-track faculty.

These examples reflect what is likely a broader and continuing trend in academia to improve the circumstances of full-time, nontenure-track faculty. For some of these groups, including lecturers and clinical faculty, it may be that their employment will come to more closely resemble that of tenured faculty. They will receive better compensation, have longer terms of appointment, and benefit from such perks as sabbatical leave that have normally been reserved to the tenured faculty. The collective bargaining process must address the appropriate balance between flexibility and stability for these faculty.

Addressing the Quality of Work-Life of Faculty

Quality of work-life is old expression with roots mainly in the goods-producing sector. At that time, the emphasis was on improving the daily existence of blue-collar workers by changing sociotechnical systems to make work less boring, more rewarding, and less dangerous. I believe the term has applicability to academia and argue that improving the quality of work-life of faculty requires attention to both workload allocation and work/life balance.

At research universities, individual faculty typically have very different workload profiles. Even within the tenured ranks, some faculty have heavy teaching loads with low research expectations while others are expected essentially to fund themselves with research grants, but engage in little teaching, particularly of undergraduates. Service in one form or another is expected of nearly all full-time faculty, but is more difficult to measure than teaching or research, which makes it particularly hard to distribute equitably. In addition, the off-campus lives of faculty vary; some may have few personal obligations, while others are overwhelmed by both child and elder care. These issues, if ignored, can lead to feelings of inequity, to interpersonal disputes, and ultimately to turnover or other manifestations of discontent. There is often also a gendered and racial angle to these matters as well. Disciplines with relatively more women are often those with heavier undergraduate teaching loads and faculty from underrepresented groups in many cases bear an unfair burden for service when institutions with relatively few such faculty—i.e. most institutions—seek diversity on nearly every committee and task force.

So, what role might collective bargaining play? Until the current agreement at my institution, there was very little language in the contract concerning workload allocation. The language merely stated that workload included research, teaching, and service and was impossible to standardize across disciplines or even individuals. From an administration perspective, opening this area of the contract was fraught. We clearly did not want to introduce language that would decrease flexibility at the department or college level by, for example, introducing language on class size, credit hours, or numbers of sections taught. Ultimately, language was incorporated into the contract that had largely existed in the university manual, but with some modification. Importantly, the language remains flexible and recognizes differences in disciplines and in individual appointments. Chairs (who are bargaining unit members) have the initial responsibility to assign workload. Deans have the right to approve assignments. Chairs should discuss workload assignments with a faculty member before making them and must consider a number of variables concerning a faculty member's duties, such as the number, level, and size of sections taught (but with no specific minima or maxima). Important to the administration was language that allows the adjustment of workload over the course of a career to maintain a proper balance of research, teaching, and service based on a faculty members' contemporaneous commitments to these three main elements of workload. The overall hope is that the new language makes chairs and deans more thoughtful when allocating and approving workload so that imbalances and inequities will be avoided.

Further, we know that being "at work" has little meaning for what faculty actually do; no one stops thinking about teaching and research when they leave campus. This fact makes attention to work/life balance particularly important in considering the quality of work-life, especially for faculty with family obligations. Parental and family leave provisions coupled with tenure clock flexibility are important for junior faculty, while elder care responsibilities may affect faculty at any point in their careers, but often fall disproportionately on mid- to late-career faculty. In the most recent round of bargaining we agreed to language that allows an automatic tenure clock extension, upon notification, for faculty who become parents by either natural birth or adoption. We also agreed that when faculty are unable to use fully their parental leave, they may receive a workload adjustment in the following semester. This change is particularly important for faculty who become parents over the summer when they are off-contract—and, therefore, gain little from six weeks of leave—but who may struggle to make up for lost research time in the fall. Elder care can be even more difficult to manage, particularly for faculty whose parents live abroad. Sometimes partial leave arrangements with the possibility of remote work are needed to handle these situations. In addition, graduate assistants and per-course faculty may also need parental and family leave options. It can be difficult to manage these situations when a graduate assistant is grant-funded, but it is important that they receive the support they need without jeopardizing their assistantships or progress toward their degrees.

Using Student Feedback Appropriately

Student evaluations of teaching have become an important issue in collective bargaining. At many institutions, methods for student evaluation were instituted in the 1970s and 1980s and remained relatively uncontroversial for some time. More recently, however, studies have revealed evidence of bias against female and minority faculty as well as against those for whom English is not the first language. Therefore, there has been a push at a number of institutions to improve, deemphasize, or even eliminate student evaluations of teaching.

During our last round of bargaining, the administration and full-time faculty union agreed to establish an *ad hoc* joint labor/management committee to discuss the issue. Both parties entered the process believing that there was an over-reliance on student evaluation scores as a means of judging teaching effectiveness. From the union's perspective, deans were too quick to draw conclusions by looking only at the summary scores or column charts attached to student evaluation results. Administrators complained that faculty often failed to include other meaningful evidence of teaching effectiveness in their dossiers, leaving little choice but to rely on student evaluation data. The union initially sought the elimination of the mandatory use of student evaluations in performance appraisal. The administration asserted that student voice should remain a mandatory component of appraisal, but should be given proper weight.

The first change the parties agreed to was semantic. We thought it important to refer to the information provided by students as "student feedback on courses and teaching" not "student evaluation of teaching", understanding that students are not always in the best position to evaluate effective teaching. Further, we amplified existing contract language that states that student feedback should not be considered the only or principal evidence of teaching effectiveness, and we developed guidance, which will be appended to the next collective bargaining agreement, with details on assembling an effective teaching portfolio. We also agreed to disallow department or college standards that impose numerical minima in annual review or promotion and tenure standards—e.g. that someone must rate 4 out of 5 on the variable "excellent teacher" on the evaluation instrument. In addition, we agreed that quantitative results may be used as a factor in promotion and tenure decisions only if they reveal a pattern, over five or more semesters, of failing to meet relevant course objectives in a majority of courses taught. Finally, we agreed that only faculty will receive the written comments of students from the student feedback instrument.

We must wait until after the COVID-19 emergency to judge whether this new system improves the evaluation of teaching effectiveness. The abrupt shift to remote teaching in the spring of 2020 and continued interruptions to in-person teaching in academic year 2020 has made it difficult to truly judge faculty member's teaching, as even renown teachers have struggled with all the changes. An unfortunate coincidence at my institution was a change in learning management system in the same year. We hope that faculty become more reflective about their teaching and that administration take a more holistic approach to evaluating teaching effectiveness, while keeping a place for student voice.

Social Justice and Bargaining

Collective bargaining has always been a tool to correct historical social injustices. Each of the topics reflected upon above are small steps to right wrongs and make the academic workplace more equitable. Consider that women are often over-represented in the ranks of nontenure-track faculty or that faculty from underrepresented groups more likely to face high service demands. As well, childcare responsibilities almost always fall disproportionately on women making work/life balance more difficult to navigate. And, as mentioned, the evidence suggests that when poorly designed or inappropriately used, student evaluation of teaching instruments may more negatively affect the performance appraisal of female and minority faculty. Through the measures taken by the parties and incorporated into our agreements we attempted to address these inequities.

Using collective bargaining to address such issues successfully requires a commitment from both parties to making the workplace more just and equitable. It also requires having the right voices at the table. And, perhaps most of all, success is more likely when relationships are strong and the parties understand their mutual interests.

Neil S. Bucklew

I will offer reflections and forecasts on the topic of academic collective bargaining by looking at some key issues over the history of this topic as well as suggest how those in this field might find it most productive to proceed as they participate in the years ahead.

Allow me to summarize my experience as a participant in academic collective bargaining from its earliest years in the late 1960s until my retirement from a career as a university administrator, including serving as president of two universities. In the late 1960s I completed my PhD degree in Industrial Relations at the University of Wisconsin – Madison. During that same time, I was serving as Director of Labor Relations for the University of Wisconsin System. The Teaching Assistants Association on the Madison Campus in 1968 petitioned the University to be recognized under the recently passed Public Sector Collective Bargaining Law. I was asked by the University to chair the university team in the negotiations that followed. This negotiation and the contract that was completed was one of the first contracts between a university and its academic staff. In 1970 I became a vice president at Central Michigan University and for the next five years one of my duties was to represent the university in negotiations with the faculty union on that campus. Over the next decades I served as a provost of two universities and president of two universities. Twice in those roles I was on a campus with a faculty union. From 1968 until my retirement I studied academic collective bargaining as a key element of my research and publication activity. In summary, my perspective of this field has been informed by my role as an active participant as well as a scholar of academic collective bargaining.

Reflections on Academic Collective Bargaining

I suggest there are four major developments impacting higher education over its recent history. As such these developments create some of the most critical issues facing the governing processes of universities including academic collective bargaining on the campuses where it exists. These developments are:

Adoption of the Business Model – Over recent decades institutions of higher education have moved away from the management structure of shared governance and are adopting a business model adapted from the general world of business. No longer is academic administration viewed as the province of seasoned faculty who have moved through the faculty ranks to become a dean, a provost and perhaps to the role of president. The top executives of the modern university are drawn more and more from those with successful careers in private and public roles. This change is not experienced only in universities but is happening in fields like hospitals and government agencies. The skills and experiences most valued are not those of scholarship and teaching excellence but those of political capabilities and management sophistication. Governing boards are more intent on finding leaders who understand how to accomplish efficiencies and build partnerships that can lead to improved economic success for the areas served by the institution.

Product Determination – Academic degrees and service programs are no longer primarily a reflection of faculty expertise and interest. Strategic plans developed under the initiative of the new breed of university leaders point the directions needed in these areas. Faculty are rewarded to an increasing degree by their interest and ability to help implement these elements of the new strategic plan. Most of these plans are designed to meet the needs and goals of improved economic vitality.

Changing Financial Patterns – Universities are large organizations and it is important to maintain successful income streams and to develop efficient ways to control expenditures. Traditional income for higher education has relied on tuition and fees as a central income source. Tuition has increased at a rate often exceeding inflation. It has slowly replaced the load of most other areas of institutional income. There are growing signs that this pattern cannot be sustained. State support has been in decline for institutions of higher education. There are simply too many competitor state-associated organizations and agencies that need the resources. States are leaning more and more toward funding projects and special programs that relate to political agendas and/or economic initiatives. Some of these are connected to a higher education institution but are not in the form of subsidy for the institutions operating budget. Federal funding in the arena of higher education is largely limited to student financial aid and national agenda-driven research funding. These are not intended for general support but follow the individual student or the research strength of a particular institution.

Social Justice Goals – It is becoming more and more clear that inequities impacting the mix of cultural groups in our nation is becoming a critical issue. This is resulting in political and social unrest. Universities have often been a leader in exposing the problems and have tended to recognize their role in improving the situation. It appears that the business world is showing a willingness to step up their efforts to improve economic opportunities in the social justice area. There is further indication that given the voting blocks represented by the diverse cultural groups and a growing sense of the need for systemic change that both state and federal government are becoming more committed to an agenda of change and improvement. This issue could become a major goal in the years ahead.

Forecast of Most Productive Patterns in Academic Collective Bargaining in Response to These Higher Education Developments

I propose three strategies for the future of higher education academic bargaining that can result in a more productive outcome for all of the parties impacted by the resulting contracts. These strategies also help manage the developments discussed earlier.

The first of these strategies is to recognize and confirm in action that academic collective bargaining will be different based on the type of higher education institution involved in the process. The goals for the negotiations process should be, and need to be, distinct given the category of institution. These categories are: community and technical colleges; undergraduate focused four year colleges both public and private; graduate and research focused universities; and for profit institutions.

An example might help in understanding this strategy. A helpful example is the topic of academic governance. A shared governance model is universal in the category of institution I identified above as graduate and research focused universities. These institutions have a long history of faculty senates which by policy and precedent play a dominant role in academic matters such as curriculum and the tenure process. In comparison the category I identified as community and technical colleges rarely have a history of shared governance of this type. The relationship is more reflective of an employer–employee arrangement. That is clearly true of the category I called for profit institutions.

In this example it is appropriate to approach the negotiating process with different intent and goals on this topic. When both parties acknowledge the strategy in play there is a much improved outcome on the horizon.

A second strategy is to recognize and confirm in action that the financial/management context for higher education has changed and will continue to move toward what might be called the business model. It is not whether you approve of this change but how the parties establish a bargaining strategy that both curbs possible excesses and endorses valuable decisions.

Again, an example might be useful. Institutions of higher education in every category have adopted the pattern of increased use of a new type of faculty other than permanent or tenure track faculty. These faculty go by many titles: adjunct, temporary, non-tenure track, clinical, etc. This approach is driven by the need for flexibility and efficiency in the face of tightening budget realities. The strategy in play here suggests that the parties create an effective structure for this new type of faculty that provides fair and needed employment safeguards for these individuals. This strategy is grounded in having both parties agree to be problem solvers not just problem identifiers.

A third strategy is to recognize and confirm in action that academic collective bargaining can be an agent for social change. The institution of collective bargaining has a history of being intertwined in social change. That is a mixed history in the United States. I am proposing that one of the keystone strategies for the future be a jointly accepted goal of moving the needle in regard to social justice practices.

In summary, higher education is changing. These developments are occurring even when they modify long-held views of how higher education should be structured and operate. External factors, such as social change, are calling for our attention. It is not an easy time for the practice of academic collective bargaining. But there are strategies that hold promise for clarifying and improving the process. This article has suggested three such strategies.

Jeffrey F. Cross

Some Fundamental Things to Consider to Make Collective Bargaining Work Better for All Concerned in Higher Education

First and foremost, every university administrator should consider that faculty unions and collective bargaining agreements (CBA) do not materialize out of thin air. They come about for a reason: perceived faculty grievances and administrative wrongs unresolved through traditional shared governance and consultative processes. Even though those past perceived grievances may have been resolved (even if years ago), the faculty union and the CBA remain, and sometimes along with remnants of charged feelings and antipathies that motivated the organization of the bargaining unit in the first place.

Considerations for Contract Negotiations

Prior to negotiating a first faculty contract, university administration essentially possessed all rights that were not otherwise constrained by law. Thereafter, a negotiated CBA lays out the sharing of those rights with the faculty's bargaining agent as specifically described in the agreement. Typically, CBAs also include an article pertaining to management rights in which the institution's governing authority reserves to itself all rights not specifically shared or consigned to the faculty union in the CBA. Consequently, the CBA should not be viewed as a comprehensive manual for how to interact with the faculty in all instances, but rather a proscribed set of rules guiding faculty administration as specifically defined and set out in the CBA. In other words, if it's not in the CBA that doesn't necessarily mean that it's prohibited. This concept is particularly important when preparing for contract negotiations with the union.

Negotiating parties are free to make a wide variety of proposals on any subject not prohibited by law. Some subjects are required by law to be negotiated. These mandatory subjects are generally wages, hours (workload), and other terms and conditions of employment. All other subjects are termed permissive subjects and are not required to be bargained unless both parties agree to negotiate them or unless previously negotiated as part of the CBA. Administratively, if some matter is not a mandatory subject, and it is not already part of the CBA, it is a right that the administration has retained and should never be an administrative proposal at the bargaining table. To make such a proposal, the university administration would effectively be bargaining for something that it already has and making an admission or declaration it does not have that right. Consequently, if negotiations do not result in agreement concerning that matter, it is no longer an administrative right.

When preparing for bargaining, the president or chancellor should consult the governing board for their perspectives and bargaining priorities, share the administration's priorities for bargaining, and determine the governing board's resolve to achieve institutional bargaining objectives. Administrative consultations in preparation for bargaining should also include: polling department heads/chairs, deans and others; reviewing grievances during the term of current agreement; reviewing ratios and benchmarks for peer institutions; consulting the chief financial officer regarding current and anticipated budget capacities; and considering anticipated external developments that could affect the institution. A part of preparing administrative objectives for bargaining a successor agreement involves careful review of matters of concern raised during the term of the current agreement. These include presidential consultations and a review of the subjects of all grievances.

When developing its bargaining objectives, university administrators should keep in mind that their union colleagues are doing the same thing. When a union's bargaining perspectives are initially presented as proposals, the proposals can often be perceived by university administrators as being over-the-top, overly ambitious, and sometimes even insulting. No matter how the union's bargaining proposals are initially presented or how they are perceived by university administrators, they will have been founded on underlying concerns for which there is usually room to negotiate. To do so successfully, the administration should present clearly defined foundational bargaining principles such as maintaining civil discourse, preserving administrative rights, and not agreeing to "dual gate keeping" provisions. Successful negotiations also often hinge on a university administration and its bargainers listening carefully and being prepared to think creatively.

From the union's perspective, there is a need to not only maintain value for its members but create additional value in terms of wages, workload, and other terms and conditions of employment. This is especially true after the Janus decision that effectively made every public employee collective bargaining state a right-to-work state. Faculty unions will likely perceive a heightened imperative to "get more" for those in their bargaining unit with each successive round of bargaining.

Administrators need to consider that faculty and academic personnel unions are private entities with interests that may, but do not always, coincide with those of the college or university. The union's interests are driven, in large measure, by its need to perpetuate itself as well as its elected leaders and to create perceived value among its constituents. Not doing so risks decertification. Each pay period members see deductions from their earnings for union fees, and the collective perception among union members must be that what they get from their union is worth the cost. This can easily lead to dissatisfaction with the status quo and to escalating demands for more compensation and/or reductions in workload with the possible exception being those circumstances that lead university administrations to seek contract concessions. In circumstances involving financial concessions, unions will often counter with demands for enhancements of so-called "non-economic" provisions of the contract. University administrators are well advised to carefully consider the ultimate costs and economic consequences of what ostensibly are termed non-economic provisions. Almost every provision of a CBA has a cost, whether it is a direct cost for compensation and benefits or an indirect managerial cost.

Who Will Bargain?

Each party to contract negotiations determines unilaterally who will bargain on its behalf. Although leaders from each party can comment on those selected to bargain, such comments are advisory and may presage how certain personalities will affect the progress of bargaining. The lead bargainer for the administration is usually the contract administrator, someone in human resources trained and experienced in collective bargaining, or an outside labor consultant or attorney. No matter who leads the administration's bargaining effort, it is important that there be a team or committee of administrative staff engaged in bargaining to bring managerial and operational perspectives to the process. Ideally, the administrative staff should represent academic department heads/chairs, deans, and fiscal officers who have knowledge of the CBA and who have experience with negotiations. Whatever interests, perspectives, and previous collective bargaining experiences are represented by those bargaining on behalf of the university administration, it is good practice to provide some comprehensive lessons learned from previous experience at the table. Nicholas DiGiovanni (2012) has distilled lessons learned that are particularly instructive.

Generally, administrative bargaining teams are smaller than faculty union bargaining teams. It is not necessary to have one-to-one parity at the bargaining table. The composition of bargaining teams or committees generally represents the major constituencies of the bargaining unit and of the administration. From an administrative perspective, who represents those constituencies on the administrative bargaining committee is very important. Although there are exceptions, neither the university president nor the provost should be at the table. Those bargaining on behalf of the university administration should have been given clearly articulated objectives and parameter limits for the negotiations. Even so, as negotiations progress, the boundaries of those objectives and limits will likely be challenged. Having authorities away from the table to consult and who can decide whether or not to compromise those objectives or stretch those limits (and by how much) is helpful and often comes into play when negotiations are in their final stages.

What communication strategies will the administration employ during bargaining with the governing authority, with other members of the administration, with the faculty, and with the community at large? There are no right or wrong ways to communicate or how frequently. However, communications away from the bargaining table cannot introduce bargaining proposals or initiatives that have not already been brought to the bargaining table. To do so would be an unfair labor practice.

Finally, the administration and the union need to determine together the manner and form for bargaining. Will it be traditional positional bargaining or some form of so-called "win-win" or "mutual-gains" negotiations such as interest-based bargaining. Irrespective of the bargaining method, all concerned need to realize and accept that not all objectives for bargaining outcomes will be achieved. This is the nature of the give-and-take of contract negotiations.

Leslie and Hu (1977) describe collective bargaining as

> ...an economically rational behavior engaged in by two competing interests: employers and labor unions. Settlement between the two parties is reached at an equilibrium point at which both employer and employee perceive that they will be better off if they agree than if they do not. In the case of college faculty bargaining, the union's major goals are improved financial compensation, job security, and reduced work loads. Institutions of higher education, however, seek to conserve their scarce resources in order to maximize productivity, particularly in regard to institutional quality.
>
> *(p. 33)*

Before an "equilibrium point" is achieved, each party may elect to exert leverage in the process. Administrations can impose a lockout, and unions can withhold their services. If negotiations stall and reach an impasse, the parties may engage in mediation by a third party, fact-finding, or arbitration in an attempt to reach an agreement. In many jurisdictions, administration can unilaterally implement its last-best offer. Although this strategy allows for some progress, it rarely, if ever, achieves the "equilibrium point" of settlement, and further negotiation over unsettled subjects often ensues.

Although most contract negotiations culminate in an agreement, before bargaining begins the administration should be prepared with a detailed strike plan including crisis communication strategies. Will classes continue? Who will teach? Who will initiate communications, with whom, and how frequently?

When negotiating a successor agreement, those at the bargaining table, both union and administration representatives, should have a good working knowledge of the current agreement and what provisions have worked and what provisions have presented problems or difficulties. Of equal importance is a good working knowledge of how provisions of the agreement affect, or potentially affect, day-to-day and term-to-term operations. If negotiations are led by an outside consultant, having operational knowledge at the table is essential to determine whether a potential provision is manageable or even desirable.

Among the components of the relationship between a university administration and a faculty union, none is more important than trust. Looking to the future, trust is foundational to finding shared interests that can lead to a viable and thriving institution. For a union to thrive, its university must also thrive. A college or university in financial distress is clearly in no position to accede to union demands for increases in compensation or reductions in workload. Public colleges and universities have experienced decades-long erosion of state appropriations and increasing constraints on tuition and other fees whether due to declining enrollments or pressure from state government. The COVID-19 pandemic will only exacerbate these constraints. In addition, higher education is increasingly seen as more of a private good than a public good further eroding public citizen support. In these circumstances, how can collective bargaining achieve mutual gains?

One avenue for mutual gains is to focus bargaining on students especially as student tuition increases as a percentage of current funds revenue. What performance measures can be bargained that will increase enrollment (and thereby tuition and fees revenue), student success, student retention, student satisfaction, and graduation? Historically, it has not been uncommon for collective bargaining agreements to link increases in faculty compensation and the overall cost of the agreement to levels of state appropriations. As burgeoning expenditure entitlements have constrained state budgets available for discretionary spending like higher education, states have turned to various forms of budgeting or funding higher education based on institutional performance. Performance-based funding has met with marginal success, and the long-term effectiveness of faculty contract provisions keyed to one or more institutional performance measures is yet to be determined. There have been a few such contract provisions, but they have been of the "bonus" variety over and above what was negotiated for across-the-board and merit salary increases. Finding institutional and student performance measures that faculty unions and university administrations can mutually embrace will not be easy. Faculty unions often consider institutional performance the purview of the administration and not the responsibility of the faculty. However, it is likely that institutional and student performance measures will become more foundational to faculty collective bargaining agreements. For institutions and faculty unions to succeed, their students must first succeed, and when students succeed, society benefits as well, thus significantly expanding the meaning and significance of collaboration and mutual gains.

Trust among university administration and union leaders helps colleagues recognize that they have many more interests in common than divergent interests. It is incumbent on faculty union leaders to publicly represent interests compiled from diverse and sometimes contradictory interests of their membership. A university's interests are often much more focused due to its scalar organizational structure. Therefore, university administrators need to appreciate the sometimes divergent voices that their union counterparts represent publicly. Faculty union leaders have an electoral and legal duty of fair representation of their members. When university and union leaders maintain a well-developed relationship founded on trust and respect, "off-the-record" confidential communications can be had. These are particularly important during negotiations and sometimes prove crucial to reaching agreement.

During contract negotiations, both union and university bargainers deal with matters across the bargaining table but also manage the interests of those on their respective sides of the table. Allison and Blitz (2018) and Winters (2018) describe the various aspects of managing negotiations on the union and administrative sides of the table respectively.

Although certain aspects of the relationship between a university and its faculty union are competitive, university and union leaders are well advised not to view their relationship as combative and totally confrontational. There is little likelihood that "fighting the union" will diminish its influence or undermine its authority. Consequently, a policy of constructive engagement provides the best avenue for successful collaboration. There are advantages to managing academic university operations in a union environment. The faculty union is the exclusive representative of the members of the bargaining unit. Even though individual members often have diverse and sometimes divergent interests (sometimes unstated and sometimes loudly articulated), university administrators in a union environment know to address matters of concern with and through designated union representatives. It then becomes the representational responsibility of union leaders to distill the divergent and sometimes contradictory concerns of its members and relieves university administration of having to deal with multiple, individual "voices" from faculty ranks.

More recently, some faculty unions have espoused equity and social justice initiatives that extend beyond the immediate interests of their members (e.g. student debt, institutional racism, etc.). The efficacy and even the appropriateness of advancing these initiatives in the context of bargaining is questionable in that they are largely to the benefit of constituencies that are not included in the certified unit definition and, therefore, beyond the scope of the bargaining agent's representational authorization. Some equity measures, however, are fully within the scope of the faculty union's certified unit definition. Negotiators typically address wages in terms of across-the-board increases, promotion in rank, merit increases, and one-time signing bonuses. Less typically, faculty salary negotiations include various forms of equity adjustments and salary increases linked to underlying market and social forces and to salary compression that may, or may not, be related to these forces. Market-based equity by discipline is an example of such an initiative and is problematic for unions to negotiate because various groups of faculty within the bargaining unit are treated differently. As a consequence, these kinds of compensation equity provisions are negotiated in addition to more traditional across-the-board increases (Blitz & Cross, 2013) and, therefore, rely on additional resources being allocated to the financial cost of the current and future agreements.

It's Not All About Bargaining

Initially developing and then maintaining a good working relationship with union leaders begins with recognition of shared academic values and mutual respect for the roles that each of the parties plays in the workings of collective bargaining. Day-to-day academic operations involve staff on several levels of an institution's organizational structure. Not all staff have the same understanding or degree of knowledge about the provisions of a CBA. Consequently, actions may be undertaken by administrative staff members, no matter how well intended, contrary to one or more CBA provisions. Recognizing that circumstances will arise wherein the parties to the agreement disagree about the intent of a given provision of the CBA, the parties will have negotiated dispute resolution provisions. These provisions typically include routine consultations as well as grievance procedures. While routine consultations usually involve those in union and university leadership roles, grievance proceedings typically begin at the department level and ask those directly involved with the disputed provision to resolve the matter. Such efforts are not often successful because those involved can be invested in actions or behaviors that resulted in the dispute in the first place.

When a disputed contractual matter escapes initial effort to resolve it, grievance procedures typically provide for escalating the grievance to a higher organizational level. University administrators are well advised to engage grievance matters with reason and careful consideration of contract language. If the grievance involves a perceived misunderstanding of contract language on the part of the union, university administration has the option to seek resolution through a variety of avenues up to and including arbitration by a third party. However, after a dispassionate and careful review of the facts, the administrative staff responsible for managing the CBA may find that administrative acted contrary to the CBA. In such instances, university administrators are well advised to own up to the error and take appropriate measures to rectify the mistake and resolve the grievance. Such open honesty can go a long way to sustaining a collaborative working relationship between university and union leaders.

The relationship with a faculty union is ongoing and will endure. The idea of "winning" a grievance or getting the better of the union in some other contested matter should be avoided because when the dust settles, the university and the union will still be there. The lesson to be taken here is the importance of finding ways to nurture relationships between those representing the interests of the university and the union. Working on these relationships does not end with the signing of an agreement or the resolution of some disputed matter through a grievance process. A relationship built on respect and collaboration does not mean that there will not be disputes between the interests of the union and those of the university. Trust in the sincere motives of each of the parties can, however, go a long way to sustaining a working and learning environment with a shared mission of organizational success.

References

Allison, John & Blitz, Jonathan (2018) "Managing Internal Tensions in Contract Negotiations: A Perspective from the Academic Union's Side," *Journal of Collective Bargaining in the Academy*: Vol. 10, Article 5. Available at: https://thekeep.eiu.edu/jcba/vol10/iss1/5.

Blitz, Jonathan P. & Cross, Jeffrey F. (2013) "Bargaining Market Equity Adjustments by Rank and Discipline," *Journal of Collective Bargaining in the Academy*: Vol. 5, Article 5. Available at: https://thekeep.eiu.edu/jcba/vol5/iss1/5.

DiGiovanni, Nicholas (2012) "This Much I Know is True: The Five Intangible Influences on Collective Bargaining," *Journal of Collective Bargaining in the Academy*: Vol. 3, Article 5. Available at: https://thekeep.eiu.edu/jcba/vol3/iss1/5.

Leslie, Larry, & Hu, T.-W. (1977). "The Financial Implications of Collective Bargaining," *Journal of Educational Finance*, 3, 32–53.

Winters, Margaret E. (2018) "Notes on the Same Side," *Journal of Collective Bargaining in the Academy*: Vol. 10, Article 6. Available at: https://thekeep.eiu.edu/jcba/vol10/iss1/6.

James M. Glaser

Reflections of a Dean Who Also Happens to Be a Political Scientist

I trained to be a political scientist. When I was in graduate school, nobody told me that I would need to understand labor relations at some point in my career. As a political scientist, however, it turns out that I have been well situated to engage in labor negotiations and to identify and articulate some lessons about bargaining with unions. After all, politics, in Lasswell's (1936) classic formulation, is "who gets what, when, and how," and labor negotiations (and indeed much of what a dean handles) is all about what is going to whom, and how and when that will happen.

Shortly before I was promoted from academic dean to dean of arts and sciences at Tufts University, the school's part-time lecturers gathered enough cards to initiate a union vote. As the new dean, I sat in the office of the regional National Labor Relations Board (NLRB) office as the ballots were counted. The administration had argued gently against the union, but it was quickly clear that our arguments had not resonated. The part-time lecturer in the room started to weep as the result was becoming apparent. She and the representatives from the Service Employees International Union (SEIU) hugged each other while we, the management representatives, sat stiffly to the side. I was certainly surprised by the depth of her emotions.

Over the next year, I learned a great deal about why she – and others – felt so strongly. She had worked at the university for decades, and it was inevitably true that the administration, and even many faculty members in her department, had never thought much about her or her colleagues. Nor did she know most of the other part-time lecturers very well. They all taught on different days and at different times. They shared offices, but were only on campus a couple of hours a week. They shared interests, but they had no way of really knowing it. The organization of the union created a community where none had really existed before. And the vote made a statement. We in the administration would have to pay attention now, and to address their newly discovered collective interests.

While it was inevitably true that part-time faculty were unhappy about their material circumstances, and desired to improve their compensation and their job security, it was also clear that they felt disrespected by the institution and by their tenured faculty colleagues. The part-timers are smart, well-educated people, oftentimes underemployed, and some of them had at one time been in tenure-track positions elsewhere. They also understood that they played an important role in educating students whose tuition dollars resourced some, perhaps most, of the university, and that our students did not recognize any difference between non-tenure stream and tenure-stream faculty. If the part-time lecturers did not fully appreciate why research and scholarship were central to our enterprise, they did understand that they were much more easily replaced than tenure-stream faculty, and that the market for their services was weak, even in university-rich Boston.

Those first negotiations yielded some important lessons, lessons that I would refine in subsequent trips to the negotiation table after our full-time lecturers and our graduate student assistants also voted to unionize. Perhaps the most important lesson was that the bargaining exercise was indeed about respect, about the lecturers no longer being an afterthought in the university. Fortunately, respect does not have to be costly. After witnessing the tears of joy and relief at the NLRB office, I elected to participate directly in the negotiations, not just delegate the responsibility to others. I hoped that my presence, and that of my academic dean, would make a statement about the importance the school placed on the negotiations, and would give us the opportunity to personally deliver the respect that had been most missing. Of course, as deans, we knew and understood the rules, processes, and practices already in place and could contribute substantively to the point and counterpoint. Because we also were teaching courses and engaged in the same activities as the lecturers, we had additional credibility in that conversation. We also could shape the solutions to be embedded in the agreement. But fundamentally, we were there to begin to repair decades of indifference.

I also learned from the strategic lawyers who led our team (and those who led the union team) that separating principles from interests is essential to the enterprise. Compromise is more easily reached on interests than on principles. It is possible to quantify interests. That is harder to do with principles. And interests are more easily divisible, allowing both sides to give some to "get to yes." As we got underway, we tried to articulate our principles and interests to guide our approach, but also to convey to the representatives of the union what mattered most to us, where we might have room to compromise, and where we could not. We also believed that the university's principles would not always be in conflict with those of the union. Indeed, they might even converge.

What were our principles? First, we wanted any structure coming out of the agreement, whether it be a pay grid or a contract schedule, to reflect what we called "clean administration." I have been a dean long enough to know that simple is better than complicated, that "easy to remember" is better than "I have to look it up." It was in our interest – and, we argued, in the union's interest – to align on this. Clean administration would mean fewer mistakes in implementing our contract. It also would provide more clarity and transparency about who would get what, when, and how, and perhaps help avoid some grievances. So, we purposefully tried to avoid "crazy quilt" solutions. We had tiers and steps, to be sure, but when complicated schemes were inevitably floated across the table, we did our best to steer back to simplicity.

Second, it was our priority to maintain flexibility in managing a tenure-stream faculty engaged in research and scholarship. As the leaders in a research-intensive university, we are deeply invested in a system that supports the creation of knowledge, not just its transmission. A vigorous marketplace exists for faculty who conduct research and produce scholarship, and we have to participate in that marketplace if we are to attract and retain the best people. To some degree, this means acknowledging a tiered system of faculty. We can pay attention to and respect the teaching faculty in new ways, but tenure-stream faculty members have broader responsibilities and are judged by their research and scholarship as well as by their teaching. The jobs are similar, but they are also profoundly different. Early on in our negotiations, the union leadership, to our relief, formally recognized this. As a practical matter, we were willing to offer the lecturers more security in the form of longer contracts, more agency in choosing what to teach and when, and earlier and more rigid deadlines for deciding upon renewals. In exchange, we bargained for the right to transform lines, even part-time lines, into tenure-stream positions. We even built into the contract that we could eliminate part-time positions to make a spousal hire, another principle being that we seek to be a family-friendly institution and hiring spouses and partners allows some families to be together.

Third, we wanted to define roles and responsibilities explicitly and carefully. For our part-time faculty, we were only paying them to teach. We had no expectations of service, advising, or research. This meant if they did advise a thesis or sit on a committee, they could rightfully expect to be paid extra for it, and we scrupulously laid out what each additional duty was worth.

This principle became even more important when we negotiated a contract with our full-time lecturers, who have faculty governance responsibilities and advise students as part of their duties. For example, when they asked for sabbaticals, we held fast that sabbaticals were intended to promote research. We did agree, however, to a limited number of professional development leaves so that lecturers could take time to improve their pedagogy, though these would not be automatic and would not enable research.

Defining roles was yet more critical when Ph.D. students serving as teaching and research assistants created a bargaining unit. It was critically important for us to ensure that all parties understood that the role of the Ph.D. students is first and foremost as students. Again, the union well appreciated our perspective and agreed that the Ph.D. students' primary affiliation with the University is as students. As a result, a number of our associated principles fell into place and facilitated our bargaining. We were able to determine when something was bargainable and when it was academic, and thus not an appropriate topic of bargaining. For instance, when the union raised the issue of academic freedom, we pushed back. Students might have academic freedom, but this would not be an appropriate expectation for bargaining unit members. We also negotiated a management rights clause that allowed a faculty supervisor to define what their assistants could teach or do, and the university retained clear control over academic decisions affecting students. The point, of course, is that these definitions circumscribed our negotiations in important ways.

So much of what I learned about union negotiations came from my colleagues at the bargaining table, smart lawyers who explained labor law to us academics, and who knew how to set the right – respectful but firm – tone. I also learned from the union's savvy negotiators. Who knew that these experiences would lead me, as a student of politics, to become interested in compromise as a topic of academic inquiry? Together with colleagues, I have since studied how the American public views, understands, and accepts compromise in politics (see Glaser and Berry, 2018 and Glaser, Berry, and Schildkraut, 2021). As we engaged our research, I encountered Senator Everett Dirksen, a masterful Senate leader from the 1950s and 1960s, who once said, "I am a man of fixed and unbending principle, and one of my principles is flexibility." That, I conclude, is perhaps the most important stance to be brought by all sides to academic labor negotiations.

References

Glaser, James M. and Jeffrey M.Berry. 2018. "Compromising Positions: Why Republican Partisans are More Rigid than Democrats," *Political Science Quarterly* 133 (1): 99–126.

Glaser, James M., Jeffrey M.Berry, and Deborah J.Schildkraut. 2021. "Education and the Curious Case of Conservative Compromise," *Political Research Quarterly* 74: 59–75.

Lasswell, Harold D. 1936. *Politics: Who Gets What, When, How.* New York: Whittlesey House.

Joseph Glover

A Provost's Reflections on Bargaining

Introduction

The relationships among the players in collective bargaining are always colored by the context in which they operate, their goals, and their perspective on the university and the profession. As an example of context, the coronavirus pandemic has introduced a relatively new phenomenon in the collective bargaining environment: substantial fear of the physical environment and demands that the university guarantee safety, sometimes to an unrealistic standard. It is important that administrators and faculty share the same worldview about the university or at least understand each other's to reduce conflict and to help each side realize what can be achieved to mutual benefit.

Context, goals, and perspective are not fixed; they morph with time, circumstances, personal growth and experience, and changes in personnel. They can determine the dynamics of the collective bargaining process. To illustrate this and to provide the reader with my own context, I will review the collective bargaining environment in the State of Florida and my own evolution in connection with it over the past 20 years.

In July 2001, Governor Jeb Bush and the Florida Legislature eliminated the Board of Regents, which had governed the state university system for the preceding 35 years. They vested the governing authority in the Florida Board of Education and Boards of Trustees that were created at each of the state's public universities. Senator Bob Graham, a previous Governor, objected to this new arrangement and led a Constitutional ballot initiative to replace the Board of Regents. The ballot initiative was successful, and the Board of Governors was born in 2003 as a constitutional entity, although the individual university Boards of Trustees also continued to exist. A certain amount of confusion ensued about the role of the Board of Governors and its relationship with the Legislature and the Boards of Trustees.

The flux in Florida's higher education governance landscape created uncertainty in the context of collective bargaining. It was not clear for some time whether there was one statewide faculty union or individual charters for each campus, and how a new process for resolving impasses through the local Boards of Trustees would operate. It was a busy and messy time through at least 2010 as all parties sought firm footing in their processes and philosophies. The new governance arrangements also meant that issues formerly decided centrally by the Board of Regents were now devolved to the local level with every campus in charge of its own destiny, at least in principle. The situation at my campus, the University of Florida (UF), was further complicated by the fact that the faculty bargaining unit includes only about one-third of the faculty. Faculty members in the six health science colleges, the Institute of Food and Agricultural Sciences, and the College of Law are not included in the bargaining unit.

I served as Associate Provost for Faculty Affairs from 2001 through 2006 as events unfolded, participating as a member of the bargaining team and writing many of the proposals pushed across the table. It is fair to say I operated in a transactional mode during this period, as we sought to establish the academic and working environment of the university with the newfound freedom and responsibility devolution brought. It is also a period in which I learned the ropes of collective bargaining with the assistance of talented individuals from the General Counsel's Office, several external consultants and policy guidance from the Provost.

In 2008, I became Provost, a position I still hold. Twelve years is a long time for someone to serve as provost at one institution. On one hand, it helps provide the university with continuity, while on the other, there is ample opportunity to evolve thinking and to shift perspective. During this time, I have also served under two presidents, and their philosophies of university management have certainly influenced mine.

As I began in 2008, the country was in the final throes of the last great recession. Much of my attention was on managing the university and minimizing damage. Within five years, the university began to have remarkable opportunities to invest in programs and faculty, and I devoted more attention to strategic opportunities for investment. Now, 12 years in, time grows short, and I have become increasingly focused on a few key initiatives that promise to advance the university for decades if there is appropriate execution and follow-through. And so, I would characterize my own evolution as moving from a transactional management mindset to one that became increasingly focused on strategic university investment opportunities to the current day, when it has sharpened to concentrate on a few key initiatives with huge transformational potential.

I write this because the evolution of my management style and increasingly finely tuned goals have influenced my attitude and behavior towards collective bargaining. I think it may be helpful for provosts to assess their own relationship with the job and reflect on how that affects what happens at the bargaining table. Above all, it is important to clearly demonstrate through speech, action, and resource allocation which initiatives will receive the highest priority.

Common Ground at the Bargaining Table

Ideally, participants on both sides of the bargaining table should negotiate based on the same set of facts and understandings about the university. This can be challenging, and it may sometimes be unachievable. But it is a goal worth pursuing. A university is most effective as a community, and a community functions most effectively when its members agree on some common principles, priorities, and goals. It is a conversation worth having.

Having held various administrative positions at UF, including department chair, associate dean, interim dean, associate provost, and provost, I am often asked which is the "best" job I have held. I always reply "provost" for one simple reason. In that position, you finally see all the forces at work on the university. You do not control them, but you understand them. In other administrative positions like dean and chair, and in faculty positions, things happen to you that you may not understand because some of the forces at work are invisible to you. This is a key point because the same dynamic is in play in collective bargaining. There are goals you, the provost, seek, actions you must take, and constraints on your actions that are clear to you. These are often unclear to the participants on the other side of the bargaining table or completely foreign to their understanding of the university. This divide can separate the two sides and provide a source of conflict. It can be bridged if sufficient trust has developed.

But trust can develop only when there is a good exchange of information. And this can be difficult, even when all parties are willing. The operations of a large public university are exceedingly complex, which is why we have administrators who specialize in finance, HR, legal, etc. Bargainers on the other side of the table, who have day jobs as teacher-scholars, often find it difficult or impossible to put in the time necessary to develop mastery of these issues.

For bargaining to be a profitable exercise, it is critical that both sides develop a set of shared understandings about the university, internally developed and externally imposed goals, and the resources and constraints in place to achieve them. These understandings create common ground for a richer conversation. Clearly elucidated university and faculty priorities will form the basis for productive trade-offs and negotiations.

What Does the Future Hold?

A provost at another university was fond of saying, "So long as God makes 18-year-olds, there will be a need for residential universities." Based on his sentiment, I believe the teaching mission of most large universities is secure. We can certainly anticipate a reexamination of the research and service missions, the university's role in creating a more just and equitable society, and concerns about financing and access. It will be important that the university administration and the faculty reach some common understanding about these issues, including goals and priorities. This will serve as a basis for productive negotiations at the bargaining table. Missing this important conversation could be a recipe for conflict in bargaining. Open and unrestrained conflict at the bargaining table will pose a great risk for universities as higher education is reexamined. It may create misunderstandings among Boards and Legislatures about the unique qualities that have made the U.S. university system so successful and the envy of the world.

James R. Johnsen

Opportunities for Collective Bargaining to Advance Higher Education through Clarity of Role and Process

American higher education institutions enjoy an unparalleled record of contribution to society through creating new knowledge, educating an informed citizenry and skilled workforce, driving innovation and economic development, supporting national security, providing health care, and advancing racial and social equity and opportunity. But our ability to extend and expand these contributions is constrained by factors from without and within.

Externally, we face declining enrollments and inadequate preparation of our incoming students, a fast changing set of employer expectations, demographic forces outside our control, never ending increases in regulation, budget cuts and corresponding pressures to reduce expenses, the imperative constantly to invest in new technologies, and demands for more equitable access to the opportunities that are created by affordable and high quality education.

Internally, our costs rise faster than inflation, we are pushed and pulled toward more on-line delivery models, our facilities are aging, pressure for increased productivity is ever on the rise while our ability to address compensation issues is limited, our bureaucracies and turf issues impede student success and faculty collaboration, our students and staff and faculty are calling for increased social and environmental responsibility, and our decision-making processes are cumbersome and constrain our ability to be nimble.

And that was before we were confronted by the combined challenges of the COVID-19 pandemic, the imperative to address racial justice, and the demand for a stepped-up contribution to economic recovery.

Fortunately, we have many assets with which to overcome these challenges as we contribute to society as only we can. Knowledge, programs, technology, facilities, and most of all, our people. Students who come to us to learn and advance their lives. Faculty who do the research, the teaching, and the outreach. Staff who provide essential support services in virtually every aspect of our work. Regents and trustees who give of their time and expertise to govern and guide our institutions. Employers who advise on our programs and employ our alumni. Alumni and donors whose generosity provides the margin of excellence and opportunity for so many of our students. And political leaders at all levels who regulate us and, in many cases, provide resources to us.

With respect to our faculty and staff (including student employees), collective bargaining has proven that it can be an effective process for setting mutually the terms and conditions of employment in support of our mission and purpose. But it also has its limits, especially when facing questions such these. How might collective bargaining promote collaboration, innovation and equity? How about contemporary social justice issues? How can outcomes of the process be evaluated and measured in meaningful ways? What are some best practices for addressing some of the most severe pressures on collective bargaining? And what impact has the pandemic had on labor management relations this past year and going forward?

I will address each of these questions in turn based on experience as a public university system president with a professional background in labor relations in the private sector and in government and higher education, on both sides of the negotiating table. But before I do, I will discuss a set of fundamental tensions that, if clarified, will strengthen the collective bargaining process as a means by which labor relations can be managed on campus.

Clarifying Roles and Processes as a Precondition for Progress

Collective bargaining in higher education can be a very complex process with multiple roles and processes for addressing specific issues. Clarifying roles and processes reduces ambiguity and conflict, and enables the parties to bring their best to the process.

The major roles in collective bargaining are the employer and the union. Seems simple enough but some of the largest universities with collective bargaining in the nation are in state systems where the union represents employees across the system and the employer is the system. In these systems with collective bargaining, while employees reasonably identify with their institution, their employer is the system. Adding to the complexity is that accreditation is tied to the institution, not to the system, when the system is the employer and the fiduciary responsible for managing the institutions in the system. Yet another complexity is that the union's status as the bargaining agent on behalf of employees typically derives from state statute, whereas management's authority is delegated from the governing board pursuant to the state constitution and/or statute. Clarity in the roles of the parties, their identity and authority, is a critical precondition if we expect our labor management processes to make progress on the important issues we face.

The major processes in labor management relations on campus are collective bargaining and university governance, especially in relation to relations with a unionized faculty. This is because faculty, in addition to collective bargaining, also engage in formal governance processes through senates and other consultative groups at each institution, usually under delegated authority from the governing board. Questions often arise over which process—collective bargaining (terms and conditions of employment) or governance (curriculum, grading, admission standards, etc.)—is appropriate for addressing a particular issue. Sometimes it is clear which issue belongs to which process. But there are many issues that may not fall clearly into one or the other. And there are issues, aspects of which are appropriately the province of the two different processes. For example, the granting of tenure typically is the prerogative of the faculty, with concurrence of management of course, through the governance structure. But the steps of the process and calendar by which a faculty member is evaluated for tenure may be provided in the collective bargaining agreement.

• A helpful basis for clarification of which issues, or aspects of issues, belong to which process is whether the issue is "academic," which requires the professional judgement of faculty or is closely tied to the mission and purpose of the employer. If so, the governance process is appropriate. If, however, the issue is a "term and condition of employment," typically defined in a state statute, then the collective bargaining process is appropriate. Clarity in which process for how an issue, or aspect of an issue, is addressed reduces confusion and potential conflict, and improves the effectiveness of both governance and collective bargaining processes.

Once these roles and processes are clearly understood, labor and management will be in a better position to make progress on the pressing issues at hand.

How Might Collective Bargaining Promote Collaboration, Innovation and Equity?

First, the parties could use interest-based bargaining methods and processes for contract negotiation. Given the importance of the issues between the parties and the critical and long-term nature of their relationship, interest-based negotiation methods are optimal, especially in as much as they highlight collaboration and innovation.

Second, the parties also could use interest-based processes for ongoing problem solving and dispute resolution rather than engaging in more traditional adversarial processes. This is not say that some disputes may require grievance arbitration, but it is to say that given the importance of the relationship between labor and management in achieving our mission and purpose, most issues would benefit from resolution through collaborative methods.

Third, a focus on shared interests in matters not necessarily within the scope of bargaining—such as student success, increasing enrollment from underrepresented populations, or streamlining administrative processes and cost reduction—can lead the parties to reach agreements on related matters within the scope of bargaining. These may include market or equity based compensation adjustments for faculty and staff retention, increased flexibility in workload or schedules to increase student access, more streamlined program review processes to enable nimble reallocation of resources, and funding in support of faculty and staff development and collaboration.

Finally, agreement between the parties to exclude certain "academic judgement" issues from the grievance arbitration process may enable those issues to be included in the collective bargaining agreement, whereas if they were subject to grievance arbitration, a more strict adherence to scope of bargaining may preclude their inclusion in the contract.

How About Contemporary Social Justice Issues?

To the extent contemporary social justice issues are not within the scope of bargaining, they are more appropriately addressed through university governance processes or labor management committees with clear scope and purpose. However, to the extent that the issue, or aspects of the issue, is clearly within the scope of bargaining, labor and management can and should address it through negotiation, whether in the contract or in supplemental agreements reached collaboratively through other labor management processes. An example might be how to increase the employment of faculty and staff of color. Clearly, such hiring decisions are the province of management and/or academic decision making, but it may be that the collective bargaining agreement could allow for recruitment incentives such as spousal hire, funding for development, special salary consideration, or workload and schedule adjustment.

How Can Outcomes of the Process Be Evaluated and Measured in Meaningful Ways?

The outcomes of the collective bargaining process can be measured quantitatively and qualitatively. On the quantitative side, examples include the cost of salary and benefits adjustments and productivity effects from changes in workload. We can measure employee turnover as it may be affected terms of the contract. And we can measure the number of issues that arise during the term of the agreement, how many become grievances and how many go onto higher steps of the dispute resolution process. On the qualitative side, surveys, focus groups, and interviews of managers and employees can tell us about morale, attitudes, priorities, successes, concerns, and intention to stay or leave.

What Are Best Practices for Addressing the Most Severe Pressures on Collective Bargaining?

First, clarify the roles and processes most appropriate for the issues between the parties. Then, work only those issues appropriate for the collective bargaining process through that process. Otherwise, it may be overwhelmed by issues that it is not equipped to handle and which are better addressed through other venues, such as the governance process.

Second, separate people from the problem, respect the other side's perspective, be open to solutions not your own, be aware of and guard against such behaviors as confirmation bias and the fundamental attribution error. And when it does get personal, do not take it personally.

Third, keep an eye on the mission, purpose, and educational values of the organization. Ultimately, university labor and management come together to provide a critical social good, advanced educational opportunities for the students and other stakeholders we serve. To this end, I would encourage the parties (jointly or separately) to develop broad, high-level goals and principles for collective bargaining that align with and support those overarching educational values. These goals and principles can serve as criteria for evaluation of options during a negotiation, they can provide a framework for managing expectations of the parties and their constituencies not "at the table," and they keep the parties eyes on how collective bargaining can advance the shared interests of the parties in serving the mission and purpose the organization.

What Impact Has the Pandemic Had on Labor Management Relations This Past Year and Going Forward?

The pandemic has had an amplifying effect on trends well under way in labor management relations in recent years.

For example, it has put increased pressure on the value of nimbleness in our ability quickly to move from face-to-face to on-line education. This required nimbleness may have implications for type of appointment, workload, schedules, faculty and staff training, and other issues in collective bargaining. As well, in response to the major financial impacts of the pandemic, there is heightened pressure to increase instructional productivity, whether through increases in student faculty ratios or through more instructional credit hours. I believe there may be an increased push for alternative forms of credit, competency-based credit for example. While in my view this is an issue for governance, aspects of it may find their way to the bargaining table.

The trend to integrate and increase collaboration among institutions within university systems, already well underway, likely will increase as legislatures, governors, and governing boards respond to cost and performance pressures. This trend will involve critical conversations between institutions and systems, and will require a reassessment of the role of institutional accreditation. And it may well impact collective bargaining.

Finally, in response to issues of social justice and racial inequity, not only are the calls for progress in higher education more compelling than ever before, in part as a result of the pandemic, I believe that our acceptance of the imperative has never been greater. To the extent we make the progress that society demands of us and that only we in higher education can provide, labor and management must work together with clarity in our roles and processes and with a joint commitment to serve our higher purpose. By demonstrating that "we can do it" together, we perform an important leadership to the society we serve.

Jason E. Lane

The Peculiar View from the Deanship: Five Lessons for Navigating the Collective Bargaining Environment and Collaborating to Advance Equity

Introduction

> "Academic administration – as we shall see – is a very peculiar art."

As a dean at a research university within the largest comprehensive system of higher education in the country, I have learned that managing within the labor contract "is a very peculiar art." These words quoted above were written more than 30 years ago by the former Harvard provost Henry Rosovosky reflecting on his 11 years as a dean. They remain relevant today even though Rosovsky wasn't dealing with a collective bargaining environment.

The purpose of this paper is to reflect on the peculiar role of the dean within the labor relations process. Below I set forth six lessons learned to help other mid-level academic leaders navigate the contractual environment and find ways to balance their role of both faculty advocate and contractual enforcer.

The role of the dean is what one might call a boundary spanner – to invoke language from organizational theory. We are both of the faculty and of the administration – though often not fully accepted by either. This can put one in a difficult situation as the job then becomes both to protect, support, and advocate for our faculty and staff as well as ensure that everyone is fulfilling their employment obligations and working to advance the mission and goals of the institution. Being in a unionized environment also means that many of the tools and levers available to administration to carry out these assignments are regulated by the employment contract. In our case, the contract is system wide and I, as dean, have no say in its negotiation; but I do sit on the front-line of how it is enacted.

It is worth noting that I came to the role of the dean from an unusual path. I had been a department chair and I had been a senior leader in the SUNY system. In that latter role, I dealt regularly with issues pertaining to the labor contract – both as a supervisor of professional staff as well supporting campus leaders in dealing with the contract. At one point, I oversaw the appeals process by which someone denied continuing appointment could appeal that decision to the system chancellor for review. The specifics of that process are not relevant for this reflection, but the lessons I learned from those cases very much inform how I approach my work as dean as well as my reflections here.

Background – A Single, Systemwide Contract

We are not the only state system with a contract covering multiple campuses; though ours may cover the most diverse set of institutional missions. This diversity results with a contract that purposefully has a great deal of flexibility and ambiguity in terms of language so to cover the many different working scenarios. It also creates a great deal of standardized language in terms of processes in attempts to ensure equity – though such is not always the case.

SUNY is a system of 64 campuses. Of those, 30 community colleges and five statutory colleges located within private universities are not part of the statewide contract. However, the United University Professions (UUP) represents all faculty and majority of other professional staff across the remaining 29 campuses, which include research universities, regional colleges, technology colleges, two standalone academic medical centers, an optometry school, and a maritime academy. The UUP claims to be the largest higher education union in the country, representing more than 37,000 members in more than 500 different job titles.

Moreover, as with most public bargaining in the state, the contract is negotiated between the governor's office of employee relations (GOER) and the union. While the SUNY system is allowed to provide input of behalf of management, the negotiations are finalized by GOER and then handed over to the system and campuses to implement. There are multiple implications of this approach. First, the UUP contract is one of several contracts with state employees and there has a been a preference to ensure comparability across contracts, at least in terms of regularly negotiated items such as raises and benefits. In fact, once one contract is negotiated, it becomes the template for the remaining contracts.

Second, after the contract is negotiated, the recent process has been to turn the contract over to the campuses to cover the costs – without any corresponding financial support. This means the campus has to find existing resources to cover the negotiated increases in salary. For one of the larger research universities, this amount might equate to around $6 million a year that needs to be covered from new revenues or existing resources. The limitations of this approach are also more poignant during times of fiscal austerity, such as has been the case due to the pandemic. While a campus's leadership and faculty may even agree on the need to postpone salary increases or to implement furloughs as a means to conserve costs and positions, such action is not possible unless it is negotiated at the statewide level by GOER.

Third, the statewide contract covers a diverse array of titles and institutional contexts. This means the contract allows for a great deal of flexibility in terms of work expectations.

Unpacking Equity in Relation to the Contract

The perch on which a dean sits is very different from that of those negotiating from the state level. At that level, one is working to develop a contract that is fair and equitable across multiple settings and role. Overall, this approach allows for flexibility – much more than I have seen in some other contracts – to set the work expectations in relation to the particular needs of the campus or academic unit. As dean, one sees how the implementation of the contract can create unintended inequities.

For example, the process for earning continuing appointment is a fundamental part of the contract. It requires that those being reviewed for continuing appointment to undergo two levels of peer review. However, in our university, not all colleges have academic departments. The result is that faculty in colleges with departments go through three levels of peer review – department, college, and university. Those without departments go through only college and university. The reasons are localized and I've not space here to delve into them; but the result is that some faculty are required to go through more levels of review – and have additional risk of a negative outcome – than others. It also means that faculty in colleges with the additional layer are required to participate in additional service requirements that their colleagues in other units do not.

The benefits of the contract can also create inequities. The contract has many benefits programs provided for faculty, ranging from professional development funding to additional developmental leave for some junior faculty. As resources are finite, these tend to be competitive programs. Often not everyone who applies or is eligible is able to take advantage of the benefit. The intent of the contract is to provide benefits to as many employees across the system as possible. As dean, though, this inevitably leads to having some employees granted additional benefits that others do not receive. This creates an inherent inequity, particularly when the received benefit might provide advantages for receiving promotion and tenure. As dean, one has to also assess whether there were inequities in the system that lead to some receiving the benefits that others did not (e.g., were their structural barriers in place, did one of have a more engaged department chair, was one already overtaxed with extra service burdens and didn't have the time to dedicate to their application).

While it is not within my authority to "fix" the contract; below are lessons I've learned along the way to try to build more collaborative and equitable environments from the decanal perch.

Lesson 1: Lean into, Not Away from, the Contract – But Not Too Much

The contract is neither foe nor friend. It is the rulebook that establishes how the management and labor interact with each other. Some academic leaders fear the union and actively avoid any action that might invoke a negative response; others see the contract as a cudgel to force compliance. My view is to use the contract as a set of guideposts to guide interactions.

My approach is to try to build healthy and effective relationships with my faculty and staff, without reliance on the contract. My work focuses on building teams to advance initiatives and creating a transparent, supportive, and inclusive organizational environment. To the extent possible, I involve department chairs and other faculty leaders in decision making and problem solving. None of this is outlined in the contract; it's based on how I want to act as a leader.

That said, even in the healthiest of organizational cultures, tension arises between management and labor. The role of the academic leader to ensure that those covered by the union contract act appropriately and perform their jobs. Some of this is more minor – assuring compliance with organizational rules such as mandatory trainings and that supervisors conduct annual performance reviews. More difficult situations may pertain to disagreements on work performance or appropriate interpersonal behavior. This is where it becomes important to lean into the contract and follow the appropriate process for addressing these tensions.

The contract does lay out requirements, such as how and when employees should be reviewed and granted permanent appointment or how work expectations can be adjusted. Those processes need to be honored. Within the process, though, you have an option about how to structure reviews – is it based on mutual respect and employee improvement or is it more punitive and focused on pointing out mistakes? How you approach this work can have repercussions for the overall organizational environment and, again, it is up to you as to your approach in implementing the contract requirements.

The takeaway here is to have a vision for how you want your organizational culture and employee interactions to look like and then work within the guideposts established by the contract to make that happen. To the extent needed, lean on the contract to carry out work; but don't the let the contract dictate who you are as a leader.

Lesson 2: Deal with Bad Behavior As Soon As Possible – and Be Prepared

As someone who has spent his professional career training leaders, I can state with a high degree of certainty that one of the roles that most academic leaders like least is dealing with bad behavior of employees. It can be uncomfortable, difficult, and awkward. However, to not deal with such behavior is unfair to other employees, can foster a toxic environment, and sends a signal to others that such behavior is acceptable. Plus, it's our job to address these issues.

Bad behavior can come in many forms from bullying to not showing up for their job. In many cases, academic leaders inherit bad behavior – often because previous leaders were unwilling to address it. One of the first things that anyone will tell you is to document the behavior in writing and keep it in a file. When I became dean, people came to me with requests to deal with problematic individuals. I immediately asked if there was a documented record. People could tell me many specific incidents that were problematic, but none of it had been officially documented. That meant we had to start from scratch, and I asked the appropriate individuals to start the documentation trail.

Once there is documentation, one then has to work through the process. This often starts with a conversation with the employee – raising the concerns and providing an opportunity to discuss the issues. If the behavior does not correct itself, then you can put the concerns in writing and direct the individual to take corrective action, which may range from stopping bullying to attending teaching seminars (if there are concerns about poor teaching). At the end of the process, and if the behaviors do not change, then one might proceed to suspension or termination. This is an oversimplification of an often lengthy process – which is why it's important to start as soon as possible. Fortunately, many times these situations are able to be resolved with a discussion or a written warning.

However, it is important to be prepared and to have a game plan worked out with HR well ahead of time. In order to be in compliance with the contract, there are things that you can and can't say at each stage of the process – and there are things that need to be said or written in order to allow you to advance to the next stage of corrective action. The employee may also be well prepared in terms of what his/her rights and responsibilities are under the contract and in many cases they might try to invoke the contract or threaten retaliation (often forbidden by the contract). Have a game plan and stick to it. Keep it cordial and to the point. Do not allow yourself to become flustered. Preparation is key.

Lesson 3: Make the Employee-Relations Specialist Your Friend

One of the most important lessons I have learned is that folks in Human Resources (HR), particularly the employee-relations specialists, are among your most important resources. Any academic leader, particularly those new in the role, should take the time to build working relationships with the HR office. These are the individuals who know the contract and work regularly with contract-related situations across the campus.

As soon as I know that I might have to take an action related to the contract, I immediately inform our employee-relations specialist. I explain the situation as best I can and my hopeful outcome. She typically has lots of questions and helps me think through different scenarios for resolution. What is most helpful is that I become more aware of what degrees of freedom I have to deal with the situation and what actions might violate the contract. As the situation changes, I keep the specialist appraised of those changes.

What I have learned is that it is better to reach out and early and that I typically have more freedom to act within the contract than I had guessed. When I first became dean, I was handed an HR review of one of my academic departments. That review detailed some hostile behaviors in the department, some of which had been in place for many, many years. I knew that I had to address the situation, but I didn't know how best to do that within the confines of the contract. HR walked me through the process, including what had to be documented and said. The conversation with the faculty members wasn't pleasant, but it was easier because I had a game plan approved by HR.

I also learned it's better to bring HR into the situation as early as possible. In another situation, I had been planning to non-renew an employee due to per- formance reasons. I reached out to HR to talk through the situation. However, before the non-renewal could happen, the employee filed for a leave of absence based on health reasons. My immediate reaction was that I might now be impeded because it could be argued I was non-renewing because of the health issue, which was not at all the case. I called HR and was reassured that we should move forward as we had planned; and HR noted that, in part, they were comfortable with moving forward with non-renew as I had disclosed to them the plan well before the health issue entered into the situation.

Few academic leaders enjoy the crucial conversations that have to be had with underperforming or badly behaving employees. Working in collaboration with HR can make these situations less stressful and help ensure that you approach in a way that honors the processes in the contract.

Lesson 4: Flexibility and (in)Equity in Workload

The contract allows for a great deal of flexibility in terms of workload assign- ments. For professional staff, there is a performance plan that is supposed to be updated annually that defines the work expectations of the individual. That does not exist for faculty, at least within my institution. While the appointment letter sets forth minimum expectations, there is a broad understanding that faculty are supposed to contribute in the areas of research, teaching, and service.

For us, as a research university with significant focus on graduate education, the standard teaching load is two courses a semester. However, over the years, the expectations in the other two areas have not been as clear and there has developed a great deal of inequity in terms of workload – while everyone tea- ches two courses, the size of those courses may vary significantly and what individuals do in the areas of service and research may also vary a great deal.

The result is that some faculty may retreat almost entirely from research and service. Others carry significant service loads necessitated by lack of engagement by those focused more on their research.

Because the contract did not require annual reviews of faculty, they were not done. Some indicated it was because the contract did not allow for it. While it was not required, it was also not forbidden. In talking with other Deans, I learned that other colleges within the University had established workload expectations and were conducting annual reviews – these were the norms I was used to at other institutions. One of the examples I learned of was that each faculty member is assumed to have six buckets of work to be allocated each semester. One of those buckets may be filled by teaching a course. Another based on producing a certain amount of research or engaging in a certain amount of service. What defines workload in each bucket was determined in collaboration between the faculty and the dean and then enforced by the department chairs. Thus, if someone is not fulfilling their research expectations over a period of time, the chair can reallocate that bucket for the faculty member to pick up an extra course. Or if the professor is carrying an extra-large set of service responsibilities, they might receive a course reduction.

Workload for faculty, who are often highly professionalized and autonomous in their work, can be difficult to manage on a day-to-day basis. However, this can also create significant inequities in terms of workload. It is important that academic leaders work with their faculty to set flexible, yet standard, work expectations for their units as a means to both set community standards and to allow academic leaders more objective processes for shifting and redistributing workloads when necessary.

Lesson 5: Honoring the Intent of the Contract

Over the years, a number of benefits have been built into the contract – from sabbaticals to developmental leaves to pools of funding for various forms of professional developments. These benefits are intended to support the career development of faculty, though they do not always come in equitable ways.

As mentioned previously, our contract provides a program that allows pre-tenured faculty, particularly from underrepresented communities, the opportunity to take a full-semester of paid leave to focus on their research in order to strengthen their case for tenure and promotion (what the contract refers to as continuing appointment). The program also provides funding for adjuncts to cover courses and some research funding. This is a competitive program as the resources are limited. So, while anyone can apply for the program, only a few are selected. As a dean, this then means that it is not uncommon to have some junior faculty who have received an extra semester of leave to work on research while others do not. Hardly an equitable situation.

As Dean, one then has a decision to try to honor the intent of the program and support all qualified junior faculty to take advantage of such a leave. While it's not required that we support the leave; it's also not forbidden. One then has a choice. I, as my predecessors, have opted to find ways to allow those individuals who were not selected for the program to have a similar benefit. We try to mirror the program as best we can both in terms of establishing expectations for how the leave would be used and for granting faculty leave from many of their typical responsibilities. Our ability to do this is, of course, constrained by our own resources, but the intent is to try to be equitable to all junior faculty.

Conclusion

Deaning within an academic labor contract is a very peculiar art. Determine the type of leader you want to be and the type of organizational culture that you want to foster. Then, work within the guideposts of the contract to realize that vision. Those guideposts may create some restrictions, but they also will create some opportunities – and protections for both you and the employee. Do not let the contract stop you from being collaborative and striving to creating equitable and more inclusive environments. My best advice, might be to leave you with the serenity prayer:

> Grant me the serenity to accept the things I cannot change, courage to change the things I can, and wisdom to know the difference.

Barbara A. Lee

Reflections from Three Sides

As a graduate student studying higher education administration, I became fascinated with the notion of faculty unions and devoted much of my early scholarly work to examining issues related to unions' impact on "traditional" governance mechanisms, the nature of faculty work and its implications for collective bargaining, and the effect of the Supreme Court's *Yeshiva University* decision on faculty bargaining in the private sector. In those days, and for the decades up to 2015, I had no intimation that I would be part of a small team managing negotiation strategy for my university in its bargaining with the faculty union that had represented me for 33 years.

State support for higher education has declined over the past two decades, and federal funding has increasingly been targeted at specific federal priorities (such as scientific research, veterans' benefits, and student financial aid). As a result, colleges in both the public and private sectors have felt considerable pressure on their operating budgets, since personnel costs represent the largest share of a college's expenditures. For unionized institutions of higher education, these budget pressures are especially difficult because agreements with their unions, particularly faculty unions, limit their flexibility in cutting the cost of faculty, primarily tenured and tenure track faculty. And although it is not unusual for negotiations over compensation to be the most difficult part of the collective bargaining process, especially in times of financial stringency, the gap between the perceived interests of unions and management appears to be largest when compensation is on the table.

Given these long-standing pressures on institutional budgets, it is not surprising that management would resist the attempts of unions to enlarge the scope of bargaining to include matters promoting "the common good." This resistance in many cases paints academic administrators into an uncomfortable corner—many of us chose academic careers because we feel a strong commitment to social justice and equity, in addition to collegial and collaborative planning and decision-making. And it is unlikely that the faculty union negotiators will be willing to trade gains in matters of the "common good" for reductions in faculty compensation.

The uncomfortable position that administrators face if the institution lacks the resources to implement even a few of the "common good" demands is exacerbated if the historical relationship between the faculty union and the administration is one of mutual distrust. A union's perception (which is sometimes well founded) that the administration has broken promises in the past, or has ignored well-meaning and genuine offers to advise and/or collaborate with the administration in planning for difficult circumstances (such as the institution's response to the COVID-19 pandemic), makes bargaining and contract administration even more complicated and divisive. And because the administration is limited in its ability to communicate directly with faculty about negotiations issues (given its need to avoid charges of "direct dealing" with the faculty), this lack of communication can convince members of the faculty bargaining unit that the union's ad hominem attacks (for example, on the "bloated" administrative salaries or perks) and theatrics (demonstrations outside the president's house) are justified.

In light of what on many unionized campuses is an environment of distrust and mutual denigration between the union and administrators, how do the parties collaborate to plan for the unexpected and the devastating, such as the pandemic that hit the U.S. generally and its higher education sector in particular in 2020? How do they retain a focus on shared goals of equity and social justice while facing financial and social challenges that the unexpected and devastating events seem to be exacerbating? Can the parties reboot their relationship?

Below is an incomplete list of strategies that administrators could employ to move toward repairing the relationship, at least during the difficult years of responding to the effects of the pandemic on individual employees and students, the institution's budget, the strategic plans that had to be shelved or modified, and in some cases, the institution's leadership.

Identify and agree with the union on common goals and values. A process of mutual gains bargaining may help the parties frame the issues in ways that allow for a more collaborative approach to negotiations.

Focus on academic values and student success as part of the common goals and values;

Admit past bad behavior by both sides.

Provide transparency with respect to the institution's budget and sources of funding (such as unrestricted reserves); be clear about the limitations the institution faces in using unrestricted endowment or reserve funds and provide examples of how reserve funds are used (for example, for faculty research accounts or startup funding).

Ensure that deans and chairs (if not in the bargaining unit) are consulted about union demands and management responses before agreements are finalized. Management negotiators, particularly those with limited experience in higher education or a lack of appreciation for academic values may not be sensitive to nuances that would concern deans and chairs and that could complicate their relationships with faculty.

If union negotiators are inexperienced, make sure that the management team has both labor negotiation expertise and members with appreciation for academic values.

Colleges and universities are facing greater financial pressure due to the impact of coronavirus and limited public funding for higher education at the same moment that the push for the "common good" is gaining momentum. The social, economic and political fallout from the pandemic has added yet another layer of issues that will very likely be raised at the bargaining table. These issues compete with the institutions' real need to use its resources responsibly and to focus on student learning and student and faculty retention. I cannot think of another time, since the initiation of academic collective bargaining, when the job of leaders on both sides of the bargaining table has been more difficult or more challenging.

Higher education is facing a tectonic shift in public confidence in the efficacy of higher education to provide upward mobility for first generation students (and even for those whose parents are college-educated). Traditional methods of delivering instruction are being questioned as technology has provided some alternatives to in-person teaching and learning, although many question whether instruction delivered remotely provides a quality learning experience. The cost of postsecondary education and student loan indebtedness will continue to factor into family decisions about whether and how to pay for their children's postsecondary education, particularly as the U.S. recovers from the harsh economic and social impact of the pandemic. These challenges suggest that both sides will need to commit to working collaboratively toward solutions that neither side will find ideal. Compromise—always an issue in negotiations—will be even more necessary in order to complete the bargaining process. It is quite likely that leaders on both sides of the bargaining table will face criticism from their constituents as they work toward resolution of what, at this time, seems like a deluge of intractable problems.

Terrence MacTaggart and Tracy Bigney

Advice to Presidents New to Unions and Collective Bargaining

"Everyone has a right to gripe, and the union protects them if you don't like what they say" are the words of a union custodian spoken to a first-time president early in his career. These words provide a pithy introduction to the importance of union protections in the minds of employees as well as a reminder of the limitations on presidential authority. Any president new to the world of organized labor should take them to heart.

Unionization across higher education is on an upswing. According to a recent report from the National Center for the Study of Collective Bargaining in Higher Education at Hunter College in the City University of New York. Between 2013 and 2019, 118 new faculty bargaining units formed at private and public institutions.

This article is intended to guide college and university presidents and trustees who come to their posts with little experience with unions and collective bargaining in higher education. MacTaggart has served as a senior then chief executive of universities and systems of public universities, all of which featured strong unions and collective bargaining. Bigney is an experienced HR professional and labor negotiator whose contributions to this piece will help chief executives work more effectively with their HR and labor relations (LR) team members.

These recommendations draw from our combined 50 years of working with public sector unionized employees of colleges, universities, and statewide systems of higher education. During that time, we have dealt with 30 different bargaining units at different institutions, participated on numerous bargaining teams, endured innumerable bargaining sessions, managed through several strikes, observed several faculty-originated no confidence votes and heard a fair number of grievances. We have also calmly paced through gauntlets of angry union members chanting and waving banners proclaiming managements' many injustices.

We came to respect most of the union leaders we worked with, admire (sometimes grudgingly) their skill in engaging the media on their behalf, engineered several "behind the scenes" accommodations that helped settle contracts, and partnered with union leaders in advocating for state financial support. We found that a problem-solving approach to union relationships works best in and outside negotiations.

Here we offer advice to presidents (and board members) beginning a relationship with higher education unions and collective bargaining.

1. Recognize that the faculty union exists to protect and advance the "wages and working conditions" of its members. Faculty unions should not be categorically vilified as uninterested in academic quality or values, but nor should they be confused with a traditional community of scholars. Union leaders view shared governance through a union lens with the practical interests of the members firmly in mind.

2. Appreciate the value union members place on the association's protections and advocacy. Jobs for faculty and staff alike were threatened well before the pandemic and have become even more at risk since the advent of COVID-19. Furloughs, layoffs, givebacks, and other job losses due to mergers, acquisitions and going out of business are painful realities. Most members know that their unions cannot prevent these dire events, but they expect the union to slow them down and ameliorate their impact on lives and livelihoods.

3. Take steps early to learn the basic legalities of collective bargaining, contract administration, and the history and tenor of relations with unions at your institution. Much of this information can come from your institution's HR/LR professionals. Consider a workshop offered by one of the university-based centers for the study of collective bargaining. We gained much from workshops offered by the City University of New York's National Center for the Study of Collective Bargaining in Higher Education and the Professions.

4. Strive to create a respectful, cordial and trusting relationship with union leaders and members. Benefits include a more positive approach to solving grievances and mutual problems as well as the possibility of opening back channels of communications. However, do not be so naïve as to expect your relationship to trump their first loyalty to the priorities of their members. One president who mistook a smile and a handshake for trust was taken aback at the lack of forewarning of a no-confidence vote.

5. Make sure that you as president and your board share the same philosophy about bargaining and how employees and their representatives will be treated. Board members with LR experience may help their fellow trustees appreciate the realities of collecting bargaining but recognize that their experience may come from other industries not especially relevant to higher education. By the same token, take steps with your board chair to limit the influence of trustees who lack constructive experience but have no shortage of misplaced opinions.

6. Be alert to anti-union bias especially if it is vociferously expressed by senior staff even in supposedly confidential meetings. Demeaning the union and its members is a bad idea that will not remain secret for long. Anger begets anger, while respect may beget respect. Tolerating negative

attitudes and speech that fuels an adversarial relationship is unprofessional and undercuts trust in the president and the board.

7. On a more positive note, take steps to ensure that your HR/LR professionals get the "big picture" of university goals and not just the specific objectives for a bargaining session. This will help ensure creativity at the bargaining table.

8. Presidents and trustees are well advised to maintain some distance from union negotiations, grievance administration and the like. In at least one state, a seat on the board is informally reserved for a representative of the AFL-CIO. Even in this case, that trustee typically keeps her or his distance from day-to-day union relations. Off-stage the president needs to deeply engage in deciding key issues like compensation, management and union rights, and the general tenor of negotiations. A board committee should confirm the boundaries for concessions and major changes, and ultimately approve the contract agreement.

9. Take care to strike the right balance between showing interest in negotiations while maintaining distance from day-to-day processes and issues. At critical times, be prepared to step in to help break an impasse. Choreograph your actions with your HR/LR team. However, beware of getting too involved with the union directly as this could easily reduce or destroy the credibility of your HR/LR team. Otherwise, before long the union will be coming to you directly to solve their problems.

10. Find legitimate means to disseminate accurate information to members, the larger academic community, and the media especially if the union distorts your positions. Labor law designates the union as the members' official representative to management. Because the members can influence the actions of union leaders and negotiators, it is important that they receive accurate, balanced information on, for example, the fiscal realities of the institution and management's proposals. Consult your staff on legitimate ways to offer accurate counterpoints. Delaying steps to correct lies and distortion in the hope that blatant misrepresentation to the members would somehow correct itself is always a mistake.

11. If the president receives a no-confidence vote from the union members or its leadership, boards should avoid extreme reactions. In most circumstances, the board should neither quickly dismiss the vote as the action of disgruntled employees nor treat it as a legitimate indictment of presidential performance. Instead, a review of the circumstances surrounding the vote by an objective outsider will clarify the motives behind the vote and provide options for the board to consider. Increasingly votes of no confidence are a consequence of faculty dismay over unpopular but necessary decisions. In these instances, the board should express its confidence in the chief executive and confirm its support. MacTaggart's article "What Confidence Should Boards Give No-Confidence Votes," Trusteeship, November/December 2012 offers a primer on dealing with these situations.

12. Where a higher education system negotiates for several institutions, campus presidents should seek to participate in negotiations planning and serve on negotiation teams. An advantage for presidents operating within a system is that they are not placed in direct conflict with the desires of campus union members. On the other hand, the president in these situations has less control over the outcome of negotiations. Systems may be more influenced by political considerations or other factors than the needs of the campus. Well-functioning systems listen carefully to their campus heads in defining the goals of negotiations and invite campus presidents to participate on negotiating teams.

13. If you are charged, as a system head or HR vice-president for example, with overseeing the appointment of negotiating teams, be sure to include academic, finance, student affairs and other frontline professionals. You will be contributing to their leadership development. A diverse team is often a more creative one when it comes to solving complex dilemmas.

14. The impact of the COVID-19 crisis calls for rethinking relationships with higher education unions. It seems certain at this writing that college and university revenues will decline further, faculty work will need to adjust to digital formats, and traditional academic programs will be reduced or eliminated as new ones are developed. The need for non-academic staff will likely decline as well. These changes and more will further stress the lives of employees and the unions that represent them. Throughout this difficult time, remember that negotiating is a give and take process. Especially when creative solutions are needed more than ever, sticking to narrow, inflexible parameters will limit the room needed to reach agreement.

15. One consequence of these disruptions could well be more intensely adversarial relationships. No-confidence votes triggered by faculty and staff reductions, and the way the cuts were selected and communicated, appear to be on the rise. However, skillful presidents with the good fortune to work with far-sighted union leaders may be able to avoid unnecessary conflict, provide safer landings for their academic colleagues and cow-orkers, and secure a brighter future for their institutions through more productive relationships with their unions. Engaging with the union in discussions of strategic directions including the hard choices, being fully transparent about the fiscal realities, and committing to open dialogue prior to making decisions that affect the lives of union members are pre-scriptions for a more successful relationship.

Patricia A. Prelock

As I consider my experience as a faculty member, a department chair, a dean and now a provost I appreciate the opportunity to reflect on the role of a union in higher education. My reflection begins, however, with a growing concern regarding the role of collective bargaining in higher education. I experience faculty as scholars—distinguished academics in a particular field of study—who work tirelessly to impart knowledge to young minds so that they might think, create and problem solve. Scholars also create new knowledge or works of art so that humanity might benefit. It is a calling with accountability as a thought leader and innovator. You continue to think, question, create and offer solutions to the world's problems. It is an honored position with great responsibility. My understanding of faculty unions is at odds with what it means to be a professor in higher education.

It is critical, however, to recognize that faculty have a crucial role in the institution that supports their success as scholars. That usually transpires through shared governance which ensures faculty have an opportunity to participate in policy development and decision making that impacts the institution. Can you have shared governance (i.e., Faculty Senate) and collective bargaining (i.e., a faculty union) on the same campus? The obvious answer is yes but the more difficult question is how does that work? Who is responsible for what and what should be bargained versus what should be part of the long history of shared governance through faculty committees in institutions of higher education?

Initially, faculty unions formed to address the challenges faculty felt in university affairs, concerns about faculty salaries and violations of academic freedom. A new approach emerged in the 1960s when institutions were experiencing economic retrenchment and its effects on salaries and working conditions. The concept of collective bargaining took hold and what evolved is a focus on salary, terms and conditions of the work environment, faculty governance (somewhat at odds with in-place shared governance models in higher education institutions), and protections for academic freedom and tenure. Importantly, unions have demanded more explicit criteria for tenure and promotion.

The American Association of University Professors (AAUP) identified freedom to teach, to engage in research, and to pursue the full rights of citizenship as core to the work of the university professor. Academic freedom is the ability to discuss, analyze, critique and debate institutional operations. Faculty believe that to educate their students, they are free to use their expertise in the classroom, defining the curriculum and to ask unpopular questions, challenge accepted beliefs, and not be punished for offending stakeholders. I suspect, whether we are talking about faculty unions or shared governance they are looking for engagement, being supported to do their job, having strong mentors and role models, and being successful in their position.

As I have learned to live and thrive in the higher education world for more than 35 years, with and without a union, and sitting at the bargaining table, I hope my reflections are helpful to those of you who will continue this challenging work with an ultimately laudable goal—providing an environment in which faculty can thrive and contribute to the common good.

I will be sharing my perspective in five key areas: 1) impact of bargaining on the provost's role; 2) what you should know about academic affairs when bargaining; 3) what collective bargaining might look like in the future; 4) how to balance labor negotiations with the institution's strategic goals in the context of both internal and external factors in higher education; and, finally 5) ways to encourage collaboration, equity and social justice.

Impact of Bargaining on the Provost's Role

Although bargaining is designed to support positive working conditions and fair salaries and benefits, decisions can both enhance and constrain the work of the Provost to lead and manage. The benefit of effective bargaining can lead to outlining clear expectations for faculty in the areas of teaching, research and service that are fair and equitable, and consistent with faculty rank. This supports the Provost's office in ensuring there is a fair process for examining the contributions of all faculty. There are two challenges, however, that should be considered when negotiating the language in union contracts. First, it is difficult to reward faculty for outstanding performance when constrained by specific contract language. Contract language often limits flexibility and has implications for a Provost's ability to retain faculty. Second, contract language creates challenges in adjusting workload based on need and performance. So, it is important that consideration is given to management about when and how workload adjustments can be made.

What About Academic Affairs When Bargaining?

It is important that there is a clear understanding of the culture of the higher education organization within which you are working. Understanding the relationship between faculty and the administration will help negotiation. Several questions should guide the bargaining process. What is working and what is not working that has impacted that relationship? How is communication established? What do the parties see as their respective roles in shared governance? The background and disciplines of the negotiating team on the faculty side are also critical to understand as their priorities may or may not be the goals of the larger faculty body. Often the requests made can have unanticipated consequences affecting other faculty across the university. It is important to talk with the Provost's Office and the Deans of colleges and schools to determine the broader impact of proposals that they bring to the table. The administrative side of the bargaining team should be clear on the boundaries for faculty decision making that relate to administrative structure and delivering the educational product students expect. Finally, the underlying financial situation of the institution is a reality that bargaining teams must understand and consider— including how the institution is aligned financially among its peers.

Future of Collective Bargaining

Higher education is changing and will require greater flexibility in moving forward. With growing student debt and greater expectations for return on investment, institutions of higher education will be expected to provide not only a high-quality education but an education that is affordable and accessible. In addition, higher education must demonstrate that its graduates are prepared for a career, whether it is providing a strong liberal arts background with transferrable skills or a professional degree. Further, institutions of higher education must establish their value in preparing a diverse workforce who will be engaged citizens. Faculty unions will need to have a shared understanding of the current state of higher education. This requires faculty to recognize that the status quo is no longer an option. Adjustments in workload expectations, changes in instructional modalities and innovative academic offerings responsive to market demands will be an expectation.

Balancing Labor Negotiations with the Strategic Goals of the Institution

To be responsive to the internal and external factors that will determine the operational realities in higher education, it is important to assess how the administration and faculty define and implement shared governance as an institution. As described earlier, institutions should clarify the role of a faculty union, which usually ensures fair working conditions, salaries and benefits whereas the faculty senate determines the curriculum and provides advice to administration on policies, structure, finance and institutional direction. Ultimately, there are shared goals for faculty and the administration. Both are committed to hiring high-quality faculty, who are compensated appropriately for the work they do. Both wish to retain these faculty and support their ability to thrive as scholars. And both recognize their responsibility to provide a high-quality education for students that is affordable and accessible. The expected balance is creating reasonable work expectations while meeting the institution's strategic priorities and not sacrificing what it means to be a scholar.

Encourage Collaboration, Equity and Social Justice

Most would agree that collaboration among faculty and the administration leads to meaningful results. Unfortunately, competing goals make that difficult to attain during union negotiations. It takes skill to weigh both the individual and collective needs of a body. There are shared goals, however, held by both the administration and the faculty. First, the recruitment and retention of faculty and students is everyone's business. Second, institutions must not lose sight of its primary role in educating students and creating new knowledge. Third, we must remember the principles upon which institutions of higher education were founded, that is, the ability to debate issues important to society, offer diverse perspectives in responding to those issues, and doing so in the context of civil discourse. Finally, as institutions of higher education emphasize the cultural, economic and social inequalities so often discussed inside and outside the classroom, there must be real actions that commit to supporting students and faculty who have had different economic resources to ensure their academic success on campus.

Summary

The state of shared governance on college and university campuses clearly has it challenges with faculty complaining that administrators are more concerned with budgets than with quality. Administrators are frustrated by the failure of faculty to realize the fiscal realities facing higher education (Rosenberg, 2014). I believe, however, that most faculty and administrators have a shared desire to provide a rich educational environment in which teaching and learning, knowledge creation and engagement occurs at a high level. Clearly, higher education's economic model is under scrutiny from students, their families, governmental officials and the larger community and with the stakes so high, the cost of inaction puts institutions of higher education at risk.

Rosenberg (2014) suggests a common role for faculty in shared governance is the "design, oversight, and teaching of the curriculum" while "co-curricular programming, student life, and, spending institutional dollars" are typically administrative responsibilities. This is a missed opportunity where deeper collaborations might be possible if faculty and administrators could find a way to share responsibility across these activities, knowing that both will have to find their way to timely decision making. This will require faculty to think with a more institutional lens and administrators to think with a more educational lens. Important decisions will require representation by faculty and administrators but should not force administrators to completely yield to faculty demands.

References

Rosenberg, B. (2014, July). Shared or divided governance. *Inside Higher Education.*

18

REFLECTIONS FROM EMPLOYEE/ UNION ADVOCATES

Ernst Benjamin, Wassim Garzouzi, Bill Lyne, Michael Mauer, Derryn Moten, Scott L. Pratt and Eve Weinbaum

Ernst Benjamin

The accelerated growth of campus academic collective bargaining in the 1970s occurred in response to the impact of the accelerated growth in enrollments and consequent demands for faculty and academic staff at that time. I participated as a union activist, chief negotiator, chapter president and national caucus chair. Faculty and staff, especially in expanding public universities but also in many private universities and colleges, sought to leverage their heightened market opportunities, not only to improve their individual conditions of employment but, through unionization, the terms and conditions of university and college employment generally. Now, a long-term decline in public financial support for higher education and a gradual shift of university resources towards administrators and non-academic personnel have reversed the process and eroded the bargaining position and terms of employment of most academic employees.

For faculty, the long-term erosion has been less evident in the inflation adjusted salaries of those fortunate enough to hold full-time tenure-track positions than in the dramatic decline in the proportion of such positions and the accelerated growth of full-time non-tenure-track, part-time and graduate assistant positions. These less costly positions are generally not only less well paid but provide less professional protection and support. The economic constraints also weaken the position of academic unions at a time when their protections are most needed and unions had in some cases been able to secure job and professional protections and support to previously unprotected faculty and staff.

DOI: 10.4324/9781003138990-21

The diminished protection of professional standards has weakened the academic institutions that increasing rely on a casual workforce who receive less support for their academic functions and often suffer chronic insecurity that has to erode professional attraction to and performance in their positions. The crisis of the pandemic, with all the attendant costs and pressures on university administrators and managers, is likely to worsen this erosion and intensify the difficulty of collective bargaining as both sides are under increasing pressure and diminishing resources. Lose-lose is all too likely to replace win-win.

Collective bargaining can serve as a problem-solving response. Nor need the parties necessarily re-invent the wheel even in these changed circumstances. Of course, some non-academic campus unions such as operating engineers and building trades may already have contracts closely drawn to the specifications of the locally prevailing terms and conditions, possibly prevailing wages of similar local employees in non-collegiate firms and institutions. In these circumstances there may be little room for bargaining although the maintenance of prevailing terms and conditions may also lead to lay-offs and reductions in staff that both parties wish to avoid. Therefore, it may be possible to discuss temporary departures from the norm where circumstances are jointly perceived to require them. On the other hand, the contracts for academic employees, as well as some non-academic employees such as cafeteria workers, custodial staff, and campus police are less constrained by ties to non-campus locals and more adaptable. I will mention one non-academic issue presently of concern to students as well as the larger community, with which I had prior experience, when the campus administration requested and our union coalition agreed to support their decision to deny to campus police the powerful long guns that they sought to negotiate for their campus patrol cars. Campus administrators, supported by the university community, may be able to negotiate and instill good practices in campus policing not always possible in the larger community. This might lead students to support, rather than oppose, as they have in some recent instances, campus policing. More generally, in view of the difficulties created by efforts to re-open campuses put at risk by the pandemic, it is in the interest of academic employees that bargaining with non-academic employees focus not only on economic issues and job security but on ensuring adequate health and safety practices and essential employee protections.

Academic employee contracts – including full-time tenure-track and non-tenure track, part-time faculty, graduate assistants and academic and administrative staff – though they may be similar to contracts in other institutions, and even based on national recommendations such as those of the AAUP, are generally less constrained than those such as the operating engineers and the trades. Comprehensive consideration of the range and variety of possibilities required that my co-editor Michael Mauer and I assemble a 400-page collection of essays outlining recommended practices and policies in our book *Academic Collective Bargaining* (AAUP/MLA, 2006), which contains much more than I can even summarize here. But it is fundamental to understand that some academic agreements markedly accord more closely with sound academic practices and professional standards than others. So, negotiators should certainly consult such essay collections but especially review the numerous contracts accessible in union and management data bases or posted online to seek out the most applicable and desirable with a view to the characteristics and needs of their specific institutions whenever formulating or considering new or revised contract language proposals. Since I have not space to conduct such a review here, I will focus here on a few general issues that seem to me particularly important in the present circumstances.

Overall, though the potential variations among academic agreements may provide greater opportunity for problem-solving in this difficult period, they may also tempt administrations to seek to impose terms and conditions that may foster disruptive union responses and/or further the decline in support for professional standards and quality. On the other hand, the unique circumstances of academic bargaining may offer the opportunity for more constructive approaches. The tradition of shared governance, for example, offers an established mechanism to explore controversial issues through joint committees of academic administrators and faculty as well as other academic staff. Such joint committees might conduct a shared exploration of the true extent and causes of budgetary short-falls, shifts in the need to deter or reverse enrollment declines, the rationale for the growth in non-academic or administrative positions, and other similarly controversial issues that are perhaps neither mandatory, or in some matters, even permissive subjects of negotiation. More traditional joint labor/management committees may also be usefully agreed upon to explore and seek to resolve, in a less adversarial setting than the negotiating table, those issues of salaries and other terms of employment that are clearly within the bounds of mandatory or permissive bargaining.

More particularly, the current pandemic has fostered an unplanned, erratically implemented, vastly increased reliance on distance learning. It seems likely that, despite the obvious discontent of many students and some faculty which should lead to a substantial return to campus instruction, greater use of distance instruction is likely to continue. Administrations may find cost-saving advantages in the opportunity to further increase part-time staff and to re-use canned lectures. Some faculty may prefer not to commute as often. Some students may prefer to set their own schedules or simply to avoid class attendance though I think most already miss direct interaction with faculty and other students. As the once Director of a Weekend College and a Dean of Lifelong Learning responsible for a TV-based adult distance learning 4-year degree program back in the early 1980s, I offer some informed cautions. First, it is very important to provide a discussion component to enable students and faculty to interact. Zoom may help but it still falls short of actual student–faculty interaction – which we provided by including an on-campus weekly small group discussion component in the evening and an opportunity for on campus lecture and discussion on a few weekends. Even so, there remain problems of providing the learning opportunities afforded by the more frequent customary classroom lecture-discussions. Faculty may understandably seek to ensure adequate classroom time as appropriate to the subject matter. They will and certainly should seek to negotiate individual or collectively bargained intellectual property protections against misuse or unlimited re-use or misappropriation of their lectures. So, I suggest again that these and similar educational issues may be better discussed in non-adversarial joint committees of academic and academic administrators. Contract negotiations may, however, be an appropriate place to establish the role and composition of such committees or even to formalize their roles and such recommendations as may be mutually agreed upon.

Above all, I think we need to recognize that the pandemic, following upon an era of increasing economic constraints, threatens to permanently diminish the quality of American higher education by limiting the opportunity for full-time scholarly teaching and learning to a very select few – not unlike the shape of higher education before the expansion of educational and professional quality as well as opportunity in the 1960s and 1970s. We need to find ways to sustain more full-time, long-term professionally supported academic positions and make them available to educate more full-time, fully involved students. If we in the academic community do not keep this goal centrally in mind, even when engaged in the difficulties of managing and negotiating in a prolonged period of financial constraints and increasing responsibilities, then no one else will.

I do not say this only to the academic administrators that I and academic unions call upon to protect and enhance the policies and budgetary priorities that sustain faculty quality and professionalism in teaching and research. I say it also to the faculty unions which need to organize and negotiate not only with a view to sustaining and improving support not only for the most fortunate few full-time faculty in research universities and elite colleges but to organize and negotiate with a view to extending appropriate professional terms and conditions broadly to all who conduct teaching and research in higher education. The emergence of separate part-time-faculty, graduate assistant and full-time faculty and academic staff unions has complicated this effort since it will not be necessarily in the interest of part-time unions to encourage a shift to increased reliance on full-time faculty. But it should be in the mutual interest of the unions and institutions, as well as the profession and the academy as a whole, to negotiate appropriate professional support as well as better salaries and essential fringe benefits for all faculty and academic staff. Reasonable job protections as well as pro-rata contributions to medical and retirement plans maintained by the institutions and/or offered by the unions themselves will benefit not only these faculty and staff but also the academic profession and the students and academic institutions they serve.

Wassim Garzouzi

Collective Bargaining in Higher Education: Debunking the Myth of Academic Exceptionalism

A well-known outcome of union certification is the sudden re-set of the existing employer–employee relationship. All at once, the paradigm of the "master and servant" relationship is replaced with—at least, in theory—an "equal parties" paradigm, where the terms and conditions of employment are negotiated from positions of relative equality. Through this process, Union representatives engage with the Employer on behalf of the collective, obviating the need for employees to plead their cases individually. Equality, collectivity, and representation, are the core values of unionism.

Equality, collectivity, and representation, are also key principles engrained within academia. Faculty seldom think of themselves as subordinate workers, but rather, as partners within their academic institutions. Principles of academic freedom provide additional independence from the traditional employer–employee relationship, while collegial governance typically means Faculty have a literal seat at the table.

Despite these common values, the parties to bargaining in higher education often consider themselves to be operating in an environment that is distinct from the typical unionized workplace. The word "association" is deemed by many Faculty to be preferable to "union." Many professionals who teach at Universities and Colleges, such as lawyers, engineers, and doctors, are excluded from labour relations statutes in their professional capacities and bring this experience with them when they become instructors.

At the same time, the Employer typically views unionism as separate from, and often at odds with, collegial governance. After all, issues of promotions and tenure are reviewed by independent peers, as are decisions impacting different departments, through Senates and other governing bodies. The notion of unionism in an academic setting is sometimes deemed offensive, changing the dynamic from collegial governance to something more base and less collaborative. A common fear is that Faculty, through their associations, will put their interests above those of the institution.

The Academic Workplace

In reality, the main concerns of academic workers more-often-than-not match the concerns of workers in other unionized work environments: namely, compensation and working conditions. In academic workplaces, in particular, working conditions, in the form of workplace standards and expectations, are often the priority for both sides when negotiating.

For example, Faculty Associations often seek to have University policies included in the collective agreement. The aim is to create greater predictability and certainty by removing the Employer's discretion to administer its affairs by amending its policies without consent. Likewise, the processes for reviewing performance, employment equity, and workload, are all issues that Faculty Associations have an interest in codifying.

From the Employer's point of view, relinquishing total control over such matters impacts its ability to provide the best delivery of services. These limitations can affect its standing, and jeopardize its reputation, a scenario—according to the Employer—that would be equally detrimental to Faculty. There is nothing new about these arguments. They mirror the arguments of industrial employers about the disadvantages of labour and employment regulations and human rights statutes.

We Are Not So Different After All: Unionization at the University of Ottawa

Is collective bargaining in higher education truly exceptional? What follows is the story of how the part-time law professors at the University of Ottawa successfully unionized. What is remarkable about this tale is not what makes is exceptional, but what makes it so familiar.

When the Association of Part-Time Professors of the University of Ottawa ("the Association") was founded in the 1980s, it organized all part-time professors at the University of Ottawa, save and except professionals who were excluded from the *Labour Relations Act* ("the *Act*"). In Ontario, lawyers are excluded from collective bargaining under the *Act*. However, over the years, a number of decisions by labour boards found that professors, who happened to be lawyers, were not excluded from academic bargaining units across the province.

As of January 2018, all full-time professors at the University of Ottawa, including law professors, were unionized. All part-time professors were also unionized: save and except law professors. The situation was untenable for several reasons. Most significantly, there was a 91% wage gap between unionized and non-unionized part-time professors. Pension benefits, grievance rights, health plans, and liability insurance, to name a few, were only available to unionized professors.

At the start of its organizing drive, the Association sought voluntary recognition from the University. The request was denied. In denying the Association's request, the University asserted its belief that the Association did not have majority support among the part-time law Faculty.

The University's opposition led to a card collecting drive. This was carried out by volunteers who scoured the University of Ottawa's online class schedule and communicated with each Faculty member individually. Once the Association was able to collect sufficient cards, it was able to apply to the Labour Relations Board for a full list of prospective bargaining unit members.

Obtaining a full list of prospective members might have posed a real challenge for the Association. In a University setting, it is never quite clear whether the listed employees are those teaching at the time of the organizing drive, during the semester, or during the academic year. For a brief period, the Ontario Liberal government had amended the *Act* to make it easier for unions to obtain employee lists. This legislative window of opportunity allowed the Association to obtain the employee list before the newly elected Ontario Conservative government revoked the amendment.

Once the Association was provided with the employee list, it still had to overcome the reluctance many part-time law professors expressed about upsetting the apple cart. Again, the Association was faced with the argument that part-time law professors were somehow "unique". Many professors claimed they were teaching for their community, or for prestige, and not for compensation. Other professors felt uncomfortable belonging to a union while representing employers in their private legal practices. Some were concerned about being outed as union supporters.

These feelings of exceptionalism, however, were overborne by feelings of disrespect when part-time law professors were shown the 91% discrepancy in compensation between themselves and their counterparts across the University.

In the end, the path to unionization was forged in the same way it has always been forged: it came down to basic fairness.

For its part, the Employer also followed a familiar path when it pleaded with its employees to think twice about unionizing. After the certification application was filed, the University issued the following communication:

> Only the vote of those who cast a ballot will matter. If you choose not to vote, this does not count as a "no" vote.
> [...]
> If 50% plus one of the part-time Professors who cast a ballot on Thursday vote in favour of APTPUO, the APTPUO will become the certified representative for all part-time Professors of the Law Faculty. Negotiation of a collective agreement will follow.
> [...]
> While the union may promise many benefits, it can only guarantee (1) the obligation to pay union dues; and (2) the presence of a third party into your relationship with the Faculty of Law. A union cannot guarantee, for example, better wages, benefits, tuition fee credits or limits to class sizes. As you know, all union demands will be subject to collective bargaining.
> The presence of a union therefore represents an important change in our relationship with you.
> Part-time Law Professors have a storied and long-standing relationship with the Faculty of Law. Most of you are practitioners and we rely on you for the special expertise you bring to the field of law. As you know, a union is

a collective organization, where the agenda that is set may or may not be one you agree with. Ask yourself whether you want the APTPUO to speak on your behalf.

In this case, the Employer argued exceptionalism to justify its opposition to unionization. In reality, there was nothing exceptional about these arguments. The University's communication resembled communications from industrial employers facing unionization in the past. For example, in a well-known decision from the Ontario Labour Relations Board, a pamphlet distributed by Wal-Mart was reproduced. That pamphlet included the following:

Q: "The union are telling people that have only 1 or 2 shifts a week that they can guarantee them more hours?"A: Don't be misled by false and misleading statements made by the union and/or rumours. Nobody can guarantee more hours since the number of hours available to associates is directly related to the store's financial performance.

Q: "If you sign the card and don't go to the meeting do they count that signature as a yes vote."

A: No. What does matter is if you vote and how you vote when the vote is held. The store will only be unionized if 50% plus one person of the total number of people who actually vote in person, choose to vote for the union.

Q: "Can a union really help this store? How? Or why not?"

A: We don't believe that it would. Your Company prides itself on being able to listen and respond to its associates directly without the need for third party intervention. Our Open Door policy allows each associate the freedom to express his or her opinion or challenge decisions he or she feels are unfair or not in your Company's best interest, without fear of retaliation. Wal-Mart is pro-associate. We consider associates to be partners in our Company's future, and believe that relationship flourishes without the need for third party intervention.

Simply put, the same tried and true tactics of dissuasion were used by the Employers in both cases.

In regards to the part-time law professors, after the application was presented at the Labour Relations Board, an electronic vote was held and 82% of voters supported unionization.

At bargaining, the three major areas of dispute between the parties were the scope of the bargaining unit, the hiring process, and compensation. These issues were referred to interest arbitration, as neither side was prepared to enact job action.

The University fought strongest on control over staffing, rather than compensation. The outcome followed suit. Professors received a 91% salary increase, whereas the University received additional discretion for its hiring practices.

Since the collective agreement was finalized, there has been industrial peace between the parties.

This story of unionization in higher education is anecdotal, but illustrative. Unions and academic institutions share core values of collaboration, equality, and representation. And yet, employers and employees in higher education settings commonly view their relationship as exceptional. However, notwithstanding how different academia considers itself from more traditional workplaces, the instincts of its main players are often the same.

More often than not, the process of collective bargaining in higher education is unique in theory, but familiar in practice. This reality should be heartening to all parties, who should feel confident that the lessons contained in Canada's rich history of industrial relations are both relevant and applicable to collective bargaining in higher education.

Bill Lyne

Stuck in the Middle with You

The legislation allowing faculty at four-year public universities in Washington state to unionize passed in 2002. Union organizers from NEA and AFT arrived on our campus at Western Washington University the next fall, and three years later, after a lot of organizing work and a series of relentless, baseless and tedious bargaining unit challenges from our administration, our faculty voted to unionize as the United Faculty of Western Washington, affiliated with both NEA and AFT. The university president—who was near retirement, had argued vigorously against our unionizing, and took our vote very personally—hired the law firm of Jackson Lewis (a firm famous for their scorched earth approach to unions) to bargain our first contract.

After 18 months of bargaining, stalemate, and arbitration, we declared impasse and the lawyer went home to Seattle, no doubt convinced that he had earned his hundreds of thousands of dollars in fees. Four days after he left, one of the vice presidents from the administration bargaining team called me and she and I settled a full tentative agreement in a three-hour session on the Sunday of Memorial Day weekend. When the expensive lawyer was informed of the details of our deal (which included basic things like grievance to arbitration and a stable workload), he strenuously urged the Board of Trustees not to ratify it. The trustees, about to hire a new president and fed up with a process that had taken so long, wisely chose to ignore him and support the university's faculty and administration.

For the next ten years, we amiably bargained successor agreements (one of which NEA called "the best contract in America") without the benefit (or expense) of a union-busting lawyer sitting between faculty and administration. Our relatively short experience with collective bargaining has revealed both its value and its limits and clarified quite a bit about the predicament of public higher education in the 21st century. If nothing else, it has helped us understand who's really on what side and why.

When we first began to organize, the university president met us with the standard tale of academic romance. Collective bargaining, she argued, would wreak havoc on our cherished values of collegiality and shared governance. Deans and faculty would no longer be able to say hello to each other in the grocery store or compete on the same bicycle race teams. Our august faculty senate would be rendered impotent. One administration spokesperson even suggested that something called "the union" might make us all wear uniforms. The whole campaign resembled that of a 1960s southern sheriff warning that Yankee agitators were coming to put crazy ideas into the heads of the local happy Negroes.

This tone deafness showed how disconnected the administration had become from faculty life on the ground and how ripe we were for unionization. Our salaries were in the 19th percentile of our peer universities, tenure and promotion decisions had become increasingly mysterious and arbitrary, tenure track faculty lines were disappearing, and carloads of new administrators seemed to be arriving every week. The faculty senate had devolved into a bi-weekly forum for complaints about parking. An actual voice in the running of the university—the thing that the administration argued we would lose with unionization—was the thing it was clear we didn't have. We spent a lot of time in committee meetings and doggedly fulfilling the requirements of empty process, but all real decisions, especially about the deployment of university resources, were made without faculty in the room.

All of that changed with collective bargaining. When recommendations from committees that administrators are under no obligation to follow metamorphose into binding and enforceable contractual agreements, the administration–faculty relationship changes dramatically. Shared governance was the impotence of faculty resolutions followed by the omnipotence of administrative decisions. Collective bargaining is nobody gets to leave the room until we have an agreement that recognizes the interests of both sides. That legal requirement made it imperative that both sides start paying more real attention to the predicament of the other. If we were going to get to a good, workable contract, we had to stop pretending that we were all on the same side with the same interests. The formal exchange of proposals that each side would actually have to live with forced both the faculty and the administration to crawl out of their own echo chambers and actually listen to the other side.

While bargaining sharpened and clarified our differences, it also began to show how much we actually had in common. And for that we owe a debt to the union-busting lawyer that the administration hired for that first contract. He was a formidable fellow, with a wealth of labor law experience, but he had done very little public sector bargaining and had no experience with higher ed bargaining. What he didn't understand was that, unlike his private sector clients, his current client actually had a lot in common with the faculty that sat across the table. This was not a situation where one side's goal was to squeeze as much blood as possible from labor and the other's was to retrieve as much of the fruits of their labor as possible. Our trustees were mostly business types, but they had no obligation to shareholders and most of them vacillated between idealistic and clueless about public higher education. The administrators who sat across the table from us were certainly subject to the neo-liberal pressures that bore down on all university bosses, but most of them had been faculty at one time and even the most mendacious among them probably still cared about students. We watched them grow frustrated and bored with their lawyer's strategy of stonewall and delay. The members of their team who engaged us in actual conversation or nodded too sympathetically at our points suddenly disappeared from the bargaining room.

The university president had been right in her warning that collective bargaining would put a third party between administration and faculty, but that third party turned out not to be the union thugs she was imagining, but rather the mercenary lawyer she had hired. Once he was gone, the rules and responsibilities still remained for both sides, and that structure along with the legal equality of the two sides at a bargaining table forced us to stop hurling blow-off platitudes past each other and get down to cases. Collective bargaining has brought us better salaries and working conditions, but perhaps the most important thing it has delivered is a vastly improved working relationship. We now have a respect for each other and a problem-solving working relationship that we never would have achieved under the old myths of shared governance.

This kind of class collaboration as the pinnacle of faculty union achievement has sent and will continue to send shivers down the spines of my faithfully radical colleagues, and rightly so. Just as collective bargaining has revealed the bankruptcy of shared governance, it has also definitively shown us that college professors are not a revolutionary class. We are mostly the children of the professional and managerial classes, our jobs require us to spend a lot of time alone with our books so solidarity does not come naturally to us, our professional training has conditioned us to suck up to authority, our political and ideological commitments vary wildly across disciplines, and within our larger class we are divided into comfortably upper middle class tenure-track professors and a large proletariat of contingent faculty who still live better and have more prospects than most Americans living below the middle class. Even those of us who teach from a radical or Marxist perspective have mortgages, drive Subarus, and contribute to a 401k plan. Ultimately, we are much more of a guild than a union, at least as a union might be imagined by the Third International or the IWW.

In this, of course, we are no different from our parent companies at NEA and AFT, who both have multi-story buildings blocks from the White House, complete with outsourced cafeterias and human resources departments. Higher education unionization fits squarely into what is left of the U.S. labor movement. We are part of a slightly left-liberal consensus, carefully regulated by state and federal labor law (the sturdy framework created by the 1937 National Labor Relations Act, amended by Taft-Hartley in 1947, and perpetuated through a series of Supreme Court decisions up to and including *Janus*), designed to give U.S. business relative labor peace. We raise millions of dollars in PAC money and are a reliable phone banking army for the Democratic party.

So it should come as no surprise that the conditions always exist for faculty unions and university administrations to work and play well together, especially when administrators can be convinced that it is worth it to trade a little bit of power for a more content faculty. And it just may be possible, especially in the current moment, that these conditions could allow faculty and administration to collaborate on something relatively radical that goes beyond guild wages, benefits, and working conditions.

The real reason that public higher education faculty need unions is the same reason that public higher education administrators behave like corporate bosses: the defunding of public higher education that began in the late 1960s and early 1970s. At about the same time that organized labor was fully defanged, college campuses became the center of progressive and radical organizing in the U.S. In the 1950s and 1960s, in the wake of the GI Bill, the Civil Rights Movement, and the Women's movement, students of diverse races, classes, and genders began showing up in public colleges in significant numbers for the first time. They brought civil rights, women's rights, and free speech movements to campus and began demanding respect and curricular change (Ethnic Studies Programs, Women's Studies Programs) in ways that began to fundamentally rearrange colleges and universities.

Business elites quickly began to recognize colleges as a problem. Lewis Powell, in his now-famous "Powell Memorandum" to the U.S. Chamber of Commerce, devoted several pages of his conservative blueprint to "The Campus," offering a detailed plan to regulate textbooks, make the faculty more conservative, and influence graduate schools of business. This turned out to be overkill, as most of his objectives could be achieved by simply defunding public higher education. Up until this time, public higher education had been essentially free. But as soon as Black and Brown, first generation and working-class students began arriving in numbers, states, led by Governor Ronald Reagan's very public attack on the University of California (especially the Berkeley campus), began the systematic disinvestment in public higher education. As the percentage of white students in public higher education has declined over the decades so has state funding, at almost exactly the same rate. This massive, nationwide act of structural racism has led to public tuition rising to private school levels and created the bankers' paradise of massive student debt.

Turning public institutions private has also no doubt shaped the careers and mindsets of college administrators. We should never mistake the time when public higher education was available to only white men as a golden age, but the job of college president in a time when the campus was fully funded by the state was surely more academic and faculty oriented. It was a job for which someone with a PhD in Physics, English, or Political Science might be relatively qualified. Today, the academic training a college president receives when they are still planning a career as a teacher and scholar has little relevance for the CEO job they have ended up with. A day filled with courting donors, building marketing campaigns to attract premium-paying out-of-state students, managing the debt-financing of fancy dorms and gymnasiums, and negotiating food service contracts with private prison vendors is a long way from that dissertation on Hawthorne or that article about molecular biology. The recent history of public higher education is what has turned administrators into managerial overseers and faculty into labor costs, putting us on opposite sides of a divide that is best bridged with collective bargaining.

And it may be that the relationships we've developed in that bargaining have prepared us to work together on something bigger than the labor/management dance. Here in Washington, the last few years have brought tangible signs that the ground of higher education may be shifting. In 2015, the Washington State Legislature, led by the *Republican*-controlled senate reduced tuition at Washington's public universities by 20%. This would not necessarily be that remarkable were it not for the fact that they also replaced the lost tuition revenue with an equal amount of new state appropriations. In 2017, the Bill and Melinda Gates Foundation began funding the College Promise Coalition, whose goal is to increase post-secondary degree attainment to 70% of Washington citizens. In 2019, the legislature instituted the Washington College Grant as an entitlement available to all students who qualify. Under this entitlement, anyone from a family of four making $50,000 or less can go to any public college in Washington for free. Any student from a family making $96,000 or less receives some grant support. This grant is funded by a tax on businesses, a tax that was strongly supported by both Microsoft and Amazon.

At the same time, there are signs that voters and policy makers are beginning to come around to the idea of higher education as a public good. In a 2020 poll conducted by the College Promise Coalition, 70% of voters, perhaps fed up with the chaos that ignorance brings, said that the most important thing higher education can do is produce well-rounded citizens who make our communities strong. And in our tech-heavy state, so far the digital giants don't seem to be trying to use the pandemic as a way to move all education online. Most people seem to be recognizing that online education is a ghost of the real thing and that digital divides create huge educational inequities.

A confluence of accidents, consequences, and intentions has brought us to a place where a fairly broad consensus is developing around the idea of making public higher education more public. In this context, we might convince our administrations that instead of hiring a token vice president for diversity, they should recruit many more low-income Black, Brown, and Native students. Together we might convince state legislatures to fund food, housing, and childcare subsidies for those students for whom free tuition is not enough. And perhaps at the bargaining table we can agree that committing to a larger percentage of tenure track faculty is the best thing we can do for students, especially those from the neglected regions of capital. If we can convince our administrative friends that we are in a place where running a college more like an educational institution and less like a business will bring them praise rather than pink slips, we might be able to turn the institutional battleship just a little bit.

And the revolution we will have to leave to our students.

Michael Mauer

Aligning Bargaining Approaches with the Academic Mission

Before diving into initial contract negotiations or negotiating a renewal contract, the parties to an academic collective bargaining relationship would do well to take a step back and undertake a comprehensive overview of their joint enterprise. The question before all of us is not just one of how the parties to the collective bargaining relationship will "divide the pie." More fundamental is determining what will help or hinder our collective effort to enhance the institution, and how the labor management relationship factors into that.

Many higher education labor relations practitioners like to think of our realm as unique, given the distinctive mission of colleges and universities and the people who work in them. But the fact is that many of the fundamentals of labor management relations in the academy are common to all unionized workforces, in both the public and private sectors, and regardless of where they are along the spectrum of blue collar to professional labor. All bargaining relationships arise in the context of the tensions that inevitably exist between those who manage the enterprise and those whose day-to-day labor enables the enterprise to "produce" what it does (whether that is tangible products or the provision of services.)

That said, the degree of success in collective bargaining always flows, at least in part, from an understanding of the particular culture of particular workplaces. The parties will go astray if they do not shape their labor management relationship to factor in how best to enable the optimal functioning of the enterprise and how to facilitate favorable outcomes.

It has long been understood that the nature of the university is one in which the faculty play a – if not *the* – central role. (The story told of Eisenhower's address to the faculty when he assumed the presidency of Columbia University – likely only partly apocryphal, as far as can be determined – is illustrative. When Eisenhower began his remarks with a reference to "you employees of Columbia University", a faculty member quickly set him straight with the clarification that "Mr. President, *we* are Columbia University.") There are only a few other corners of American workplaces, such as the skilled building trades, in which there is not a commonly accepted underlying belief that the boss makes the rules, and the workers earn their pay by complying with directives. Despite the fact that there surely has been some erosion of this in recent years, those who toil in the academy do so with the understanding that the faculty (and related academic professionals) are entitled to a prominent role in all decision-making.

By AAUP's lights, the framework for this decision-making is the scheme laid out in our policy statements. The bedrock is the 1966 Statement on Governance of Colleges and Universities, which articulates the interdependent roles for faculty, administrators, and boards. Each of these groups participates in formulating and finalizing all decisions, with one body having primary responsibility in each area. For academic decision-making that primacy of decision-making rests with the faculty.

Faculty traditionally have exercised these responsibilities through the structural mechanisms of shared governance. At least ideally, through the instrument of academic or university senates faculty use their expertise to take the lead in promulgating institutional policies on academic matters. Though "ultimate managerial authority" does not rest with the faculty, the governing board and president of an institution are expected to "concur with the faculty judgment except in rare instances and for compelling reasons which should be stated in detail." In a complementary fashion, the president and board use their areas of primary expertise to take the lead in addressing questions of resources or administration, with faculty input then being accorded appropriate weight.

With the addition of a union to the decision-making equation, faculty add a second structural framework for their role in academic decision-making. While it's seemingly easy to state a clear distinction between the bailiwicks of senates and unions – the former deals with academic matters, the latter with traditional terms and conditions of employment – in practice, a Venn diagram would reveal that most matters are in the shared category. For example, a move to online instruction clearly involves things that are central to the bread and butter of faculty jobs: workload, provision of needed equipment and training, compensation, and so on. But there's also an indisputable academic component: how such instruction is best delivered, how the different nature of online instruction affects grading, and so on. A second example would be academic freedom. Surely a senate has a central role in determining what an institution's policies on free expression ought to be. But equally surely, a union's responsibilities to its members include obtaining contractually guaranteed job security protections for the exercise of academic freedom. The same description of overlapping responsibility applies to promotion and tenure and a myriad of other issues.

This distinctive role that academic workers play in the functioning of the academy commends two approaches to higher education labor relations practitioners.

First, there is the question of how best to define the respective roles that faculty play in governance bodies and in their union, and how this shapes relationships with the administration. Since there is no clear bright line separation between which faculty body has an interest in the various matters that may arise, it behooves the faculty, collectively, to work out a common understanding. And concurrence also must be reached on the part of all involved parties, not just the governance and union mechanisms, but also the administration. It's quite unproductive for endless discussions to take place between the senate and the administration as to whether a particular matter is or is not within the senate's bailiwick. Likewise, it diverts the parties' attention and leads to confusion and muddled decision-making for disputes to continually arise at the bargaining table over whether the administration should more properly address concerns addressed in a union proposal with the senate.

As a practical matter, two sets of discussions should take place. One is for the union and the senate to hammer out a common understanding of which matters are best handled exclusively by one body or the other, and which are of such common concern that they are best processed jointly. (And as to the latter, how such matters will be addressed in a practical sense: how the senate and the union will attempt to formulate a joint position, which body takes the lead in dealing with the administration, and so on.) And all three bodies would do well to establish a mutually agreed-upon framework for structuring administration – senate relations, and administration – union relations.

And the parties would be well served to memorialize both content and structure of overlapping working conditions and academic matters in the collective bargaining agreement. Confusion and disputes can be obviated, at least in part, if the contract sets forth clear standards and mechanisms. For example, what are the processes for promotion and tenure determinations, and for challenging unfavorable outcomes? Or what structural framework will apply to the functioning of governance bodies, such as any changes thereto? The AAUP refers to this approach as "bargaining the Redbook", and promotes it as a means of enshrining roles and responsibilities in our workplaces. (A discussion of how the range of such issues typically are dealt with can be found in "The Collective Agreement: Negotiating Redbook Principles", in *Academic Collective Bargaining*, Ernst Benjamin and Michael Mauer (co-editors), Modern Language Association, 2006.)

The second approach to healthy academic collective bargaining that flows from the distinctive role of faculty in their workplace pertains to how "the scope of bargaining" is dealt with. Though the legal frameworks in various jurisdictions set forth different parameters, in general there are three categories of issues that can be addressed in bargaining. *Mandatory subjects*, the terms and conditions of employment, are those that are generally thought of as the essential bread and butter concerns of a union. Any matter fitting within that definition compels a party to bargain over a proposal forwarded by the other party. *Permissive subjects* are those considered to have a less direct connection to day-to-day working conditions. Proposals addressing such topics may be introduced at the bargaining table by either party, but there is no legal compunction for the other to engage if it chooses not to do so. (A third category, *illegal subjects*, is self-explanatory and in fact arises only rarely.)

The almost reflexive employer response to a union proposal that deals with a permissive subject of bargaining is simply to decline to engage. No counterproposal is offered, with the employer instead asserting its "management rights" to determine unilaterally how policy will be formulated and carried out. When this path is chosen, unions typically respond by engaging in pressure tactics (both at the bargaining table and often away from the table) in an attempt to force the employer to respond with a counterproposal. Taking into account the distinctive role and the particular expertise of faculty and academic professionals in the work setting of a college or university, having the dispute play out in this fashion leads to problematical results.

First, simply declining to engage forces discord and antagonism, both then and there and during the life of the collective bargaining agreement that eventually is produced. Though some discordance is inevitable in any collective bargaining relationship, it is never the most desirable state of affairs. The second consideration was expressed by Langston Hughes: "What happens to a dream deferred? Does it dry up like a raisin in the sun? … *Or does it explode?*" That is to say, if the administration does succeed in blocking a union attempt to address a matter of concern at the bargaining table, that problem does not cease to exist. Rather, it will undoubtedly surface during the life of the contract. At this point the parties will have no previously agreed-upon way of dealing with the problem, with this leading to adversarial stances and a power struggle. Similarly arguing in favor of broad contract coverage of areas of possible dispute is the question of what pathways will exist for resolving matters of contention that arise during the life of the contract. If the contract provides no dispute resolution mechanism, then aggrieved parties to disputes over promotion and tenure, discrimination, or other matters will have their only recourse in the judicial system. But the existence of a contractual grievance/arbitration mechanism serves both parties well in providing a less costly, less time consuming, and usually less contentious way of resolving disputes.

So, for all these reasons, wisdom lies in the parties' default position in bargaining to be that they will attempt, in good faith, to address and resolve any legitimate matter of concern that is put forth by either party.

The peculiar nature of collective bargaining relationships in the academy lead to a greater level of complexity than that found in other types of workplaces. But the complications, if addressed thoughtfully, can yield more powerful solutions to enhancing the parties' collective enterprise.

Derryn Moten

The South is home to all but a handful of historically Black colleges and universities (HBCUs). The South also has a well-established aversion to organized labor with its history of plantation slavery coupled with feudal peonage labor and Big Mule politics. White paternalism replaced white philanthropy at HBCUs and white male presidents and white male boards of supervisors lorded over many of these Black schools until the twentieth century. As G. David Houston opined in a 1920 *Crisis* article, "Neither the prestige nor the income of any Negro college has ever been appreciably augmented by the administration of a white president."

I teach at Alabama State University, a HBCU located in Montgomery, Alabama, the Cradle of the Confederacy, and the Birthplace of the Montgomery Bus Boycott. Dr. Martin Luther King, Jr. understood the inequity of Black labor in America. That realization became abundantly clear during the Boycott where the overwhelming Black ridership of Montgomery buses in 1955 were Black maids, porters, gardeners, and one iconic seamstress. Despite Alabama's early history of union organizing, as historian Wayne Flynt reminds us, "Democratic Redeemers in 1875, fixed their attention on low taxes, banishing labor unions, and bolstering cheap labor including the nefarious convict lease system." In 1953, the democratically controlled Alabama Legislature passed a Right to Work bill becoming the fourteenth state to codify such laws. Alabama outlawed boycotts in 1921 as an anti-strike measure.

Created in the wake of the Civil War to educate newly freed enslaved African Americans, most Black colleges began as normal schools and teacher training institutions. Of the current 103 HBCUs, Talladega College in Alabama became the "first American college for Negroes authorized to confer the baccalaureate degree." It did so in 1895. The State's two Black public universities, namely, Alabama A & M University, a land-grant college, and Alabama State University, a teacher's college, are affiliates of the NEA and the AFT, the National Education Association and the American Federation of Teachers, respectively. A & M is the only higher education local of the Alabama Education Association, the Alabama affiliate of NEA. ASU holds the similar distinction for AFT. The serpentine history of union work on both campuses is storied.

When mainline teacher associations and teacher unions eschewed Southern Black educators, these Black women and men created the National Association for Teachers in Colored Schools (NATCS), 1907–1937. NATCS moved its operations to the campus of Alabama State College where Dr. H. C. Trenholm served as president of the Black college. In time, Black Alabama educators represented 40 percent of NATCS members. George Washington Trenholm, H. C. Trenholm's father, preceded his son as President of Alabama State College. The elder Trenholm co-founded NATCS and helped start the Alabama

State Teachers Association, ASTA, the largest Black teachers' association in the South. Another founder was William Hooper Councill, the president of the State Normal School at Normal, Alabama, now Alabama A & M University. George Washington Trenholm and John Beverly, the first Black president of Alabama State College, made the school the locus of ASTA activity. In 1969, ASTA merged with the Alabama Education Association.

In May 1986, the NEA dedicated the H. Councill Room at its Washington, D. C. headquarters. NATCS changed its name to the American Teachers Association in 1937. H. Councill Trenholm served that organization for 31 years as executive committee member, trustee, president, executive secretary, and editor of its official organ, *The Bulletin*. NEA credits H. C. Trenholm with orchestrating the merger between the two segregated associations, ATA and NEA. The ATA encompassed Black state teacher associations from Alabama, Arkansas, Florida, Georgia, Louisiana, Mississippi, North Carolina, South Carolina, Tennessee, Texas, and Virginia. These deep-South groups had names such as the Palmetto Education Association, and the Tennessee Education Congress. When ATA and NEA combined, these ATA affiliates consolidated with their white counterparts. Prior to the mergers, Black educators depended on the NAACP, not the AFT, AAUP, or NEA to litigate pay inequities between Black and white teachers.

In Alabama, Arthur Shores, the Black attorney who litigated Autherine Lucy's and Pollie Anne Myers' admission to the University of Alabama as its first Black students, defended the wrongful termination of school principal Mrs. Ruby Jackson Gainer, five-term president of the Jefferson County Negro Teachers Association. The school board indicted Mrs. Gainer with dereliction of duty, and insubordination. Gainer countered arguing that the board terminated her for "personal and political reasons" arising out of her federal lawsuit for salary parity. The Jefferson County Negro Teachers Association is now the Jefferson County AFT, Local 2143, the largest K-12 AFT local in Alabama.

Howard University became the first HBCU to unionize its teaching corps and the first to affiliate with the American Federation of Teachers. AFT chartered the Howard University Teachers' Union, Local 33, in November 1918. The headline for the *Washington Herald* read "Unionism Reaches to the Ranks of Professors." Holding its first meeting in Founder's Library, charter members included Mary Church Terrell, noted clubwoman and the first president of the National Association of Colored Women. Local 33 disbanded in 1921. Few documents remain attributing the work of Local 33 and its officers; however, at the January 2, 1920 AFT annual meeting in Chicago, delegates of the Howard University Teachers' Union read a resolution from the floor calling AFT to lobby Congress for adequate HBCU funding "to carry out a constructive educational program of vast importance to the colored people of America…" Dr. Emmett Scott, 18-year personal secretary to Tuskegee Institute Principal Booker T. Washington, was the Howard University Teachers' Union delegate at that Chicago meeting.

Howard formed a chapter of the American Association of University Professors, AAUP, in May 1933. Dr. Alain L. Locke, the father of the New Negro Movement, was its president. Twelve years later, AAUP chapters existed on Black campuses at Atlanta University, Hampton Institute, Lincoln University (Missouri), North Carolina College for Negroes, West Virginia State College, and Xavier University. Florida A & M University had an AAUP chapter in 1957.

In 1965, an Oregon State University Sociology professor and AAUP member wrote an op-ed on the ten principles of the organization. Number 10 was "Providing advice and assistance to faculty members and administrators at junior colleges, state colleges, Negro colleges, Catholic institutions, which are undergoing fundamental changes." AAUP seemingly separated Academic Freedom from racial freedom. In 1945, Dr. W. E. B. Du Bois terminated his AAUP membership in protest of AAUP meetings held at hotels that denied service to Blacks. Du Bois was a charter member of the Atlanta University AAUP Chapter in 1938.

In 1953, Lincoln University in Missouri had an AAUP chapter for 19 years, becoming the second longest at an HBCU. Currently, AAUP represents five HBCUs: Delaware State University, Edward Waters College in Florida, Central State University in Ohio, Wilberforce University in Ohio, and Lincoln University. AFT and NEA jointly represent Florida A & M University.

In January 1936, the second iteration of the Howard University Teachers' Union affiliated with the American Federation of Teachers becoming a joint AAUP/AFT affiliate. Local 440 counted folklorist Dr. Sterling Brown and Black Nobel laureate Dr. Ralph Bunch among its members. Like its predecessor, Local 440 pushed AFT to inveigh racism. In February 1938, Local 440 joined fellow unionists, the United Federal Workers, American Women's Trade Union League, and the Worker's Alliance of America in objecting to a reshowing of D. W. Griffith's "Birth of a Nation" at a local DC theater.

At the 23rd Annual meeting held in Buffalo, New York in September 1939, Local 440 denounced DAR's, Daughters of the American Resolution, denial of Marian Anderson's request to perform at DAR's Constitutional Hall. The contralto performed before 75,000 from the steps of the Lincoln Memorial on Easter Sunday as a fundraiser for Howard University's School of Music.

Local 440 dissolved in 1944.

The unionization of Black faculty and staff at HBCUs has been a dream deferred. Like the Langston Hughes' poem, organizing Black campuses seems to be a "heavy load" for AFT, AAUP, and NEA. When AFT chartered the Faculty-Staff Alliance at Alabama State University, Local 4866, in 1994, ASU faculty and staff bore the burden. The FSA is only the third HBCU organized by AFT in the union's history. The Florida A & M faculty organized under the United Faculty of Florida, an AFT/NEA merged local.

The Faculty-Staff Alliance at Alabama State University does not have a collective bargaining agreement and negotiates through "meet and confer." FSA and university administration meet to discuss workplace matters in good faith.

These discussions require a level of finesse and adroitness for both parties. Talks around salary equity are perennial. Lacking a state law requiring university administration to the table, FSA officers sometimes employ moral suasion to lesser or greater success. We have coalitions with local organizations who come to our aid when requested. We lobby politicians and we solicit support from local and state newspapers and media outlets. Our members serve on the faculty senate and several served as senate presidents. And lastly, we stage actions. Our most successful was a "silent protest" we staged in 2002. FSA members, university staff and students stood in silence in front of the administration building to protest pay inequities at Alabama State University. We held placards that read, "Fair Pay, Fair Play," and "I AM A MAN," and "I AM A WOMAN," reminiscent of the protests put on by sanitation workers in Memphis, Tennessee. The result was the largest pay increase in school history.

In his 1993 Rutgers University dissertation, Gregory Michael Scott ponders unionization at a fictive HBC, Eastern State College. His thesis, "Faculty Unionization at a Black Public College: A Case Study in the Evolution of Academic Governance" explores the difficulties of collective bargaining at institutions once known for autocracy. Faculty at Eastern State College believed unionizing was their best chance to influence important decisions on campus. Yet, the Easton State president seldom responded to faculty requests. "A 12-member group of senior Black faculty composed of administrators, department chairmen, and teaching faculty, collaborated with the president to dominate the college's decision making" (p. 133). Eastern State is certainly not the first campus where faculty members parley with administration to curry favor.

HBCUs find themselves at a crossroads. Outside of the Black Church, the second most significant entity within the Black community is the Historically Black College or University. It is impossible to imagine Black progress and achievement without these schools. They produced our most important teachers, scholars, musicians, artists, writers, politicians, ministers, scientists, physicians, athletes, union leaders, and the list goes on. Scott argues, "The pattern of social relations, including governance, at Black public colleges suggest the need to understand the extent to which it was caused by forces associated with segregation" (p. 4). HBCUs have always fought for autonomy from either white supervision or Black conservatism. The history of segregation challenges the notion that collective bargaining under the guise of white labor unions or white professional associations is the most efficacious solution.

Racial stigmas abound. Black Lives Matter. Ole Jim Crow is dead, but his progeny haunts boardrooms, courtrooms, classrooms, emergency rooms, and union halls throughout America. In *Plessy v Ferguson*, Chief Justice Henry Billings Brown opined "If the two races are to meet upon terms of social equality, it must be the result of natural affinities...." Unions created a democratic past fostering interracial, multi-cultural affinities; the question now becomes whether unions will foster that democratic promise for America's present and future.

Scott L. Pratt

Shared Governance and Collective Bargaining

The evolution of shared governance in United States higher education runs counter to faculty appeals to history to justify their claims to authority in their institutions. Higher education, the appeal goes, began in days when leadership of the university was made up of teachers and scholars willing to step away from their work for a time. These dedicated leaders took up the necessary tasks of keeping the lights on (or the candles lit), making sure that the campus was in good repair, and managing the paperwork necessary to enroll and graduate their students. Efforts by administrators in recent years to confine faculty to narrow "academic matters," the story goes, are somehow a violation of founding principles. For colleges and universities to succeed in their mission of research, teaching, and service, the faculty must take up leadership roles and hold professional administrators accountable. While the former claim is false, the latter claim remains true but as the result of a different history.

The real story is that American higher education was founded in response to local conditions. As Labaree (2017) has argued, colleges and universities were the product of land deals, market forces, and politics. Leadership was usually vested with an external governing board (mostly local) that appointed a president or chancellor whose role was to govern the university but whose responsibility was to the supervising board. Charters and bylaws confirmed this structure. Rather than a history of faculty authority steadily eroded, the history of American higher education affirms the limits of faculty governance and the idea that, at least historically, independent authority has been with boards and presidents. As Geiger (2015, 26) observed, "The American model of a strong president under the authority of an external governing board with a relatively weak faculty was the product of evolution rather than design."

The model began to change in the face of what Geiger (2015, 326) called "the academic revolution" that emerged in the late 19th century with the rise of disciplines that solidified their importance by establishing publishing venues and professional associations. The disciplines became the key to peer review which in turn became the ground for the knowledge creation and innovation that marks American higher education. Despite the growth and success of higher education, tension between administrations and faculty in their disciplines, combined with rapidly transforming undergraduate programs (Geiger, 2015, 365), led to new problems of management and the firing of faculty who resisted administrative decisions (Tiede, 2015).

In January 1915, months after the beginning of World War I and after what the founding members viewed as ongoing assaults on the academic freedom of faculty by governing boards, philosophers John Dewey and Arthur Lovejoy joined with other faculty to form the American Association of University

Professors (AAUP). By December of that year the AAUP produced the *Declaration of Principles on Academic Freedom and Academic Tenure* which concluded

> [o]nce appointed, the scholar has professional functions to perform in which the appointing authorities have neither the competency nor moral right to intervene. The responsibility of the university teacher is primarily to the public itself, and to the judgment of [their] own profession.
>
> *(Seligman et al., 1915, 26)*

Writing in 1918, Veblen described the relationship that many faculty members thought followed from a commitment to academic freedom:

> In order to their best efficiency, and indeed in the degree in which efficiency in this field of activity is to be attained at all, the executive officers of the university must stand in the relation of assistants serving the needs and catering to the idiosyncrasies of the body of scholars and scientists that make up the university.
>
> *(Veblen, 1918/1957, 63)*

In 1925, after joint meetings with the AAUP, the American Council on Education issued a set of recommendations that would become the standard tenure structure and part of what faculty viewed as essential to protecting academic freedom and the teaching and research missions of higher education (Geiger, 2015, 494). Faculty resistance that emerged with the academic revolution had achieved a new model of shared governance.

In the 1920s, as a result of organized faculty resistance to the received model of governance, "the trustee domination they attacked was receding ... and faculty power was making inroads against autocratic presidents" (Geiger, 2015, 494). The system of governance that emerged in response to the increasing importance of faculty governance in research, teaching and tenure, in some ways balanced the demands of academic freedom with the growing role of professional administrators charged with managing the university. The result was the development of a higher education system that, despite being "a decentralized, uncoordinated process" at its core (Geiger, 2015, 326–7), nevertheless became the envy of the world and had the practical effect of producing world-changing research and generations of graduates who transformed the character of the nation and the economy.

Despite struggles in the 1950s, 1960s, and 1970s that tested limits of the new model of governance tied to academic freedom, the nation and economy began to turn their backs on the system of education that had sustained them and emphasized a new conception of higher education marked by decreased public funding and greater reliance on philanthropy, grants, and tuition. For a variety of reasons, the democratic expansion of access to higher education after the Second World War and the social reforms of the 1960s and 1970s gave way to a movement to change higher education again. While continuing to expect colleges and universities to sustain large enrollments and produce transformative research, especially in the sciences, donors, legislators, and some of the public began to demand that universities rely less on public funding and "operate like a business," catering to the "customer," the investor, and government demands, regulatory and otherwise. The resulting "corporate university" and the growing ranks of career administrators took over more and more university functions that had become reserved for the faculty and protected by the road concept of academic freedom.

By the 1990s, it became clear at many public universities that the commitments that had framed the project of higher education since the beginning of the century were at risk. The role of the faculty in shared governance, systematically reduced with the rise of the corporate university, no longer included the authority to set the university's agenda or resist the decision-making power of deans and central administrators. At my own university, beginning in the 1990s, the senate operated under a constitution that left the last word on senate decisions to the president and to a state board (later an independent board). This new world of the corporate university also saw the nature of the faculty change. Teaching by tenured-related faculty was at first augmented by and then later was often replaced by faculty with contingent appointments who lacked job security and the protections essential to academic freedom enshrined in the 1925 statement (and later statements as well). The university senate objected to these developments but found that they had little power to direct, let alone protect, the mission of their university as responsible "primarily to the public."

The union movement, led by the AAUP and AFT among others, organized faculty to adopt collective bargaining and the faculty at many universities voted for unionization as a new dimension of shared governance. With the advent of collective bargaining, faculty, through the mechanisms of labor law, could reassert some control over important aspects of their work as teachers, scholars, and researchers.

There are, I think, three lessons that deans and central administrators can learn by recognizing this history of faculty resistance to the original American conception of university governance. First, and perhaps most important, unionization of the faculty is a further step in a long history of faculty working to make universities better by increasing their role in governance. Some have argued that labor unions and academic associations are distinct and so unions are an obstacle to such success. AAUP cofounder, Arthur O. Lovejoy, for example, argued in 1938 that, despite superficial similarities unions and the AAUP were dramatically different in their interests. The evolution of higher education and the wider political context of the last several decades, however, have led faculty to want a say in both academic matters and the working conditions that make academic work possible.

In American higher education, unionization and labor law have provided a means to address changing circumstances. Instead of allowing presumptions that all unions are alike and that they are primarily interested in the benefits delivered to the worker regardless of the impact on the employer (the claim made by Lovejoy), administrators should understand that faculty unions recognize the role faculty have in the work of the university already established in the academic revolution of the late 19th century. The university is not a separate body that hires faculty to do its work, but rather a body composed of faculty who are the university. Consistent with the history of colleges and universities, administrators are hired to be of service and to ensure that the work of the university, defined by the faculty, can be accomplished. Faculty members who unionize, at least in my experience, come to union membership because they do not have the ability to control their work and to realize their commitment to the project of higher education and research.

When the union formed at my university, it was a response to the failure of the administration and governing board to allow faculty a meaningful role in shared governance, an administration with its own agenda disconnected from the faculty, and a state board out of touch with the university. As a member of the union organizing committee and then a member of the union's first bargaining team, I heard again and again that the reason faculty joined the union effort was because they loved their work and wanted support to accomplish it. After years of a partially enforced salary freeze, no ability to affect institutional spending priorities, and a remarkable lack of stability for contingent faculty, the faculty as a whole decided that the situation called for something new. As we formed the union, we decided that our bargaining unit would include both tenure-related faculty and non-tenure-related faculty and that the combination, with the commitment to the success of our work together, would give all faculty a stronger voice and bargaining power.

While the administration resisted the union's formation, in the first years after its ratification, several senior administrators (also long-serving tenured professors) decided to work with the union to address the circumstances of the contingent faculty (now called Career Instructors and Researchers) to solve other problems around promotion and merit reviews and to address a general lack of written policies. As a result of those first collaborations between the faculty and the administration, members of the union leadership and senior administrators co-presented their work at conferences on labor in higher education. Faculty and administrators worked together to improve the university's reputation as a nationally and internationally recognized research university. The size of the tenure track faculty increased, and career faculty gained longer contracts, promotion reviews, and long-overdue raises. Problems remained, but the willingness of both sides to focus on solving shared problems meant changes that benefited the bargaining unit faculty, the administration, and the university as a whole.

The second thing administrators should recognize is that the union is a new pillar in the management of the university alongside the administration and faculty academic governance through a senate (or other governing body) and its related committees. A robust and independent faculty senate is essential to achieving the university mission. As the body that governs the academic program at the heart of the university, faculty senates must make decisions informed by their public trust to provide education and research that benefit the whole community. The role of a union is to bargain for working conditions of the faculty that will support the success of that academic mission since, as the slogan goes, "faculty working conditions are student learning conditions" (Osborn, 2012). Academic decisions about teaching, courses taught, grading, awarding degrees and so on are all intimately connected to employment matters. It is key to the university's success that the connections are recognized so that decisions of the senate are compatible with the demands of faculty employment. Further, where faculty governance is often limited in its ability to enforce its decisions, when those decisions become part of the working conditions specified in the collective bargaining agreement, they have the force of law. Administrators must recognize this fact and respect the work of the senate as a faculty body and avoid using it as a way to bring faculty to heel through tension with the union.

The balance between faculty academic governance and the responsibilities of the union to bargain on behalf of most of the faculty is a challenge. While work assignments, including course load, advising expectations, research, and service responsibilities, are part of the conditions of employment and so a union matter, they are also elements of how the university carries out its mission of teaching, research, and service and so a faculty matter taken up through the senate. It is easy to see how faculty leadership in the university's senate can imagine that the union and the senate are at odds. For example, policies about performance reviews are a key element of faculty conditions of employment, but standards for those reviews are key to achieving the university's mission. The former are determined by collective bargaining but the latter need to be developed by faculty in their disciplines as part of academic governance. The administration likewise has a role to play to ensure that reviews are carried out properly and that faculty judgment is primary. In general, the presence of a faculty union means that shared governance assigns advocacy of faculty working conditions to the union, academic matters to the senate, and management of the resulting system to the administration.

Finally, administrators should recognize that, as a result of these two factors—that unionization is a part of a new model of governance and that it has a specific function in that new model—bargaining itself ought to be conceived differently. The more-or-less standard starting assumption is that "there is an inherent conflict of interest between employees and employers that derives from the clash of economic interests between workers seeking high pay and job security and employers pursuing profits" (Katz et al., 2017, 4–5). If the faculty are, in a real sense, the university, then the interests of the university are more or less the interests of the faculty senate and the union. If this is so, then the administration's responsibility is to work with the faculty to realize faculty goals where those goals are both an academic matter and a matter of employment. The corporate university has undermined the structure, but unionization has provided one means of recovering that relation. Administration sought to use their best judgment to carry out the faculty-determined mission of the university even as the union is obliged to represent faculty concerns and seek to address them.

Bargaining itself must be conceived as the effort to achieve shared results. Where conflicts emerge (for example, over how best to achieve mission goals), the response should be two-fold. On one hand, bargaining represents an effort to clarify goals and solve the problem of realizing them through an agreement between the union and the administration. On the other, should the goals remain out of reach, the parties to the discussion should work to evolve new goals that can be achieved in whatever situation has led to the problem. Rather than conflict and compromise, which necessarily means that some goal of the university is not being achieved, bargaining should aim to integrate the concerns of both the faculty and administration in order to develop a new goal (Follett, 1918/1998, 114; Follett, 1924/1930, 164). The outcome of bargaining in this way does not give up something, but rather fosters something new that is shared by the university as a whole.

Mary Parker Follett, a philosopher in the early 20th century whose work led her to be an early labor relations consultant, argued that collective bargaining ought to be seen as a matter of fostering power, not "power over" one side or the other, but "power with" where the interests of both sides are integrated into shared goals and agreements aim to achieve those goals (1924/1930, 179 ff.). A bargaining mistake is to suppose that such integration is not possible either by deciding in advance that unions have no place in the academy—though history assures us that they do—or by misunderstanding the idea of integration as compromise. If faculty unions are part of the shared governance of the university, then agreements will emerge with creative ideas for solving problems and a vision for the university's future. Commenting on the disagreements that emerge in bargaining, Follett concludes, "Our 'opponents' are our co-creators, for they have something to give which we have not. The basis of all cooperative activity is integrated diversity" (Follett, 1924, 174).

Many find it easy to conclude that faculty unions are somehow outside entities whose interests are fundamentally opposed to those of the university. I have argued that faculty unions are the product of changing circumstances in the governance of American higher education and in the present world, they are better seen as internal, as a third element of shared governance. While the place of unions in higher education is a more recent development, teachers' unions emerged at the beginning of the 20th century under similar conditions. Speaking about the constructive role of such unions in a 1922 interview, John Dewey concluded:

> we should all welcome the appearance of the Teachers' Union in the field…. It is standing for human freedom at the very point where freedom is most essential. It is standing for the right to develop thinking power. It is standing for fearlessness as opposed to dogma, for education as opposed to propaganda, and for reliance upon the great power of human intelligence to solve life's problems rather than upon traditions and superstitions which have so conspicuously failed.
>
> *(Dewey, 1922/1988, 429–30)*

By recognizing faculty unions as continuous with the evolution of shared governance, bargaining becomes an opportunity to bring together faculty interests in the project of higher education and administrative responsibilities for achieving them.

References

Dewey, John. 1922/1988. Report of Interview with John Dewey, by Charles W. Wood. In *The Middle Works of John Dewey*, Volume 13. Edited by Jo Ann Boydston. SIU Press.

Follett, Mary P. 1918/1998. *The New State: Group Organization the Solution of Popular Government.* Forewords by Benjamin R. Barber and Jane Mansbridge, Introduction by Kevin Mattson. Pennsylvania State UP.

Follett, Mary Parker. 1924/1930. *Creative Experience.* Longmans, Green and Co., New York.

Geiger, Roger L. 2015. *The History of American Higher Education: Learning and Culture from the Founding to World War II.* Princeton UP.

Katz, Harry C., Alexander Colvin, and Thomas A. Kochan. 2017. *An Introduction to U.S. Collective Bargaining and Labor Relations.* ILR Press, Cornell UP.

Larbaree, David F. 2017. *A Perfect Mess: The Unlikely Ascendancy of American Higher Education.* University of Chicago Press.

Osborn, Eliana. 2012. "Faculty Working Conditions Are Student Learning Conditions." *Chronicle of Higher Education*, 30.

Seligman, Edwin R. A., *et al.*1915. General Report of the Committee on Academic Freedom and Academic Tenure. *Bulletin of the American Association of University Professors* (1915–1955), December, Vol. 1, No. 1, pp. 15–43.

Tiede, Hans-Joerg. 2015. *University Reform: The Founding of the Associate of American University Professors.* Johns Hopkins UP.

Veblen, Thorsten. 1918/1957. *The Higher Learning in America.* Sagamore Press, New York.

Eve Weinbaum

Slow Thinking in Faculty Collective Bargaining

Universities are often exhorted to be nimble, forward-thinking, and open to rapid change. This is especially true for public institutions whose budgets and priorities fluctuate with the whims of the economy, student demographics, and state legislatures. Unions are often accused of slowing down the process and preventing quick decision-making; unions require negotiation, consultation, and ratification by stakeholders. But what if this very process – slowing down institutional change – turns out to be a great strength? Evidence shows that administrations that collaborate closely with academic unions often make better decisions that serve the long-term interests of the institution, the faculty and staff, the students, and the wider community.

In 2002, Daniel Kahneman won the Nobel Prize in Economics for his research on decision-making in circumstances of uncertainty. Contrary to "rational choice" theories in social and behavioral sciences, Kahneman and his colleague Amos Tversky demonstrated that smart people often made illogical and counterproductive choices. In 2011, Kahneman published Thinking, Fast and Slow, a groundbreaking exploration of behavioral economics. Among other insights, he differentiated "System 1" – fast, intuitive, experience-based reactions – as opposed to "System 2" – systematic, focused, fact-based delib- eration. System 1 works well for some areas of life, when familiar heuristics are sufficient. Their research demonstrates, however, that System 1 fails in complex situations, when the future is uncertain, or when a problem demands more elaborate thought processes and analysis of multiple interactive variables – which is almost always the case in universities. Kahneman and Tversky's research has been applied to many fields, but rarely to labor relations. The idea of "thinking slow" is particularly valuable for university collective bargaining, where research offers important lessons for unions and administrators.

Slow thinking is hardest in a time of crisis or rapid change. In the spring of 2020, for example, as the extent of the COVID-19 emergency emerged, uni- versity campuses across the U.S. faced unprecedented uncertainty. Adminis- trators struggled to protect the safety of students, faculty, and staff, while simultaneously panicking about the financial implications of emptying dorms, losing international students, and moving the curriculum online. The COVID- 19 crisis presented a moment to test Kahneman and Tversky's theories about making rational decisions in conditions of uncertainty. University administrators had every incentive to think fast – to implement immediate layoffs and budget cuts – although in fact, they had no idea what was likely to happen next. Campuses with unions were forced to slow down, at least a little bit. While the negotiations process may have been frustrating to administrators, it resulted in better decisions and less damaging conflict on campus. Slowing down the process to get input from multiple sources – including the state and federal governments, students, families, and staff – and to take into account the short-term and long-term interests of the university proved the best and most rational course of action, preventing unnecessary pain and involving the community in a productive conversation.

Analyzing past decisions provides evidence for the benefits of slow thinking in collective bargaining. We can look at previous disputes and choices made in conditions of uncertainty, and we can evaluate the long-term consequences. Two examples from my own experience with collective bargaining at the University of Massachusetts Amherst (UMass Amherst) show how the administration's immediate impulses and short-term cost-benefit analysis would not have led to the best long-term outcomes for the university. In each case, taking time to collaborate with the union led the university to a more rational and productive course of action.

The first example involves one of the thorniest labor issues on most campuses: non-tenure-track (NTT) or adjunct faculty status and benefits. As the percentage of NTT faculty increased on most campuses in the 1990s, some joined existing faculty unions while others formed their own adjunct unions. At UMass Amherst, the union representing tenure-system faculty, the Massachusetts Society of Professors (MSP/MTA/NEA) expanded our ranks to include all NTT faculty, including part-time adjuncts. The union was clear that the best way to prevent a race to the bottom, to protect wages and benefits as well as tenure itself, was to make it as expensive as possible for the university to hire NTT faculty. Our proposals mirrored the advantages of tenure: proportional benefits; regular promotions with a corresponding salary increase after six years of service; continuous appointments with job security after the third-year review; just cause protections; and, most recently, professional improvement leaves that are equivalent to sabbaticals. Through many rounds of negotiations, administrators fought strongly against all of these proposals, arguing that the expense would harm programs and make it impossible to deliver the curriculum, and that it made no sense to give NTT faculty as much job security as tenured faculty. Years later, however, administrators told us the exact opposite. In fact, generous benefits for NTT faculty had made UMass Amherst a "destination of choice" for scholars. Administrators told us how they brought the MSP collective bargaining agreement to professional associations and used it to recruit new faculty with promises of job security, promotions, and paid professional leaves. They lured prospective hires by arguing that NTT jobs at UMass were just as good as – or better than – tenure-track jobs at most universities. What had seemed unreasonable to the experts turned out to be the best long-term policy for the university.

A second example resulted from a series of negotiations around parental leave and family benefits. Two decades ago, UMass Amherst was one of the first universities in the U.S. to offer a comprehensive set of "family-friendly" policies for faculty and librarians, including a semester of leave at full pay when someone gives birth or adopts a child, childcare subsidies, a partner employment program, and automatic delay of the tenure decision year (reversed if the individual chooses). Unlike most universities, UMass's policy did not require the faculty or librarian to be the primary caregiver of the child; men and women with children were eligible. This became a source of contention in the next round of negotiations, when the administration argued that they never intended for both parents to take a semester of paid leave; the policy was intended to support women as a step toward gender equality in academia. The union presented data showing that women were much more likely to take advantage of parental leave if men in their department were also eligible – arguing for a universal benefit rather than one provided to women on the "mommy track" (Lundquist et al., 2012). Furthermore, the research showed that parental-leave policies created norms of support for balancing work and family and changed the culture of departments to be less competitive and more caring (O'Meara and Campbell, 2011). Faculty reported increased loyalty to the institution and the data showed higher retention rates among faculty members, especially women, notably in fields where women were underrepresented. A few years later the national COACHE survey showed that UMass Amherst was in the top ten percent of public research universities for supporting faculty to raise children while in a tenure-track position. UMass was listed in the *Chronicle of Higher Education* "Great Colleges to Work For," and celebrated for its family-friendly policies. Once again, the union's extensive organizing persuaded the administration to agree to generous policies that later became a point of pride for the university. Benefits that the administration was loath to provide – because of assumed short-run costs and feared conflicts – ended up strengthening recruitment and retention, improving morale, and enhancing UMass's reputation, as well as supporting women and promoting equity.

After the COVID-19 crisis passes, universities will face more crises, as we always do: uncertain economies at the federal and state level, demands for "multi-modal" or hybrid online education, the demographic "cliff" that is shrinking the college population, the student debt crisis, climate change, and more. Kahneman's research shows that we cannot rely on intuition or previous knowledge to choose a path forward in unpredictable situations; overconfidence about our predictive abilities leads to poor decisions. When faced with a new situation, those in power should not rely on "System 1" fast thinking. The less agile, more cumbersome, sometimes conflictual processes of "System 2" – collaborating with stakeholders, hearing contrary opinions, and collecting information from more sources – provide the data necessary to arrive at good decisions.

How do unions force slow thinking in universities? First, unions require a process of negotiations. Negotiations require taking into account different perspectives, looking at proposals, and considering options. When done well, negotiations require analyzing costs and benefits into the future. This type of analysis is more likely to result in good decisions than intuitive guesses, even expert guesses. Second, unions are democratic. Democracy is slow. Union agreements must be ratified by members, which means educating faculty and staff about the situation. While two chief negotiators could make quick decisions between the parties, a union bargaining team is accountable to its entire membership. Third, academic unions are not monolithic but represent diverse viewpoints: tenured, untenured, non-tenure-track, and adjunct faculty; librarians and staff; research and clinical instructors; STEM disciplines, humanities and professional schools; graduate and undergraduate educators; men and women and others; faculty/staff of various racial and ethnic groups. Unlike other groups on campus, the union must represent everyone in the bargaining unit. This diversity is the union's strength and a goldmine of information for the administration. Especially in the age of *Janus*, unions have a strong incentive to be responsive to their members, and an effective union is in constant communication with its members across campus. The bargaining process provides the administration with an opportunity to hear the experiences and concerns of these multiple constituencies.

Truly innovative collective bargaining agreements are rare in academia; they usually result from collaboration between progressive activist unions and administrators who come into office with a social-justice agenda of their own. In those cases, unions can be powerful allies to administrators who are interested in – or at least open to – making change. But even when administrators are just muddling through and trying to keep an institution afloat, unions can be essential partners. Better decisions result from a process that requires more data and a clearer understanding of the impact on all community members within a campus or university system. Unions can facilitate crucial conversations and force slow thinking, which results in better decisions for all stakeholders.

References

Daniel Kahneman, *Thinking, Fast and Slow.* New York: Random House, 2011.

Jennifer H. Lundquist *et al.*, "Parental Leave Usage by Fathers and Mothers at an American University," *Fathering*, Volume 10, Number 3, Fall 2012, pp. 337–363.

KerryAnn O'Meara and Corbin M. Campbell, "Faculty Sense of Agency in Decisions about Work and Family," *The Review of Higher Education*, Volume 34, Number 3, Spring 2011, pp. 447–476.

INDEX